Studies in Art, Heritage, Law and the Market

Volume 1

The book series *Studies in Art, Heritage, Law and the Market* provides an international and interdisciplinary forum for volumes that

- investigate legal, economic, and policy developments related to arts, heritage, and intellectual property;
- critically assess how and for whom art and heritage values come about;
- promote novel forms of user engagement, participatory presentations, and digitalization of arts and heritage;
- examine the processes that transform cultural objects and practices into arts and heritage; and
- highlight new approaches in preservation and conservation science.

The series addresses a need for research and practice in the fields of art, culture, conservation, and heritage including a focus on legal and economic aspects. It deals with complex issues such as questions of authenticity and provenance; forgery and falsification; the illicit trade, restitution, and return of cultural objects; the changing roles of museums; the roles of experts and expertise; and the ethics of the art market.

More information about this series at http://www.springer.com/series/16197

Naomi Oosterman • Donna Yates
Editors

Crime and Art

Sociological and Criminological Perspectives of Crimes in the Art World

Springer

Editors
Naomi Oosterman
Department of Arts & Culture Studies
Erasmus University Rotterdam
Rotterdam, The Netherlands

Donna Yates
Criminal Law and Criminology
Maastricht University
Maastricht, The Netherlands

ISSN 2524-7425 ISSN 2524-7433 (electronic)
Studies in Art, Heritage, Law and the Market
ISBN 978-3-030-84855-2 ISBN 978-3-030-84856-9 (eBook)
https://doi.org/10.1007/978-3-030-84856-9

This Springer imprint is published by the registered company Springer Nature Switzerland AG.
The registered company address is: Gewerbestrasse 11, 6330 Cham, Switzerland

Contents

About the Contributors

Francesco Angelini is a Post-doc Researcher at the Department of Statistical Sciences 'Paolo Fortunati', the University of Bologna (IT) and an Adjunct Professor at the University of Bologna and at the Ca' Foscari University of Venice (IT). His research is focused on pricing and value formation in the cultural market and in the digital market.

Diāna Bērziņa is a Junior Researcher on the project 'Trafficking Transformations: Objects as Agents in Transnational Criminal Networks' based in the Department of Criminal Law and Criminology, Maastricht University. In 2018, Diāna graduated with MSc in Criminology and Criminal Justice from the University of Glasgow. Her research focused on the ways how the digital world and digital communications are used to legitimise art crime and antiquities trafficking.

Neil Brodie is an Archaeologist who has published widely on issues concerning the market in cultural objects, with more than 50 papers and book chapters devoted to the subject. He is presently a Senior Research Fellow on the Endangered Archaeology in the Middle East and North Africa project at the University of Oxford's School of Archaeology.

Rodrigo Christofoletti is a Cultural Heritage Professor with graduation and post-graduation in History from the Universidade Federal de Juiz de Fora (UFJF), Minas Gerais, Brazil. A leader of the research group Heritage and International Relations (CNPq) and Collaborator with the Transdisciplinary Research Centre 'Culture, Space and Memory' (CITCEM-FLUP). He holds a Doctorate in History, Politics, and Cultural Heritage from the Getulio Vargas Foundation (FGV-CPDOC) and researches the interface between History and International Relations focusing on cultural heritage. He is an editor, along with Marcos Olender, of the book *World Heritage Patinas: actions, alerts and risks*. With Maria Leonor Botelho, he published the book *International Relations and Heritage: patchwork in times of plurality*.

Katherine Davidson is a doctoral candidate at the Carleton University, where her research focuses on object elicitation, understudied archaeological collections, and community engagement. She employs digital ethnographic methods to connect communities in Northern Ontario to their material culture at institutions in Southern Ontario. Her MA thesis featured the first formal analysis of the Fort Severn HBC post site, alongside a community engagement project with students from Fort Severn First Nation.

Lauren Dundler is an interdisciplinary researcher broadly concerned with art and antiquities crime, and ethical academic practice. In 2017, she submitted her Master of Research thesis—An Analysis of the Internet Market for Papyrus—which won the department award for best thesis. Currently, Lauren is developing a framework for ethical engagement with the ancient world for her doctoral research due for completion in 2021.

Anya Eber is a doctoral candidate in Criminology at the University of Oxford. Her research investigates the role of specialised art and antiquities law enforcement units in preventing the illicit antiquities trade in the United Kingdom and the United States. Anya holds an MSc degree in Criminology and Criminal Justice from the University of Oxford, an Art History MSc degree in Collecting and Provenance in an International Context from the University of Glasgow, and an AB in Archaeology and Art History from Brown University.

Michelle D. Fabiani is an Assistant Professor of Criminal Justice at the University of New Haven and co-director of the Cultural Resilience Informatics and Analysis (CURIA) Laboratory. Her research focuses on developing tools, methods, and data to mitigate and prevent crime as a means of confidence building. Her research has been published in *Global Crime, Arts,* and *Sociological Science,* among others.

Shawn Graham is a Digital Archaeologist where his research focus is on the creative application of digital methods to reuse archaeological or historical archives, using techniques from sonification to generative adversarial networks. His current major SSHRC-funded research project explores computer vision techniques for understanding how social media intersects with the trade in human remains as it takes place online.

Fiona Greenland is an Assistant Professor of Sociology at the University of Virginia. She studies the politics of national heritage. Her book, *Ruling Culture: Art Police, Tomb Robbers, and the Rise of Cultural Power in Italy*, traces Italy's historical entanglements of cultural elites, tomb robbers, and the state. Her new work examines cultural destruction and civilian deaths in the Syrian war.

Damien Huffer was a Postdoctoral Fellow (2017–2019) within the Osteoarchaeological Research Laboratory, Department of Archaeology & Classical

Studies, Stockholm University. During 2014–2016, he held the Stable Isotope Postdoctoral Fellowship at the Smithsonian's Museum Conservation Institute/Division of Anthropology. As a co-founder of The Alliance to Counter Crime Online, an interdisciplinary antiquities trade scholar, and an emerging museum professional, he is passionate about helping to raise public awareness of the existence and complexities of the 'niche' market that is the global traffic in human remains.

Simon Mackenzie is a Professor of Criminology and Head of the School of Social and Cultural Studies at Te Herenga Waka–Victoria University of Wellington. Simon's research is in the fields of white-collar crime and organised crime. His latest book is *Transnational Criminology: Trafficking and Global Criminal Markets (2020)*

James V. Marrone is an Economist at the RAND Corporation. His antiquities-related research has been published in the *Journal of Law and Economics*, *International Journal of Cultural Property*, and other outlets. Other cultural heritage-related work includes assisting the recovery of cultural resources in Puerto Rico after Hurricane Maria, and assessing how the COVID-19 pandemic affected working artists.

Francisco Romeo Marugan finished his studies in history, specialising in archaeology, in 1992. He wrote a thesis in 1997 on Iberian defensive systems. He worked as a professional archaeologist between 1992 and 2004 directed more than 200 excavations. Since 2005 Romeo Marugan has worked as an archaeologist for the Government of Aragon where he currently coordinates the analyses of the impact on the cultural heritage of public and private works. He regularly collaborates with the National Police and Civil Guard in the fight against archaeological plundering, participating as a judicial expert in several cases.

Naomi Oosterman is a Permanent Lecturer at the Department of Arts and Culture Studies, Erasmus University Rotterdam and an affiliated researcher at the research group Heritage under Threat of the Centre for Global Heritage and Development. Her research interests include the policing of art and heritage crime and the trafficking of antiquities.

Mackenzie Priest is a current J.D. candidate at Fordham University School of Law, class of 2024. Prior to attending law school, Mackenzie served the Manhattan District Attorney's Office's Antiquities Trafficking Unit as an Investigative Analyst. She specialises in cases relating to the preservation and collection of cultural property.

Vitória dos Santos Acerbi holds a master's degree in Latin American Studies from the University of Salamanca (Spain), with an Erasmus year at the Paris School of International Affairs of Sciences Po (France). She is a member of the research group International Law Without Borders, researching law and decoloniality. She also holds a bachelor's degree in History, with an emphasis on Cultural Heritage, from UFJF (Brazil).

Emiline Smith is a Lecturer in Criminology at the Scottish Centre for Crime and Justice Research, University of Glasgow. She is a Fellow at the Centre for Criminology, University of Hong Kong. Her research focuses on the trafficking of cultural and natural resources and plastic waste disposal.

Erin L. Thompson holds a PhD in art history and a J.D., both from Columbia University. She is an associate professor of art crime at the City University of New York.

Federica Villa holds a BA in archaeology at the University of Turin, Italy, and an MA in Art of Africa, Oceania and the Americas at the SRU—UEA, UK. She worked as an assistant director at the Raimondi Museum in Lima, Peru between 2018 and 2020, and she is currently collaborating as a Registrar with the Museum of Cultures in Milan, Italy. Her main interests concern the market of antiquities, museum studies, provenance research, and Peruvian antiquities.

Donna Yates is an Associate Professor in the Department of Criminal Law and Criminology, Maastricht University. Her research is focused on the transnational illicit trade in cultural objects, art and heritage crime, and white-collar crime. She is a founding member of the Trafficking Culture Research Consortium that produced evidence-based research into the illicit trade in cultural objects, and she is the principal investigator of the European Research Council-funded Trafficking Transformations project, which considers the role objects play in criminal networks.

Introduction

Naomi Oosterman and Donna Yates

Criminologists and sociologists are poorly represented in academic discourse on art and heritage crimes. Within criminology and sociology, art crime is considered an ultra-niche topic, a subject of focus for few,[1] of passing interest for some, and usually relegated without much elaboration to some broader categorisation of crime: white collar crime, organised crime, etc. It does not exist as a delineated space of contemplation and research.

Yet in parallel disciplines, the nexus between art and crime is approached as a clear topic of focus in its own right. Art law, which, of course, includes criminal law, is a growing academic and practical field: universities throughout the world offer law masters programmes on the topic, there are a number of focused art law journals, and professional law societies have incorporated art law into their standard pantheon of processional development offerings. In art historical and museums studies, provenance research methods particularly related to artworks collected during mass atrocities (e.g. colonialism or theft of art by the Nazis) are taught at an undergraduate level, are the subject of focused master's programmes, and are considered to be among the most important contemporary disciplinary concerns. In archaeology, professional activism at an international level against the global illicit trade in cultural objects has existed in force since the 1960s, with teaching heritage crime being a component of the standard undergraduate archaeology curriculum, and

[1] To name names would risk accidentally omitting someone, suffice to say their work is reflected in the bibliographies contained within this volume.

N. Oosterman (✉)
Department of Arts & Culture Studies, Erasmus University Rotterdam, Rotterdam, The Netherlands
e-mail: oosterman@eshcc.eur.nl

D. Yates
Criminal Law and Criminology, Maastricht University, Maastricht, The Netherlands
e-mail: d.yates@maastrichtuniversity.nl

N. Oosterman, D. Yates (eds.), *Crime and Art*, Studies in Art, Heritage, Law and the Market 1, https://doi.org/10.1007/978-3-030-84856-9_1

heritage crime prevention/mitigation considered an archaeologist's professional duty.

Within front-line policing, again art and heritage crimes are distinct. Many countries (as will be discussed by several authors in this volume) have dedicated art and heritage crime police units, customs, and border security units, as well as specialist agents within anti-money laundering, fraud, and financial crimes units who are specifically tasked with dealing with art-related crimes. Indeed, art and heritage crimes are distinct crimes within the criminal codes of many countries, and at the time of writing the International Criminal Court is consulting to develop its approach to heritage crimes.

Even in popular culture, art and heritage crime is both ubiquitous and clearly "a thing" in the public consciousness. To take one example, at the time of writing (June 2021 during the COVID-19 pandemic) three different art crime documentaries are currently popular on the media platform Netflix,[2] and the fictional series *Lupin*, which portrays a gentleman thief who steals from museums, became the most-watched non-English language series on the platform.

Exactly why criminology and sociology have not embraced art crime research as the lawyers, art historians, archaeologists, police, and Netflix viewers have is unclear. However, empirical research drawn from criminology and sociology's disciplinary frameworks is vital to understanding topics like theft, security, trafficking, forgery, vandalism, offender motivation, the efficacy of and results of policy interventions, and the effects art crimes have on communities. Conversely, the often strange, provocative, and intangible qualities of art inspire crimes that often exist outside of standard criminological understandings of such basics as offender motivation and crime opportunity. If, as artist Agnes Martin said, "art is the concrete representation of our most subtle feelings", then what is art crime. . .a violation of those most subtle feelings? Studying violations against art, with art being one of the few tangible manifestations of the intangible essence that makes us human, brings us closer to the ultimately impossible goal of understanding what, exactly, crime is.

With this volume, we seek to encourage not only an increased focus on art crime within criminology and sociology, but also to promote the utility of criminological and sociological frameworks and tools for art crime research. There is a tendency in published works on this topic to focus commentary on particular case studies. Through a largely descriptive review of the case, authors highlight interesting points of law, certain notable practices, and provide recommendations for future research, with these recommendations serving as a stand-in for actually conducting said research or placing the case within a more complex theoretical or analytical context. Such chapters are easy to write (we have written several ourselves) and are often fun to read, but they do little to either build our knowledge about the phenomenon of art

---

[2] *Murder Among the Mormons*, which documents bombings committed by a forger of rare historical documents; *Made You Look: The True Story About Fake Art*, which tells the story of a fake artworks scandal that shuttered the famous Knoedler Art Gallery; *This is a Robbery: The World's Biggest Art Heist*, about the 1990 Isabella Stewart Gardner Museum robbery and went 'viral'.

crime or allow the unique and notable aspects of art crime to further the disciplines of legal studies, heritage studies, anthropology, art history, or in our case, criminology and sociology.

In developing the concept of this volume, we sought contributions which moved decidedly beyond case studies, towards methodological or theoretical advancement. We called for chapters that pushed boundaries, considered new questions, and reframed existing understandings of 'art crimes'. Using criminology and sociology as unifying themes, we selected chapters that focused on elaboration, not description; experimentation, not reporting. We told contributors that they could get 'weird' if they wanted to. The results, as the reader will soon see, are both interesting and exciting.

Along with our focus on advancement came a conscious decision on our part as editors to showcase the work of early career researchers within this volume. Edited volumes, conferences, and journal special issues focused on art crime research often feature the same cast of characters: experienced scholars whose work is well known and who are at the centre of the academic and policy development networks that have developed in this field. This leads to a lack of diversity in the discourse and a degree of conservatism when considering new methodological, theoretical, and analytical approaches. Here, the reader will find contributions from scholars at every career stage reflecting the high quality of criminological and sociological work on art crime not just from senior scholars, but up-and-coming innovators.

The following chapters are divided into three parts: "Methods" which includes chapters focused on developing novel methods for investigating art crime; "Theory" which includes chapters that develop or expand theoretical frameworks for understanding art crime; and "Data Applications" which includes chapters that present the results of new empirical research in this field. Yet, these distinctions are largely artificial. Most chapters in this volume could be placed in two or even all three parts, as they use data from empirical research to advance theory, apply novel methodologies to generate empirical data, and all other combinations of the three. Indeed, the parts and the chapter ordering in this volume are there mostly so the reader and our publisher do not think we are lazy. The useful architecture offered by this volume is not found in the subtleties of chapter ordering, rather within the chapters themselves.

This book begins with a chapter by Michelle D. Fabiani and James V. Marrone who performed a social network analysis on the market of Egyptian, Near Eastern, and Classical antiquities. Having analysed over 30,000 items for sale that transited through three auction houses and 20 dealers, they uncovered the pathways of these items within the market, the relationship between sale outcomes and the re-emergence in the market, between auction houses and dealers. As they aptly demonstrate, applying an existing methodological framework on 'art crime data' uncovers new perspectives of the market here under investigation. In relation to their discussion on legitimisation, they argue that the more times an object is auctioned, specifically when it's also sold, the legitimacy of the object (e.g., its provenance or ownership history) can become higher, outweighing possibly questionable origins. Fabiani and Marrone furthermore provide a detailed and substantive discussion on how to utilise social network analysis in future art crime related research.

In a variation of the social network analysis, the next chapter by Katherine Davidson, Shawn Graham, and Damien Huffer discusses the illicit market for human remains on social media. They show that sellers on social media platforms actively utilise the legal grey area and lack of enforcement concerning the trade on these platforms. They argue that posting on social media is a form of performance, and that through the analysis of both textual and visual elements of posts that sell human remains, they can identify differences in performances of taste. When examining the different aesthetic styles of posts on Instagram, Davidson et al. note that various small online communities, to agree, share communal taste patterns, interests, and aesthetics.

The following chapter by Francisco Romeo Marugan brings us 'on the ground' as he discusses a novel methodology to map archaeological items in such a way that allow for the identification of the place of origin of stolen or looted archaeological items. Illustrating this methodology, he discusses, in detail, the *Helmet* operations that took place in Spain, and how the application of these novel techniques determining temperature, proximity, and dispersion of objects can result in a better determination of object origin, and thus improve expert aid in judicial proceedings of archaeological plundering.

The next chapter, by Emiline Smith, provides a discussion of the possible uses and implementations of *Photovoice* when studying the illicit trade of cultural objects. She argues that this 'participant-centred' and highly visual approach to research is an ideal avenue for art crime research, as it places those who are most affected by the crime at the core of the research process. In her chapter, Smith provides examples and best practices for the implementation of Photovoice by illustration of her previous field work undertaken in Nepal.

The final chapter of this part is by Lauren Dundler, who, in a qualitative variation of the themes developed by Marrone and Fabiani, and Davidson et al, discusses the construction of art dealer 'personas'. She uses a thematic analysis to study the ways in which dealers' construct, use, and perform their persona within the internet market for antiquities. She noticed that dealers are invested in creating a persona that is trustworthy, knowledgeable, discreet, but above anything else: that their role in the online antiquities trade is morally and legally acceptable. Dundler meticulously 'deconstructs' these carefully constructed personas, showing that many dealers in her analysis not only sell themselves and their antiquities, they also try to sell a certain lifestyle.

The next part of the book focuses on novel applications of sociological and criminological theory in the field of art crime research.

This part of the book starts off with Neil Brodie discussing scholarly engagement with unprovenanced cuneiform tablets, in particular, how scholars publicly justify researching objects that they must know are illicit. While prior art crime research has focused on how white-collar actors neutralise their participation in the grey market for antiquities, Brodie uses Luc Boltanski and Laurent Thévenot's theory of justification to shed light on the markets peripheral, but important participants. That academics are able to effectively justify the study and publication of looted archaeological material results in direct material harm in Iraq, the focus of Brodie's chapter, and beyond.

Donna Yates and Simon Mackenzie provide a highly original discussion of actor network theory in relation to art objects. By focusing on three key locations of the art market: the gallery, the museum, and the auction house, they propose that art worlds can be thought of as "desirescapes" where the ways in which art objects are displayed, portrayed, and in other ways presented, invoke the desire of individuals to own said objects. However, rather than focusing on a 'traditional' discussion of agency, that remains human-centred, Yates and Mackenzie move to a post-human discussion of the human-object relationship where objects develop 'organic properties' resulting in a form of relative independence from the original intentions by human actors.

The following chapter provides an equally thought-provoking discussion of the portrayal and presentation of objects, focusing on the discussion of 'constructed authenticity' in the backdrop of Peruvian antiquities. Federica Villa, in a variation of the human-object relationship as discussed by Yates and Mackenzie, discusses the ways in which auction houses use 'authenticity markers', by applying narratives in their catalogues that centre around primitivism and 'pastness', embedded within a Western art historical discourse. Villa notes that, in her discussion of *Moche* vessels, that authenticity is constructed through two different discourses, as the title of her chapter so clearly states: either as 'authentically primitive' or 'authentically beautiful'.

Rodrigo Christofoletti and Vitória dos Santos Acerbi's chapter discusses the history of the patrimonialisation and restitution of Afrobrazilian sacred items, specifically those objects labelled as the 'Black Magic' collection that were formerly part of the Civil Police Museum in Rio de Janeiro, Brazil. Discussing this collection through a lens of colonialism, decolonialism, and institutional racism, Christofoletti and dos Santos Acerbi diligently guide us through the history of this collection, starting with the illegalisation of 'black magic' and the subsequent confiscations of objects in 1891, to the current debates of restitution and decolonial justice, exemplified by the careful, but not nearly complete, implementation of these objects as objects of 'national heritage'.

The final chapter in this part is a work by Fiona Greenland that centres around the 'myth of violence' in relation to art crime. By analysing the workings of Italy's Art Squad, and examining art crime data from Interpol and the FBI, Greenland argues that human-artefact relationships in art crime policing are increasingly evaluated in terms of state violence and control. She aptly shows, by combining theoretical perspectives on cultural codes and empirical data from the three biggest policing initiatives concerning art crime, that art crime is more often than not a non-violent crime. Therefore, Greenland argues, thinking about art and archaeological policing, inaccurately, as organisations needing to display, or act on, violence and power, reinforces other persistent stereotypes concerning class, geography, and race.

The final part of this book focuses on data applications, presenting new empirical advances in the field of art crime. The part starts with a chapter by Erin Thompson and Mackenzie Priest who have evaluated the American Alliance of Museums

(AAM) guidelines concerning archaeological material and ancient art. They come to the rather shocking—nevertheless "unsurprising" according to the authors—conclusion that, of the 67 AAM museum members surveyed, many either lack compliance to the AAM guidelines and/or refrain from disclosing full transparency concerning their collection policies and ownership documentation. They exemplify why this is problematic through an in-depth analysis of the David Owsley Museum of Art in Muncie, Indiana, the United States.

The subsequent chapter by Anya Eber focuses on Routine Activities Theory and the broader discussion of 'guardianship' of specialised art, antiquities, and cultural property units in the United States and the United Kingdom. She focuses specifically on the antiquities market and provides a detailed account of the role of specialised art crime units and their different roles in the pro-active policing of art crime.

The next chapter by Diāna Bērziņa takes a novel, empirical approach by focusing on the low-end antiquities trade. She provides, in yet another variation of the theme concerning human-object relationships, that within the low-value antiquities trade, emphasis on financial gains excludes possible different motivations on engagement with these crimes. As exemplified in her snapshot analysis of Russian treasure hunter forums, most of the 'gains' of treasure hunting far outweigh the costs that treasure hunters make when engaging with their 'hobby'. Why then, Bērziņa asks herself, engage with the crime at all? And additionally: what is the risk of not policing this crime purely based on (low) financial indicators? Indeed, she offers an interesting addition on the often-heard *low risk, high reward* narrative in art crime research by studying those crimes that are, in financial terms, considered as not highly rewarding.

The next chapter by Michelle D. Fabiani focuses on offender motivations. She observes that many general studies on offender motivations lack empirical scrutiny, often ascribed to a lack of data, and that most prior research into offender motivations within art crime focus on the market, not on source-end offenders. After a detailed discussion and conceptualisation of criminological theory concerning offender motivations, she provides an extensive description on how to falsify theoretical propositions concerning, and the empirical investigation of, motivations for looting. She then continues to exemplify, using her own research undertaken between 2015 and 2017 on Lower Egypt, how the collection and analysis of spatiotemporal data infers motivations for looting in this region.

The final chapter of this part and book has Naomi Oosterman and Francesco Angelini analysing a unique data source: the 'dark marketplace' *Evolution.* In their analysis, rather than focusing on 'traditional' cultural objects central to art crime research, they focus on the often-overlooked category of luxury goods. In their analysis, these goods are conceptualised as 'conspicuous': namely those goods that are consumed by the wealthy elite to distinguish themselves from lower classes. In their analysis of the dark market structure for these goods, Oosterman and Angelini notice that on the dark marketplace these goods, counterfeit or original, are subject to price mechanisms associated to branding. They argue that sellers on this market are aware of the conspicuous 'qualities' of these goods, and subsequently brand, and price, them accordingly: as goods that are criminogenic desirables.

The various quantitative studies in this volume, which is an uncommon phenomenon in art crime research, show that, besides specialised art crime databases, various forms of data can be utilised to learn more about the scope of, and motivations for, art crime. Researchers tend to overlook art crime statistics due to factors such as poor- and under-reporting, and tend to dismiss quantitative research altogether because of the persisting idea that, especially criminal (especially police) data, is 'untrustworthy'. However, broadening our vision, as the authors in this volume do, to include perhaps not so straightforward or 'obvious' sources of data, tells us about the way the different crimes under the 'art crime umbrella' are structured, what networks exist, and sometimes quite literally where objects originate from. It is clear therefore from the authors in our book that a macro-analysis of art crime does pay off. Additionally, the many qualitative studies in this chapter show that, by scrutinizing, deconstructing, or just by simply asking different actors in the field the right questions, we understand so much more about the day-to-day practices in the art world in relation to art crime.

The study of art crime, as previously mentioned, deserves a delineated space of contemplation and research. With this volume, in addition to the existing legal, historical, and archaeological discussions of art crime, we provide empirical and original contributions embedded within sociological and criminological perspectives. This book has showcased that on the one hand, sociological and criminological theory, and on the other hand both quantitative and qualitative modes of enquiry, serve as an enrichment to the knowledge we have about art crime.

Part I
Methods

Transiting Through the Antiquities Market

A Social Network Analysis of Auctions

Michelle D. Fabiani and James V. Marrone

Abstract The antiquities market repeatedly raises concerns about money laundering, forgeries, and illicit trafficking. Auction houses' and dealers' roles in these activities are heavily studied, but there has been little research looking at connections between these market participants. We show the potential for social network analysis illuminate new aspects of the art market. In this case study, we track 30,000 individual items based on catalogued provenance information indicating their prior transit through various auction houses and dealers. The network inferred from these data allows us to address basic questions about the structure of the antiquities market, such as the rate of transit for items in the market, the pathways taken by items between auction houses, and the relationship between sale outcomes and re-appearance at auction. There are two types of objects that reappear at auction: those that failed to sell and are re-auctioned very quickly, and those that are held by a collector for about a decade before returning to auction. We also show that private dealers play a relatively important role in "vetting" certain objects, lending them legitimacy. Finally, we discuss additional uses of social network analysis and possible data sources for future art market researchers.

1 Introduction

As with many markets, the trade in antiquities does not readily provide a means for gathering primary data about the aspects of market structure that are of greatest interest to public policy. In the case of antiquities, the structures of interest are the supply chains by which items transit from the ground to their final sales in the market. These supply chains are implicated in both ethical and legal questions

---

M. D. Fabiani
Henry C. Lee College of Criminal Justice and Forensic Sciences, University of New Haven, West Haven, CT, USA

J. V. Marrone (✉)
RAND Corporation, Santa Monica, CA, USA
e-mail: jmarrone@rand.org

N. Oosterman, D. Yates (eds.), *Crime and Art*, Studies in Art, Heritage, Law and the Market 1, https://doi.org/10.1007/978-3-030-84856-9_2

surrounding the trade of cultural property. However, the market structure must be inferred from observable data due to the difficulty in observing the pathways by which archaeological objects exit their countries of origin directly (although some exceptional papers provide evidence of looting activity and the prices garnered by looters (Brodie, 1998; Brodie & Sabrine, 2018; Fabiani, 2019; Farchakh-Bajjaly, 2008; Greenland et al., 2019; Rose & Burke, 2004)). The literature commonly uses observable variables from auction sales to develop or substantiate hypotheses about various aspects of the supply chain. Though these studies provide valuable insight, their limited focus and methods can make it difficult to draw broad conclusions about market dynamics.

Social network analysis (SNA) provides an alternative for visualising and analysing market structures that can complement the findings from previous studies. SNA has increasingly been applied to a variety of markets, generating valuable insights into market activity and the relationships between market participants that form the foundation for market transactions. SNA has been used to explain firms' exposures to exogenous shocks (Uzzi, 1997), to understand firms' cost constraints due to their position in the supply chain (Borgatti & Li, 2009), and to analyse the art market's financial structure (Agrawal et al., 2015) and mechanisms for participation in dubious markets (Bichler et al., 2013). Network analysis is both feasible and useful in explaining market prices and other outcomes for both densely populated and sparse networks, since transactions may be determined in large part by the strength of relationships between market participants.

Although formal SNA methods have been applied to other black markets (Bright et al., 2012; Reid et al., 2007), few studies have taken a formal network approach to the auction market (see Bichler et al., 2013 for an exception). In this chapter, we apply SNA methods to a set of roughly 30,000 antiquities sold at auction and show how these methods illuminate new aspects of the art market. In particular, we find that a minority of objects reappear at auction a second time, but those that do follow two main paths: (1) they are re-auctioned at the same house within a short time frame (often 6 months) after failing to sell initially or (2) they that sold initially and were re-auctioned after several years without mention of the initial sale. In addition, our network analysis shows dealers play an important role in providing the first verifiable provenance for many objects. Auction catalogues rarely list an object's location prior to its having passed through the hands of a dealer, meaning that the dealer is lending the object *de facto* legitimacy.

Beyond the substantive findings, our analysis shows how social network methods may be to the art market to study the dynamics of object movement and patterns of sale. As we discuss further in the conclusion, there are several reasons art market research may benefit from SNA methods. The methods are naturally suited to looking at social relationships, including how the characteristics of those relationships correlate with material flows of objects and money. SNA methods can also make use of many types of data, including rich text data that encodes quantitative information. Our analysis provides one example of how auction catalogue text can be turned into a visual network of antiquities flowing between auction houses and dealers over time and space.

Our study follows several others that use auction sales and provenance information to deduce temporal patterns in looting or trafficking behaviour (Brodie, 2014a; Davis, 2011). Several other studies have examined the degree to which provenance information conforms with various market regulations (Beltrametti & Marrone, 2016; Brodie, 2019; Topçuoğlu & Vorderstrasse, 2019). A few other studies have performed empirical analyses of actual trafficking pathways (Brodie & Sabrine, 2018; Mackenzie & Davis, 2014) or relations between traffickers (D'Ippolito, 2014).

But many aspects of market structure—such as the importance of major collectors in generating supply and demand (Brodie, 2014b; Brodie, 2016), or the role of minor auction houses in sourcing material to later be sold by large auctioneers—remain largely the subject of speculation. The challenge of identifying the inner operations of auction markets has restricted the literature on this sector of the illegal antiquities market to either take a structured but high-level view of the market, where auction houses are but one actor in a system (Bichler et al., 2013), or to focus on conceptual models of market relations, from the ground to the final buyer (Campbell, 2013; D'Ippolito, 2014; Kersel, 2007; Polk, 2014). Many of these studies emphasise 'soft' relationships (such as the strength of ties between market participants). These relationships undergirding the market are undoubtedly important, a fact to which several book-length studies attest (Felch & Frammolino, 2011; Watson, 1997); however, soft relationships are difficult to study systematically and on a large scale, and they are not the only source of information about important aspects of market structure. The SNA approach adopted here begins to address some of these gaps by examining the movement of items over time in terms of a network.

The remainder of the paper discusses the data and how it was transformed into a meaningful social network format, then the SNA methods we used and the main empirical results.

2 Data

As with prior studies of provenance, our data came from antiquities sales catalogues. We recorded individual items sold at the semi-annual antiquities sales at Bonhams, Christie's, and Sotheby's, between 2007 and 2015.[1] Items at art auctions are sold in 'lots', which contain one or more individual objects. When there were multiple objects in a lot, we distinguished the individual objects based on catalogue descriptions.

Auction catalogues published prior to the auction provided information about the items in each lot, including details about each item's provenance, or ownership history.[2] Provenance documentation varies in quality, in terms of whether the

[1] These were the most recently available data during the data collection phase of this project.

[2] We use the word provenance when referring to an object's ownership history because that is the term used in auction house catalogues. There is a scholarly debate regarding the appropriate terms to

Table 1 Summary statistics for auction lots

	Total	Bonhams	Christie's	Sotheby's
# Lots	16,422	8249	6494	1679
Average low estimate (Jan. 2021 USD)	20,043	5483	26,641	70,801
Average high estimate (Jan. 2021 USD)	29,753	7817	39,892	105,382
% Sold	72.3	71.2	70.0	86.4
Average sale price (Jan. 2021 USD)	53,389	6847	51,084	252,848
Average # items	2.15	2.82	1.50	1.33

information is specific and can be independently verified; provenance information has been known to be falsified by collectors and dealers (Gerstenblith, 2019, discusses several examples), but it is often just vague. The catalogued provenance is hardly ever complete, in that it does not document every possessor of an object all the way back to the day and location it was excavated (Brodie & Manivet, 2017). This means that reconstructing an item's exact ownership history is generally impossible based solely on the information in the catalogue. However, auction sales serve as 'signposts' for an item's provenance: if a catalogue claims that an item was sold at a prior auction, then the catalogue for that earlier auction can be consulted to verify the claim. The earlier catalogue may provide historical prices and additional provenance information as well.

When the catalogued provenance indicated an item was previously offered for sale at another auction house (including some houses besides the three studied here or at auctions that were not dedicated solely to antiquities), we consulted the prior auction catalogue to record the prior sale price and any additional provenance information. The process was continued until each item ceased to be traceable on the auction market. The resulting data set consists of 31,654 unique items offered at auction a total of 33,709 times.

From the sales data, we constructed a social network of individual antiquities. This network, like any social network, consisted of nodes and edges connecting the nodes. In this case, the combination of individual items and individual auction houses yielded a bipartite network, i.e., a network with two types of nodes. Some nodes were items, other nodes were auction houses, and the edges (lines) connecting them indicated the item was sold at the auction house (see Borgatti et al., 2013, for additional details on bipartite networks). The network itself should be considered a snapshot of the market in 2007–2015, along with the historical connections between items in that snapshot and other auctioneers who sold those items before 2007.

Tables 1 and 2 summarise the baseline data set of sales between 2007 and 2015; the full dataset also included sales of these items that took place prior to 2007, as

denote an archaeological object's ownership history since excavation vis-à-vis its archaeological and stratigraphic context or its history since creation. See Gerstenblith (2020) for a history of this debate and the related complexities of an object's legality and authenticity.

Table 2 Summary statistics for individual items

	Total	Bonhams	Christie's	Sotheby's
# Objects	33,709	22,205	9459	2045
% Previously offered at auction	14.5	10.0	20.4	35.4
% No provenance	5.1	7.6	0.3	0.3
% Previously sold by private dealer	13.9	6.5	28.7	26.8

indicated in the catalogues. The network was constructed at the item level, which means that lot-level characteristics like price could not be disentangled easily—although it is known that items sold alone in a lot are different in many ways from items sold in large groups (Marrone, 2018). The tables show differences across auction houses with prices adjusted to January 2021 United States dollars. The tables do not distinguish between locations within a house (such as Christie's London versus Christie's New York) because the differences in prices and sales rates across houses are larger than the corresponding differences across locations of a given house.

First, Table 1 shows differences in lots put up for auction. During this time period Bonhams was high-volume but lower price, offering roughly 25% more lots than Christie's and nearly five times more lots than Sotheby's. It also had more items per lot—nearly three on average, compared to about 1.5 for Christie's and 1.3 for Sotheby's. On average, the high estimates at Christie's and Sotheby's are 5 and 12 times higher than at Bonhams; if the lot successfully sells to a bidder, the prices are 7 and 37 times higher than Bonhams. Conversely to Bonhams, Sotheby's was the low-quantity, high price auction house.

Table 2 shows differences in individual items. Auction houses have a differential propensity to source material from prior auctions, to research objects' ownership histories in order to identify prior sales, and to report extensive provenance information in their catalogues. On average, 14.5% of items were offered in at least one prior known auction (including possibly prior to 2007 when our observation window started); Bonhams had the smallest and Sotheby's had the largest proportion. Yet 5.1% of items have no provenance at all—not even unverifiable information such as "Private European collection." Most of these items came from Bonhams, at which 7.6% of items had no provenance; only 0.3% of items at Christie's and Sotheby's fit this category. Finally, for 14% of items the catalogue description noted a prior sale by a private dealer. Again, Bonhams has the lowest fraction. Christie's has the most, with almost 29% coming (at some point in the past) from these private sellers.

3 Method

To get a better sense of the data and how patterns of sale varied over time, the data were structured into valued 2-mode edgelist and edgearray[3] datasets with multiple attributes for each. The data were visualised both for the overall network and for the subset of items that were put up for auction multiple times. Only the subset network was examined across time periods.

To look at multiple time periods, we aggregated the data into 16 unique time periods representing 6-month intervals. Generally, auction houses have two auctions per year—one in the spring and one in the fall. When analysing the data, a yearly interval had too little variation between time periods to be useful, so instead we segmented the data at 6-month intervals to align with the auction cycle. Bonhams' auctions occur at less-regular intervals, so we aggregated the Bonham's data in 6-month intervals. Only two cases were identified where an item was auctioned more than once in the same 6-month period. As such, the use of 6-month intervals is a reasonable breakdown of time periods.

Additionally, we created new variables for both the vertices and for use as attributes using information provided in the raw data. Specifically, we created a new variable that combined auction houses and their locations (for example Bonhams Knightsbridge and Bonhams New Bond Street). The new attribute variables included:

1. A binary variable indicating if an item sold at each auction, versus failing to meet the reserve price.
2. A binary variable indicating if there was a known dealer associated with the item.
3. A binary variable indicating if there was any provenance information listed.
4. Categorical variables indicating whether an item changed location and/or auction houses if it was put up for auction more than once.
5. Categorical variables indicating whether an item's dealer history and/or provenance information changed if the item was put up for auction more than once.[4]
6. A variable recording the number of years between auctions, for those items put up for auction multiple times.

[3] An edgearray dataset allows for visualisation of networks by type of relationship by structuring data as a series of stacked matrices that account for multiple levels of relationships at once (Borgatti et al., 2013).

[4] Both variables looking at auction house and/or location movement include four categories with values 0–4 in ascending order: (0) item not auctioned, (1) no change in the house and location, (2) a change in the house with no change in the location (e.g., an item is auctioned at Bonhams in London and is then auctioned at Christie's in London the next time) (3) a change in the location with no change in the house (e.g., an item is auctioned at Bonhams Knightsbridge and then Bonhams New Bond Street), and (4) a change in both the house and the location.

4 Analysis

We structured these data and new variables into an edgelist dataset (for the overall network) and an edgearray dataset (for the subset of the network comprising items offered for sale more than once), which were then visualised as 2-mode networks. For the subset network, we used NetDraw,[5] as it can work with a valued 2-mode edgearray dataset as well as multiple node attributes. To visualise and analyse the movement of these items between and within auction houses and their locations, we visualised the data based on combinations of dealer and provenance information as well as time between sales and auction house and/or location movement. Visualisations of each of these combinations looked specifically at changes both between the first and second time and the second and third time an item was put up for auction. Additionally, we supplemented the network visualisations with descriptive statistics on the patterns of sale. NetDraw (and UCINET[6] more generally) have a limit of roughly 32,600 nodes and lose functionality around 10,000 nodes. The overall network with data from 2007–2015 in one snapshot contains 31,654 nodes. As such, we used a software specifically designed to accommodate and visualise large datasets (up to millions of nodes), Pajek, to visualise the overall network.

Valued 2-mode network datasets are best suited for descriptive analyses where the primary interest is in visualizing movement or changes in relation to events, groups, or time periods. The calculation of network statistics (e.g. measures of centrality) has limited utility for 2-mode networks. By default, the most central nodes in a 2-mode network will be the events or groups the other nodes are attached to. In the case of our data, the auction houses will be the most central by construction. Moreover, since the purpose of the visualisations here is to demonstrate movement and changes between periods when items go up for auction, network descriptive statistics will not add any substantive value to the analysis. As such, they are not included in this study.

This approach to modelling the network reveals the degree of connectedness of the market—the degree to which items transit through multiple different sellers or if they tend to be sold by just one. Looking at how auction houses are related to each other through object sales highlights how the three largest firms are connected to each other and to various dealers and lower-tier auction houses. In turn, this connectedness can speak to whether these three large auction houses appear to maintain relationships with a unique set of dealers and collectors who buy and sell only through that house. If the network is not connected and each auction house appears to maintain exclusive relationships with its own consignors, then each

[5]NetDraw is a free social network analysis visualisation software that was developed to work alongside the analytical software UCINET. For more information, see http://www.analytictech.com/products.htm.

[6]UCINET is a windows-based software package for analysing social networks, developed by Lin Freeman, Martin Everett and Steve Borgatti. For more information, see https://sites.google.com/site/ucinetsoftware/home.

auction house's catalogues would provide insight into separate supply chains, with the items at each house being sourced from distinct sets of consignors and agents. On the other hand, if the network is interconnected then auction houses are competing for consignments and auctions do not tell much about the buyer/seller relationships undergirding the unobservable private market. As such, looking at the art market from a network perspective can be useful for revealing patterns and dynamics that might otherwise be difficult to observe or model.

5 Results

Figure 1 shows the entire network. Auction houses and their locations are labelled with white squares while grey circles represent individual items put up for auction.[7] Edges represent whether each item was put up for auction at a given auction house and location. Most of the items auctioned at these three houses from 2007–2015 have been put up for auction once and do not return prior to 2015. These are the large clouds of grey nodes surrounding each black node denoting an auction house. Yet if all items followed this pattern, then there should be no edges connecting auction houses. Instead, a not-insignificant portion of nodes are connected to multiple auction houses and locations, shown by the grey nodes with long edges spanning between different clouds. Specifically, 3.4% of items accounting for 6.4% of sales were offered at more than one auction house from 2007–2015. There are also peripheral auction houses: the black dots with just a handful of edges are smaller auction houses that sold items prior to their appearance at Bonhams, Christie's or Sotheby's.

Figure 1 shows that some items are 'moving' through auction houses and locations. It is not uncommon for items to be auctioned multiple times over an extended period of time. However, there a relatively limited literature looking at whether there is a difference in, on the one hand, the time between the auction of an item that legally transfers it among collectors, and on the other hand, the laundering of items through auction houses. Network analysis is one way to begin to look at this question by examining how items 'move' between auction houses over time. To look at this in more depth, we consider the subset of nodes that had multiple connections to auction houses and locations.

There are 1035 items that were put up for auction more than once, totalling 2104 observations in the data (33 items were auctioned three times, the others just twice). Figure 2 shows the distribution of these items by auction house and season. As the figure demonstrates, there is heterogeneity in when and where items are offered for

[7] A few black dots represent locations such as Christie's Paris, which does not normally hold stand-alone antiquities auctions. The presence of these nodes is because they sold antiquities in other auctions, and those antiquities later sold at one of the major antiquities auctions from which we gathered data.

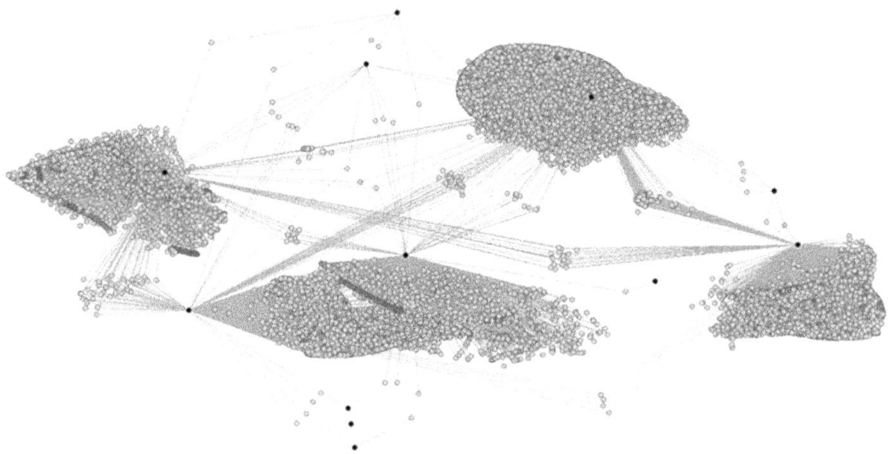

Fig. 1 Complete Network 2007–2015. Black nodes indicate auction houses and grey nodes represent items put up for auction. Starting at the top centre (clockwise), the auction houses are: Christies Amsterdam, Bonhams London NBS (New Bond Street), Bonhams OXF (Oxford Street), Bonhams London KB (Knightsbridge), Sotheby's Paris, Sotheby's NY, Bonhams SF (San Francisco), Sotheby's London, Bonhams LA, Christie's NY, Christie's London, Christie's Paris

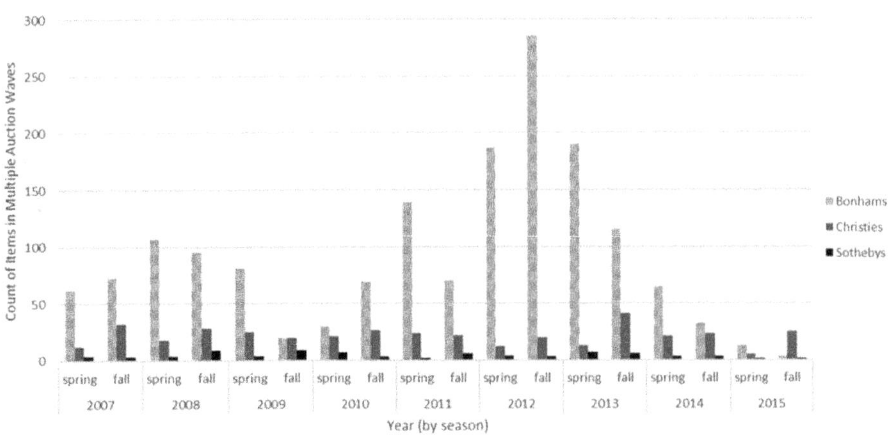

Fig. 2 Appearances of items auctioned multiple times by auction house and season

sale. Bonhams has the most, relative to the other houses, and the 2012 seasons contain the most items put up for auction multiple times (see Fig. 2). This is partly because Bonhams often resells antiquities that failed to find a buyer in the previous season's auction (a practice we only observed at Bonhams, with the exact same picture and description pasted from the prior season's catalogue). But it could also indicate movement of items from other auction houses to Bonhams. Thus, it is

Table 3 Prior performance of re-auctioned items and time between sales

	Number of items	Average time since prior sale
Did not find buyer in previous auction	732	0.9 years (almost 11 months)
Did find buyer in previous auction	336	3.6 years

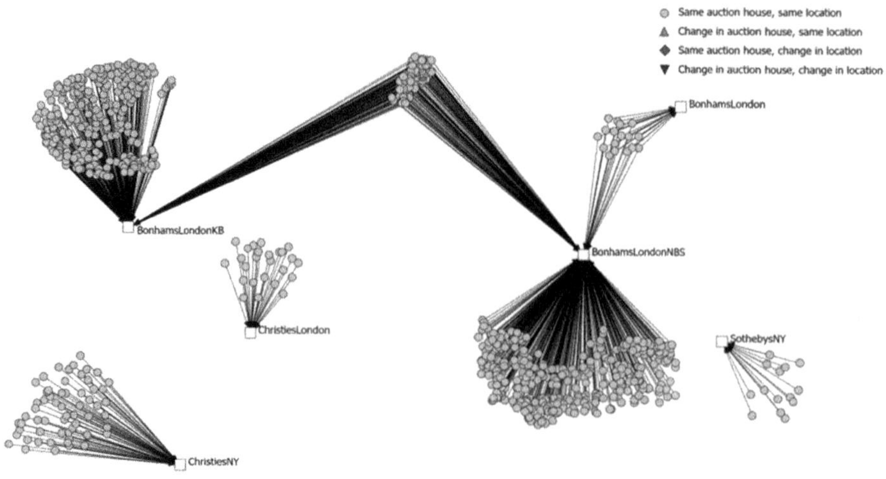

Fig. 3 No movement between or within auction houses and locations between item's first and second time at auction. Items remained at the same auction house and in the same location. Note that Bonhams has multiple London locations and so those are connected

important to look more closely at the relationship between these items and the auction houses and their locations.

One factor that may influence whether an item is put up for auction a second or third time is whether it successfully sold the previous time. In this respect, the data show two general types of objects, listed in Table 3. Of the subset of items that were auctioned more than once, 732 items failed to find a buyer the first time; they reappeared, on average, less than one year later. By contrast, when items found a buyer they reappeared on average 3.6 years later.

Among the items that are auctioned more than once, over 80% were re-auctioned at the same house and in the same location. Yet, there is also evidence of overlap and 'communication' between and within auction houses. Figures 3, 4, 5, 6, and 7 show changes in auction house and/or location between successive appearances at auction. Nodes are coloured and shaped according to the object's movement between auctions. Circles represent no change in auction house or location (e.g., an item at Bonham's London Knightsbridge location twice in a row). Upward triangles represent a change in the auction house but no change in the location (e.g., an item first at Bonham's Knightsbridge and then Christie's London). Diamonds represent a change in location within the same house (e.g., an item first at Bonham's Knightsbridge and then at Bonham's LA). Downward triangles represent a change in both the house and location for the item (e.g., an item first at Bonham's Knightsbridge then at Sotheby's

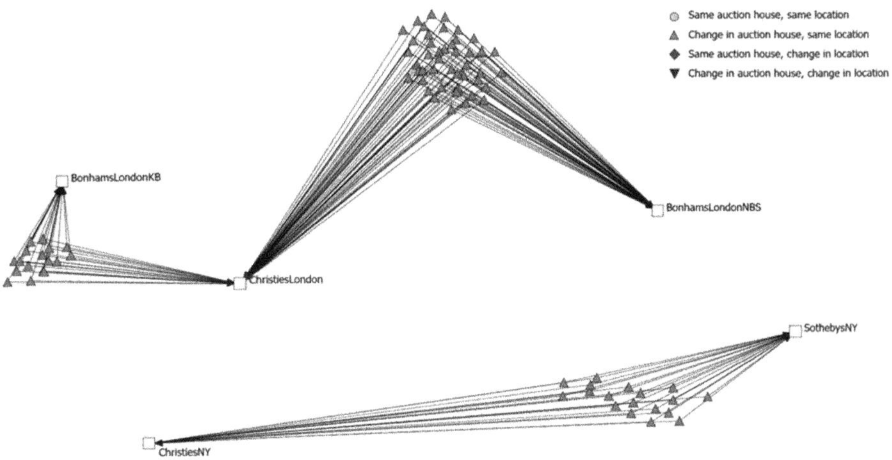

Fig. 4 Movement between auction houses, but not locations between item's first and second time at auction. Items changed auction houses but remained in the same location

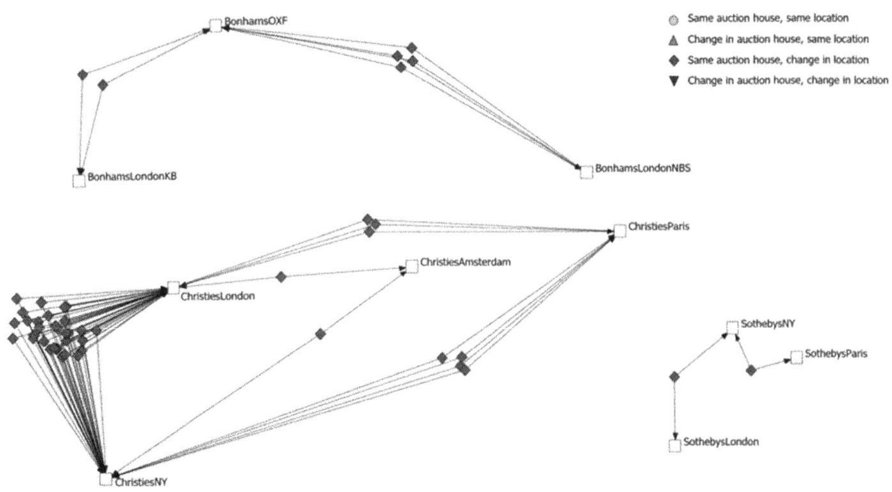

Fig. 5 No movement between auction houses, but a change in location between item's first and second time at auction. Items remained in the same auction house, but changed locations

NY). Thus, the symbols represent the flow of items both geographically and between firms.

Overall, most items appear to have been auctioned within the same auction house and the same location (circles) between successive sales. Roughly 8% of items changed houses in the same location (upward triangles), 5% moved within the same house to a different location (diamonds), and 6% changed both houses and locations (downward triangles). Additionally, in line with Table 3 the majority of

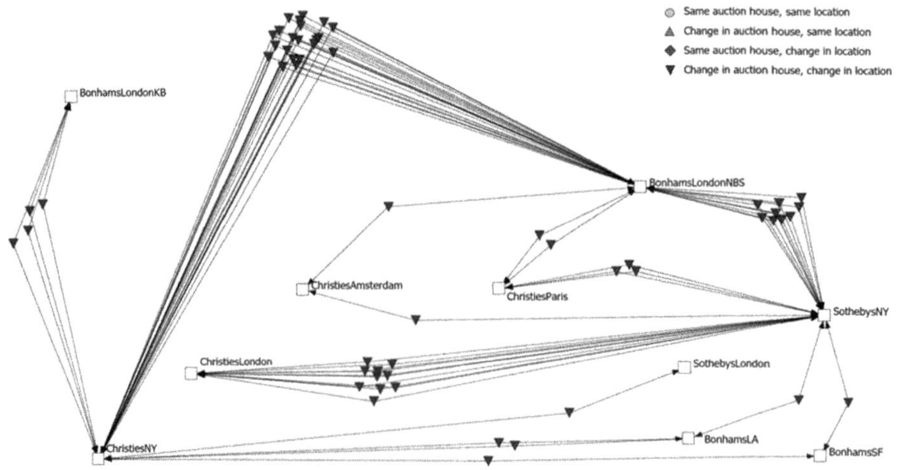

Fig. 6 Movement both between auction houses and in locations between item's first and second time at auction. Items changed auction houses and changed locations

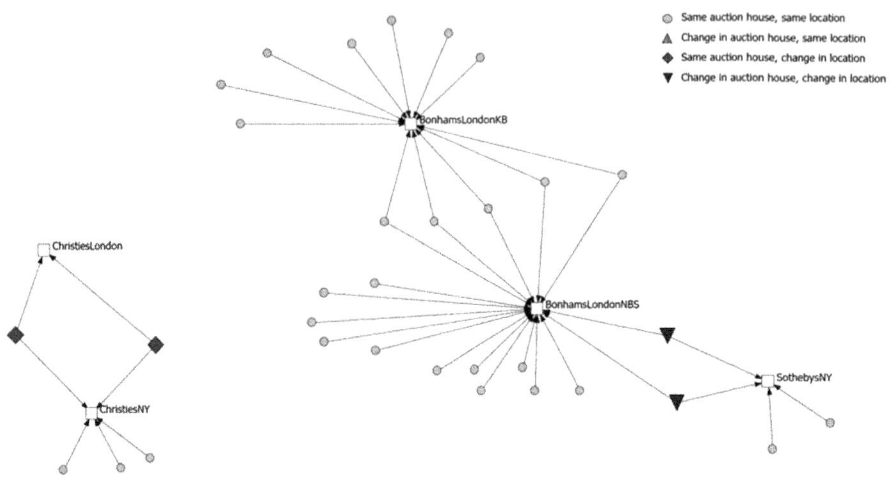

Fig. 7 Movement between and within auction houses and locations between items' second and third time at auction

these items are re-auctioned very soon after their first auction: over half (56.6%) of items are sold again at the next auction 6 months later.

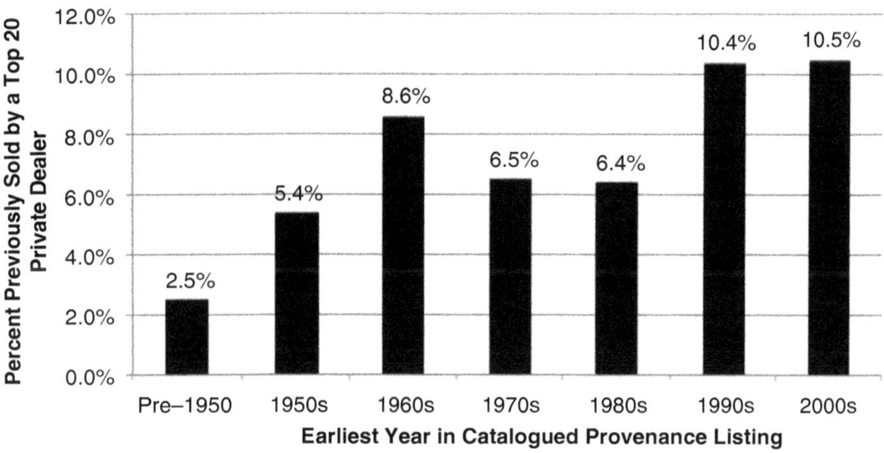

Fig. 8 Proportion of items at auction associated with one of the 20 most common private dealers, based on the earliest date of provenance

6 The Importance of Dealers

Auction houses are just one type of transit point for items on the antiquities market. Private dealers handle a large quantity of items but comprise a market segment that is difficult to observe. Many dealers do not publish catalogues, and they do not provide public records of their sales (it should be noted that auction houses, too, engage in private sales). Though auctions take place regularly, information on the items going up for sale is closely guarded by the auction houses. Often, auction catalogues are one of the only sources of information about antiquities that are bought and sold on the market. As such, auction catalogue provenance provides one of the few ways to see, retrospectively at least, how important dealers are in terms of sourcing antiquities and giving them a provenance. Of the dozens of dealers listed in the provenances of our database, we examined the 20 dealers who appeared most frequently.[8]

Figure 8 shows the fraction of items that passed through these dealers based on the earliest decade of provenance. It is not necessarily the case that the dealers sold the items in the decade listed but rather that they sold items that could be traced back to that decade. The figure shows these dealers sold few items overall (less than 10%),

[8] We partly focus on just 20 because they are identifiable as dealers (provenance information is not always clear on whether someone was a dealer or collector, or what the full name of the dealer is). We also focus on these 20 because they are highly prominent and therefore presumably lend some credibility to the object's authenticity and may add prestige to the object itself. We ignore items that were noted to have been in a dealer's private collection, as dealers can act as collectors in their own right.

but they are relatively more likely to have sold items with more recent provenance. Whether or not the pattern is intentional, the upshot is that dealers are more likely to offer a veneer of legitimacy to items with thinner documented ownership histories. This is somewhat troubling, given that many of these dealers were quite active between 1960 and 1980, and many major private collections were formed during that time. To the extent that dealers kept records that are available to provenance researchers, auction houses are not reproducing that information in their catalogues.

Still, if dealers were doing their own provenance research or deliberately sourcing antiquities from well-documented historic collections (such as antiquities collected on the Grand Tours of the eighteenth century, as discussed in Black, 1996, 2010), it would presumably be in the auction house's best interest to record as much in auction catalogues. Not only does such information raise an object's desirability (and hence its price), but it can help to prove that the object was not recently looted and is being sold in compliance with relevant international laws. Instead, auction catalogue provenance often traces objects back to dealers, but no further. This means dealers, when mentioned, are likely to be the first documented location of objects on the market. In this way dealers become de facto sources of 'sufficient' provenance, with catalogues leaving a mystery from where the dealer received the object and to whom they sold it.

One problem with relying on dealers to legitimise an object is that they can be a source of illegitimate or illegal transactions. Several of the 20 dealers that comprise our sample have known links with the illicit trade (for examples of dealers' complicity with illegal transactions see Brodie, 2012; Watson & Todeschini, 2007). We are not claiming this is true of every object sold by these dealers, but the sale patterns in conjunction with these illicit connections reinforce existing doubt on the means by which many items came to the market. Although some scholars and critics of the antiquities market claim that virtually any item without a documented find-spot must have been illegally procured (Brodie & Renfrew, 2005 provide a more nuanced discussion of the potential relationships between lack of provenance, looting, and collecting trends), it has been difficult to identify exactly what share of antiquities were looted and at what time in the past looting occurred.[9] Our data, of course, cannot provide any conclusive evidence for looted or laundered goods, but insofar as dealers might act as clearinghouses for 'new' antiquities this analysis shows they are connected to a small but important chunk of goods that make their way to auction.

---

[9]A documented archaeological origin is referred to as *provenience*, as opposed to provenance, which is a history of the object since excavation. The distinction is important when considering objects' scientific value, as opposed to just aesthetic value or legality. Regardless of how far back provenance research can track an object, most of the time they still come to the market with no provenience. The foundational studies are Muscarella (1977) and Chippindale and Gill (1993).

7 Using Social Network Analysis in Future Art Crime Research

Taken together, our findings suggest that there are likely multiple different processes at play in the patterns of auction and sale of antiquities and art in these auction houses. First, there may be important differences between items that are re-auctioned and those that are not. The more times an item is auctioned (and especially sold), the more current and legitimate history of ownership an item acquires, which can outweigh any questionable origins the item may have. Second, there may be differences between items that move between houses and/or locations and items that stay within the same house and location. It may be that changing locations and/or auction houses provides the seller with more freedom in the type of information listed with the item, such as changing the provenance descriptions, including any exhibitions, publications, or known collectors associated with the item.

In addition to the substantive findings above, this analysis speaks to the utility of social network analysis as an approach to studying the art market. Here we were able to examine connections between market participants over time and space in a way that would otherwise have been difficult to study quantitatively. Future research should consider network methods to study the art market for three reasons.

First, network analysis encourages asking questions that focus on how objects, events, and people relate to each other. The art market is inherently social in construction and so is well suited to research looking at such questions. For example, social network methods allow for relatively easy analysis of how art objects move between art collectors, dealers, and other market participants. Other questions could focus on how the structure of the art market facilitates the sale of certain objects (e.g., through dealer-auction house relationships), the laundering of money or objects, or the transit of objects through trafficking networks. Still other questions could focus on the role of trust or power dynamics in the trafficking of objects through to the market, for example by comparing familial to transactional relationships (Von Lampe & Johansen, 2004) or by comparing the length of time a relationship lasts (Molm et al., 2009). These types of questions all have their roots in conceptualising and explicitly looking at how social relationships are structured. Exploring these or other such questions in the context of the art market could provide valuable insight into its dynamics. In turn, this information can be used to develop more effective means of intervening in the acquisition, movement, and sale of illicit art and antiquities.

Second, this method is flexible both in the types of data it requires and how the data are used. Data can be derived from many sources in network analysis, including court records, seizure data, interviews, investigative journalism, qualitative case studies, and more. Anything that speaks to a relationship between objects, people, or events can be coded into a matrix for network analysis. Equally relevant to the art market, network analysis methods can incorporate qualitative attributes for both nodes (actors, objects, events) and edges (relationships). Thus, this method can visually display complex relationships and dynamics in an intuitive format. It can also accommodate many definitions of a relationship—transactional, familial relationship, rivalries, friendships, informant-police relationships, and more. This flexibility makes network analysis particularly useful in the art market where there may be varying qualities and quantities of data available and relationships of interest.

Finally, network analysis is increasingly able to incorporate dynamic modelling and spatial movements. Historically, network analysis has been limited to looking at snapshots in time, which limited the ability of studies seeking to analyse the evolution of decision-making within networks. More recently, studies have demonstrated new ways of modelling dynamic decision-making in covert networks (see e.g., Bichler & Malm, 2013). Similarly, the ability to incorporate spatial relationships into studies of networks has become more common, particularly looking at illicit market flows (see e.g., Berlusconi et al., 2017). Given the constantly evolving nature of the art market and its transnational scope, the ability to incorporate both temporal and spatial dimensions into future research could prove invaluable. Understanding the decision-making process within the art market as well as in the trafficking networks could help to develop better methods for countering crimes in this area.

References

Agrawal, A., Catalini, C., & Goldfarb, A. (2015). Crowdfunding: Geography, social networks, and the timing of investment decisions. *Journal of Economics and Management Strategy, 24*(2), 253–274.

Beltrametti, S., & Marrone, J. V. (2016). Market responses to court rulings: Evidence from antiquities auctions. *Journal of Law and Economics, 59*(40), 913–944.

Berlusconi, G., Aziani, A., & Giommoni, L. (2017). The determinants of heroin flows in Europe: A latent space approach. *Social Networks, Crime and Networks, 51*, 104–117. https://doi.org/10.1016/j.socnet.2017.03.012

Bichler, G., Bush, S., & Malm, A. (2013). Bad actors and faulty props: Unlocking legal and illicit art trade. *Global Crime, 14*(4), 359–385.

Bichler, G., & Malm, A. (2013). Small arms, big guns: A dynamic model of illicit market opportunity. *Global Crime, 14*(2–3), 261–286. https://doi.org/10.1080/17440572.2013.787928

Black, J. (1996). Italy and the Grand Tour: The British experience in the eighteenth century. *Annali d'Italianistica, 14*, 532–541.

Black, J. (2010). *The British and the Grand Tour*. Routledge.

Borgatti, S. P., Everett, M. G., & Johnson, J. C. (2013). *Analyzing social networks*. SAGE Publications.

Borgatti, S. P., & Li, S. (2009). On social network analysis in a supply chain context. *Journal of Supply Chain Management, 45*(2), 5–22.

Bright, D. A., Hughes, C. E., & Chalmers, J. (2012). Illuminating dark networks: A social network analysis of an Australian drug trafficking syndicate. *Crime, Law and Social Change, 57*(2), 151–176.

Brodie, N. (1998). Pity the poor middlemen. *Culture Without Context, 3*, 7–9.

Brodie, N. (2012, August 21). Organigram. Blog post. *Trafficking Culture*. Retrieved May 31, 2021, from https://traffickingculture.org/encyclopedia/case-studies/organigram/

Brodie, N. (2014a). Auction houses and the antiquities trade. In S. Choulia-Kapeloni (Ed.), *3rd International conference of experts on the return of cultural property* (pp. 71–82). Archaeological Receipts Fund.

Brodie, N. (2014b). The antiquities market: It's all in a price. *Heritage & Society, 7*(1), 32–46.
Brodie, N. (2016, May 14). Rich and powerful collectors (1). Blog post. *Market of Mass Destruction*. Retrieved May 31, 2021, from http://www.marketmassdestruction.com/rich-and-powerful-collectors-1/
Brodie, N. (2019). Through a glass, darkly: Long-term antiquities auction data in context. *International Journal of Cultural Property, 26*(3), 265–283.
Brodie, N., & Manivet, P. (2017). Cylinder seals at Sotheby's and Christie's (1985–2013). *Journal of Art Crime, 17*(Spring), 3–6.
Brodie, N., & Renfrew, C. (2005). Looting and the world's archaeological heritage: The inadequate response. *Annual Review of Anthropology, 34*, 343–361.
Brodie, N., & Sabrine, I. (2018). The illegal excavation and trade of Syrian cultural objects: A view from the ground. *Journal of Field Archaeology, 43*(1), 74–84.
Campbell, P. B. (2013). The illicit antiquities trade as a transnational criminal network: Characterizing and anticipating trafficking of cultural heritage. *International Journal of Cultural Property, 20*(2), 113–153.
Chippindale, C., & Gill, D. W. J. (1993). Material and intellectual consequences of esteem for Cycladic figures. *American Journal of Archaeology, 97*(4), 601–659.
D'Ippolito, M. (2014). New methods of mapping: The application of social network analysis to the illegal trade in antiquities. In W. Kennedy, N. Agarwal, & S. J. Yang (Eds.), *Social computing, behavioral-cultural modelling and prediction* (pp. 253–260). Springer.
Davis, T. (2011). Supply and demand: Exposing the illicit trade in Cambodian antiquities through a study of Sotheby's auction house. *Crime, Law and Social Change, 56*(2), 155–174.
Fabiani, M. (2019). Building a baseline: Unifying spatial and temporal methodologies to understand archaeological looting in Egypt. Doctoral Dissertation, University of Maryland. Digital Repository of the University of Maryland (DRUM).
Farchakh-Bajjaly, J. (2008). Who are the looters at archaeological sites in Iraq? In L. Rothfield (Ed.), *Antiquities under siege: Cultural heritage protection after the Iraq war* (pp. 49–56). Altamira.
Felch, J., & Frammolino, R. (2011). *Chasing Aphrodite: The hunt for looted antiquities at the world's richest museum*. Houghton Mifflin Harcourt.
Gerstenblith, P. (2019). Provenances: Real, fake, and questionable. *International Journal of Cultural Property, 26*(3), 285–304.
Gerstenblith, P. (2020). Provenience and provenance intersecting with international law in the market for antiquities. *North Carolina Journal of International Law, 45*(2), 457–496.
Greenland, F., Marrone, J. V., Topçuoglu, O., & Vorderstrasse, T. (2019). A site-level market model of the antiquities trade. *International Journal of Cultural Property, 26*(1), 21–47.
Kersel, M. M. (2007). Transcending borders: Objects on the move. *Archaeologies: Journal of the World Archaeological Congress, 3*(2), 81–98.
Mackenzie, S., & Davis, T. (2014). Temple looting in Cambodia: Anatomy of a statue trafficking network. *British Journal of Criminology, 54*(7), 722–740.
Marrone, J. V. (2018). Quantifying the supply chain for Near Eastern antiquities in times of war and conflict. *Journal of Cultural Heritage, 33*, 278–284.
Molm, L. D., Schaefer, D., & Collett, J. L. (2009). Fragile and resilient trust: Risk and uncertainty in negotiated and reciprocal exchange. *Sociological Theory, 27*(1), 1–32. https://doi.org/10.1111/j.1467-9558.2009.00336.x
Muscarella, O. W. (1977). 'Ziwiye' and Ziwiye: The forgery of a provenience. *Journal of Field Archaeology, 4*(2), 197–219.
Polk, K. (2014). The global trade in antiquities: Some new directions? In L. Grove & S. Thomas (Eds.), *Heritage and crime: Prospects, progress, and prevention* (pp. 206–223). Palgrave Macmillan.
Reid, E., Hsinchun, C., & Xu, J. (2007). Social network analysis for terrorism research. In H. Chen, T. S. Raghu, R. Ramesh, A. Vinze, & D. Zeng (Eds.), *Handbooks in information systems, book 2: National security* (pp. 243–270). Elsevier.

Rose, J. C., & Burke, D. L. (2004). Making money from buried treasure. *Culture Without Context, 14*, 4–8.

Topçuoğlu, O., & Vorderstrasse, T. (2019). Small finds, big values: Cylinder seals and coins from Iraq and Syria on the online market. *International Journal of Cultural Property, 26*(3), 239–263.

Uzzi, B. (1997). Social structure and competition in interfirm networks: The paradox of embeddedness. *Administrative Science Quarterly, 42*(1), 35–67.

Von Lampe, K., & Johansen, P. O. (2004). Organized crime and trust: On the conceptualization and empirical relevance of trust in the context of criminal networks. *Global Crime, 6*(2), 159–184. https://doi.org/10.1080/17440570500096734

Watson, P. (1997). *Sotheby's: The inside story*. Bloomsbury.

Watson, P., & Todeschini, C. (2007). *The Medici conspiracy: The illicit journey of looted antiquities—From Italy's tomb raiders to the world's greatest museums*. PublicAffairs.

Exploring Taste Formation and Performance in the Illicit Trade of Human Remains on Instagram

Katherine Davidson, Shawn Graham, and Damien Huffer

Abstract The Digital Age has greatly expanded the scope of the illicit trade of art and antiquities—including human remains from archaeological and other contexts. From the Dark Web to social media platforms, the online world has become a marketplace fostering the creation of new trade networks, exchanging objects as well as ideas. Vendors on social media continue to benefit from the legal grey area and lack of enforcement around trading human remains, posting images of their objects for sale and leaving the responsibility for adhering to state laws to the buyer. As an image-based social network, Instagram is one such space where the exchange of ideas and the creation of 'taste'—through image content, composition and hashtags—are evident through visual and metadata trends. This chapter explores an approach to measuring the visual similarity of posts within the illicit trade of human remains on Instagram, along with the textual content of those posts, towards a way of tracking the development and evolution of taste formation in this trade. We employ a 'distant viewing' approach using machine vision to trace influence within illicit trade networks on Instagram to witness the development of taste and the expansion of the market.

K. Davidson
Department of Sociology and Anthropology, Carleton University, Ottawa, ON, Canada
e-mail: KatherineSDavidson@cmail.carleton.ca

S. Graham (✉)
Department of History, Carleton University, Ottawa, ON, Canada
e-mail: shawn.graham@carleton.ca

D. Huffer
Department of History, Carleton University, Ottawa, ON, Canada

School of Social Sciences, University of Queensland, St Lucia, QLD, Australia

N. Oosterman, D. Yates (eds.), *Crime and Art*, Studies in Art, Heritage, Law and the Market 1, https://doi.org/10.1007/978-3-030-84856-9_3

1 Introduction

The trade of human remains has a colonial and exploitative history. Colonial collection practices perpetuated violence against marginalised groups, and the proliferation of collector communities represents history repeating itself (Huffer & Graham, 2017, p. 4). In particular, the history of 'medically prepared specimens'—terminology often used by vendors in the bone trade—are grounded in colonialism and built on the literal bodies of the poor and marginalised across the world (Davidson, 2007, p. 194). Jayakumar et al. emphasise that anatomical dissection was supplied with cadavers by using unclaimed bodies—the bodies of those in poverty, the mentally ill, victims of war, and immigrants (2020, p. 872). Halling and Seidemann (2016) and Graham, Lane, et al. (2020) identified potential victims of war crimes and regions with civil unrest as potential sources of remains in the trade of human remains. In large part, the abuse of corpse laws that exist now (see below) were formed because of the medical malpractice and unsavoury activity that led to antique medical skeletons being made in the first place (Doughty, 2019).

Over nearly two decades, heritage professionals and forensic anthropologists have witnessed a flourishing trade of human remains created in online spaces (e.g., Huffer & Chappell, 2014; Huxley & Finnegan, 2004). Social media sites are the latest space where people participate in this illicit trade, forming communities around discussions and sales of human skulls from a variety of origins. Digital methods—including computer vision—can be used to study these networks of trade, by examining the relationships formed through social media connections: likes, follows, hashtags, and the raw text of the posts (Graham & Huffer, 2020; Huffer & Graham, 2017).

2 The Online Trade of Human Remains

Considerable research has been conducted into understanding the nature and mechanisms of the online trade of human remains, by scholars from multiple disciplines (see Cumback, 2018; Doughty, 2019; Halling & Seidemann, 2016; Huxley & Finnegan, 2004; Jayakumar et al., 2020; Marsh, 2016; Seidemann et al., 2009; State Burial Laws Project, 2020), and by members of the Bonetrade Project[1] (see Graham & Huffer, 2020; Graham, Lane, et al., 2020; Graham, Huffer, & Blackadar, 2020; Huffer & Graham, 2017).

Vendors either do not know or actively obfuscate the origin of the remains they sell (Graham, Lane, et al., 2020; Halling & Seidemann, 2016, pp. 1324–1325). Typically, vendors employ three 'main tropes' when discussing the origins of skulls for trade—remains made into medical supply specimens; ethnographic specimens

[1] A Social Sciences and Humanities Research Council of Canada funded project into the trade in human remains online, led by Graham and Huffer, https://bonetrade.github.io.

within the 'tribal art' market; or remains looted from archaeological sites, cemeteries, clandestine burials or happenstance. Those participating in this trade—who can be summarised as specialist vendors, generalist vendors and enthusiast onlookers (Huffer & Graham, 2017, pp. 17–18)—continue to insist that this is all perfectly legal, and not explicitly a crime, except in certain jurisdictions. That vendors (especially in the United States) claim this is the case is due to the outdated public discourse about the trade, the ambiguous status of dead humans before the law, and the uneven application of enforcement of e-commerce guidelines (see Stroud, 2018). Vendors sometimes do know better, however. In an interview with National Geographic, a vendor stated that "there are times when you receive a photograph of a skull that someone's wanting to sell that's very clear that it's been dug up" (Hugo, 2016). Yet, it is not clear, who has jurisdiction over human remains, and where, and how; as Halling and Seidemann (2016, p. 1325) note, there is a common trope that New York, Georgia, and Tennessee are the only states in which importing or exporting human remains is restricted, a trope which was outdated even in 2016. The *lingua franca* of the trade is English; major vendors are known to be based in the United Kingdom, Canada, and the United States (we suspect this is strongly a reflection of the history of tech platforms and their wider adoption in particular countries and accidents of first-use: a particular vendor decided to use Instagram, and others followed suit to keep up). For this reason, when we discuss legislation in this chapter, we will restrict our comments on legislation to the United States and Canada for the most part.

Halling and Seidemann's article is often cited as influential in the establishment of legislation such as the restrictions introduced in Louisiana and eBay's policy against selling human remains (Vergano, 2016; eBay, 2020). Although this practice is regulated regionally in the United States rather than federally, federal law in Canada requires documentation or ministerial permission to import or export human remains (Canada Border Services Agency, 2020). In the United States the Native American Graves and Repatriation Act (NAGPRA) is sometimes cited by vendors, to the effect that a given skull is not of an Indigenous person; this is taken as a kind of *carte-blanche* by the vendor, a sort of lay (mis)understanding that if the remains are not Indigenous then NAGPRA does not apply (NAGPRA, 2020). However, Graham et al. suggest that skulls sold online are not what vendors say they are, and that the chance that Native American remains are actively being traded is a staunch possibility that warrants investigation (see Graham, Lane, et al., 2020 for the full discussion).

Even if selling human remains is not illegal in a certain state, Halling and Seidemann point out that "disturbance or desecration of grave spaces" is, as is selling human remains that were donated as part of the Uniform Anatomical Gift Act (Halling & Seidemann, 2016, p. 1325). The Criminal Code of Canada also makes it a crime to offer an indignity to or interfere with human remains (Criminal Code of Canada, 2021; Stroud, 2018, pp. 16.4–16.5). The American University Washington College of Law keeps a list of legislation related to burials in the United States, highlighting laws in each state and their penalties for unlawful selling, purchasing, possessing, or excavating (State Burial Laws Project, 2020).

Vendors rarely offer, or even claim, that no documentation is needed to import, export or sell a skull. Nevertheless, the 1970 UNESCO Convention and its stipulations against the import or export of artifacts and cultural materials (UNESCO, 1970) would certainly seem to apply, alongside other conventions aiming to regulate the import, export, deaccessioning and transportation of human remains (see Huffer & Graham, 2017, p. 5). Canadian federal export laws prohibit the exporting of objects removed from soil, including human remains, except with express permission (Government of Canada, 2020). While vendors and experts both acknowledge that the likelihood of documentation existing for human remains is slim, it is a red flag in the context of antiquities specialists (Ferry, 2020; Halling & Seidemann, 2016). Remains willed through the Uniform Anatomical Gift Act or its off-shoots will have a decree with the donor's signature (Martinez, 2013). Legally importing and exporting human remains between countries will always have some form of import/export permission control (Canada Border Services Agency, 2020). And finally, any human remains deaccessioned from museum collections must have been deaccessioned in a particular manner that would generate documentation about the deaccessioning (Canadian Museums Association, 2020;; Ingenium, 2017, p. 3; Smithsonian Institution, 2005, p. 173; see also Skidegate Repatriation & Cultural Committee, 2007).

2.1 Social Media Moderation

Although social media is not the only avenue for the trade in human remains, it is where the networks of trade are gaining the most traction at present. These trade networks are pervasive on social media due in part to the irregular enforcement of policies in these spaces. Etsy and eBay have both been discussed at length by researchers, due to their introduction of policies banning the trade of human remains (Cumback, 2018, p. 335; Halling & Seidemann, 2016; Huffer & Graham, 2017; Huxley & Finnegan, 2004; Seidemann et al., 2009). EBay's "Human Body Parts Policy" prohibits the sale of human remains and has done since it was implemented in 2016 (Cumback, 2018, p. 335; eBay, 2020). Similarly, Etsy's "Prohibited Items Policy, Section 2: Animal Products and Human Remains" has seen the trade prohibited since 2012 (Cumback, 2018, p. 335; Etsy, 2020). We can see through the increase of posts on Instagram, among other platforms, that the introduction of restrictions by Etsy and eBay led to the trade of human remains moving elsewhere (as far as we can tell, to other open social media platforms), rather than disrupting the chains of supply and demand entirely (Graham & Huffer, 2020; Huffer & Graham, 2017).

Facebook and Instagram succeeded Etsy and eBay as the go-to places for vendors of human remains because of the sites' apparent lack of enforcement of restrictions on this trade. If we examine the deeply integrated terms of service between Facebook and Instagram, we can see that there are at least some policies in place that the sale of human remains would violate. The extent of prohibitions on selling human remains can be found in Instagram's Community Guidelines and Terms of Service; they state that users must follow the law, and stipulate that nothing unlawful may be posted on the platform (Instagram, 2020a, 2020b). But Instagram also has a policy that users are to follow Facebook's platform terms, as Facebook has owned the platform since 2012 (Rusli, 2012) and directs users through Facebook's web of policies (Facebook, 2021a, b; Instagram, 2020b). The sale of human body parts is against Facebook's rules, as per the "Facebook Commerce Policies, Prohibited Content Section 5: Body Parts and Fluids" (Facebook, 2020a). Facebook's Community Standards stipulate explicitly that they prohibit certain regulated goods (Sect. 4: Regulated Goods, under Part I. Violence and Criminal Behaviour), including prohibiting the sale of objects listed in Facebook's Commerce policies, along with historical artefacts (Facebook, 2020b).

Instagram offloads responsibility to the page owner/seller to "follow the law". Facebook, Etsy, and eBay all say that certain types of transactions are prohibited, and that failure to comply could result in a page or account being removed, but these can always be remade/reposted (we have seen vendors with more than one account, where the second account is explicitly labelled 'a backup in case Instagram deletes me'), and it is unknown whether reporting illicit activity ever results in notifying the authorities. Instagram does not appear to back up their policies banning the use of their platform for unlawful purposes, regarding many types of activities (Huffer & Graham, 2017, p. 5). This could be due in part to the small size of the communities and the relatively small number of social media pages trading in human remains. Faust hypothesises that creators with lower profiles/fewer followers may evade Instagram's moderation by virtue of the smaller amount of traffic on their feed, and therefore smaller amount of visibility, compared with 'influencers' or creators with higher visibility (Faust, 2017, p. 160). Faust compared individual female influencers with large followings to those with small followings, who made posts on Instagram about the experiences of female bodies. The pages she looked at, had over 300,000 followers (Faust, 2017, pp. 162–164) which is over ten times the number of followers of the largest account selling human remains examined in this study. If Faust's theory is correct, and based on our observations of bone trade networks, then the community of people buying and selling human remains is still too small to attract the attention of Instagram's moderation algorithm or its few human moderators.

The second evident issue is that of sellers offloading the responsibility for knowing local laws to buyers, and many state that it is "perfectly legal" to own human remains (Marsh, 2016), while skirting the obvious questions: according to the law of what jurisdiction? Based on secure provenance? How can they possibly know? Or, vendors offer one interpretation of their own local laws, and state that they are doing everything in their 'power' to be ethical. Language around this includes terms such as "ethically sourced", "medically prepared", "professional antiques", and "research quality" (based on Instagram scraping descriptions and tags from this research).

2.2 *The Ethics of Social Media Research*

To whom do we owe a duty of care when we monitor, map, and analyse the online trade in human remains? Clearly there is an ethical duty to the peoples whose remains are being traded; that duty underpins everything else. But social media as an arena for research also presents ethical dilemmas, and consensus has yet to be reached (Tiidenberg, 2018, pp. 2–4). When we scrape Instagram to study the trade in human remains, we do end up collecting posts by individuals who are not known to be active participants in the trade. And while morally we might find the trade abhorrent, it is not always illegal, and we cannot necessarily know which laws of which jurisdictions apply at all times. Thus, we have to extend an ethical duty of care to all persons whose materials we end up algorithmically collecting.

In the context of university-driven research, obtaining ethics clearance often requires a demonstrable informed consent process. Tiidenberg (2018, p. 5) notes that sensitive research includes research into "illegal activities, everything pertaining to sexuality, abuse, death, and illness". The traders whom we study, whose illicit activities we bring to light, are being exposed to potential legal vulnerabilities through our research. Dennis notes that digital methods are seen as "have[ing] no 'participants' that may be harmed", prompting people to overlook ethics clearances altogether (2020, p. 215). Huffer and Graham indicate that, even though profiles may be accessible publicly, users have not explicitly made their profiles available to researchers (2017, p. 6). Thus, we remove identifying details as a matter of practice when discussing this research.

3 A Methodology for Mapping Taste Performance

Online networks themselves are unique in that they exist within both the infrastructure *and* the regulations of corporations. One aspect of these groups operating in quasi-legal spaces online is their ability to create a kind of 'atmosphere' or taste-setting. A group may be visited by someone who never participates in looting or buying and selling, yet who becomes interested in the mythos associated with the activities. Huffer and Graham (2017) were able to generate a network of individuals through their patterns of 'liking' various posts. There was nothing to indicate that these people bought or sold remains themselves (yet), but by providing an audience, and a data trail of what appealed to them, they provided fodder for Instagram's programming, which gives these posts added traction within the algorithm's suggestions. Thus, the visuals and the visual aesthetic of posts of human remains matter in terms of the discoverability of accounts.

Using different metadata, such as hashtags and follows, allows us to model these networks of influence. This is because part of participating in taste performance (whether as buyer, seller, collector, or 'just looking') is also about understanding which terminology is used in the community, and how pages' link to each other through common tags (Venturini et al., 2018). The practice of putting multiple hashtags into a post is called 'hashtag stuffing' or 'keyword stuffing', and this is often replicated between pages that are influenced by each other, sometimes down to the exact order of hashtags (Huffer & Graham, 2017, p. 20). Liu's analysis of the formation of "taste statements" in social media profiles included an analysis of common consumable media, activities, etc., which were part of the culture of MySpace in the Aughts (Liu, 2007). These consumables included things like books, movies, music, and television, and Liu observed four types of different taste statements, which he called prestige persona, differentiation persona, authenticity persona, and theatrical persona. (Liu, 2007, pp. 262–263). Liu has described different "taste neighbourhoods", akin to digital communities of practice, that are comprised of profiles linked through shared interests or "interest tokens", as performed on individual MySpace profiles (Liu, 2007, p. 255). Our experiment here aims to trace the same taste neighbourhoods through visual similarity on Instagram, and examines how similar images are to each other, suggesting potential influence in ways other than just hashtags and follows.

Examining the different aesthetic styles of images, posts and text help us to understand how these interactions are created and maintained. Social network profiles are a form of performance; this takes place through the "textual performance of self" (Liu, 2007) as well as through the curation and aesthetic of visual media. Of this, Liu argues that the creation of an online self, whether written or illustrated, is an essential part of becoming fully real in digital spaces (Liu, 2007, p. 253). Similarly, Faust highlights that Instagram is equally for photo and video sharing as it is for mobile social networking (Faust, 2017, p. 160). How people construct their profiles or their digital selves on Instagram and other social media platforms, constrained by the infrastructure of the platform, is intentionally crafted as a performance that reflects the user's taste. These taste performances, in turn, reflect the communities that users become a part of in the virtual world. Bourdieu argued that membership in a certain socioeconomic class would lead to shared formative experiences, creating common understandings of class identity, and by extension, taste (Bourdieu, 1984, as cited by Liu, 2007, p. 256). Conspicuous consumption has been highlighted as one way of demonstrating participation in a class based on taste performance, especially regarding costly goods, which evoke feelings or symbolism of higher-class status (Veblen, 1899, as cited by Liu, 2007, p. 255; human remains are marketed as 'one of a kind', with stories that promote that uniqueness, and can be considered a kind of Veblen good). Similarly, Gans (1999) offered that society could be grouped based on shared aesthetic and cultural traits, which he called "taste publics" (as cited by Liu, 2007, p. 256). It is also possible to extend the membership in taste groups to people consuming the media surrounding it, not just those engaged in trade and monetary exchange. Through liking, commenting, and following, people who may not own human remains are still participating in the "digital sensorium" and emotional affectivity of this community (Graham, Huffer, & Blackadar, 2020, p. 4).

The desire to belong to networks of collectors and enthusiasts, along with the desire for the comfort of nostalgia in a time of social unrest, could be the reason why collecting has thrived in the context of the COVID-19 pandemic. In the context of the COVID-19, collection practices around human remains have increased in scale by a considerable margin (Graham & Huffer, 2020, p. 5). Not only did the collecting of human remains in 2020 more than double the apparent scope of trade from the previous year, but many other collecting specialisations also saw a revitalisation and new investments (Hernandez, 2020). Many of the posts examined in this research referenced the pandemic, and specifically the liquidation of previously unavailable or private specimens, alongside the importance of supporting local businesses (see Post Metadata below).

4 Teaching Machines to Understand Visual Similarity as Taste Performance

Visual similarity can be measured computationally and used to create a network of similar images and by seeing which images are most central in this network or which connect disparate parts of it, we can identify the taste-makers and trends for the consumption of these illicit materials. This approach, called "distant viewing" by Arnold and Tilton (2019), uses convolutional neural networks to detect stylistic similarities in a corpus of photographs.

A convolutional neural network is a series of mathematical functions (or neurons) that take as their input the output of a previous layer of neurons. The 'convolutional' part expresses the way the original photograph is fed into the first layer of neurons—it is rather like a filter being passed over a small subset of pixels, left to right, top to bottom. Each layer reacts to different aspects of the image data, the presence or absence of straight lines, curves, areas of colour, areas of absence. When these networks are 'trained', they are exposed to multiple examples of the same kind of 'thing'. The network responds to the image data in different ways, lighting up different neurons and links with differing strengths. Feed it images of dogs, note the aggregate patterns that light up (the vector or list of 2048 numbers) when exposed to the idea of 'dog', and that pattern can be labelled as 'dog'. When the network is next exposed to an image it has not seen before, it can then compare its reaction to what it knows is a 'dog' and return a probability that the image is indeed that of a dog.

For our purposes, we do not need the labels. Instead, we can use a pre-trained model and strip away the last layer that does the labelling, and just focus on the pattern that lights up instead (the vector). When we expose an image to the model, the resulting vector can be measured in terms of its similarity to other vectorised images. We can thus visualise a corpus of images as a network of nodes, connected to its most similar neighbours (say, every image where there is at least 80% similarity). We can then find the most influential images using network statistics. In terms of social media, since we also know when the images were posted, we can add that metadata to our network. If images on social media did not influence the composition of other images, we would expect that in the network of visual similarity, an image would have an equal chance of being connected to its nearest neighbour regardless of when that image was created. We expect that the composition of images related to the trade in human remains on Instagram are influenced by earlier posts within their network; newcomers might take their cue from established accounts even if there is no evidence elsewhere on Instagram that this person follows that person. In this way, we can begin to investigate the formation of tastes and affinity groups at scale.

Arnold and Tilton analysed the Farm Security Administration–Office of War Information corpus of photographs (photos taken in the 1930s and 1940s to document government programmes) in this way. Photographs that appeared visually similar when represented as a network often occurred in chains with a historical dimension—a photographer's early work was visually most similar with the work of their mentor and suggested new avenues to explore by highlighting hitherto unknown connections amongst subgroups of photographers (Arnold & Tilton, 2019). Another example of this kind of approach comes from a study of print advertising, where the investigators analysed hundreds of thousands of historical advertisements from newspapers, finding groupings and evolutionary paths over time for these groups (Wevers & Smits, 2020, pp. 195, 198–199).

4.1 Building the Network

We scrape Instagram using a program to retrieve the underlying metadata for every post, including the direct URL to the image and the image file itself. We begin the scrape by querying for the tag '#humanskullforsale'. Our one-day scrape produced 2984 pictures from 1308 unique posts, the majority of which dated to 2020, but some of which go back to 2014. Of these posts, nine were videos (and so were removed from the analysis), leaving us with a corpus of 1299 posts. Following Duhaime (2017), we vectorise the images using the neural network and then measure the similarity between all pairs of images, resulting in a list of each image's most similar images. The list is transformed into a network format where we understand 'this image' is nearest to 'that image' with nearness being the strength of the similarity (between 0 and 1; also known as the 'weight' of the relationship). We can then query the network. The steps for measuring and expressing networks of visual similarity are relatively straightforward and are gathered together in a computational notebook at https://github.com/o-date/Identifying-Similar-Images-with-TensorFlow-notebooks for readers' reuse.

5 Results and Discussion

Examining the resulting network in Fig. 1, there are many loosely connected visual clusters within the trade of human remains on Instagram. These clusters are determined by measuring patterns of similar interlinkages, a metric called 'modularity'.

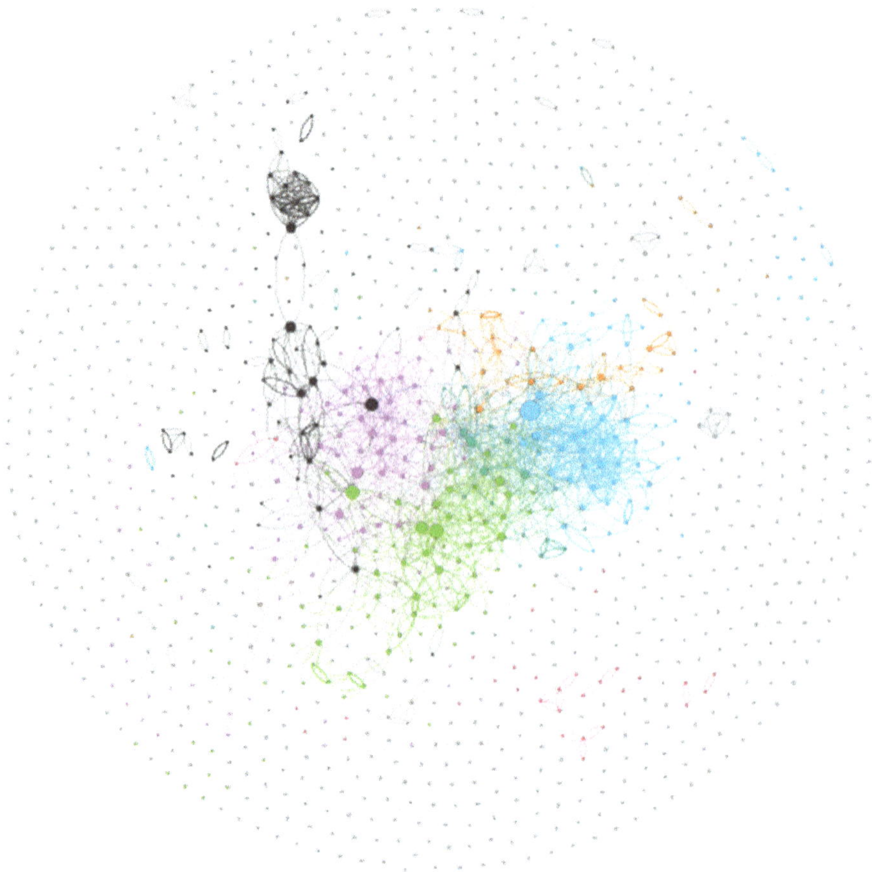

Fig. 1 Network of visual similarity of all images from a scrape of the tag #humanskullforsale, coloured by modularity (sub-community) and scaled according to eigenvector centrality

The result shows a diverse selection of small communities that share visually similar interests and aesthetics. There are also many images that appear as 'isolates', unconnected from the broader patterns. In some cases, the images are of sufficiently different subject matter—crystal skull charms, for example—that they have no other images that score high on visual similarity.[2] Other 'isolates' are indeed of human remains for sale but are either exceptional in terms of cultural modifications made to them (whether authentic or a more modern skull modified to look 'ethnic'), or exceptional in how they are displayed (for instance, customised *'wunderkammer'* cabinets). There are also very small otherwise unconnected clusters of images that

[2] Although the original post metadata shows that these images used the #humanskullforsale hashtag, which we might interpret as a bit of marketing to get these tchotchkes in front of a suggestible audience. A similar strategy is used for posts selling taxidermied animals.

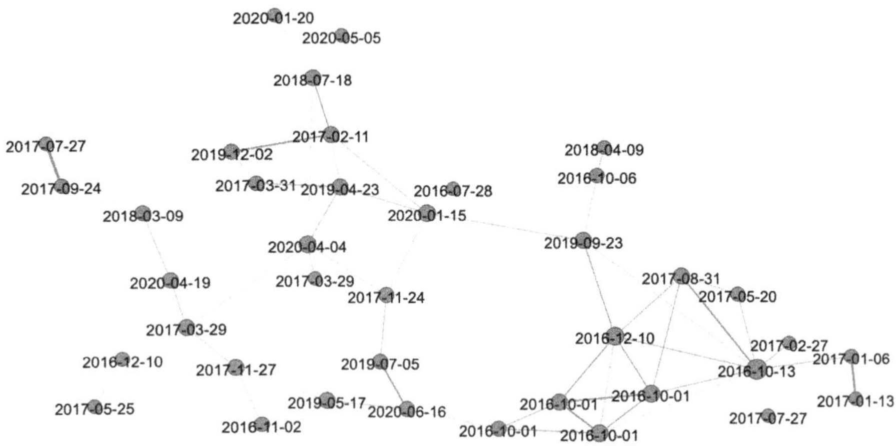

Fig. 2 Modules are first calculated against the entire network. Then the largest module is displayed and then filtered so that the *strongest (>0.85) relationships* are displayed

upon inspection prove to be multiple views on a single skull, coming from a single multi-image Instagram post.

The larger groupings (or ‘modules’) are where we might look to see if we can spot visual influence flowing from older images to newer images. Take the largest ‘module’, which is reproduced in Fig. 2 but filtered to show just the strongest relationships. The vast majority of posts in this module all come from a single vendor, which implies a uniformity of style that evolves over time (other posts by this vendor can be found elsewhere in the larger graph). The earliest dated posts are from October 2016; they depict skulls without mandibles, square to the camera, on a simple shelf. The later posts are done with from the same aspect, but with more ‘style’ in terms of background props, old leather-bound books, dribbly candles, dark red velvets, and more composite images are used later on (composite images, pulled together from earlier images, complicate the visual similarity scores). In this case, it does seem that visual similarity gives us insight into the vendor’s evolution of style and marketing. It is worth noting that this particular vendor is an individual with well over 40,000 followers and that this module (when unfiltered) is the largest in the dataset. This vendor’s images also appear in other modules, creating points where their visual aesthetic reaches and shapes other traders.

Other modules do not appear so neat to interpret. The second largest module in our graph for instance contains a motley of different vendors, and the neat interconnections of older posts to newer posts is not so readily apparent (though it appears to happen in some sub-areas of the module). Instead, what unifies this module is an apparent *thematic* unity: many shots are taken *as if* the person holding the camera is performing Hamlet’s speech over the skull of Yorick, and the photographer’s arm and hand are frequently visible in the classic pose. Where an image does not depict the photographer’s arm and hand, the angle and distance to the skull remain largely the same. Also, in this module, we find that the posts with the highest betweenness centrality score (that is, they sit on the majority of shortest paths between every other post) do tend to be the earliest posts, but not always. We might see that some individuals are influenced by others' Hamlet-play, while the idea occurs spontaneously to others. When we examine how these different 'modules' interconnect, we find the articulation points (where a node is connected to two or more nodes in other modules) tend to be amongst the earliest posts we have in this particular dataset, and the individual vendors are those individuals like the vendor in module 1, who have large followings on Instagram.

This limited experiment does suggest that we can trace the formation of taste for human remains on Instagram through visual similarity, to a degree. Some individual vendors have a very distinct 'style' that is apparent to a computer; other vendors perform visual tropes from other cultural domains (the theatre, the macabre) in marketing their materials—a little performance of taste. This method of analysis suggests connections that may not have been evident in other methods of analysis using Instagram analytics such as tags or text analysis. It also demonstrates that the trade of human remains exists in a cross-section between groups that self-identify in a variety of ways: a trader who posts discussions about taxidermy may be influenced by traders posting about gothic subculture or osteology.

Arnold and Tilton conveyed relationships of visual similarity as a network of unidirectional, outward-branching relationships (2019, p. 9). This is consistent with what we are able to see in Fig. 2. However, unlike Arnold and Tilton's model, we can see that there is often more than one node between branches. This suggests that visual similarity can take several paths of influence, drawing from many sources, or from just a few. Some images are highly interconnected with each other, while others are connected to one or two images in their neighbourhood and no others. This seems consistent for participation in online communities; some Instagram profiles will be highly interconnected, while others exist on the margins. The resulting network suggests that people are learning how to visually represent the sale of human remains, sometimes from many popular pages, and other times from smaller, niche vendors.

6 Post Metadata

In the actual text of the posts we scraped, several themes within the discussion of buying and selling human remains were evident: the COVID-19 pandemic, legal implications of the trade of human remains, and discussions around four sub-themes related to origin; culture, taxidermy, aesthetic, and osteology. These are similar to the communities identified by Huffer and Graham (2017, pp. 17–18), examining networks of following/followers and the text of their posts; they identify three communities: specialists ('accounts selling mostly bones'), generalists ('accounts selling more things in addition to bone'), and enthusiasts ('who enjoy looking at pictures of human remains'). With the onset of the COVID-19 pandemic in the

United States and Canada in early spring 2020, many Instagram user pages began to align themselves textually with membership in the 'support local' movement. Antiquities dealers included themselves in the ranks of businesses struggling with imposed shut down orders in many regions. Posts note that many of these businesses offer national shipping or regional pick-up options. Within the text of posts, legal restrictions—or vendors' opinions about them—were often mentioned (emphasising the vendors' mis/understandings of the relevant laws as we noted earlier). Many posts also use the term "medically prepared" as a qualifier for the legitimacy of the trade of skulls. This, along with other terms such as "research quality" or "ethically sourced", seek to add an appearance of legitimacy to skulls being traded online. With regard to 'culture' were posts about cultural groups who headhunted, and skulls in the aesthetic style of the New Guinean Asmat or Dayak material culture (as Huffer says in Schwartz, 2019: likely "osteologically real, but culturally fake"). Others were often not human remains at all but used the relevant hashtags. Many of these images were of animal bones, and it seems that certain taxidermy specialists also moonlight in the occasional sale of human skulls. The extent of the crossover between animal taxidermy and human remains vendors warrants further research. Then there were posts that discussed different subculture aesthetics, such as goth, witchcraft, or the occult. Finally, posts that discussed osteological specimens from a research or educational perspective were also identified. These posts highlighted specific points of interest on skulls, and some of them were clearly not posts made by vendors, but osteology enthusiasts.

These themes reflect how participants in these networks identify themselves to other bone enthusiasts, and how they use expressive coherence to demonstrate their knowledge within this community (Liu, 2007, p. 258). Measuring visual similarity is complemented by both textual and network analysis. We can see that posts may have either text and tags in common, or visual similarity, or both; this is consistent with the networks of "small traders" identified by Huffer and Graham (2017).

7 Conclusion

Taste performances can be replicated based on aesthetic or text and are performed on a small scale; in this way, the trade of human remains can remain a niche, tight-knit community with limited access to outsiders. The network generated from visual similarity and its interpenetration with the thematic content of the posts suggests small communities centred around taste performances. This is consistent with previous examinations of social media using digital methods (Huffer & Graham, 2017; Liu, 2007), and therefore reinforce the current understanding of the creation and behaviour of communities online. The use of multiple types of data to trace these connections allows us to identify how networks of influence span both visual and textual modes within the community. Finally, these methods need to be applied to other avenues for the illicit trade of human remains, namely other social media platforms such as Facebook, and the darkweb. Paul (2018) suggests that the modelling and tracing of illicit trade networks needs other methods of data scraping that can trace the "untraceable" interactions than those used here. Visual similarity could be used to identify influence, between seemingly unrelated posts and users on the darkweb.

Acknowledgements This chapter draws on research supported by the Social Sciences and Humanities Research Council of Canada.

References

Arnold, T., & Tilton, L. (2019). Distant viewing: Analyzing large visual corpora. *Digital Scholarship in the Humanities*. https://doi.org/10.1093/digitalsh/fqz013

Canada Border Services Agency. (2020). Memorandum D19–9-3: Importation and Exportation of Human Remains and Other Human Tissues. Retrieved December 29, 2020, from https://www.cbsa-asfc.gc.ca/publications/dm-md/d19/d19-9-3-eng.pdf

Canadian Museums Association. (2020). Canadian Museums Association Deaccessioning Guidelines. Retrieved February 5, 2021, from https://www.museums.ca/site/deaccessioning_guidelines

Criminal Code of Canada. (2021). 182b Nuisances–Dead body, R.S., 1985, c. C-46, s. 1822019, c. 25, s. 63. Retrieved February 5, 2021, from https://laws-lois.justice.gc.ca/eng/acts/c-46/page-41.html#h-118691

Cumback, K. (2018). A bone to pick with international law: The Ghoulish trade in human remains. *Michigan State International Law Review, 26*(2), 335–372.

Davidson, J. M. (2007). "Resurrection Men" in Dallas: The illegal use of black bodies as medical cadavers (1900–1907). *International Journal of Historical Archaeology, 11*, 193–220.

Dennis, L. M. (2020). Digital archaeological ethics: Successes and failures in disciplinary attention. *Journal of Computer Applications in Archaeology, 3*(1), 210–218.

Doughty, C. (2019). *Will my cat eat my eyeballs?* W. W. Norton & Company Ltd..

Duhaime, D. (2017). Identifying similar images with TensorFlow. Retrieved October 2, 2020, from http://douglasduhaime.com/posts/identifying-similar-images-with-tensorflow.html

eBay. (2020). Human body parts policy. Retrieved December 29, 2020, from https://www.ebay.ca/help/policies/prohibited-restricted-items/human-remains-body-parts-policy?id=4325

Etsy. (2020). Prohibited items policy—Our house rules. Retrieved December 29, 2020, from http://www.etsy.com/ca/legal/prohibited/

Facebook. (2020a). Commerce policies. Retrieved December 29, 2020, from https://www.facebook.com/policies/commerce/prohibited_content/body_party_fluids. Accessed 29 December 2020.

Facebook. (2020b). Community standards. Retrieved December 29, 2020, from https://www.facebook.com/communitystandards/regulated_goods

Facebook. (2021a). Platform terms. Retrieved January 1, 2021, from https://developers.facebook.com/terms/

Facebook. (2021b). Terms of service. Retrieved January 1, 2021, from https://www.facebook.com/legal/terms

Faust, G. (2017). Hair, blood and the nipple: Instagram censorship and the female body. In U. U. Frömming, S. Köhn, S. Fox, & M. Terry (Eds.), *Digital environments* (pp. 159–170). Transcript Verlag.

Ferry, J. (2020). Why doesn't my human skull come with paperwork? Retrieved January 1, 2021, from https://www.jonsbones.com/blog/why-doesnt-my-human-skull-come-with-paperwork

Government of Canada. (2020). Canadian Cultural Property Export Control List (C.R.C., c. 448): Objects recovered from the soil or waters of Canada. Government of Canada. Retrieved January 1, 2021, from https://laws-lois.justice.gc.ca/eng/regulations/C.R.C.,_c._448/page-2.html

Graham, S., & Huffer, D. (2020). Reproducibility, replicability, and revisiting the Insta-Dead and the human remains trade. *Internet Archaeology*. https://doi.org/10.11141/ia.55.11

Graham, S., Lane, A., Huffer, D., & Angourakis, A. (2020). Towards a method for discerning sources of supply within the human remains trade via patterns of visual dissimilarity and computer vision. *Journal of Computer Applications in Archaeology*. https://doi.org/10.5334/jcaa.59

Graham, S., Huffer, D., & Blackadar, J. (2020). Towards a digital sensorial archaeology as an experiment in distant viewing of the trade in human remains on Instagram. *Heritage, 3*(2), 208–227.

Halling, C. L., & Seidemann, R. M. (2016). They sell skulls online? A review of internet sales of human skulls on eBay and the laws in place to restrict sales. *Journal of Forensic Sciences, 61*(5), 1322–1326.

Hernandez, P. (2020, November 6). Pokémon cards are hot again, now that Charizard can make you rich. *Polygon*. Retrieved November 6, 2020, from https://www.polygon.com/2020/11/6/21551503/pokemon-card-charizard-appraisal-shadowless-collection-first-edition-prices

Huffer, D., & Chappell, D. (2014). The mainly nameless and faceless dead: an exploratory study of the illicit traffic in archaeological and ethnographic human remains. *Crime, Law and Social Change, 62*(2), 131–153.

Huffer, D., & Graham, S. (2017). The Insta-Dead: The rhetoric of the human remains trade on Instagram. *Internet Archaeology*. https://doi.org/10.11141/ia.45.5

Hugo, K. (2016, August 23). Human skulls are being sold online, but is it legal? *National Geographic* Retrieved December 28, 2020, from https://www.nationalgeographic.com/news/2016/08/human-skulls-sale-legal-ebay-forensics-science/

Huxley, A., & Finnegan, M. (2004). Human remains sold to the highest bidder! A snapshot of the buying and selling of human skeletal remains on eBay®, an internet auction site. *Journal of Forensic Sciences, 49*(1), 1–4.

Ingenium. (2017). Deaccessioning and disposition of collection objects, guideline # 100-B. Retrieved February 5, 2021, from https://ingeniumcanada.org/ingenium/doc/content/cstmc/CSTMC%20-%20Guideline%20Number%20100-B%20-%20Deaccessioning%20and%20Disposition%20of%20Artifacts%20-%202017-07-25.pdf

Instagram. (2020a). Community guidelines. Retrieved December 29, 2020, from https://help.instagram.com/477434105621119

Instagram. (2020b). Terms of use. Retrieved December 30, 2020, https://help.instagram.com/581066165581870/?helpref=hc_fnav&bc[0]=Instagram%20Help&bc[1]=Privacy%20and%20Safety%20Center

Jayakumar, N., Athar, S., & Ashwood, N. (2020). Where do these cadavers come from? *Clinical Anatomy, 33*(6), 872–875.

Liu, H. (2007). Social network profiles as taste performances. *Journal of Computer-Mediated Communication, 13*(1), 252–275.

Marsh, T. (2016). Internet sales of human remains persist despite questionable legality. Retrieved December 28, 2020, from https://funerallaw.typepad.com/blog/2016/08/internet-sales-of-human-remains-persist-despite-questionable-legality.html

Martinez, B. (2013). Uniform Anatomical Gift Act (1968). *Embryo Project Encyclopedia*. Retrieved December 29, 2020, from https://embryo.asu.edu/pages/uniform-anatomical-gift-act-1968

Native American Graves and Repatriation Act. (2020). Pub. L. No. 101–601, 25 U.S.C. 3001 et seq., 104 Stat. 3048. Accessed 5 February 2021.

Paul, K. (2018). Ancient artifacts vs. digital artifacts: New tools for unmasking the sale of illicit antiquities on the Dark Web. *Arts*. https://doi.org/10.3390/arts7020012

Rusli, E.M. (2012, April 9). Facebook buys Instagram for $1 Billion. *The New York Times*. Retrieved December 30, 2020, from https://nyti.ms/2jD6Z3i

Schwartz, O. (2019, July 18). Instagram's grisly human skull trade is booming. *Wired*. Retrieved January 1, 2021, from https://www.wired.co.uk/article/instagram-skull-trade

Seidemann, R. M., Stojanowski, C. M., & Rich, F. J. (2009). The identification of a human skull recovered from an eBay sale. *Journal of Forensic Sciences, 54*(6), 1247–1253.

Skidegate Repatriation & Cultural Committee. (2007). Canadian Museum of Civilization. Retrieved February 5, 2021, from http://www.repatriation.ca/Pages/Canadian%20Museum%20of%20Civilization.html

Smithsonian Institution (2005). Acquisition and disposal of collections. Retrieved February 5, 2021, from https://www.si.edu/content/opanda/docs/Rpts2005/05.04.ConcernAtTheCore.Disposal.pdf

State Burial Laws Project. (2020). American University Washington College of Law. Retrieved December 29, 2020, from https://www.wcl.american.edu/burial/

Stroud, E. (2018). Law and the dead body: Is a corpse a person or a thing? *Annual Review of Law and Social Science, 14*, 16.1–16.11.

Tiidenberg, K. (2018). Research ethics, vulnerability, and trust on the internet. In J. Hunsinger, L. Klastrup, & M. M. Allen (Eds.), *Second international handbook of internet research* (pp. 1–15). Springer Netherlands.

UNESCO. (1970). Convention on the means of prohibiting and preventing the illicit import, export and transfer of ownership of cultural property 1970. Retrieved December 29, 2020, from http://portal.unesco.org/en/ev.php-URL_ID=13039&URL_DO=DO_TOPIC&URL_SECTION=201.html

Venturini, T., Bounegru, L., Gray, J., & Rogers, R. (2018). A reality check(list) for digital methods. *New Media & Society, 20*(11), 4195–4217.

Vergano, D. (2016, July 12). eBay just nixxed its human skull market. *Buzz Feed. Scholarship in the Humanities, 35*(1), 194–207. Retrieved February 5, 2021, from https://www.buzzfeednews.com/article/danvergano/skull-sales

Wevers, M., & Smits, T. (2020). The visual digital turn: Using neural networks to study historical images. *Digital Scholarship in the Humanities, 35*(1), 194–207.

#antiquitiesdealers

The Construction and Use of "Dealer Persona" in the Internet Market for Antiquities

Lauren Dundler

Abstract Antiquities dealers have always occupied unique positions of authority and trust within the market, requiring them to portray themselves as professionals who can guarantee the authenticity, quality, and legality of antiquities offered for sale. In the twenty-first century, this compels the ongoing online performance of the professional self, which can be understood through the analytical concept of the persona. This chapter introduces the concept of "dealer persona": the online persona that antiquities dealers use to operate in the internet market for antiquities. These personas are presented differently across various social media and internet platforms, requiring this analysis to examine the ways in which antiquities dealers construct and use online personas across various social media profiles, sales-hosting websites, and their own professional websites. Based on an examination of 26 internet antiquities dealers, four categories of dealer persona are identified: (1) the performance of trust and discretion through use of authenticity guarantees and collecting advice; (2) the performance of professional expertise in the form of credentials, professional biographies, and collaboration with academics or scientific laboratories; (3) the performance of legitimate relationships with the ancient world including autobiographical narratives, photos, and other media to convey their connection with the past; and (4) the performance of professional ethics demonstrated through the expression of awareness of the relevant legal context when dealing in antiquities, the development of professional ethics policies. Insights from this analysis demonstrate the intersection between the marketplace and scholarship, whilst highlighting ongoing ethical and legal issues with the internet antiquities market.

1 Introduction

> Personas are mutable public masks worn, not to obscure our features, but to present them to the world. For many, the deployment of a persona is deemed to be superficial, a frontage that

---

L. Dundler (✉)
Department of History and Archaeology, Macquarie University, Sydney, NSW, Australia
e-mail: lauren.dundler@hdr.mq.edu.au

N. Oosterman, D. Yates (eds.), *Crime and Art*, Studies in Art, Heritage, Law and the Market 1, https://doi.org/10.1007/978-3-030-84856-9_4

> is as flimsy as appearance. And yet personas have the ability to move us, to convey great affect, and embody deeply held personal values. (Marshall et al., 2020, p. 75).

Antiquities dealers have always occupied unique positions of authority and trust within the market, requiring them to portray themselves as professionals who can guarantee the authenticity, quality, and legality of antiquities offered for sale (Mackenzie et al., 2020). The emergence of the internet and social media as platforms for facilitating sales of antiquities have presented new business and networking opportunities for emerging and existing dealers (Brodie, 2017). However, users of online marketplaces have their own expectations and interpretations of authority and trustworthiness that must be acknowledged by dealers if they are to be successful in adapting to digital commerce. This necessitates the ongoing online performance of the professional self, which can be understood through the analytical concept of the persona emerging "from the close study of the performance and assemblage of the individual public self" (Marshall et al., 2020, p. 17).

This chapter introduces the concept of 'dealer persona': the online persona that antiquities dealers use to operate in the internet market for antiquities. These personas are presented differently across various social media and internet platforms, requiring this analysis to examine the ways in which antiquities dealers construct and use online personas on various social media profiles, sales-hosting websites, and their own professional websites. Insights from this analysis demonstrate the intersection between the marketplace and scholarship, whilst highlighting ongoing ethical and legal issues with the internet antiquities market.

2 The Internet Antiquities Market

The modern antiquities market is the product of centuries of collecting practices (Arnold, 2006; Pearce, 1995; Thompson, 2016). When examining the history of collecting antiquities, a pervasive set of actions and values can be observed, which have been shaped and reshaped over time and place (Pearce, 1995; Thompson, 2016). Supporters of the market often acknowledge the relationship between the modern antiquities trade and the *Wunderkammer* kept by the wealthy European elite (Arnold, 2006). However, the private ownership and public display of antiquities is deeply entrenched in the history of colonialism (Procter, 2020) and conquest (Miles, 2008).

Since the 1960s, research has highlighted how the acquisition of antiquities involves the commission of multiple crimes. These crimes include the looting of archaeological and heritage sites, the trafficking of cultural objects from source to the destination market, and the laundering processes which transform looted antiquities into legal commodities (Mackenzie et al., 2020). The looting and trafficking of antiquities is now recognised as damaging and harmful, destroying archaeological information and depriving communities of access to their cultural patrimony. Restrictions on the export of cultural heritage have existed since the nineteenth century, however, it is the second half of the twentieth century which saw the development of international legal frameworks aimed at combatting illicit cultural trafficking.

In 1970, the UNESCO Convention on the Means of Prohibiting and Preventing the Illicit Import, Export and Transfer of Ownership of Cultural Property was adopted, and upon celebrating its 50th anniversary it had been ratified by 140 states. State parties are required to adopt protection measures in their own territories, including drafting appropriate national legislation guided by the principles of the convention; control the movement of cultural property, for example through the introduction of a system of export certificates; and return stolen cultural property at the request of the State Party of origin. In the early 1990s UNIDROIT was tasked with developing a new legal instrument in response to concerns about the limitations of the 1970 Convention, resulting in the promulgation signing of the Convention on Stolen or Illegally Exported Cultural Objects in 1995. As part of the ratification process, states are required to adopt domestic law which implement the convention's focus on "the creation of private rights of action" (Gerstenblith, 2014, p. 7428). Importantly, the convention states that in most circumstances stolen and illegally exported cultural objects should be returned to the original owner or the state of origin.

The late twentieth century and early twenty-first century saw the rise of digital economies, and the use of e-commerce became commonplace in an increasingly global marketplace. Antiquities dealers are amongst the varied types of businesses who began to take advantage of the connectivity, accessibility, and ease offered by the internet. Existing auction houses like Sotheby's, Christie's, and Bonhams established web presences where they began to host live digital auctions, supplementing their existing services (Lidington, 2002). Independent dealers took advantage of newly emerging auction and sales hosting websites, such as eBay, or developed their own websites with storefronts or advertisements to their existing brick-and-mortar businesses (Lidington, 2002). In recent years, antiquities sales have been found to occur widely on social media platforms (Al-Azm & Paul, 2019; Dundler, 2019).

There are a number of key issues with the internet market for antiquities that must be acknowledged here, including the incompatibility between existing legal and regulatory frameworks and digital marketplaces (Bieron & Ahmed, 2012); the online disinhibition effect allowing individuals to engage in criminal, unethical, or otherwise risk-taking practices online (Suler, 2004, 2015); and the removal of traditional barriers between source and market afforded by the internet (Lidington, 2002). For example, buyers and potential buyers who can communicate with antiquities looters and traffickers on the ground in Syria and Iraq to request certain artefacts (Al-Azm & Paul, 2019). There is also the belief that the internet market is more vulnerable to the dissemination of fakes and forgeries (Fay, 2011)—a belief which requires internet antiquities dealers to develop strategies for ensuring the authenticity of their wares in order to gain consumer trust.

Nowadays, most auction-hosting websites and social media platforms have internal policies prohibiting users from buying and selling illicit or otherwise restricted objects. Some sales-platforms, such as eBay, explicitly restrict the sale of antiquities in their policy statements (Brodie, 2017). The issue, however, is how well these internal policies are enforced by the platforms, and whether they possess loopholes which can be exploited by market participants. Further, commentators have highlighted that these regulated goods policies are rarely immediately visible when navigating these sites (Brodie, 2017), and that these platforms do not provide users with the necessary tools to report posts or sales listings which violating their own policies (Paul, 2020). Overall, these failings to regulate the internet market for antiquities creates an environment where illicit or otherwise morally dubious sales occur in plain sight.

3 The Role of Antiquities Dealers

Professional individuals and businesses dedicated to facilitating the sale of antiquities have always played vital roles in the market. In their comprehensive examination of the illicit antiquities trade, researchers of the Trafficking Culture consortium argue that there are many aspects of the modern marketplace that seem to exist in contradiction to theories of regulation and economics (Mackenzie et al., 2020, p. 11). These archaic features of the modern antiquities market can be traced to the ideas of class, wealth, and discretion germane to the Enlightenment and post-Enlightenment periods. The most typical example of this is the practice of offering an antiquity for sale without provenance: information about the object's discovery and history of ownership which can attest to its authenticity and legal status.

In a market obsessed with authenticity this practice seems contradictory. Market commentators have argued that antiquities with extensive ownership histories or "good provenance" are seen as more valuable to collectors (Borodkin, 1995; Cannon-Brookes, 1994), but there is little evidence to suggest this is actually the case (Brodie, 2014). In reality, antiquities are purchased for substantial sums of money with little to no provenance, rendering it all but impossible for a potential good-faith buyer to ensure legal and ethical acquisitions. Instead, the market extends the previous owners of antiquities a veil of anonymity which is inherently linked to the socio-political values of the eighteenth and nineteenth centuries. These acts of discretion allowed "cash-strapped gentry to unload the family collection without a public declaration of financial insolvency" (Mackenzie et al., 2020, p. 11). Antiquities dealers, then, occupied—and continue to occupy—a position of personal trust through their assurances of anonymity and discretion.

In his psychoanalytic exploration of collecting, Werner Muensterberger emphasises the significance of the relationship between collectors and dealers. Muensterberger argues that whilst dealers do provide collectors with guidance on what to purchase, the main role these professionals perform is one of encouragement in order to negate any feelings of anxiety and guilt involved in acquiring new collectables (Muensterberger, 1994, pp. 236–238). Thus, the relationship between collector and dealer is one of emotional support and assurance, often featuring a "finely tuned interplay between the needful collector-acquisitor and the astute [. . .] empathetic dealer-provider" (Muensterberger, 1994, p. 238). This dynamic of emotional support involved in antiquities dealing is an integral feature in the development and use of dealer persona—an idea which will be explored throughout this chapter.

4 The Construction and Use of Dealer Persona

In an increasingly digital world, antiquities dealers have access to a much wider potential customer base than ever before. To be successful in the internet antiquities market these individuals and businesses must construct, utilise, and maintain a dealer persona: a performance of the public and professional self. Emerging from the multidisciplinary landscape of cultural, media and, celebrity studies, social psychology, and sociology, is the field of persona studies. Whilst the concept of persona is not new by any means, persona studies and its approach to the public self is an emergent discipline. Marshall and colleagues define persona as the public self we construct, fabricate, produce and present: a "technologically mediated but naturalised identity that we inhabit individually and collectively" (Marshall et al., 2020, p. 2) Drawing on the works of Hannah Arendt, Judith Butler, and Irving Goffman (Arendt, 1958; Butler, 1999; Goffman, 1959), they argue the persona is the public self we perform in our everyday lives, formed and reformed in response to our constantly changing world.

Throughout their work, Marshall et al. (2020) emphasise how the internet and social media technologies have fundamentally changed the ways in which persona is constructed and used by individuals and corporations. Within the broader concept of persona, they identify three registers of the performance of persona—professional, personal, and intimate—as well as five dimensions of persona: the public, mediatised, performative, collective and intentional value (also known as VARP: Value, Agency, Reputation, Prestige). The VARP is a series of "overlapping facets of personal investment or value" that act "not as sub-dimensions but equally important examples of what represents intentional speculation and investment in the public self" (Marshall et al., 2020, p. 72; Marshall, 2016; Moore et al., 2017). It is within the framework of the VARP that we can understand how internet users form and evaluate connections with others to maximise the investment of an online persona. Whilst this idea has been applied by Marshall and his colleagues to the public persona of celebrities, it is becoming an increasingly relevant tool to explore questions of "engagement, authenticity, and reputational legitimacy" (Marshall et al., 2020, p. 73). All professionals who operate in digital spaces require this awareness of both the monetary and reputational value of constructing and using an online professional persona. Antiquities dealers are no exception.

5 Dataset

This analysis of dealer persona is based on a dataset of 26 internet antiquities dealers, developed through the monitoring of the online market for antiquities over a period of three years (2017–2020). Dealers were identified via Google searches for "antiquities for sale" and "antiquities dealers"; targeted searches for types of popular antiquities (e.g., shabtis) on auction and sales hosting websites eBay, Facebook Marketplace, invaluable.com, and Live Auctioneers; and via the #antiquitiesdealer and #antiquitiesforsale hashtags on Instagram. Whilst there were many more than 26 internet antiquities dealers identified through these searches, there were three key selection criteria that were applied in order to formulate the dataset.

Firstly, the person in question had to personally identify as a dealer or seller of *antiquities* rather than an *antiques* dealer who may sell the occasional antiquity, or a casual seller making a one-off sale.[1] This criterion was necessary in ensuring the dataset was representative of only professional antiquities dealers in order to develop the most robust understanding of antiquities dealer persona. Secondly, the dealers had to either operate their business via their own professional website or have an additional web presence outside of a sales hosting platform. This criterion was determined by the limitations of some sales hosting platforms, which may restrict the amount of professional information a person can include about themselves. Data garnered from either a website controlled by the antiquities dealer, or a combination of platforms was preferred as it offers a fuller picture of professional persona. Thirdly, to limit the scope of this study, the search terms and hashtags used were only in English. This criterion skewed the dataset to include antiquities dealers from English-speaking regions including the United Kingdom and North America, which represented eight and 13 dealers respectively. Outside of these regions there was a single dealer in Grafton, Australia, and another in Jerusalem, Israel. Two dealers also identified as operating out of multiple locations across different countries: one out of both London and New York and another out of London, Hong Kong, Los Angeles, and Seoul.

The goal of this study is to demonstrate how the 26 internet antiquities dealers construct and utilise professional persona, and this is achieved through a thematic analysis of their web pages and social media profiles. However, in order to give a broader understanding of the social media platforms represented in the dataset, this discussion of dealer persona is preceded with an overview of these demographics. The majority of dealers—19 of 26—had public Facebook presences associated with their business. One dealer had a private group for "Facebook friends, friends, fans and customers". Both Instagram and LinkedIn were used by 16 of the 26 dealers in the dataset. The next most-represented social media platform was Twitter, with

[1] Antiques are objects which are at least 100 years old, however, the term is often used to describe any object which is "old". Antiquities are objects originating in the ancient world. Both are valued for their rarity and because they are capable of representing the historical period in which they were created.

13 dealers having public accounts associated with their businesses. Out of the 26 dealers in the dataset, 10 had Pinterest accounts linked to their businesses. There was also one dealer with a Flickr account. One-fifth of the dealers had YouTube accounts associated with their businesses. There were two further examples of professional websites used by the dealers, including two Academia.edu profiles and one IMDb page. Finally, whilst many dealers had blogs built into their own websites, four also have public blogs hosted on Medium, paper.li, Weebly, and WordPress.

6 Results

Based on an examination of 26 internet antiquities dealers, four categories of dealer persona are identified:

1. the performance of trust and discretion through use of authenticity guarantees and collecting advice.
2. the performance of professional expertise in the form of credentials, professional biographies, and collaboration with academics or scientific laboratories.
3. the performance of legitimate relationships with the ancient world including autobiographical narratives, photos, and other media to convey their connection with the past.
4. the performance of professional ethics demonstrated through the expression of awareness of the relevant legal context when dealing in antiquities, the development of professional ethics policies.

6.1 The Performance of Trust and Discretion

One of the most common ways of communicating trust and discretion is the guarantee of authenticity. Discourses of authenticity have always been central to the antiquities market, especially in the post-industrial and increasingly digital world. According to Baudrillard (1968), the modern status of ancient objects is intimately linked with our obsession with our own origins. In the case of ancient objects, the site of birth is in antiquity and the older an object is, the greater its symbolic value. This obsession with origins also extends to a fixation with authenticity, certainty, and the moment of creation.

Authenticity is then intimately linked to value in the antiquities market as it is what guarantees a connection with the past and with the ancient world. Collectors of antiquities collect the past through its tangible remains and thus seek this connection above all other qualities. A fake, regardless of its quality, lacks this connection with the ancient world and what Yates calls "past-based value" (Yates, 2015, p. 75). Paradoxically, most buyers of antiquities lack the expertise to accurately determine authenticity independently and are therefore reliant on the expertise of others (Yates, 2015). In order to be successful in the antiquities market, dealers must therefore develop and use a number of strategies to prove the legitimacy of their wares.

These strategies—employed by all but five of the dealers in the dataset—take a variety of forms, ranging from simple declarations ("100% genuine ancient artefact") to the provision of authenticity certificates, often constructed by the dealer themselves. Such guarantees include the assurance of a refund if an antiquity purchased by a buyer was proven to be inauthentic, which may require testimony from a relevant academic or scientific testing facility. For example, dealer based in Washington D.C.:

> provide a lifetime, unconditional guarantee of authenticity and provenance. Every artifact purchased from us is accompanied by a Certificate of Authenticity, stating culture, provenance, and age.

Similarly, a United Kingdom-based dealer states:

> You can shop confidently knowing that we are 100% committed to **Safe** and **Reliable** transactions
>
> All items offered for sale are **AUTHENTIC** and unconditionally **GUARANTEED** to be **GENUINE**
>
> Feel confident about your purchase with our 100% purchase price money back guarantee of authenticity.

The use of authenticity guarantees and certificates are often complemented by additional strategies which are designed to encourage consumer trust. Antiquities dealers have long played an advisory role to collectors and casual buyers of antiquities, and in the internet market this role is performed in unique ways. For example, the provision of how-to-guides for collectors, ranging from topics of provenance, preservation, and the best places to seek out authentic antiquities. Such tips and tricks are disseminated through the dealers' blogs, publications, newsletters, Facebook posts, and even YouTube videos.

One New York-based dealer has a public YouTube account with 2900 subscribers and 116 videos: a mixture of advertisements for coins for sale, how-to-guides on topics like collecting and photographing coins, effectively selling on eBay, and a fifteen-minute-long video about why ancient coins make the "best gifts" for "Him & Her Women and Children for Holidays & Christmas". A North Carolina-based dealer has a total of 17 subscribers and four videos, on topics including ancient coins, oil lamps, provenance, and authenticity. The YouTube account for a Colorado-based business has 319 subscribers. In a series of videos posted between 2015 and 2018, the dealer presents a number of how-to-videos for collectors, including: "Adding Religious Art to Your Collection", "Displaying Ancient Art", and "Using Smell to Authenticate Ancient Art". These videos and how-to-guides are a tangible demonstration of dealer expertise, making them an effective method of engendering consumer trust.

In addition to providing guidelines for acquiring and preserving antiquities, some of the dealers offer support to customers and potential customers for navigating the internet antiquities market. eBay is often the target of these e-commerce specific guidelines. For example, a United Kingdom-based dealer includes in their "Collectors' Resources" a section entitled "Buying on eBay", which starts with the following three bullet-points:

- Ebay can be fun and interesting things can be found there but for the newcomer it can also be risky.
- The majority of antiquities dealers are honest and knowledgeable but
- fraudulent selling of fakes and forgeries is very common on eBay.

At face value these videos, how-to-guides, and authenticity guarantees are clearly utilised by internet antiquities dealers to engender trust in consumers who operate in a market of uncertainty. These strategies, however, present the dealer as more than just trustworthy. Instead, they are an opportunity for dealers to model their own version of ideal values and behaviours for consuming the past. Further, upon transacting with these dealers a purchaser is not only buying antiquities for collecting, but also being deemed worthy of collecting in the first place. As argued by Muensterberger (1994), the main role of the dealer is to alleviate the guilt and shame of collecting, and this is how internet antiquities dealers accomplish this feat.

6.2 The Performance of Expertise

Expertise is the most common way to assert authenticity and quality in the antiquities market. The careful eye of the connoisseur, the authority of a trained scholar, or the legitimacy of a scientific laboratory generates consumer confidence. This process, however, requires the dealer to perform their expertise, or position themselves to the expertise of another.

The most common communication of expertise is a description of the dealer/s provided on the website, which usually includes the length of time the dealer has been in the industry for, the forms of training they have, and any famous clients, such as well-known national collecting institutions, they may have worked with.

For example, a London-based dealer provides the following description of their experience:

> Under the tutelage of the great Dr Colin Kraay of the Ashmolean Museum and the Art lover Dr Eva Frommer, [they] entered the world of collecting at a very young age. Funding [their] own collection through trading in ancient coins, [they] founded the company in 1971 and has been dealing in the antiquities and numismatic business ever since. [They have] handled enormous numbers of coins and antiquities, enabling [them] to lead at the forefront of the industry. [They are] currently serving as Vice Chairman of the Antiquities Dealer Association (ADA) and Chairman of the British Numismatic Trade Association (BNTA). [They have] also been appointed by the Culture Secretary to sit on the Treasure Valuation Committee for a five year term, starting in 2016.

Here, the dealer starts by positioning themselves to the professional reputation of well-known figures in the art and antiquities world, which has the effect of enhancing their own standing in the market. They then connect this expertise to their company, explicitly stating the age of the business to emphasise the dealer's professional experience. Finally, the dealer lists a number of professional roles they maintain in the antiquities trade, supporting their claim that they "lead at the forefront of the industry."

Collectively, these individual pieces of information produce the public and professional self that the dealer wishes to be seen by potential customers. The use of such strategies which highlight personal expertise and/or the proximity of the expertise of others are recurring in the dataset of internet antiquities dealers. Fourteen dealers present themselves as members of various professional dealer associations, while 16 have a LinkedIn profile where potential buyers or clients can see that they have been endorsed by other users for their skills in authenticating and cataloguing antiquities. Similarly, other dealers in the dataset are also eager to build their professional reputation by publicising their relationships with well-known individuals and institutions. The majority of dealers in the dataset utilised the expertise of others in various ways to promote the legitimacy of their businesses, with only three dealers making no reference whatsoever to the academic or professional expertise of an external individual or institution.

Whilst allusions to other collectors or scientific laboratories which perform authenticating tests on antiquities were made, the most common examples of this practice were references to academic publications. This is most often done within the context of a description for an antiquity being offered for sale, usually for the purpose of providing an example of a comparative artefact which has been studied and published. In some cases, however, the antiquities being offered for sale have been the subject of academic research and this is always highlighted by the dealer. A New-Jersey based dealer includes both a list of their "9000 customers and counting" and the pieces in their sales lots featured in academic publications. The latter list is concluded with the statement: "DePaul University lists our site as an online archaeological reference." Dealers in the dataset also utilised Facebook and Twitter to maintain the appearance of staying abreast with academic publications and archaeological discoveries, providing further context to the antiquities offered for sale whilst simultaneously situating the dealer's expertise within the world of scholarly expertise.

The academic facilitation of the antiquities market has been the subject of research (Brodie, 2011a, 2011b; Prescott & Munch Rasmussen, 2020), including an examination conducted by Neil Brodie of the professional relationship between one of the dealers in the dataset and Professor Wilfred Lambert (Brodie, 2011b). The dealer offers the following description of their working arrangement:

> [The Dealer] has secured the services of Professor Lambert (University of Birmingham), a renowned expert in the decipherment and translation of cuneiform, to examine and process the information on these tablets.

This statement precedes both a description of the cuneiform text and Lambert's translation, and can be found in the sales listings of 188 of 218 cuneiform objects available on the dealer's website. A further 15 listings mention Lambert in the item description, in the form of the assertion: "Description and translation kind provided by Professor W.G. Lambert."

Prior to his death in 2011, Lambert was Professor of Assyriology at the University of Birmingham for thirty years, making him an ideal choice to produce consumer confidence in the market for cuneiform objects.

Academic expertise is always of value in the modern antiquities trade; however, this is especially true when discussing the market for text-based artefacts such as papyrus and cuneiform objects when the value of an object is enhanced by expert translation (Brodie, 2011a, p. 130). In his study of illegally looted and exported Iraqi antiquities, Brodie argues academics facilitate the antiquities market by supporting "a credible pricing regime by establishing the quality, interest and rarity of the pieces on offer, and maintain customer confidence by keeping the market free of fakes" (Brodie, 2011a, p. 129). The relationship is also mutually beneficial, with academics not only financially compensated for their expertise, but receiving academic credit through the publication of objects they authenticate (Brodie, 2011a).

Recent controversies, however, have drawn attention to the ethics of academic involvement with the antiquities market. Cases including the Gospel of Jesus' Wife (Sabar, 2020), and the conduct of academics who have worked with and for the Museum of the Bible (Hicks-Keeton & Concannon, 2019; Moss & Baden, 2017) exist within a much broader context of unethical, and even illegal, academic conduct. Such involvement can vary from the common practice of researching and publishing antiquities without investigating their provenance to outright law-breaking. In response to this growing awareness of how academia intersects with the problematic commodification and consumption of antiquities, many academic organisations, institutions, and individuals have developed ethics policies to limit contact with the market and foster less harmful professional practice.

6.3 *The Performance of Legitimate Relationships with the Past*

"In late 2004, I set off on a month-long expedition through Egypt and Jordan," says a California-based dealer. On their business website, this dealer provides a travelogue of their modern-day Grand Tour, which they describe in the following words:

> Every day was an adventure—we avoided the "beaten path" and overly-touristed locations and instead stuck to ancient maps and writings to find our destinations.
>
> We roamed the vast Sahara Desert where the mummies still lay upon their burial slabs, lived in tents with Bedouins who guided us through their discoveries, and rode by horse and donkey through the cliffs of Petra, Jordan [. . .].

The dealer, who first entered the "fascinating world of ancient artifacts, exploration and travel" via their work writing and producing History Channel documentaries, presents a travelogue in seven parts. Each entry is accompanied by a series of photographs, including images of significant sites featuring ancient cultural and human remains. All the photos are accompanied with a caption, such as the description of a 'discovery' at the Temple of Amarna:

> Way deep in a tomb in Amarna. Only our torches to light the way. No clue how to get back.
>
> Until we found...
>
> Pottery and bones way way way down in this tomb at Amarna.

Many of the photos feature the dealer themselves or their companions posing in front of a hieroglyphic column or leaning against the "undergraound [sic] remains of One library at Alexandria". In one photo from part six, Siwa Oasis, the dealer is featured sitting on the ground, leaning against a wall. The caption reads:

> The actual room where Alexander and the Oracle met
>
> I am not kidding.

These 'antiquities selfies' and the inclusion of a travelogue on a business website is a deliberate strategy employed by this dealer and other antiquities dealers to legitimise themselves not only as trustworthy sellers of ancient objects, but as conduits of antiquity itself. Their expert knowledge of the objects they deal in is not merely a product of years of experience or training, instead it is informed by a deep and intimate rapport with the ancient world which they often trace back to childhood or their own modern-day Grand Tours. Communicating this relationship is a key component in the construction and use of antiquities dealer persona, and this is accomplished through a number of recurring strategies.

References to travelling appear three more times in the dataset: An Ohio-based dealer claim their collecting expertise was established during travels throughout Europe, Turkey and Asia in the 1960s; a dealer based in North Carolina has "travelled extensively in the ancient Mediterranean world and visited countless archaeological sites"; and a New York-based dealer's collection of videos depict a trip to Italy posted in 2015. Two other dealers include photos of themselves posing with ancient sites, including one dealer posing at the Roman ruins located in Sevilla, Spain, and another in front of an unidentified Egyptian pyramid.

In addition to travel narratives the dealers in the dataset offered descriptions of how they first encountered the ancient world. These autobiographical accounts are often featured in the "About Us" sections of their websites, such as the following from a London-based dealer:

> [their] interest in archaeology was stirred at the age of just six when [they] swapped [their] pocket money for ancient coins with an antiques dealer on the King's Road in London.

Another United Kingdom-based dealer offers the following description:

> My interest in the past began as a child when visiting historic houses and castles in England and Wales. I began buying antiques about 30 years ago and then one day I had the opportunity to handle some ancient pottery. I've never looked back.

There is also an intergenerational component in some of these narratives. For example, from a different United Kingdom-based dealer:

> It all began with a small group of roman silver coins being handed down to me by my grandfather when I was a young [child]. They fuelled the passion to acquire more pieces to add to my ever increasing collection.

Likewise, a Canadian dealer acknowledges their:

> [. . .] grandfather and father [who] helped spark this passion decades ago near the shores of the Mediterranean in a country where two of the seven ancient wonders of the world originated—Egypt.

These intergenerational narratives further legitimise the relationship between the dealer and the ancient world. For these dealers have not just inherited collections of antiquities or dealerships from their family members, but that 'spark' which embodies their passion for antiquity, which is what distinguishes them from others.

We can also see these attempts to establish a dealer persona on the foundations of legitimate relationships with the past in the naming of businesses after ancient words, phrases, and individuals. Eleven of the 26 dealers in the dataset adopted this strategy, with the most common type of names being deities or mythical figures including and Orientalist clichés designed to conjure images of the ancient 'East'. Like the antiquities selfies and autobiographical narratives, the use of ancient words, phrases, and names by internet antiquities dealers contributes to the overall performance of possessing an authentic and unique relationship with antiquity. Together these strategies produce a public and professional self which conveys that these dealers not only have intimate knowledge of the ancient world, but also an ownership of it. They are positioning themselves as the ideal custodian of the tangible remains of antiquity; the true inheritors of the past who possess the moral and legal right to determine who will best appreciate and protect antiquities against modernity.

6.4 *The Performance of Professional Ethics*

Two dealers in the dataset make the following claim on their websites: "our company maintains a zero-tolerance approach to illicit, fake or smuggled antiquities." This statement is an example of what can be termed a performance of professional ethics, which is a core component of the public and professional persona used by internet antiquities dealers. Like the claims of expertise and personal relationships with antiquity, the dealers of the dataset achieve this image through a series of related strategies. Firstly, declarations of professional ethics, like the one featured above, are commonplace in the dataset, with only five dealers failing to make any type of statement. Such declarations can include a single sentence, whilst others adopt their own Code of Conduct, for example:

> [The dealer is] proud to uphold the following Code of Conduct:
>
> We undertake to make, to the best of our ability, all purchases in good faith.

> We undertake not to purchase or sell objects until we have established, to the best of our ability, that such objects were not stolen from excavations, architectural monuments, public institutions or private property. [. . .]
>
> To the best of our ability, we guarantee authenticity and provenance of all objects offered for sale.

These declarations of professional expertise are supplemented by the communication of awareness of the legal frameworks which inform the contemporary trade of antiquities. Again, this can take form of a brief statement:

> All items from these places of origin have come from old collections brought into the USA prior to 1969 and the UNESCO convention and related antiquities laws. I strictly adhere to these laws and make no exceptions.

Other dealers offer far more detailed guidelines about the legal obligations of antiquities collectors, as demonstrated by a New Jersey-based dealer who provides guidelines for legally acquiring antiquities, encouraging customers and potential customers to "seek a qualified attorney for specific legal advice." In addition to mentioning the role of the 1970 UNESCO and 1995 UNIDROIT Conventions, the dealer provides a list of all the relevant Memoranda of Understanding (MoUs) between the United States and 18 countries (as of August 2017) concerning the trade of cultural property.

The dealers in the dataset also employed the use of different social media platforms and blogging websites to engage in ethical discussions with their followers. A dealer based in North Carolina uses a WordPress account to discuss cultural heritage issues and their opinions on legislative changes to combat the looting of antiquities; a London-based dealer shares links on their Facebook account on topics including conservation of heritage sites during the COVID-19 pandemic; and a dealer from Colorado has a YouTube account which features a video entitled "Cultural Patrimony & Legal Collecting" posted in 2016, with the following description:

> [The dealer] explains the basics of Cultural Patrimony and how to avoid running afoul of law enforcement agencies when collecting antiquities.

Finally, dealers perform professional ethics by demonstrating their connections with the professional ethics of others. For example, the dealer based in Canada declares:

> We are proud members of CINOA [Confédération Internationale des Négociants en Oeuvres d'Art] and AADLA [Art and Antique Dealers League of America] and adhere to the strict standards and code of ethics.

Elsewhere, however, I have demonstrated that these testimonies of professional ethics and legal awareness do not necessarily translate to ethical dealer practice (Dundler, 2019). Through a comparison of the standards of provenance and the levels of legal awareness demonstrated by a dataset of 45 internet antiquities dealers, I argued that legal obligations in this context do not operate as a tool of checks and balances, but instead can be understood "as an act of branding, a performance of values and ethics to support the dealer's reputation in the market" (Dundler, 2019, pp. 2323–2324). It is also an expression of what Marshall et al. identify as agency: a tool for understanding how personas "express, incorporate, resist, and embody power" (Marshall et al., 2020, p. 75; Marshall, 2013). Such posts and statements of ethics, professional conduct, and other forms of market commentary are enforced by the influence dealers hold in the modern antiquities market. Just like celebrities using their platform to promote awareness of charities, these internet antiquities dealers form their online persona with the intent of enforcing personal and professional beliefs.

7 Conclusion

The use of dealer persona is not only for guaranteeing sales of antiquities but is ultimately an advertisement of the dealer themselves. The strategies implemented in the construction and maintenance of a dealer persona are designed to carefully navigate the expectations of buyers and potential buyers. These expectations are built on a combination of traditional market values and consumer demands which are now germane to e-commerce. Every post, every webpage, and every selfie in front of ancient ruins contributes to the overall messages antiquities dealers wish to disseminate: that they are trustworthy, discreet experts with unique relationships to the past, and, above all, that their role in facilitating the private ownership of cultural objects is legal and morally acceptable.

In their introduction to persona studies, Marshall et al. argue that persona is both the "cause and effect" of reputation (Marshall et al., 2020, p. 77). Internet antiquities dealers, like all professionals navigating the twenty-first century, highlight specific qualities which they perform in order to "produce a particular type of reputation" (Marshall et al., 2020, p. 77). When we view dealer persona collectively the online reputation which is actively managed by these individual dealers becomes a communal endorsement for the modern antiquities market. These dealers are not only selling antiquities and themselves; they are selling an aspirational lifestyle. YouTube video how-to-guides, discussions of ethics in Facebook posts, and Grand Tour travelogues invite consumers into privileged spaces with direct access to both antiquity and the elite world of Renaissance and post-Renaissance collecting. However, these are invitations which often conceal the colonial legacies of the antiquities trade, inadvertently endorsing historic and contemporary crimes and unethical market practices.

Acknowledgments This chapter was researched and written on the lands of the Cammeraygal and Ngunawal peoples. I pay my respects to their Elders, past, present and, emerging. I also acknowledge the contribution of Professor Malcolm Choat, who kindly reviewed this chapter.

References

Al-Azm, A., & Paul, K. A. (2019). Facebook's black market in antiquities. Report. Retrieved October 29, 2020, from http://atharproject.org/wp-content/uploads/2019/06/ATHAR-FB-Report-June-2019-final.pdf

Arendt, H. (1958). *The human condition. Charles R. Walgreen foundation lectures*. University of Chicago Press.

Arnold, K. (2006). *Cabinets for the curious: Looking back at early English museums*. Ashgate.

Baudrillard, J. (1968). *Le Système des objets*. Gallimard.

Bieron, B., & Ahmed, U. (2012). Regulating E-commerce through international policy: Understanding international trade law issues of E-commerce. *Journal of World Trade, 46*, 545–570.

Borodkin, L. (1995). The economics of antiquities looting and a proposed legal alternative. *Columbia Law Review, 95*, 377–417. https://doi.org/10.2307/1123233

Brodie, N. (2011a). The market in Iraqi antiquities 1980-2009 and academic involvement in the marketing process. In S. Manacorda & D. Chappell (Eds.), *Crime in the art and antiquities world: Illegal trafficking in cultural property* (pp. 117–133). Springer.

Brodie, N. (2011b). Congenial bedfellows? The academy and the antiquities trade. *Journal of Contemporary Justice, 27*, 411–440. https://doi.org/10.1177/1043986211418885

Brodie, N. (2014). Provenance and price: Autoregulation of the antiquities market? *European Journal on Criminal Policy and Research Policy, 20*, 427–444. https://doi.org/10.1007/s10610-014-9235-9

Brodie, N. (2017). How to control the internet market in antiquities? The need for regulation and monitoring. Antiquities Coalition Policy Brief.

Butler, J. (1999). *Gender trouble tenth anniversary edition* (2nd ed.). Taylor & Francis.

Cannon-Brookes, P. (1994). Antiquities in the market place: Placing a price on documentation. *Antiquity, 68*, 349–350. https://doi.org/10.1017/S0003598X00046688

Dundler, L. (2019). "Still covered in sand.looked very old."—Legal obligations in the internet market for antiquities. *Heritage, 2*, 2311–2326. https://doi.org/10.3390/heritage2030142

Fay, E. (2011). Virtual artifacts: Ebay, antiquities, and authenticity. *Journal of Contemporary Criminal Justice, 27*, 449–464. https://doi.org/10.1177/1043986211418887

Gerstenblith, P. (2014). UNESCO (1970) and UNIDROIT (1995) Conventions. In C. Smith (Ed.), *Encyclopedia of global archaeology* (pp. 7428–7432). Springer.

Goffman, E. (1959). *The presentation of self in everyday life*. Anchor Books.

Hicks-Keeton, J., & Concannon, C. (2019). *The Museum of the Bible: A critical edition*. Rowman and Littlefield.

Lidington, H. (2002). The role of the internet in removing the 'shackles of the saleroom': Anytime, anyplace, anything, anywhere. *Public Archaeology, 2*, 67–84. https://doi.org/10.1179/pua.2002.2.2.67

Mackenzie, S., Brodie, N., Yates, D., & Tsirogiannis, C. (2020). *Trafficking culture: New directions in researching the global market in illicit antiquities*. Routledge.

Marshall, P. D. (2013). Personifying agency: The public-persona-place-issue continuum. *Celebrity Studies, 4*, 369–371. https://doi.org/10.1080/19392397.2013.831629

Marshall, P. D. (2016). *The celebrity persona pandemic*. University of Minnesota Press.

Marshall, P. D., Moore, C., & Barbour, K. (2020). *Persona studies: An introduction*. John Wiley & Sons.

Miles, M. M. (2008). *Art as plunder: The ancient origins of debate about cultural property*. Cambridge University Press.

Moore, C., Barbour, K., & Lee, K. (2017). Five dimensions of online persona. *Persona Studies, 3*, 1–11. https://doi.org/10.21153/ps2017vol3no1art658

Moss, C. R., & Baden, J. S. (2017). *Bible nation: The United States of Hobby Lobby*. Princeton University Press.

Muensterberger, W. (1994). *Collecting: An unruly passion*. Princeton Legacy Library.

Paul, K. A. (2020). Instagram just created reporting for endangered species—Almost one year after it was listed in their community guidelines. Blogpost. Medium. Retrieved November 29, 2020, from https://medium.com/alliance-to-counter-crime-online/instagram-just-created-reporting-for-endangered-species-almost-one-year-after-it-was-listed-as-3a1fa7a01278

Pearce, S. M. (1995). *On collecting: An investigation into collecting in the European tradition*. Routledge.

Prescott, C., & Munch Rasmussen, J. (2020). Exploring the "Cozy Cabal of Academics, Dealers and Collectors" through the Schøyen Collection. *Heritage, 3*, 68–97. https://doi.org/10.3390/heritage3010005

Procter, A. (2020). *The whole picture: The colonial story of art in our museums & why we need to talk about it*. Cassell.

Sabar, A. (2020). *Veritas: A Harvard Professor, A Con Man and the Gospel of Jesus's Wife*. Double Day.

Suler, J. (2004). The online disinhibition effect. *CyberPsychology & Behavior, 7*, 321–326. https://doi.org/10.1089/1094931041291295

Suler, J. (2015). *Psychology of the digital age: Humans become electric*. Cambridge University Press.

Thompson, E. (2016). *Possession: The curious history of private collectors from antiquity to the present*. Yale University Press.

Yates, D. (2015). Value and doubt: The persuasive power of 'authenticity' in the antiquities market. *Platform for Artistic Research Sweden, 2*, 71–84.

Evaluating the Transformative Potential of Photovoice for Research into the Global Illicit Trade in Cultural Objects

Emiline Smith

Abstract Criminologists are increasingly considering 'the visual' within their research, both as objects of study and through the use of visual methodologies. Within this trend, Photovoice provides an innovative, collaborative, and empowering visual research method that allows for in-depth engagement with lived experiences, particularly with underrepresented and previously 'unseen' communities, with the intention to foster social change. Photovoice relies on meaningful collaboration between researchers and stakeholders, so that the research is co-created between researchers and participants, therefore democratising the knowledge generation and exchange process. This chapter considers the use and potential effectiveness of Photovoice as a visual research method to further our understanding of art crime. It is argued that criminological enquiry into the illicit trade of cultural objects would benefit from utilising Photovoice to shed light on un(der)represented perspectives and lived experiences to better inform the debate around the production, protection, trade and ownership of cultural objects.

1 Introduction

Participatory visual research methods aspiring to foster social change by providing a platform to marginalised individuals and communities are gaining popularity in criminological research. One example of this is Photovoice, a method whereby researchers facilitate participants to capture photographs which reflect their day-to-day experiences and then discuss their perceptions and emotions surrounding the capture (Wang & Burris, 1997). The participant-generated photographs and discussions held throughout the research process provide unique insight into "real flesh and blood life experience" (Becker, 2002, p. 11). This chapter discusses how Photovoice can be used in criminological inquiry into the global illicit trade of cultural objects. The global illicit trade in cultural objects involves items "of importance for

E. Smith (✉)
Scottish Centre for Crime and Justice Research, University of Glasgow, Glasgow, UK
e-mail: emiline.smith@glasgow.ac.uk

N. Oosterman, D. Yates (eds.), *Crime and Art*, Studies in Art, Heritage, Law and the Market 1, https://doi.org/10.1007/978-3-030-84856-9_5

archaeology, prehistory, history, literature, art or science" (UNESCO, 1970: Art. 1), such as archaeological material, art, parts of architectural structures, and even human remains. These cultural objects are traded for financial gain, ending up in private and public collections around the world. This chapter draws on experiences from the author's fieldwork in Nepal for a 2019–2021 Scottish Government-funded project into post-earthquake community crime prevention methods against the looting and trafficking of cultural objects, and reflects on how Photovoice might have benefitted this research. It argues that Photovoice could be a valuable tool in the criminological toolkit for the study of the illicit trade in cultural objects.

Landlocked between Tibet and India, Nepal is a multi-ethnic, multi-lingual, and multi-cultural country in South Asia. The country's 240-year-old monarchy was abolished in 2008, but the subsequent democratisation process has proven an arduous task (Thapa & Sharma, 2009). The two primary religions of Nepal are Hinduism and Buddhism, which has engendered centuries of sacred objects and architecture, including temples, shrines, and statues of deities (Bangdel, 1989). As a representation of the artistic fusion of both religions and their continued use as living sacred locations, several monument zones within Kathmandu Valley have been listed as part of the UNESCO World Heritage List in 1979 (Tiwari et al., 2017). Bangdel (1989) likened the abundance of Nepal's sacred art and architecture to an enormous open museum, where cultural objects are scattered around temples, shrines, monasteries, old palaces, private courtyards, streets, open fields, water fountains, etc.

Even though cultural objects are protected under Nepal's 1956 Ancient Monuments Protection Act, foreign market demand was and continues to be too strong to prevent the looting of Nepal's cultural heritage (Yates & Mackenzie, 2018). The looting and theft of cultural objects from Nepal is well-documented, reaching its peak in the 1970s and 1980s when Hindu and Buddhist iconography entered Western popular culture (Liechty, 2017). During this time, celebrated art historian Lain S. Bangdel and art connoisseur Jürgen Schick independently set out to photographically document the rapid disappearance of Nepal's cultural objects. So dire was the situation that Schick (2006, p. 66) warned "the land of the gods" may quickly be "emptied to the point where nothing remains". With their pioneering publications, *Stolen Images of Nepal* (Bangdel, 1989) and *The Gods are Leaving the Country* (Schick, 2006), they intended not only to evidence the looting and theft of cultural objects throughout the country, but also to provide proof in case the objects would turn up on the global market. Indeed, their efforts have paid off, as stolen Nepali objects continue to be identified in foreign-held public and private collections, with some already having been repatriated on the basis of these two books (e.g., Sijapati, 2021).

As will be explored below, research into the illicit trade of cultural objects is inherently visual. However, the visual element is underexplored as a tool and method, resulting in gaps in our understanding of this topic. This chapter therefore calls for an expansion of the methodological toolkit of research into this topic through the use of Photovoice. The following sections describes how images and photographs have historically been used in criminological enquiry, and research into the illicit trade of cultural property specifically. The third section provides an overview of the Photovoice method, whereas the fourth section considers how research into the global illicit trade of cultural objects would benefit from visual research methods to capture its nature, scale and consequences. Overall, it argues that Photovoice can provide a useful tool in adopting a stakeholder-centred approach to research design, implementation, and dissemination in research into the illicit trade of cultural objects.

2 Academia's Visual Turn

Photography plays an increasingly important role in social sciences as a research method and as the object of study (see Pauwels, 2010, for an overview). Photographs are deemed repositories of meaning that visualise social power relations by way of their representation and reception, i.e., how we do and do not see (e.g., Rose, 2016). How images are created and how the viewer makes sense of them depends upon cultural assumptions, personal knowledge, and the context in which the picture is generated and presented (Dicks et al., 2006; Edwards, 2012). They are visual representations of subjective experiences, rather than objective statements (Bal, 2003): they are ontologically fallible and partial, like language (Carrabine, 2014).

A key point of debate here is image agency: instead of focusing on images as representations, or on questions of intention and meaning, the possibility of images affecting and being affected by cultural and social contexts is explored (e.g., Bal, 2003; Edwards, 2012). Images are ascribed an agentic role: for example, Mitchell (1996, p. 82) proposes that images be "seen as complex individuals occupying multiple subject positions and identities" and "not merely a by-product of social reality but actively constitutive of it". The concept of agency has also been extended to photography. Azoulay (2008) claims that photography exists as a socio-political event through which political relations between 'agents' (such as photographer, photographed subject, and spectator) are created and negotiated. The act of taking photographs and the images themselves are key sources of critical thinking and feeling about social issues. They invite the participants (both photographers and viewers alike) to slow down and consider what they are seeing and what they do not see, and why this is the case (Grimshaw, 2001; Linfield, 2010). As such, photographs can "encode an enormous amount of information in a single representation" (Grady, 2004, p. 20). Because of this, visual data facilitates new insights into social phenomena "which oral, aural or written data cannot provide" (Bolton et al., 2001, p. 503): it can provide unique insights or deepen our understanding of spoken and written information.

Criminology has also recognised the pervasive visuality of contemporary culture and the need to engage with the visual. Visual exploration had been an underused approach, often regarded as supportive or illustrative of textual accounts, instead of being recognised to 'speak for itself' and its capacity to bring a distinctive contribution to sociological or criminological enquiry (Bolton et al., 2001; Pauwels,

2017). However, recently there has been a "remarkable visual turn in criminology" (Carrabine, 2012) to overcome what Harper (2012) calls the "visual/non-visual divide in research" by giving attention to alternative visions, representations and images of crime, control, and harm. Fitting within a broader disciplinary move towards a social and cultural approach to criminology, this has resulted in a visual criminology, a branch of criminology concerned with the visual as primary site of analysis to explore the role of vision and the visual in relation to crime, harm and control (see e.g., Carrabine, 2012; Hayward, 2010). Similarly, visual sociology explores the visual dimensions of social life (Harper, 2012; Traue et al., 2018; Wagner, 2002).

Visual criminology, under the umbrella of cultural criminology, extends its gaze to social harms that 'traditional' criminology has often omitted due to its narrow definition of crime (Brown, 2014; Hayward, 2010). This is particularly well-documented for crimes and harms against the environment (as studied under the heading of 'green criminology'). For this reason, Brisman (2017) argues for a 'cross-fertilization of green criminology and visual criminology' through visual understandings of environmental crime and harm, arguing that "spectacles of suffering" (Carrabine, 2011, p. 19) of the planet possess the potential to transform the way we live on and with the planet. Brisman (2018) further concludes that developing a visual representation for environmental harms is paramount to inspiring action. The same arguments for visual research into environmental harms could be applied to the study of the global illicit trade in cultural objects. Gaining a visual understanding of the crimes, harms, practices, narratives, and emotions connected to cultural objects has the potential to transform how we approach their ownership, trade and protection.

As visual criminology matured, there emerged a recognition of the potentially constitutive and agentic role of images, beyond their use as mere "epiphenomenal supplements" or "representational objects in need of decoding" (Young, 2014). In her work on unauthorised image-making (i.e., street art and graffiti writing), Young (2010, p. 83) therefore advocates a paradigm of "criminological aesthetics", in which both the image itself as well as the relation between the spectator and the image is analysed. The encounter between the image and the spectator involves a dynamic process in which images are judged and contested and tracing the affective nature of our connection to images can generate a greater understanding of the processes by which spectatorship exist "between thought and image, perception and action" (Bennett, 2012, p. 188). This recognition of the entanglement between the social world and the image, and how meaning is derived from the affective nature of the spectator's encounter with the image, ensures "the image is conceptualised as a point of attachment and identification—as a subject position through which we speak and think 'crime'" (Young, 2014, p. 160). It is argued here that Photovoice, a participatory action research method that promotes participant engagement as a catalyst for community-driven social change, is particularly well-suited to assist in thinking through the conflicting legal and cultural responses to looting, trafficking, trading, and repatriating of cultural objects by way of participant-generated image analysis.

One of the challenges of studying and employing the visual is the risk of confirming, reproducing or amplifying old, dominant, and unhelpful narratives while ignoring others: what Armstrong (2017) calls the "politics of visibility". Consequently, Armstrong (2017, p. 417) invites (visual) criminology to consider its role in the making of desired worlds, to reflect on its relationship to the imagery of crime and how this enables particular ways of seeing: "one task of a visual criminology ought to be stirring the imagination, stimulating new ways of seeing and therefore thinking about crime and punishment". One way of committing to this call for activism is by using innovative tools such as Photovoice that employ the visual as a data source, method and output in the study of crime and its societal impact. For example, instead of focusing on the materiality of looted objects, visibilising past and present injustices and resistance against these injustices in relation to cultural objects could incite new methods for their protection and repatriation.

3 The Role of the Visual in Research into the Illicit Trade of Cultural Objects

The visual as connected to heritage has brought about a wide array of scholarship to explore representation and signifying practices (see Watson & Waterton, 2010b, for an overview). The production, use, and consumption of visual imagery is herein considered to be a platform for engaging with heritage and its contexts. Watson and Waterton (2010a, p. 3) hold that visuality is at the core of meaning-making processes related to heritage but note that heritage scholarship is "obsessively" concerned with materiality instead of visuality. This materiality, they argue, obscures the socio-cultural role of heritage or even actively suppresses it. This is in line with Smith (2006), who states that "the physicality of heritage also works to mask the ways in which the heritage gaze constructs, regulates and authorises a range of identities and values by filtering that gaze onto the inanimate material heritage" (Smith, 2006, p. 53). She therefore proposes to shift the focus from the heritage object to the processes underpinning the transformation of things, places, acts and experiences related to heritage. Through this, the visual is deemed an active agent, either through representation or response, in understanding the past in the present and understanding the present through the past.

Visual representations of material culture have often played a powerful role in disconnecting the cultural objects from the social and physical environments in which they were used and produced (Wagner, 2020). The visual has therefore aided the commodification and fetishisation of cultural objects (see e.g., Baudrillard, 1970, 1997; Marx, 1976)—think, for example, of the sterilised images of cultural objects in auction house and museum catalogues (whether physical or virtual) which highlight only the object's aesthetic value and materiality. In the context of the museum, the object is ascribed a performative function: it is "at once venerated and at the same time denied any other past that the one that is selected for it" (Watson &

Waterton, 2010a). It is therefore key to explore the life beyond this materiality—and its commodification—as symbolic, non-material dimensions of culture are an implicit complement to the world of things (Wagner, 2020).

Academic inquiry into the illicit trade of cultural objects is inherently visual because of its materiality-focused approach: it considers how and why cultural objects are looted, stolen, trafficked, and illegally traded, and how this violates legal and ethical frameworks (see Brodie et al., 2013 for an overview). The visual is used in various ways to explore these topics: for example, to document the harmful consequences of looting on archaeological sites (e.g., Contreras, 2010; Contreras & Brodie, 2010; Parcak et al., 2016) or to trace the trade of objects through (online) museum, private collection and auction house records (e.g., Brodie, 2014a, 2014b, 2019; Coggins, 1969; Gilgan, 2001; Gill & Chippindale, 1993; Nørskov, 2002). More often, studies in this area rely on documentary research, for example to consider the legal basis for ownership and protection (e.g., Elia, 1997; Merryman, 1986); and qualitative methods such as interviewing and observation, for example to consider the perspectives and motivations of stakeholders (Hollowell-Zimmer, 2003; Kersel, 2012; Mackenzie, 2005; Mackenzie & Yates, 2016; Matsuda, 1998). Although these studies engage with communities to explore their perspectives, the project design of these studies has primarily been researcher-led (even though a community-based, civic engagement approach is commonly used in other heritage research, including archaeology, see e.g., Atalay, 2012; Colwell, 2016). It can therefore be argued that 'traditional' research into the illicit trade of cultural objects has overall employed fairly conventional methods of enquiry, based primarily on oral, aural and written data and research outputs, resulting in gaps in our understanding of the narratives and practicalities related to this illicit trade that could be explored through the visual.

In my own research, I have encountered the limitations of 'traditional' research methods in studying, recording, communicating and disseminating the problematic narratives that surround cultural objects. For example, interviews with stakeholders (e.g., dealers, collectors, law enforcement representatives, community activists, archaeologists and museum staff) of the illicit trade of cultural objects in Nepal exemplified the wide range of emotions and perspectives attached to the repatriation of foreign-held cultural objects: from those favouring the objects to be repatriated to Nepal as it was the rightful thing to do, to those arguing against repatriation because the cultural objects were desecrated, could easily be replaced, or did not fit with Buddhist anti-materialism. These different viewpoints were represented by three female temple guardians in Kathmandu Valley in an interview on the topic of foreign-held Nepali cultural objects: Divya[1] wanted 'her' gods back as they belonged in Nepal and could not properly be appreciated or taken care of abroad; Prabha stated they should stay abroad to represent Nepal and educate the world about their culture; while Alisha felt it did not matter what happened to the objects as (Buddhist) spirituality comes from within and does not depend on materialism or

[1] Please note: pseudonyms are used throughout this chapter to protect the identity of participants.

physicality. However, in the course of our conversation, Prabha and Alisha also mentioned several times that the statues should "of course" come back, replicating the dominating narratives within press and government (e.g., Sijapati, 2021) without further elaboration.

This project employed traditional research methods: fieldwork consisted of semi-structured interviews, (participant) observation and ethnography, paired with secondary data analysis (e.g., court documents, law enforcement statistics, newspaper articles, etc.). These semi-structured interviews were intended to co-construct knowledge (e.g., Koro-Ljungberg, 2008), but such interviewing has been critiqued as it is based on what researchers' designs and activities can afford while potentially restricting spontaneity and authenticity (e.g., Birch & Miller, 2002).

As will be explored below, the use of Photovoice as an alternative research method could have enabled my understanding of participants' viewpoints and social worlds on their terms without the constraints of the interview (e.g., Capous-Desyllas & Forro, 2014; Young, 2014). In this, photographs could have served as a bridge between the distant social and cultural worlds of the participants and the researcher (e.g., Wagner, 2002). Photovoice could also have assisted in the denaturalisation of their social worlds to promote critical assessment by the participants themselves (Prosser, 1998). Moreover, although community collaboration was at the forefront of the research design process, there were limitations to the amount of control participants had over the research design and dissemination methods. In addition, there were power imbalances between the researchers and the participants, as well as between participants, as is common in cross-cultural research using traditional research methods (e.g., Liamputtong, 2010): this calls into question the representativeness and authenticity of the interviews, and problematises the research and data dissemination process. Photovoice would have been more effective at operationalising the plans for collaborative engagement by promoting power-sharing, trust and sustainability, and committing to community capacity, advocacy and policy change. Through this, Photovoice could have functioned as a platform for knowledge exchange between participants like Divya, Prabha and Alisha, within their wider communities and with other stakeholders, and could have led to more impactful social change.

4 Control, Collaboration, and Social Action: An Introduction to Photovoice

Photovoice is a form of Community-Based Participatory Research (CBPR) or Participatory Action Research (PAR) that centres on research *with* communities rather than *about* communities. Participatory research methods attempt to "promote active involvement in every stage of the research process by those who are conventionally the focus of research" (Chataway, 1997, p. 457). Developed in the field of public health, Photovoice uses reflective photography to enable people to record and reflect their community's strengths and concerns; promote critical dialogue and knowledge about important issues through large and small group discussion of photographs; and reach policymakers (Wang & Burris, 1997, p. 369). It can be used to research a particular question important to community members, or in a more exploratory way to assess community needs and assets and build relationships (Dedrick, 2018). The taking of a photograph often provokes critical thinking, bringing to the surface feelings about social issues as participants question their perspectives and experiences and how they would like to represent them (Woodgate et al., 2017). The contemporary familiarity of taking and talking photographs facilitates this process. To ensure the robustness of this information is captured for each image, the Photovoice method also incorporates individual storytelling and critical group discussion processes. The method honours knowledge grounded in experience but acknowledges the multiplicity of knowledge from individuals within and outside of communities, in which knowledge is co-constructed as "a 'polyvocal composite' through which multiple voices are raised and subjectivities are performed" (Lykes, 2010, p. 250).

Photovoice can be extremely useful in the study of emotive topics like the global trade in cultural objects. Unlike research-driven photography where photographs are created by the researchers, Photovoice's participant-driven photography turns participants into so-called 'co-researchers' or 'co-producers': a term reflecting the participatory nature of the research process and the increased control they have over the research process and its outcomes (as compared to e.g., observational practices). The participant is the expert, as manifested through a democratic process of involvement which distributes power between the researcher and the researched (Wang, 1999). As a result, participants are involved in the project's conception, design, recruitment and planning, to maximise community ownership and individual empowerment, as well as to establish rapport and build trust (Castleden et al., 2008). Wang and Burris (1997) proposed Photovoice as a pathway for 'insiders' to communicate their perspectives and realities through the camera lens, in order to potentially inform policy and be a catalyst for change in their own communities. This proposed process increases the likelihood that policy reflects participants' needs instead of outsiders' assumptions. Through this method, participants are considered collaborators who possess agency and are given a platform to communicate their impressions, experiences and feelings in order to "identify, represent, and enhance their community" (Wang, 1999, p. 185). As such, Photovoice can provide insight into difficult, emotional, sensitive topics and experiences, where text may fall short or where photography provides a 'neutral' base for discussion, and can therefore provide deeper, more complex understandings of lived experiences (Capous-Desyllas & Forro, 2014).

Photovoice therefore allows for the refining, enriching and democratizing of the knowledge creation process and grounds research findings in real community needs and expertise (Fals-Borda & Rahman, 1991; Liebenberg, 2018). Because of this, Photovoice has been heralded as an unobtrusive way to visualise the lived experiences of individuals and communities, which may be hidden, uncomfortable or unknown (Keller et al., 2008). As a result, Photovoice use in criminological research has been instrumental in the exploration of a variety of social issues, ranging from understanding the effects of surveillance, supervision and social control (e.g., Fitzgibbon & Healy, 2019; Fitzgibbon & Stengel, 2018; Healy & Fitzgibbon, 2020) to the socio-legal responses to unauthorised images in public space in the form of street art and graffiti (Young, 2014). Sensitivity to the subject is already advocated by many researchers in the field of art crime research, particularly when it comes to topics like the (colonial) looting of cultural objects and their potential repatriation, but this also complicates research practices in this field. Photovoice offers a way to prioritise subject sensitivity on participants' terms, while being guided by their lived experiences.

In sum, the Photovoice method is committed to principles of empowerment, collaboration, inclusivity, equity, and social action (Healy & Fitzgibbon, 2020). It therefore builds on core CBPR principles such as community capacity building, empowerment, and balancing research and action. If done properly, Photovoice has a transformative potential, offering "a powerful and evocative method of gaining trust and hearing participants' stories as they choose to share them, making the invisible visible literally and emotionally" (Fitzgibbon & Healy, 2019, p. 22). By relinquishing power and decision-making control over the study, researchers open themselves up to increased community ownership, trust building, and equity. As art crime research often involves cross-cultural research, considerations around maximization collaboration, researcher reflection, equity and trust-building, are paramount. The current push for decolonisation includes a quest for a more equitable decision-making process around how cultural objects are owned, preserved, studied, displayed, stored, traded and protected (see e.g., Tythacott & Ardiyansyah, 2021). This should obviously include control over the way in which the narratives attached to these cultural objects are researched, recorded and represented. Photovoice can facilitate these efforts by forefronting the perspectives of underrepresented individuals and communities through a democratic research design and dissemination process.

5 Potential Use of Photovoice for Research into Illicit Trade of Cultural Objects

As outlined above, Photovoice centres around the coproduction of knowledge grounded in equity and usefulness for all involved actors. Trust-building and community engagement is at the core of doing research into sensitive topics or in risky environments (e.g., Wong, 2015). Photovoice can help develop trust with community members and identify their priorities for the future, the obstacles they face, and their perspectives on and definitions of cultural heritage (Dedrick, 2018). This could engender community-directed discussion of the issues surrounding the ownership, trade and protection of cultural objects, highlighting taken-for-granted or underrepresented issues and perspectives.

The visual plays a key but underexplored role in the scholarship around the illicit trade in cultural objects. In Nepal, such scholarship is complemented by the key contributions of the work of Nepali and foreign activists and scholars, in which the visual takes centre stage as object as well as method of study in order to spark discussion about the theft of Nepal's cultural objects and elicit their repatriation. For example, curator Roshan Mishtra founded the online 'Global Nepali Museum', dedicated to objects "that are away and housed in the museums around the world" (Global Nepali Museum, n.d.). Cultural Conservationist Rabindra Puri conceptualised the 'Museum of Stolen Arts', to be opened in 2022, in which replicas of Nepal's stolen deities aim to increase awareness around the looting of Nepali cultural objects (Sijapati, 2020). Additionally, artist Joy Lynn Davis documented community responses to looted sculptures through a series of photo-realistic paintings—repatriating them visually to their sites of origin—and continues her engagement in this area through a dedicated website that includes a database of thefts (Remembering the Lost, 2021). Their efforts make clear that an image-based approach to the study of illicit trade of cultural objects can unlock in-depth engagement with the meaning-making processes that surround these objects to highlight their cultural significance.

Photovoice offers a way to explore the social and cultural contexts of objects beyond their materiality. For example, the participant-generated photographs and interviews can assist in revealing community perceptions or align views about specific topics related to heritage. This can be as basic as allowing for a shared understanding of terminology: for example, what does cultural heritage mean to people? In my own research, I have found that assumptions about shared understandings of concepts and terminology like 'cultural heritage', 'antiquity' and 'crime' are quickly proven false when conducting cross-cultural qualitative research (Smith, 2018). Moreover, it could provide visual representations of concepts where words may fall short. This is particularly important as the illicit trade of cultural objects can be a very emotive and sensitive topic for stakeholders due to the destructive, exploitative system it is based upon, the various values attached to these cultural objects and its connection to physical and emotional violence, loss, collective trauma, intergenerational harm, and insecurity, as well as individual and collective pride and social justice (e.g., Colwell, 2017; Van Beurden, 2021). Photovoice could therefore offer insight into the meaning of cultural objects beyond their materiality: for example, of the emotions and experiences that contextualise the cultural objects; how they should be used, owned, protected and preserved; what constitutes crime and illicit behaviour in relation to cultural heritage; what repatriation means, and how it could (not) restore justice; what the emotional and practical consequences of looting and theft of cultural objects are.

'Traditional' methods fall short when researching and representing the rich narratives attached to cultural objects, and particularly the lived realities of those at the forefront of the global illicit trade. Take for example Bijay, a dealer of Himalayan art and antiquities based in Kathmandu Valley. Over the course of our two 1.5-h interviews, he proudly showed off his collection of cultural objects, including those with 'questionable' provenance. He also guided me around the community temple in his backyard he helps take care of, which is seemingly at odds with his business. We spoke at length about his motivations for participating in the global illicit trade in cultural objects: his passion for the objects, his expertise, how he rationalised his participation in a harmful practice (see Mackenzie & Yates, 2016). On the one hand, he argued for stricter regulation to protect Nepal's cultural heritage, while on the other hand he complained about increasing stigma and tighter governmental oversight attached to his business. He claimed he had never been interviewed about these topics before.

Although I spent as much time as I could with Bijay and other stakeholders in the trade in Nepali cultural objects, my recording of their perspectives and lived realities was restricted by the usual practical constraints of fieldwork for an externally-funded academic project (such as time, money, mobility, and language capacity). Current knowledge, based on 'traditional' methods such as ethnography, (participant) observation, and interviewing, scarcely represents views of the 'intermediaries' between source and market (although see Mackenzie, 2005; Mackenzie & Davis, 2014). Photovoice as a research tool and process can encourage expression and engagement of marginalised groups; highlighting knowledge, issues and perspectives that may otherwise be overlooked (Masterson et al., 2018). It can offer different or deeper insights into the lived experiences of stakeholders, eliciting unique perceptions and concerns and identifying strategies for change (Dedrick, 2018; Young, 2014). Building on the affective potential of images, Photovoice can be particularly helpful in offering direct, tangible ways of understanding these experiences and perspectives that may not be accessible to policymakers and other audiences otherwise (Milne & Muir, 2020). Here, Photovoice would have offered a possibility to represent 'on the ground', lived experiences of those involved at the frontline of the illicit trade of cultural property that are excluded from governmental and academic discussions about these topics. This would have given underrepresented research participants much more control over the research process, including data dissemination, and could have therefore stimulated participation, engagement and representation. Instead of passive objects of study, they become empowered co-creators of data. Photovoice can therefore assist in depicting the hidden, complex and often neglected (in)tangible connections to cultural objects; highlight plural perceptions of the socio-legal frameworks that govern the ownership, protection and trade of cultural objects; and uncover issues of access and control over cultural objects and related intellectual property.

Photovoice can also assist in the challenging of assumptions, stereotypes and stigma, and help researchers to reframe their approach to research in this field, in order to start thinking about more impactful and empowering research pathways. Research into the illicit trade of cultural objects to date has primarily been conducted by researchers from North America, Europe, and Australia. Although impacted individuals and communities may have assisted in the design or practical implementation of a project, these projects' focus and framework are still often driven by 'outsiders'. Understanding this power imbalance, the Photovoice process and method offers researchers, particularly criminologists, an opportunity to democratise the research process by viewing co-researchers as the experts who should co-define the research focus and process, including dissemination of the research findings. This allows for inclusion of currently underrepresented, unseen and taken-for-granted perspectives and lived experiences of a variety of stakeholder groups in this illicit trade, including collectors, auction house representatives, museum curators, community activists, religious leaders, etc. Through this, we gain insight into what is and what matters in communities that are often excluded from discussions around the protection, ownership and use of cultural heritage. Moreover, the current debates around the decolonisation of museums and the repatriation of foreign-held cultural objects taking place across the globe indicate that discussions around illegal removal and trade of cultural objects demand an equitable representation of diverse voices (see e.g., Tythacott & Ardiyansyah, 2021). This demands new, innovative ways to explore these stories. Photovoice's focus on equity and social change therefore make it particularly suitable for research into the trade and trafficking of cultural objects.

6 Conclusion

Photovoice presents a timely means of conducting research into the illicit trade of cultural objects. This chapter has argued that the main contributions of Photovoice to the criminological study of the illicit trade in cultural objects could be found in taking a stakeholder-centred (as opposed to object-centred) and participant-led (as opposed to researcher-led) approach; shedding light on un(der)represented perspectives, practices, and experiences; and creating a platform to incite community-driven social change. Effectively implemented, the approach draws on participatory photography to facilitate a collaborative knowledge creation process that can facilitate deep exploration of taken-for-granted, underrepresented lived experience. The generated photographs and the co-creation of knowledge throughout the Photovoice process can result in accounts *of* rather than merely *about* stakeholders. Through this, Photovoice can help visualise the complex entanglements between physical objects and their various social and cultural contexts.

As Armstrong (2017, p. 423) notes, visual criminology needs to engage critically with what is difficult to visualise, and "visibilizing the underrepresented aspects of crime and punishment requires inventive tactics of showing which would enable seeing". Photovoice answers to this call by allowing for the 'visibilzing' of realities, experiences and practices that currently remain at the periphery of our inquiry into the global trade of cultural objects, and of the criminological discipline more generally. Moreover, it allows for a recentring of that inquiry to issues and topics that stakeholders of the trade in cultural objects want to shed light on and want to effect social change in. As an interdisciplinary and novel field of study in itself, research into the trafficking and trade of cultural objects is ripe for employing dynamic, innovative visual research methods such as Photovoice. Through this, researchers would position themselves at the forefront of a unique and interesting emerging paradigm for the study of such harmful practices.

Acknowledgements This fieldwork was supported by the University of Glasgow and the Scottish Funding Council through the Global Challenges Research Fund. I wish to thank the individuals and organisations who generously shared their time, experience and perspectives for the purposes of this project.

References

Armstrong, S. (2017). Seeing and seeing-as: Building a politics of visibility in criminology. In M. Brown & E. Carrabine (Eds.), *Routledge international handbook of visual criminology* (pp. 416–426). Routledge.
Atalay, S. (2012). *Community-based archaeology: Research with, by, and for indigenous and local communities*. University of California Press.
Azoulay, A. (2008). *The civil contract of photography*. Zone Books & MIT Press.
Bal, M. (2003). Visual essentialism and the object of visual culture. *Journal of Visual Culture, 2*(1), 5–32.
Bangdel, L. (1989). *Stolen images of Nepal*. Royal Nepal Academy.
Baudrillard, J. (1970). *The consumer society*. SAGE Publications.
Baudrillard, J. (1997). The system of collecting. In J. Elsner & R. Cardinal (Eds.), *Cultures of collecting* (pp. 7–24). Reaktion Books.
Becker, H. (2002). Visual evidence: A seventh man, the specified generalization, and the work of the reader. *Visual Studies, 17*(1), 3–11.
Bennett, J. (2012). *Practical aesthetics: Events, affects and art after 9/11*. IB Tauris.
Birch, M., & Miller, T. (2002). Encouraging participation: Ethics and responsibilities. In M. Mauthner, M. Birch, J. Jessop, & T. Miller (Eds.), *Ethics in qualitative research* (pp. 91–106). SAGE.
Bolton, A., Pole, C., & Mizen, P. (2001). Picture this: Researching child workers. *Sociology, 35*(2), 501–518.
Brisman, A. (2017). Representations of environmental crime and harm: A green cultural criminological perspective on human-altered landscapes. In M. Brown & E. Carrabine (Eds.), *Routledge international handbook of visual criminology* (pp. 523–539). Routledge.
Brisman, A. (2018). Representing the "invisible crime" of climate change in an age of post-truth. *Theoretical Criminology, 22*(3), 468–491.
Brodie, N. (2014a). The internet market in precolumbian antiquities. In J. Kila & M. Balcells (Eds.), *Cultural property crime: An overview and analysis on contemporary perspectives and trends* (pp. 237–262). Brill.
Brodie, N. (2014b). Auction houses and the antiquities trade. In S. Choulia-Kapeloni (Ed.), *3rd international conference of experts on the return of cultural property* (pp. 71–82). Archaeological Receipts Fund.
Brodie, N. (2019). Through a glass, darkly: Long-term antiquities auction data in context. *International Journal of Cultural Property, 26*(3), 265–283.
Brodie, N., Dietzler, J., & Mackenzie, S. (2013). Trafficking in cultural objects: An empirical overview. In S. Manacorda & A. Visconti (Eds.), *Beni culturali e sistema penale* (pp. 19–30). Vita e Pensiero.
Brown, M. (2014). Visual criminology and carceral studies: Counter-images in the carceral age. *Theoretical Criminology, 18*(2), 176–197.
Capous-Desyllas, M., & Forro, V. A. (2014). Tensions, challenges, and lessons learned: Methodological reflections from two Photovoice projects with sex workers. *Journal of Community Practice, 22*(1–2), 150–175.
Carrabine, E. (2011). Images of torture: Culture, politics and power. *Crime, Media, Culture, 7*(1), 5–30.

Carrabine, E. (2012). Just images: Aesthetics, ethics and visual criminology. *The British Journal of Criminology, 52*(3), 463–489.
Carrabine, E. (2014). Seeing things: Violence, voyeurism and the camera. *Theoretical Criminology, 18*(2), 134–158.
Castleden, H., Garvin, T., & Huu-Ay-Aht First, N. (2008). Modifying Photovoice for community-based participatory Indigenous research. *Social Science & Medicine, 66*(6), 1393–1405.
Chataway, C. F. (1997). An examination of the constraints on mutual inquiry in a participatory action research project. *Journal of Social Issues, 53*(4), 747–765.
Coggins, C. (1969). Illicit traffic of pre-columbian antiquities. *Art Journal, Fall*, 94–98.
Colwell, C. (2016). Collaborative archaeologies and descendant communities. *Annual Review of Anthropology, 45*, 113–127.
Colwell, C. (2017). *Plundered skulls and stolen spirits: Inside the fight to reclaim native America's culture*. University of Chicago Press.
Contreras, D. (2010). Huaqueros and remote sensing imagery: Assessing looting damange in the Virú Valley, Peru. *Antiquity, 84*(324), 544–555.
Contreras, D., & Brodie, N. (2010). Quantifying destruction: An evaluation of the utility of publicly-available satellite imagery for investigating looting of archaeological sites in Jordan. *Journal of Field Archaeology, 35*, 101–114.
Dedrick, M. (2018). Photovoice as a method for the development of collaborative archaeological practice. *Journal of Community Archaeology & Heritage, 5*(2), 85–100.
Dicks, B., Soyinka, B., & Coffey, A. (2006). Multimodal ethnography. *Qualitative Research, 6*(1), 77–96.
Edwards, E. (2012). Objects of affect: Photography beyond the image. *Annual Review of Anthropology, 41*(1), 221–234.
Elia, R. J. (1997). Looting, collecting, and the destruction of archaeological resources. *Nonrenewable Resources, 6*, 85–98.
Fals-Borda, O., & Rahman, M. A. (1991). *Action and knowledge–Breaking the monopoly with participatory action-research*. Apex Press.
Fitzgibbon, W., & Healy, D. (2019). Lives and spaces: Photovoice and offender supervision in Ireland and England. *Criminology & Criminal Justice, 19*(1), 3–25.
Fitzgibbon, W., & Stengel, C. M. (2018). Women's voices made visible: Photovoice in visual criminology. *Punishment & Society, 20*(4), 411–431.
Gilgan, E. (2001). Looting and the market for Maya objects: A Belizean perspective. In N. Brodie, J. Doole, & C. Renfrew (Eds.), *Trade in illicit antiquities: The destruction of the world's archaeological heritage* (pp. 73–88). McDonald Institute.
Gill, D., & Chippindale, C. (1993). Material and intellectual consequences of esteem for Cycladic figures. *American Journal of Archaeology, 97*(4), 601–659.
Global Nepali Museum. (n.d.). *About Us* [online]. Retrieved June 9, 2021, from https://globalnepalimuseum.com/about-us/
Grady, J. (2004). Working with visible evidence: An invitation and some practical advice. In C. Knowles & P. Sweetman (Eds.), *Picturing the social landscape: Visual methods in the sociological imagination* (pp. 18–31). Routledge.
Grimshaw, A. (2001). *The ethnographer's eye: Ways of seeing in modern anthropology*. Cambridge University Press.
Harper, D. (2012). *Visual sociology*. Routledge.
Hayward, K. (2010). Opening the lens: Cultural criminology and the image. In K. Hayward & K. Presdee (Eds.), *Framing crime: Cultural criminology and the image* (pp. 1–16). Routledge.
Healy, D., & Fitzgibbon, W. (2020). Different ways of seeing: Exploring audience reactions to images of probation supervision. *Qualitative Social Work, 19*(4), 663–684.
Hollowell-Zimmer, J. (2003). Digging in the dirt: Ethics and "low-end looting". In L. J. Zimmerman, K. D. Vitelli, & J. Hollowell-Zimmer (Eds.), *Ethical issues in archaeology* (pp. 45–56). AltaMira Press.

Keller, C., Fleury, J., Perez, A., Ainsworth, B., & Vaughan, L. (2008). Using visual methods to uncover context. *Qualitative Health Research, 18*(3), 428–436.
Kersel, M. (2012). The value of a looted object: Stakeholder perceptions in the antiquities trade. In R. Skeates, C. McDavid, & J. Carman (Eds.), *The Oxford handbook of public archaeology* (pp. 253–272). Oxford University Press.
Koro-Ljungberg, M. (2008). A social constructionist framing of the research interview. In J. Holstein & J. Gubrium (Eds.), *Handbook of constructionist research* (pp. 429–444). Guilford Press.
Liamputtong, P. (2010). *Performing qualitative cross-cultural research*. Cambridge University Press.
Liebenberg, L. (2018). Thinking critically about Photovoice. *International Journal of Qualitative Methods, 17*(1), 1–9.
Liechty, M. (2017). *Far out: Countercultural seekers and the tourist encounter in Nepal*. University of Chicago Press.
Linfield, S. (2010). *The cruel radiance: Photography and political violence*. University of Chicago Press.
Lykes, B. M. (2010). Silence(ing), voice(s) and gross violations of human rights: Constituting and performing subjectivities through PhotoPAR. *Visual Studies, 25*(3), 238–254.
Mackenzie, S. (2005). *Going, going, gone: Regulating the market in illicit antiquities*. Institute of Art and Law.
Mackenzie, S., & Davis, T. (2014). Temple looting in Cambodia: Anatomy of a statue trafficking network. *British Journal of Criminology, 54*(5), 722–740.
Mackenzie, S., & Yates, D. (2016). Collectors on illicit collecting: Higher loyalties and other techniques of neutralization in the unlawful collecting of rare and precious orchids and antiquities. *Theoretical Criminology, 20*(3), 340–357.
Marx, K. (1976). *Capital: Volume 1*. Penguin Books.
Masterson, V. A., Mahajan, S. L., & Tengö, M. (2018). Photovoice for mobilizing insights on human well-being in complex social-ecological systems: Case studies from Kenya and South Africa. *Ecology and Society, 23*(3). https://doi.org/10.5751/ES-10259-230313
Matsuda, D. (1998). The ethics of archaeology, subsistence digging, and artifact looting in Latin America: Point, muted counterpoint. *International Journal of Cultural Property, 7*(1), 87–97.
Merryman, J. H. (1986). Two ways of thinking about cultural Property. *American Journal of International Law, 80*(4), 831–853.
Milne, E.-J., & Muir, R. (2020). Photovoice: A critical introduction. In L. Pauwels & D. Mannay (Eds.), *The SAGE handbook of visual research methods* (pp. 282–296). SAGE.
Mitchell, W. (1996). What do pictures "really" want? *October, 77*, 71–82.
Nørskov, V. (2002). *Greek vases in new contexts: The collecting and trading of Greek vases—An aspect of the modern reception of antiquity*. Aarhus University Press.
Parcak, S., Gathings, D., Childs, C., Mumford, G., & Cline, E. (2016). Satellite evidence of archaeological site looting in Egypt: 2002–2013. *Antiquity, 90*(349), 188–205.
Pauwels, L. (2010). Visual sociology reframed: An analytical synthesis and discussion of visual methods in social and cultural research. *Sociological Methods & Research, 38*(4), 545–581.
Pauwels, L. (2017). Key methods of visual criminology: An overview of different approaches and their affordances. In M. Brown & E. Carrabine (Eds.), *Routledge international handbook of visual criminology* (pp. 62–73). Routledge.
Prosser, J. (1998). Photographs within the sociological research process. In J. Prosser (Ed.), *Image based research: A sourcebook for qualitative researchers* (pp. 115–127). Falmer.
Remembering the Lost. (2021). About. Retrieved June 7, 2021, from http://rememberingthelost.com/
Rose, G. (2016). *Visual methodologies: An introduction to researching with visual methodologies*. SAGE.
Schick, J. (2006). *Gods are leaving the country: Art theft from Nepal*. Orchid Press.

Sijapati, A. (2020, February 21). Replicating Nepal's stolen gods. *Nepali Times*. Retrieved from https://www.nepalitimes.com/here-now/replicating-nepals-stolen-gods/

Sijapati, A. (2021, January 28). Nepal's gods return from exile. *Nepali Times*. Retrieved from https://www.nepalitimes.com/banner/nepals-gods-return-from-exile/

Smith, E. (2018). *Illicit markets in the global city: The cultural property trade in Hong Kong*. (Unpublished doctoral thesis). University of Glasgow, United Kingdom.

Smith, L. (2006). *Uses of heritage*. Routledge.

Thapa, G., & Sharma, J. (2009). From insurgency to democracy: The challenges of peace and democracy-building in Nepal. *International Political Science Review, 30*(2), 205–219.

Tiwari, S., Shreshta, P., & Bjønness, H. (2017). Local right in World Heritage Sites: Learning from post-earthquake rehabilitation dynamics in the Kathmandu Valley. In P. Larsen (Ed.), *World heritage and human rights* (pp. 135–152). Routledge.

Traue, B., Blanc, M., & Cambre, C. (2018). Visibilities and visual discourses: Rethinking the social with the image. *Qualitative Inquiry, 25*(4), 327–337.

Tythacott, L., & Ardiyansyah, P. (Eds.). (2021). *Returning Southeast Asia's past*. NUS Press.

UNESCO. (1970). *Convention on the Means of Prohibiting and Preventing the Illciit Import, Export and Transfer of Ownership of Cultural Property*, No. 11806, 823 U.N.T.S. 231 (14 Nov 1970).

Van Beurden, J. (2021). *Ongemakkelijk Erfgoed: Koloniale collectives en teruggave in de Lage Landen*. Walburg Pers.

Wagner, J. (2002). Contrasting images, complementary trajectories: Sociology, visual sociology and visual research. *Visual Studies, 17*(2), 160–171.

Wagner, J. (2020). Seeing things: Visual research and material culture. In L. Pauwels & D. Mannay (Eds.), *The SAGE handbook of visual research methods* (pp. 76–95). SAGE.

Wang, C. (1999). Photovoice: A participatory action research strategy applied to women's health. *Journal of Women's Health, 8*(2), 185–192.

Wang, C., & Burris, M. A. (1997). Photovoice: Concept, methodology, and use for participatory needs assessment. *Health Education & Behavior, 24*(3), 369–387.

Watson, S., & Waterton, E. (2010a). Reading the visual: Representation and narrative in the construction of heritage. *Material Culture Review, 71*, 84–97.

Watson, S., & Waterton, E. (2010b). *Culture, heritage and representation: Perspectives on visuality and the past*. Routledge.

Wong, R. (2015). A note on fieldwork in 'dangerous' circumstances: Interviewing illegal tiger skin suppliers and traders in Lhasa. *International Journal of Social Research Methodology, 18*(6), 595–702.

Woodgate, R., Zurba, M., & Tennent, P. (2017). Worth a thousand words? Advantages, challenges and opportunities in working with Photovoice as a qualitative research method with youth and their families. *Forum Qualitative Sozialforschung, 18*(1). https://doi.org/10.17169/fqs-18.1.2659

Yates, D., & Mackenzie, S. (2018). Heritage, crisis, and community crime prevention in Nepal. *International Journal of Cultural Property, 25*(2), 203–221.

Young, A. (2010). The scene of the crime: Is there such as thing as 'just looking'? In K. Hayward & M. Presdee (Eds.), *Framing crime: Cultural criminology and the image* (pp. 83–97). Routledge.

Young, A. (2014). From object to encounter: Aesthetic politics and visual criminology. *Theoretical Criminology, 18*(2), 159–175.

A New Method of Forensic Archaeology

Identification of the Origin of Archaeological Materials Seized in Police Proceedings

Francisco Romeo Marugán

Abstract In judicial proceedings on archaeological plundering, judges usually request an expert to identify the place of origin of seized items. This can be a serious problem, because these items are usually out of their archaeological context and no provenance data are available. This paper describes a method used successfully by experts of the regional Government of Aragon (Spain) under the judicial proceedings related to the Helmet operations carried out by the Central Operational Unit of the Spanish Guardia Civil. The method was designed specifically for items found with a metal detector. The greater the number and variety of the seized items, the more accurate will be the results. In this method, crime geometry and the Tobler Law are used to analyse mappings of archaeological items; the creation and analysis of temperature, proximity and dispersion maps of specific typologies of archaeological materials have allowed the identification of the place of origin of most of the stolen items. These maps and the determination of the origin of the items recovered in the Helmet operations have been key evidence in the prosecution of the defendants.

1 Helmet: The Background

The Helmet case has been the most prominent in the Spanish state in recent times. Carried out by the Historical Heritage Group of the Central Operational Unit of the Guardia Civil, the Helmet case, with the operations Helmet I and Helmet II, put an end to the archaeological plundering of an area of the Celtiberia (see Fig. 1) which had caused particularly harsh damage to the city of Aratis, as was finally demonstrated.

F. R. Marugán (✉)
Cultural Heritage Prevention Section, Directorate General for Cultural Heritage, Government of Aragon, Aragon, Spain
e-mail: fromeo@aragon.es

N. Oosterman, D. Yates (eds.), *Crime and Art*, Studies in Art, Heritage, Law and the Market 1, https://doi.org/10.1007/978-3-030-84856-9_6

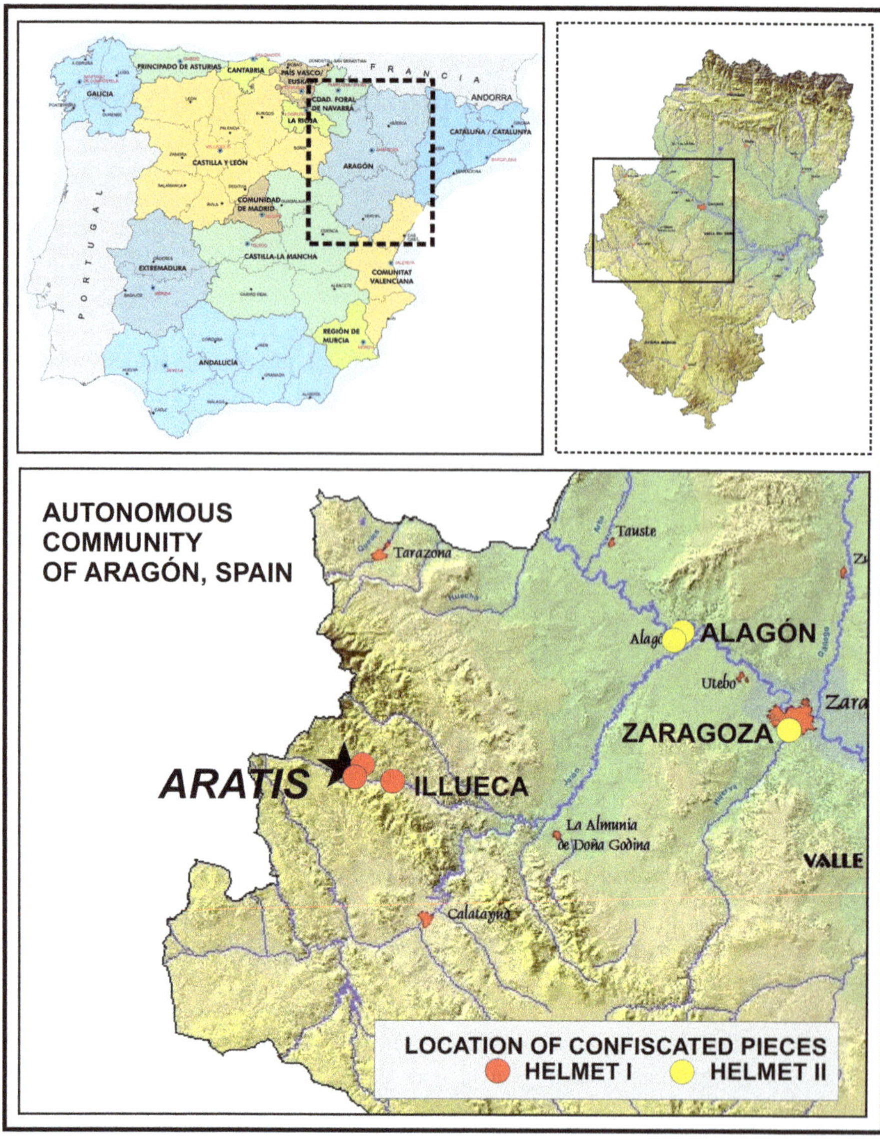

Fig. 1 Location of confiscated pieces

It is essential to begin the presentation of the following forensic archaeology system with a brief summary of the main events of the *Helmet* case,[1] during which it

[1]For more information, see Esteban et al. (2019), pp. 116–117; Graells et al. (2014), pp. 1–6; Lorrio et al. (2019), pp. 107–115.

was specifically developed and successfully applied within the judicial process that has recently ended with the conviction of the two defendants.[2]

Between June 1989 and May 1990, a Spanish antique dealer in Geneva, Fernando Cunillera Cunill, offered Marcus Egg of the Römisch-Germanisches Zentralmuseum in Mainz a set of helmets whose origin was eventually revealed: a rocky slope in an archaeological site in the Aragonese town of Aranda de Moncayo (Egg, 2002; Müller-Karpe, 2014, p. 148). The helmets were rejected by the museum and finally acquired by Alex Guttmann, a Berlin-based businessman and art collector. After Guttman's death in 2001, the pieces began to appear in various auction rooms (Lorrio et al., 2019, pp. 109–110).

On November 25, 1993, the Government of Aragon was informed of archaeological plundering at a site in Aranda de Moncayo. After the inspection, movement and extraction of earth with heavy machinery was verified at the site of Castejon I–El Romeral—an unauthorised action that had affected the wall and other structures. Likewise, it was possible to recognise the existence of numerous holes dispersed throughout the deposit, presumably made with the use of metal detectors since they corresponded to the usual patterns of metal detector use (Romeo & Matas, 2020). On the same dates, a local publication (Moya, 1993, p. 226) recorded the finding "without archaeologists being aware of it [...], of a large number of Celtiberian helmets".

Unfortunately, the denunciation by the Government of Aragon had no effect. Later, in 2003, an auction house in Munich put up for sale several Hispanic Chalcidian helmets which reactivated the investigation. Interpol contacted the Bundeskriminalamt in Wiesbaden (Lorrio et al., 2019, p. 108). H. Born, delegate of the Guttmann collection, stated that the pieces had been bought from Cunillera who had owned them since the beginning of 1970 (Müller-Karpe, 2014, p. 148). At that point, police actions were paralysed. From then until 2009, several helmets from the Guttman collection were auctioned.

In October 2010, the General Direction of Cultural Heritage of the Government of Aragon was informed of the auction in the same auctionhouse in Munich of some archaeological pieces from the Guttman collection, probably from Aranda de Moncayo. That same day, the Ministry was informed of Aragon's maximum interest in this matter, since, in Spain, the Autonomous Communities do not have competence in cross-border matters (Pomed, 2001; Villagrasa, 1999). In April 2012, the Guardia Civil informed Aragonese institutions that they would resume investigations on the subject, requesting maximum discretion.

---

[2]Ruling of the Criminal Chamber No. 335/2010 of the Supreme Court of the Administration of Justice of Spain of 19 June 2020.

2 Operations *Helmet I* and *Helmet II*

On 13 February 2013, agents of the Historical Heritage Group of the Central Operational Unit of the Guardia Civil proceeded to search three properties and arrest the alleged perpetrator of the looting, with the seizure of 6835 archaeological pieces. This was *Helmet I*. On 30 July 2013, the same unit proceeded to raid three properties of another suspect; two in the town of Alagón and another in Zaragoza. This was *Helmet II*. In this operation, 2429 archaeological objects were located and seized. The materials seized were deposited in a vault of the Government of Aragon.

Once the judicial procedure had started, the Court requested that the Government of Aragon determine the importance of the Celtiberian site of Aranda de Moncayo (Zaragoza), determine the details of the seized objects, and determine that Aratis was the origin of both the pieces in the museum of Mainz and the auctioned ones.[3]

Two lines of action were designed to respond to the court. First, the study, cataloguing, documentation, inventory, and valuation of all the materials seized to analyse the relationship between the pieces and Aratis and between one another. Second, an archaeological intervention was carried out in the area affected by the removal of land, to accredit and assess the damages produced (Romeo et al., 2017) and determine the reasons for the spoliation of that particular area of the site.

A fundamental part of the expert's report was the identification of the pieces. Was an extremely complex process due to their diversity, since the pieces correspond to all the chronologies and cultures of the Iberian Peninsula, and due to the pieces' decontextualisation. The requirement to keep the details of the investigation secret made any kind of specific consultation with other archaeological specialists impossible. The economic valuation of the pieces, which was fundamental for the trial, followed an objective procedure, applying a rigorous methodology developed specifically for the economic valuation of looted archaeological objects that we had successfully applied in a case of looting at the Cueva de Chaves in Huesca, among others (Romeo et al., 2017, pp. 258–263; Romeo, 2021).

The expert's report was presented to the court on 11 February 2015. After analysing this report, the Court ordered the expansion of the archaeological excavations, which were carried out between October and November 2015, and allowed for the determination of the reason for the removal of the land. By extending the

[3]On 1 April 2013, the Court of First Instance and Instruction No. 2 of La Almunia de Doña Godina issues a Ruling in relation to the Preliminary Proceedings of Abbreviated Procedure 0000288/2013, with the following content: "(. . .) the object of the referred expertise consists of the determination of the historical-archaeological importance of the Celtiberian deposit of Aranda de Moncayo (Zaragoza) as a possible deposit of Celtiberian weapons, as well as its possible illegal exploitation with determination, if possible, of the type, quantity and economic valuation of the stolen pieces, the determination as originating from this site of the existing pieces both in the RGZ DE Mainz museum and the ones auctioned by the Hermann Historical Auction House in Munich, damages caused and their relevance and current state. Likewise, the experts of the entity are authorized to unseal the bags that contain the seized material and that are in the vault of the DGA for the realization of the expert's report".

Fig. 2 Auxiliary disc of a Celtiberian disc shell (*kardiophylakes*) split in two

intervention, it was possible to detect the remains of a necropolis under the floors of the Celtiberian houses destroyed by the machinery. This necropolis belonged to the first urban nucleus of Aratis and was sealed by the expansion of the city at the end of the third century or beginning of the second century B.C.

Machinery was used to remove the tough layer of archaeological levels of housing and thus to gain access to plunder the necropolis.[4] Sentence 199/2018 of the Provincial Court of Zaragoza of 16 July 2018, is devastating since it gives as certain facts the plundering and the continuous damage at Aratis, detailing the seizure of eight metal detectors, three of them in the trunk of the offender's car.[5] It is also true that he proceeded to extract earth by mechanical means on 24 November 1993, to access and plunder one of the necropolises of *Aratis.*[6]

The sentence details, in relation to the Hispano-Chalcidian helmets, that a resident of Illueca began to extract these helmets from the site in 1989, taking them to the protagonist of Operation *Helmet II* so that he could restore them and, with the antiques dealer Cunillera, proceed to their sale. In fact, the ruling states that the first person convicted sold most of the stolen goods to the second person convicted, as evidenced by one piece, an auxiliary disc of a Celtiberian disc shell split in two (see Fig. 2), the halves of which were seized in different locations, one from each of the

[4] Metal detectors have a limited range, even those with plates like the one seized in Helmet I. Their detection range is no more than about 130 cm (Romeo & Matas, 2020) and the necropolis was under an average of 250 cm of sediments.

[5] We are not going to enter in this work into the analysis of the criminal figure and the use of metal detectors in relation to archaeological plundering. In this regard, see, among others Rodríguez (2000, 2004, 2012); Rodríguez et al. (2015); Romeo and Matas (2020); Yánez and Rodríguez (2018).

[6] A minimum of five necropolis zones have identified for this Celtiberian city (Lorrio et al., 2019, pp. 114–115).

condemned. The identification of the correspondence of these two fragments to a single piece, being both separated into independent lots, shows, firstly, the degree of detail of the work carried out and, secondly, the need to proceed in expert studies with this degree of detail. This has been one of the fundamental proofs of the relationship between the two convicts, who claimed not to know each other, and between the two sets of archaeological pieces that had been seized.

The latter would be the intermediary between the direct plunderer of the site and the distribution channels, as indicated by the profile of the materials seized from him, which were predominantly Roman and pre-Roman weaponry. The relationship of the two defendants with the Hispano-Chalcidian helmets is proven by the fact that up to seven fragments of this exceptional type of helmet were located in the possession of each of the defendants.

When the sentence was appealed, the Supreme Court finally ratified all the proven facts, but did not consider a charge for the crime of money laundering appropriate in this case. This classification comes from article 301.1 of the Spanish Criminal Code, which defines as such "the possession and transfer of property in the knowledge that it has its origin in criminal activity". In its place, the Spanish Supreme Court states on page 25 of its sentence 335/2010 that "instead of a money laundering crime we consider that, in effect, as the appellant advocates, the correct qualification is that of reception of Article 298 of the criminal code", the High Court continues to state that:

> the principle of validity obliges us to give a content, a field of application to reception, that classic crime with deep roots and tradition, which seems to have been swallowed up by the impetuous voracity of the new typology of money laundering that has been progressively conquering territories and spaces, above all legal, but also jurisprudential, despite its relatively short life. A brutal growth has characterised its overwhelming evolution.

Lesson learned: in Spain, it is not advisable to abuse the criminal charge of money laundering in relation to archaeological heritage.[7]

3 The Need to Locate the Origin of Archaeological Materials; Legal Context in Spain

One of the usual tasks for experts in criminal proceedings relating to archaeological plundering in Spain is to determine the exact place of origin from where the archaeological objects were seized. We can consider this demand almost a bipolar attitude on the part of the magistracy, since the Spanish normative framework makes clear in any case the public character (*res publica*) of the archaeological objects (Alegre, 1997, pp. 121–122). Only those objects for which there is documentation accrediting their possession prior to 25 June 1985 are excluded from this

[7]A comprehensive study on the law of sanctions in relation to offences against archaeological heritage in Spain in Yánez (2018).

consideration—in the case of Spain, the date of the publication of Law 16/1985 on Spanish Historical Heritage.[8]

The measures contemplated in this regulation are not applicable retroactively, but some solid documentary evidence of the possession of these pieces prior to the law must be provided. The fact that this situation cannot be proven would be sufficient to consider the possession of archaeological objects as irregular or illegal, but the lax principle *in dubio pro reo* applies especially when no force has been used and there is no specific physical victim (Serebrennikova et al., 2018), although, in this case, the victim is the State itself and, by extension, all its citizens.

Nevertheless, the fact that the seized archaeological pieces belong to a specific archaeological site is a prosecution test with specific weight for the courts, among other facts (Rodríguez, 2012, p. 289; Romeo, 2018). In any case, the object of this work is not the legal analysis of the importance of determining the concrete origin of seized archaeological materials, but the development of a system for the geographical determination of the same, since the location of seized archaeological materials in records is usually required by the courts, as has been said.

The characteristics of numerous archaeological objects seized in Helmet I and Helmet II, as we shall see, allowed them to be attributed to specific cultures and chronologies. These are objects that appear in specific geographical areas, which has made it possible to draw up maps that are decisive in this procedure. In fact, the results obtained have been so relevant that we consider that this system presented here can be a procedure that can be used successfully to determine the area of origin of minimally large sets of archaeological pieces without information regarding their provenance.

4 Criminology and Crime Maps

Bringing together concepts such as archaeology and criminology is a recent process, so many concepts have yet to be defined. Criminology is a discipline based on interdisciplinary methods for the study of crime (Redondo, 1988) and the use of maps by this discipline dates back to the beginning of the nineteenth century (Guerry, 1883; Quetelet, 1842; Stangeland & Garrido, 2004, p. 48). Similarly, archaeology has used maps and planimetry since its origins. For this reason, it is striking that, until now, cartographic representations have not been used as tools for analysing and trying to define the origin of plundered objects for which there is no other data than the place of seizure.

The system presented in this work is based on the concentric circle model developed by Burgess (1925) which focused on the location and prediction of

[8]The Constitutional Court has used the argument of arbitrariness for a law, but not in this case (Romeo, 2018, p. 266). We have a summary of the doctrine regarding the arbitrariness of the legislator in the sentence 233/1999 of 16 December of the Law of Local Treasuries, FJ 12.

crime in cities. Years later, several researchers from what is now known as the Chicago school, such as Phillips, assessed the influence of the environment on the distribution of crime, developing maps as instruments for data collection, crime analysis, evaluation of results, and prediction of crime risks (Phillips, 1972).

The appearance of new technologies has been a real revolution that has made crime maps one of the most valid tools in criminological studies and analyses, with the systematic use of geographical information systems and the use of big data (Andresen, 2017; Olaya, 2014). Maps must clearly reflect the information that is considered relevant (Harries, 1999), and it is essential to avoid subjectivity when transferring the data that is being used and to avoid unnecessary elements that can make the map unreadable or even erroneous (Tufte, 1983). These types of crime maps were defined by Harries (1999), who classified them into point maps; statistical maps; choropleth maps, which are those that show values in delimited areas that are represented with different colours; isoline maps, with areas that are delimited by lines that separate categories that share the same value; surface maps; and line maps.

For the study of this particular case, I decided to use the isoline maps as a basis for developing surface and heat maps (Eck et al., 2005). We started from the need to visually transmit information in a diaphanous way, which requires a certain level of abstraction (Tufte, 1983, 1990). For the analysis of the data that are provided by the isoline maps, we have used Tobler's intuitive law, which states that 'everything is related to everything else, but things that are near are more related than things that are far away' (Tobler, 1970, p. 236). The principle of decay with distance has also been taken into account, based on the opportunities for crime that exist within a spatial structure (Brantingham & Brantingham, 1981). It can be said that people normally make the minimum effort to perform any task, from which the inverse relationship between the distance travelled by the offender and the frequency of his activity can be deduced (Simon, 1957, 1982).

5 Development of a Forensic Method for Determining the Origin of Archaeological Repertoires; Selection of Types, Zoning, and Overlapping of Layers as a Method

As previously mentioned, it is very difficult to establish the exact provenance of archaeological objects if both the archaeological context and direct information about the place of origin are lacking. This was the case with Helmet I and II; the provenance of more than 9000 seized objects was unknown due to the lack of cooperation of the accused and later convicted.

The state of conservation of the objects, including the soil traces adhering to them and their level of corrosion, confirmed their extraction from the ground, and, as this extraction was not authorised, their illegal origin. The fact that among the seized pieces there were objects from all the cultures of the Iberian Peninsula did not make it easy to determine their specific provenance.

However, the characteristics of pre-industrial societies and the existence of relatively limited distribution networks, in addition to the handcrafted nature of a large part of the archaeological materials, make it possible to establish more or less defined areas of origin for them, especially in ancient chronologies, in which the commercial circuits were less intense than in later times. This was the reason for selecting pieces from pre-Roman times, above all. Materials with specific typologies were chosen for which there were reliable archaeological studies that determined specific areas of dispersion for the objects (Quesada & Baena, 1997).

Analysing the described systems of crime maps, it was decided to capture the areas of presence of these archaeological pieces on different isoline maps and, in a second phase, to superimpose the isoline maps to produce heat maps, trying to identify the area most likely to be the origin of the pieces that had been seized. We had the advantage of knowing, above all for Helmet I, that most of the artefacts must have come from Aratis, due to the seizure points themselves and the known routine of the condemned man (two locations were at the foot of the site and his home was about 13 km away), but this was an element that was never taken into account in the analysis; we worked completely ignoring this data.

The materials seized in Helmet I and Helmet II were analysed separately, the results of which were compared to determine the relationship between both collections of pieces, as well as the relationship between the detainees, who claimed to not know each other. The best-known pieces were selected, with scopes of dispersion defined at the time that the expert report was written between 2013 and 2014. These maps, presented in Figs. 3, 4, 5, 6, 7, 8 and 9, were analysed by drawing up environments with maximum concentration criteria to ensure the objectivity of the procedure.

The repertoire of pieces selected for Helmet I was as follows:[9]

- Hispano-Chalcidian helmets and Alpanseque-Almaluez type helmets (see Fig. 4)
- Shell discs or kardiophylakes (see Fig. 5)
- Navarre Aquitaine brooch (see Fig. 5)
- Pre-Roman and Roman Republican and Imperial numismatics (see Figs. 6, 7, and 8)
- Arcobriga type plates (see Fig. 9)

On the maps, the areas of origin of the known specimens of Hispano-Chalcidian and Alpanseque-Almaluez type helmets, the armour discs, and the dispersion of the Aquitanian Navarrese type fibulas and Arcobriga type plates have been delimited (Lorrio & Sánchez, 2009, pp. 209–223). On all maps, the places of seizure and the location of the Celtiberian city of Aratis have been indicated.

In the case of the helmets and the shell discs, the distribution of the findings shows the existence of a nuclear area located at the confluence of the current Spanish provinces of Soria (Arlegui, 2014; Graells & Lorrio, 2013), Teruel, Zaragoza, and

[9] I will not carry out an archaeological study of each of the pieces; they will only be briefly contextualised, providing basic bibliography.

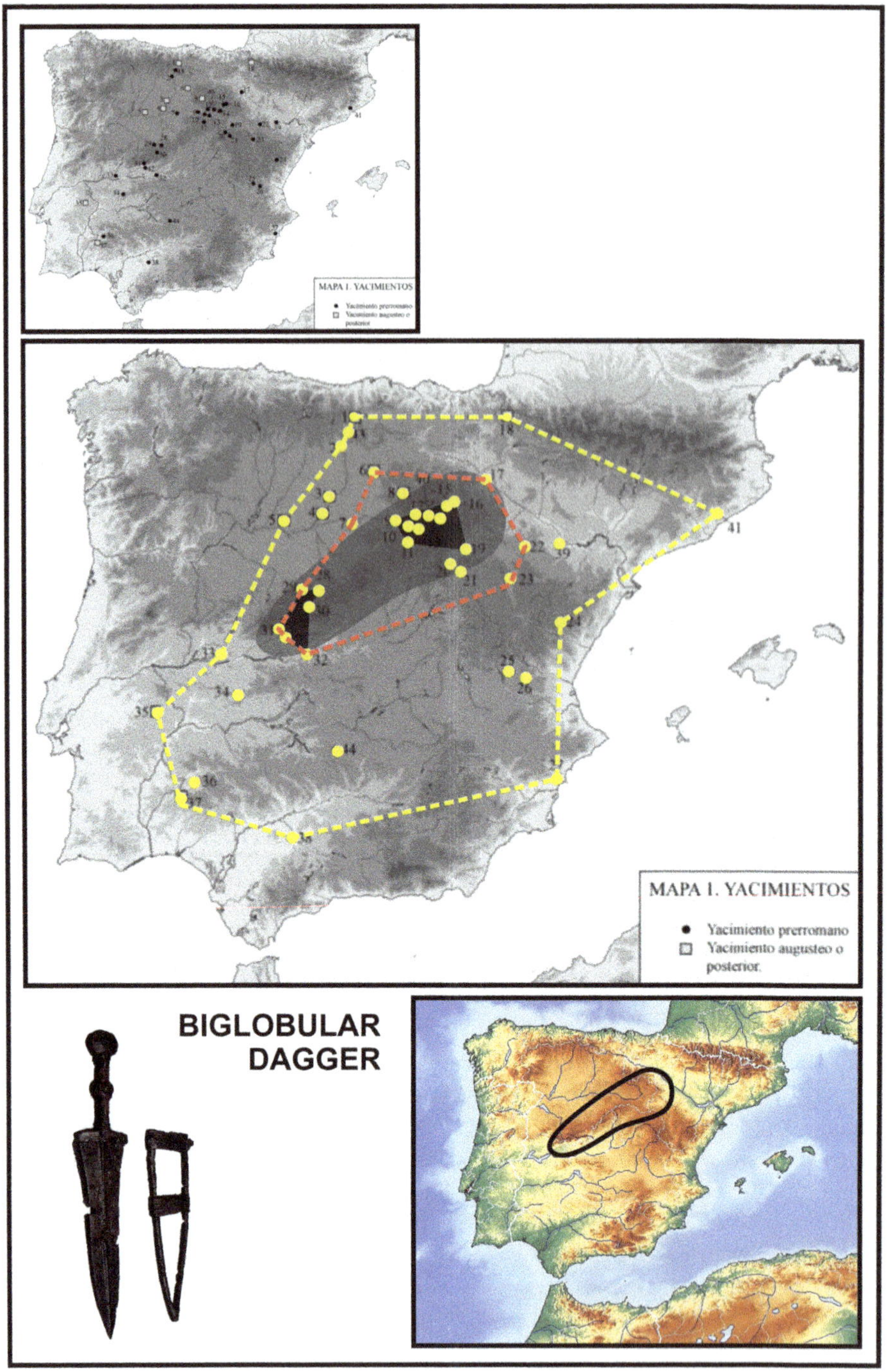

Fig. 3 System for determining areas of maximum concentration of archaeological pieces

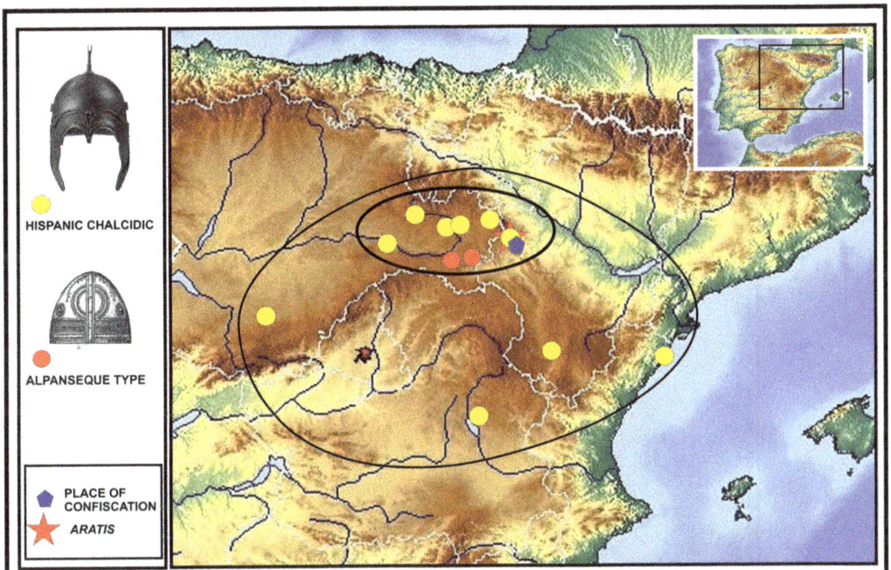

MAP 1. HELMET I. DISPERSION OF HISPANIC CHALCIDIC HELMETS, ACCORDING TO GRAELLS, LORRIO AND QUESADA 2014. THICKER LINE, CONCENTRATION AREA.

Fig. 4 Dispersion of Hispano-Chalcidian helmets and Alpanseque-Almaluez type helmets, according to Graells et al. (2014)

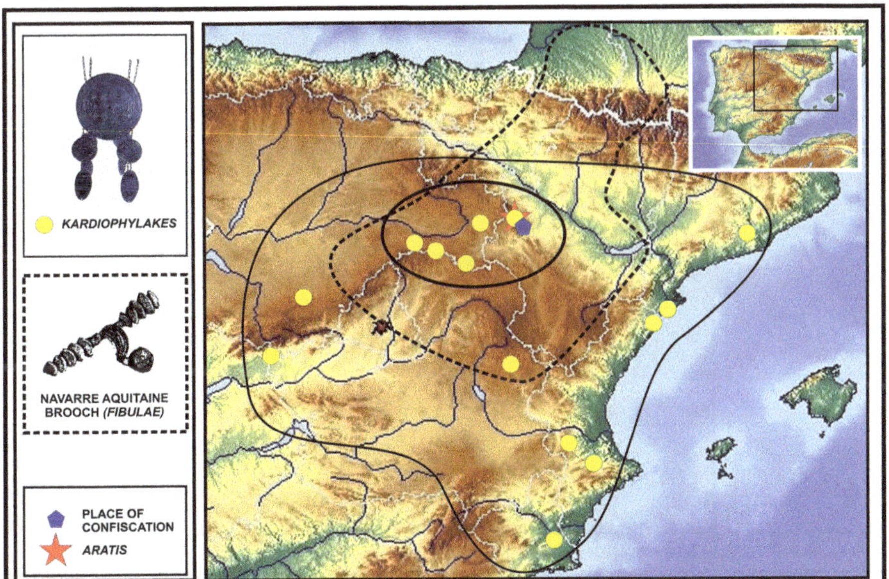

MAP 2. HELMET I. DISPERSION OF *KARDIOPHYLAKES*, ACCORDING TO GRAELLS 2014. THICKER LINE, CONCENTRATION AREA. DISPERSION OF NAVARRE AQUITAINE BROOCH, ACCORDING TO CERDEÑO y CHORDÁ 2004.

Fig. 5 Helmet I. Dispersions or *kardiophylakes*, according to Graells (2014), and Navarre Aquitaine brooch, according to Cerdeño and Chordá (2004)

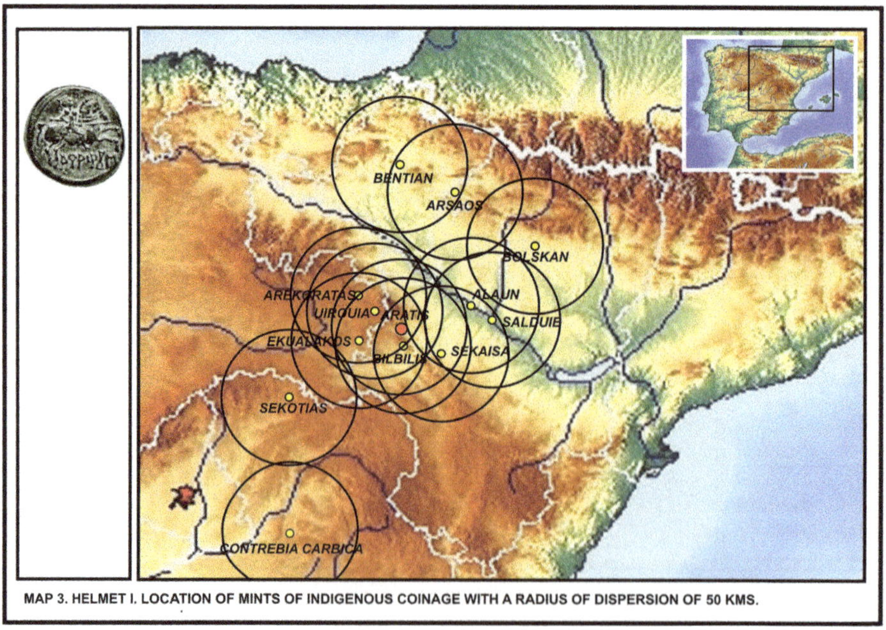

Fig. 6 Helmet I. Location of mint of indigenous coinage, with a radius of dispersion of 50 km

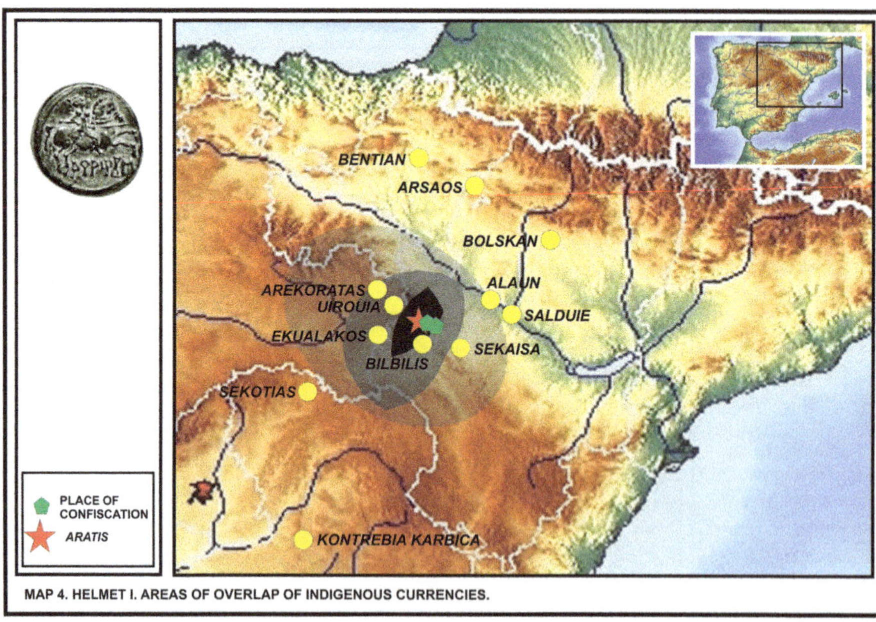

Fig. 7 Helmet I. Areas of overlap of indigenous currencies

Guadalajara (Fatás et al., 2014; Graells, 2014; Graells & Marzoli, 2016). This delimitation is more restricted in the case of the Arcobriga type plates (Fig. 9),

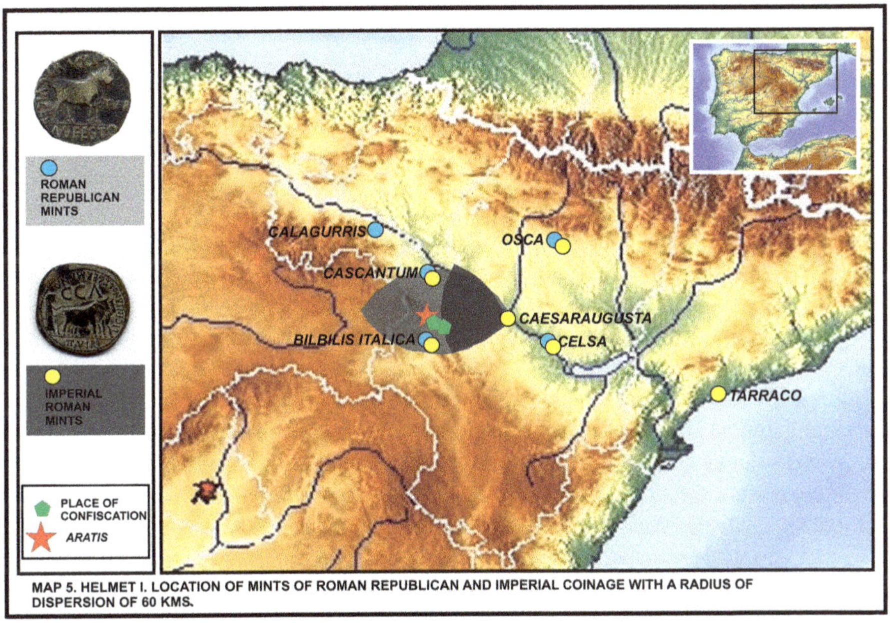

Fig. 8 Helmet I. Location of mints of Roman Republican and Imperial coinage, and areas of overlap with a radius of dispersion of 60 km

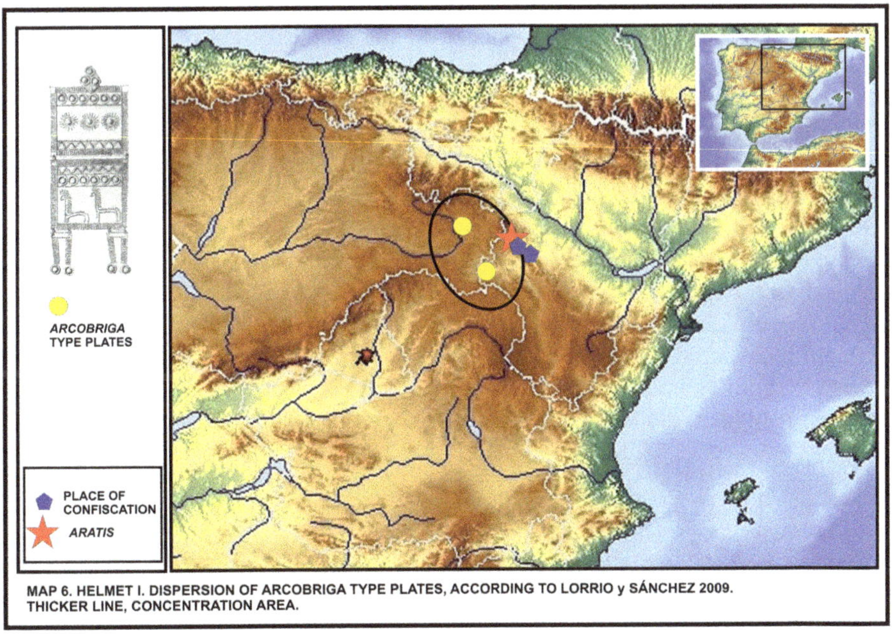

Fig. 9 Helmet I. Dispersion of Arcobriga type plates, according to Lorrio and Sánchez (2009)

while it is much wider for the Navarre-Aquitaine type fibulas as presented in Fig. 5 (Cerdeño & Chordá, 2004).

A specific study methodology has been developed for numismatics, addressing the spatial analysis of indigenous, Roman Republican and Roman Imperial coins—and leaving aside coins from later periods, due to their wide geographical dispersion. In fact, in Helmet I, out of a total of 6835 objects recovered, 1986 were coins, 29.05 percent of the total.

The analysis of the pre-Roman coins has been particularly relevant, since the diverse but small number of mints that are represented in the seized material, and the limited geographical dispersion that these pieces usually have when compared with coins from other chronologies, made these productions the most suitable for spatial analysis. We used the system of concentric circles and projected perfect circles with a radius of 50 km (see Fig. 6). This distance is due to several factors, although mainly the establishment of a reduced proximity in which the dispersion of the indigenous coins was relevant, beyond the tendency of the coins of the middle Ebro valley to flow towards the west (Stefanelli, 2012). However, another element that determined this radius of dispersion was the optimisation of the available data. As mentioned before, a certain level of abstraction is necessary to achieve relevant data. A larger radius would have delimited an enormous area that would not contribute anything, and a smaller radius would have made many of the circles not even touch each other, without providing any information. The results were surprising since the seizure points and Aratis appear at the epicentre of the delimited area (see Fig. 7).

The same analysis has been carried out for Roman coins of Republican and Imperial chronology (see Fig. 8). In this case, the identified mints are much smaller. We have extended the area of dispersion of these coins, as their circulation and dispersion was greater than that of the indigenous coins. However, to maintain the same criteria, we used a diameter of 120 km for the identified mints. As the dispersion is less relevant, as mentioned above, their concentration is again significant. The overlap between the areas of the indigenous and Republican coins can be seen clearly. This overlap is not incidental, as can be deduced from the analytical process that was carried out. The concentration of the Imperial coins must be assessed taking into account the few identified mints and their wide dispersion. This leaves a clearly defined area with an epicentre in Aranda de Moncayo, very close to Illueca and extending mainly towards the west and south.

More types of archaeological pieces were assessed in Helmet II; some of them were present in Helmet I, and therefore the dispersion maps are identical in these cases. In particular, the following types of archaeological pieces were analysed:

- Hispano-Chalcidian helmets (see Fig. 4 above).
- Armour discs or kardiophylakes (see Fig. 5 above).
- Arcobriga type plates (see Fig. 9 above)
- Falcatas and Bronze Age swords (see Fig. 10)
- Bidiscoidal daggers and Monte Bernorio type swords (see Fig. 11)
- Shields of Quesada's group 2 and Soliferrea (see Fig. 12)

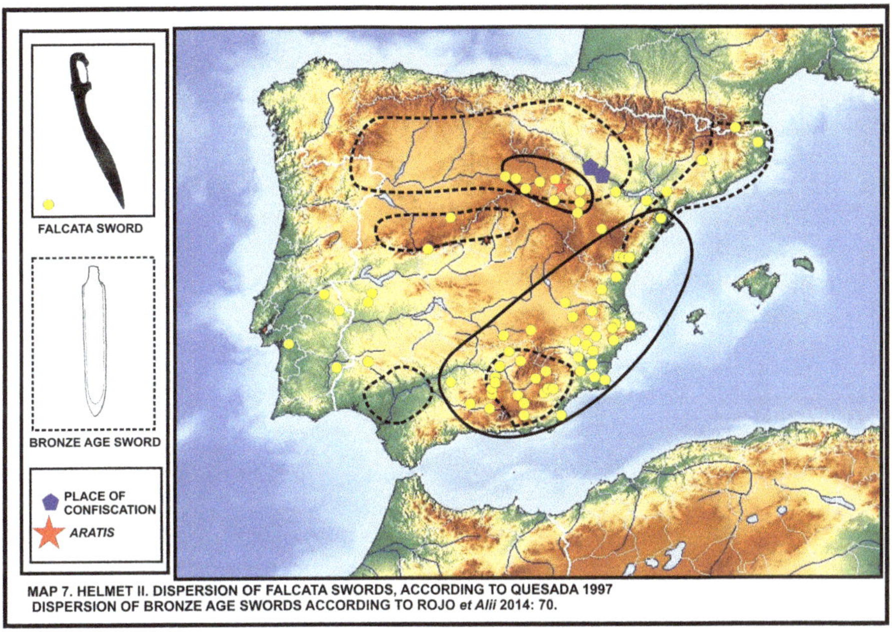

Fig. 10 Helmet II. Dispersion of falcata, according to Quesada (1997), and bronze age swords, according to Rojo et al. (2014)

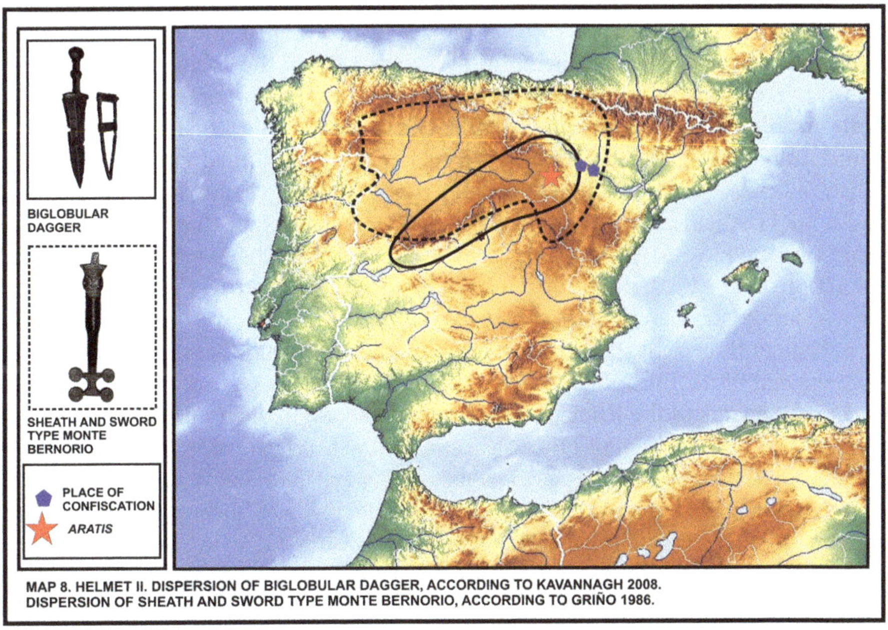

Fig. 11 Helmet II. Dispersion of biglobular dagger, according to Kavannagh (2008); and sheath and swords Monte Bernorio type, according to Griñó (1986)

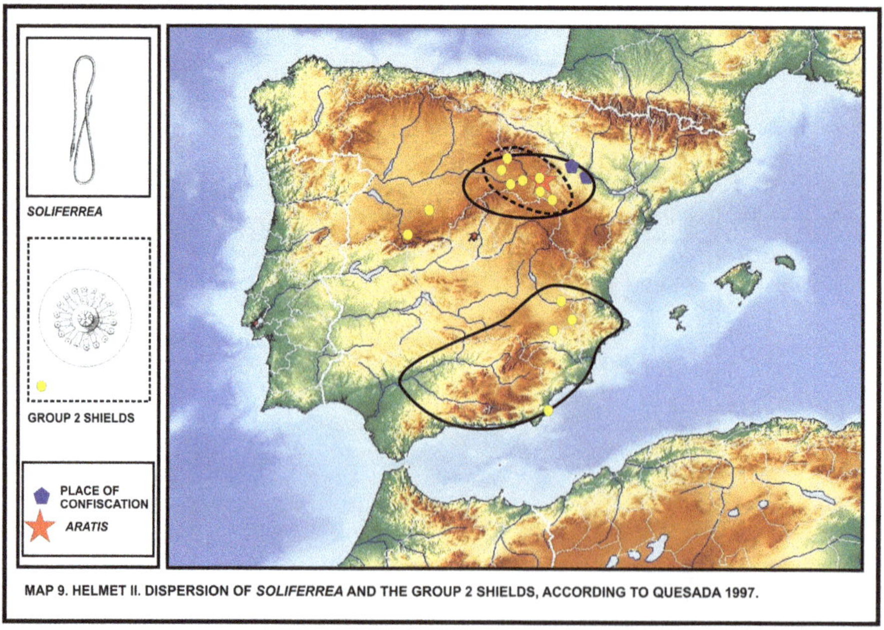

Fig. 12 Helmet II. Dispersion of *soliferrea* and the shields of Quesada's group 2, according to Quesada (1997)

The *falcata* is a sword from the Iberian Peninsula which is characterised by its curved shape. In fact, its name comes from the Latin term *falx*, meaning sickle. Until a few years ago, it was considered to be exclusively of the Iberian world, but its presence is common in Celtiberian contexts (Lorrio, 2016, p. 239; Quesada, 1997), in the area between the upper course of the Duero and the middle stretch of the River Jalón. Among the material seized in the area, a complete folded falcata stands out, which indicates that it undoubtedly comes from a funerary context.

Another particularly relevant piece is a bronze sword blade that we identify as a reed sword, typical of bell complexes with a chronology between 2200 and 2000 B.C. (Rojo et al., 2014, p. 70). It is usually concentrated in an area that is located on the northern plateau and the right bank of the Ebro.

In Helmet II, several specimens of bidiscoidal daggers appear, with a chronology from the end of the third to the first century B.C. These pieces are considered to be direct antecedents of the Romans' *pugio* sword and were widely disseminated from the middle of the third century B.C. (Kavannagh, 2008). There are variants present in Helmet II, which consist of pieces with a short leaf and sleeve, resolved with a simple spike, and a marked central nerve. These are pieces whose pommel, grip, and guard make them very similar to La Tène type swords. García comments that this type of piece is common in Celtiberian contexts from the third to the first century B.C. (García, 2012, p. 267).

Another important element in the group studied are the circular coats of arms of the so-called "Aguilar de Anguita variant A" or group II of Quesada. These are iron umbos with a truncated cone shape and an engraved cross on the base with a smaller diameter from which radii end in discs. It is especially present in the Eastern Plateau, between Guadalajara and Soria, in sites such as Aguilar de Anguita, from which it takes its name: La Cerrada de los Santos, Alpanseque, Carratiermes, La Mercadera, La Cerrada de los Santos, El Inchidero, or Quintanas de Gormaz among others. It is also documented in an isolated manner outside this area in the Iberian zone. They would be dated between the fifth and third centuries B.C. (Lorrio, 1997; Quesada, 1997).

The *soliferrea* (Quesada, 1997) are also common in Celtiberian areas (Lorrio, 2016, p. 245). These are spears made entirely of iron, which gives this weapon much greater potential than spears with wooden shafts.

6 Conclusions

The overlapping of the different maps allowed us to produce heat maps for Helmet I (Fig. 13) and for Helmet II (Fig. 14). The comparative analysis of both (Fig. 15) allowed us to establish clear links between the lots that were seized from the convicts.

The results of the maps were especially revealing and conclusive; it was possible to show that both groups of seized artefacts came from the same area, with the epicentre in the Celtiberian city of Aratis and its immediate surroundings. Specifically, after superimposing the areas of greatest concentration of the typologies

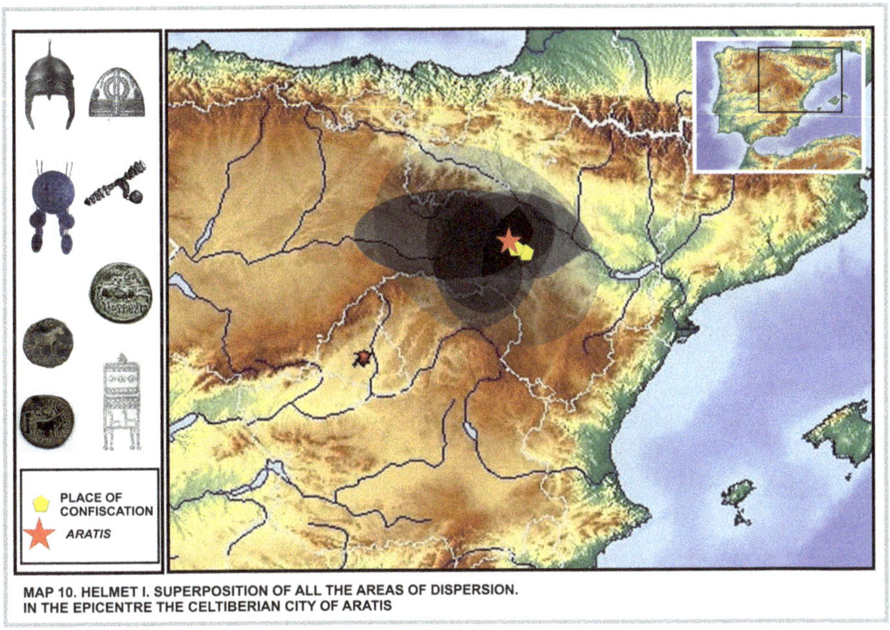

Fig. 13 Helmet I. Superposition of all areas of dispersion. In the epicentre, the Celtiberian city of Aratis

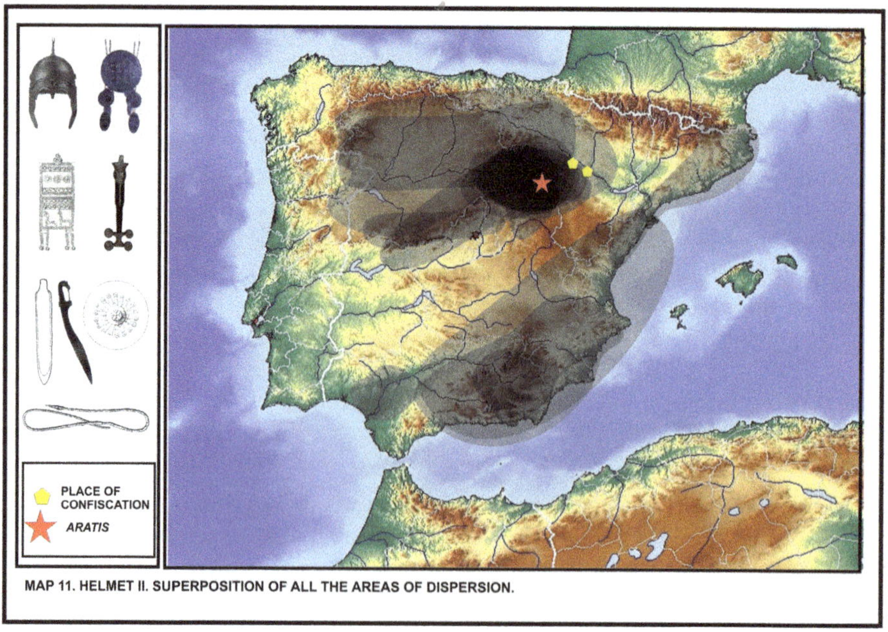

Fig. 14 Helmet II. Superposition of all areas of dispersion. In the epicentre, the Celtiberian city of Aratis

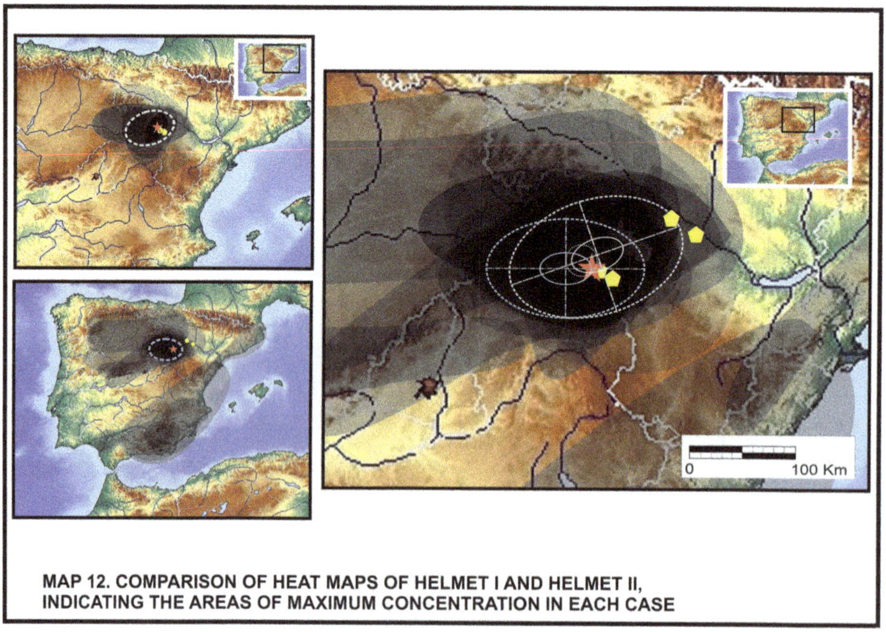

Fig. 15 Comparison of heat maps of Helmet I and Helmet II, indicating the areas of maximum concentration in each case

analysed, and projecting the epicentres, an area of maximum probability of origin of 11 km radius was defined. Aratis is inside (see Fig. 15). This fact, together with other evidence, such as fragmented pieces that were dispersed in both lots (see Fig. 2), the results of the archaeological interventions carried out in Aratis in 2013 and 2014, and other data from the summary of the process, were necessary elements for the definitive sentence of the two accused.

This objective method, which is presented as a first, will be improved with the development of specific software in a dedicated Geographic Information System (GIS). The method should be tested in other contexts, in other cases of archaeological plundering. It only has two requirements: that there be a wide repertoire of typologies of seized archaeological objects and that there be reliable archaeological studies on the dispersion of the appearance of each of the typologies. In this sense, the numismatic analysis, especially of the pre-Roman coins, was conclusive. Moreover, it is precisely these coins that are often one of the most common pieces in the collections that are seized in archaeological plundering procedures in many parts of the world.

Acknowledgements I would first like to thank Samuel Hardy for his help with my English manuscript. To Luis Fatás, archaeologist of the Government of Aragón, who was the best possible travel companion in the Helmet case, and to Donna Yates and Naomi Oosterman, for their confidence and time they devoted to the correction and improvement of this work.

References

Alegre, J. M. (1997). El Patrimonio Arqueológico: Aspectos de su régimen jurídico. *Patrimonio Cultural y Derecho, 1*, 121–131.

Andresen, M. A. (2017). Mapping crime prevention: What we do and where we need to go. In B. LeClerc & E. Savona (Eds.), *Crime prevention in the 21st century*. Springer.

Arlegui, M. (2014). *Museo numantino*. Soria.

Brantingham, P. J., & Brantingham, P. L. (1981). *Environmental criminology*. Sage.

Burgess, E. W. (1925). The growth of the city: An introduction to a research project. In R. E. Park, E. W. Burgess, & R. D. McKenzie (Eds.), *The city*. University of Chicago Press.

Cerdeño, M. L., & Chordá, M. (2004). Fíbulas de tipo navarro-aquitano en el área celtibérica. *Cuadernos de Arqueología de la Universidad de Navarra, 12*, 161–175.

Eck, J., Chainey, S., Cameron, J., & Wilson, R. (2005). *Mapping crime: Understanding hotspots*. Report. Washington D.C.: United States Department of Justice.

Egg, M. (2002). Eisenzeitliche Waffenwihungen im mittleren Alpenraum. In *Kult der Vorzeit in den Alpen: Opfergaben, Opferplätze, Opferbrauchtum* (pp. 961–984). Tiroler Landesmuseum Ferdinandeum.

Esteban, C., Romeo, F., & Fatas, L. (2019). El campo de túmulos de Peñas Pasera de la ciudad celtibérica de Aratis (Aranda de Moncayo, Zaragoza) y el calendario celta. *Zephyrus, 84*, 115–137.

Fatás, L., Graells, R., Lorrio, A. J., & Romeo, F. (2014). Dos nuevos cascos hispano-calcídicos en contexto urbano: los oppida celtibéricos de Aratis (Aranda de Moncayo, Zaragoza) y Contrebia Carbica (Villas Viejas, Cuenca). *Boletín del Seminario de estudio de Arte y Arqueología, LXXX*, 13–51.

García, G. (2012). El armamento de influencia La Tène en la Península Ibérica (siglos V–I a.C.). Dissertation, Universitat de Girona.
Graells, R. (2014). Discos coraza de la Península Ibérica (s VI–IV a.C.). *Jahrburg RGZM, 59*, 85–244.
Graells, R., & Lorrio, A. J. (2013). El casco celtibérico de Muriel de la Fuente (Soria) y los hallazgos de cascos en las aguas en la Península Ibérica. *Complutum, 24*(1), 151–173.
Graells, R., Lorrio, A. J., & Quesada, F. (2014). *Cascos Hispano-calcídicos. Símbolo de las élites celtibéricas*. Römisch-Germanischen Zentralmuseums.
Graells, R., & Marzoli, D. (2016). *Armas de la Hispania prerromana*. Römisch-Germanischen Zentralmuseums.
Griñó, B. (1986). Los puñales tipo Monte Bernorio Miraveche. *Zephyrus, 39*, 297–306.
Guerry, A. M. (1883). Essai sur la statistique morale de la France. Paris.
Harries, K. A. (1999). *Mapping crime: Principle and practice*. United States Department of Justice.
Kavannagh, E. (2008). El puñal bidiscoidal peninsular: tipología y relación con el puñal militar romano (pugio). *Gladius, XXVIII*, 5–85.
Lorrio, A. J. (1997). *Los celtíberos. 2ª edición ampliada y actualizada*. Publicaciones UCM.
Lorrio, A. J. (2016). La guerra y el armamento celtibérico: estado actual. In R. Graells & D. Marzoli (Eds.), *Armas de la Hispania prerromana* (pp. 229–272). Römisch-Germanischen Zentralmuseums.
Lorrio, A. J., Graells, R., Müller-Karpe, M., Romeo, F., & Royo, J. I. (2019). La destrucción del patrimonio celtibérico. El caso del valle del rio Huecha y de la Sierra del Moncayo. In G. Munilla (Ed.), *Musealizando la protohistoria peninsular*. Publicaciones UB.
Lorrio, A. J., & Sánchez, M. D. (2009). La necrópolis celtibérica de Arcobriga. Monreal de Ariza. *Caesaraugusta,* 80. Zaragoza: Publicaciones de la Cátedra José Galiay.
Moya, F. (1993). Historia de la Almunia hasta la Reconquista. *Ador* 2, Zaragoza: Centro de Estudios Almunienses.
Müller-Karpe, M. (2014). Antikenhandel/Kulturgüterschutz–Fortsetzung von KUR 2012, 195 ff., Kunst und Recht (KUR). *Journal für Kunstrecht, Urheberrecht und Kulturpolitik, 6*, 147–153.
Olaya, V. (2014). *Sistemas de Información Geográfica*. Retrieved June 14, 2021, from http://volaya.github.io/libro-sig/
Phillips, P. D. (1972). A prologue to the geography of crime. *Proceedings of the Association of American Geographers, 4*(1), 86–91.
Pomed, L. (2001). La ley del Patrimonio Cultural Aragonés en el contexto competencial. In L. Pomed (Ed.), *Estudio sistemático de la Ley del Patrimonio Cultural Aragonés*. Ediciones Cortes de Aragón/derecho, Zaragoza.
Quesada, F. (1997). El armamento ibérico. Estudio tipológico, geográfico, funcional, social y simbólico de las armas en la Cultura Ibérica (siglos VI-I a.c.). Montagnac: Monographies Instrumentum 3.
Quesada, F., & Baena, J. (1997). Mapas temáticos a partir de cartografía digitalizada. In C. Blasco, J. Baena, & F. Quesada (Eds.), *Los SIG y el análisis espacial en arqueología*. Universidad Autónoma de Madrid.
Quetelet, A. (1842). A treatise on man and the development of his faculties. Edinburgh.
Redondo, S. (1988). Prólogo. In V. Garrido & A. M. Gómez (Eds.), *Diccionario de criminología*. Editorial Tirant lo Blanch.
Rodríguez, I. (2000). Los detectores de metal y el expolio del patrimonio Arqueológico. Algunas propuestas de actuación en Andalucía, PH. *Boletín de Instituto andaluz de patrimonio histórico, 30*, 32–49.
Rodríguez, I. (2004). El uso de detectores de metales en la legislación cultural española. *Patrimonio Cultural y Derecho, 7*, 233–260.
Rodríguez, I. (2012). *Indiana jones sin futuro. La lucha contra el espolio arqueológico*. JAS Arqueología editorial.
Rodríguez, I., Yáñez, A., & Ortiz, M. (2015). Arqueología y el uso de detectores en España: el caso de Andalucía. *La Linde, 5*, 53–73.

Rojo, M., Garrido, R., Tejedor, C., & García, I. (2014). Calcolitico: Puñales-cuchillo, en Arlegui (coord.). *Museo Numantino. Guía*, volumen 2, 70–72.
Romeo, F. (2018). La regulación del uso de detectores de metales en la Comunidad Autónoma de Aragón: 69 bis LPCA. Criterios, procedimientos y valoración tras casi tres años de gestión. In A. Yánez & I. Rodríguez (Eds.), *El expoliar se va a acabar* (pp. 264–280). Editorial Tirant lo Blanch.
Romeo, F. (2021). Reflexiones acerca de un sistema de tasación objetivo de piezas arqueológicas dentro de procedimientos judiciales. In A. Yáñez & I. Rodríguez (Eds.), *La valoración del patrimonio arqueológico*. Madrid.
Romeo, F., & Matas, F. (2020). La tecnología de los detectores de metal: principios de funcionamiento y análisis de los escenarios de expolio arqueológico. *Journal of Cultural Heritage Crime*. Retrieved June 14, 2021, from https://www.journalchc.com/2020/10/01/la-tecnologia-de-los-detectores-de-metal-principios-de-funcionamiento-y-analisis-de-los-escenarios-de-expolio-arqueologico/
Romeo, F., Royo, J. I., Gonzalvo, I., Angás, J., & Fatás, L. (2017). Un nuevo sistema para la valoración económica de los daños en yacimientos arqueológicos expoliados. *Revista Patrimonio Cultural y Derecho, 21*, 231–267.
Serebrennikova, A. V., Trefilov, A. A., Kharlamov, D. D., & Zuykov, A. V. (2018). The correlation of in dubio pro reo and in dubio pro duriore principles in the criminal proceedings of Switzerland and Russia. *Revista Publicando, 5–15*(2), 229–240.
Simon, H. A. (1957). *Administrative behavior: A study of decision-making processes in administrative organization*. Macmillan.
Simon, H. A. (1982). *Models of bounded rationality*. MIT Press.
Stangeland, P., & Garrido, M. J. (2004). *El mapa del crimen. Herramientas geográficas para policías y criminólogos*. Editorial Tirant lo Blanch.
Stefanelli, F. V. (2012). Dispersión del numerario de Sekia. *Saguntum, 44*, 155–166.
Tobler, W. R. (1970). A computer movie simulating urban growth in the Detroit region. *Economic Geography, 46*(1), 234–240.
Tufte, E. R. (1983). *The visual display of quantitative information*. Graphics Press.
Tufte, E. R. (1990). *Envisioning information*. Graphics Press.
Villagrasa, M. M. (1999). Notas sobre la tramitación parlamentaria de la Ley de Patrimonio Cultural Aragonés. *Revista de relaciones laborales, 7*, 221–232.
Yánez, A. (2018). *Patrimonio arqueológico y derecho sancionador*. Editorial Tirant lo Blanch.
Yánez, A., & Rodríguez, I. (2018). *El expoliar se va a acabar*. Editorial Tirant lo Blanch.

Part II
Theory

Cuneiform Exceptionalism?

Justifying the Study and Publication of Unprovenanced Cuneiform Tablets from Iraq

Neil Brodie

Abstract Through the 1990s and 2000s thousands of cuneiform tablets were looted from archaeological sites in Iraq and acquired by private collectors. Since then, scholars with expertise in reading cuneiform inscriptions (who call themselves Assyriologists) have been studying and publishing the texts. This scholarly engagement with what is generally understood to be illicitly-traded material has been controversial, and many Assyriologists have made public statements justifying their work. This chapter presents a brief overview of the controversy over publication, before using Luc Boltanski and Laurent Thévenot's theory of justification to examine the justificatory statements of Assyriologists for what they reveal about their reasons for engaging with illicitly-traded material. The chapter concludes by considering the harms such scholarship might cause to Iraq.

1 Introduction

Through the 1990s and 2000s, civil society in Iraq was stretched to breaking by a destructive cycle of war, economic sanctions, invasion, and occupation. Archaeological sites were badly looted for their valuable antiquities that were sold on the international market (Emberling & Hanson, 2008; Rothfield, 2008; Stone & Farchakh Bajjaly, 2008), with on-the-ground reporting and satellite imagery highlighting the desirability of cuneiform tablets (Atwood, 2003; Breitkopf, 2006; Farchakh Bajjaly, 2008; Stone, 2008). Cuneiform tablets are made of clay and carry texts written in cuneiform script, which was invented towards the end of the fourth millennium B.C. in the area of what is today is often termed Mesopotamia, centred on Iraq, eastern Syria, and immediately adjacent territories in Turkey and Iran. Over time, cuneiform was used to write a number of languages until its use began to decline in the late first millennium B.C. It was deciphered during the middle years of

N. Brodie (✉)
EAMENA Endangered Archaeology in the Middle East & North Africa, School of Archaeology, University of Oxford, Oxford, UK
e-mail: neil.brodie@arch.ox.ac.uk

N. Oosterman, D. Yates (eds.), *Crime and Art*, Studies in Art, Heritage, Law and the Market 1, https://doi.org/10.1007/978-3-030-84856-9_7

the nineteenth century. Today, scholars who translate and study cuneiform inscriptions are known as cuneiformists or Assyriologists and work within the academic discipline of Assyriology.

The trade in cuneiform tablets from Iraq is, and has been for a long time, illegal (Brodie, 2006, 2008a, 2008b; Foster et al., 2005). Under Iraq's domestic law, unexcavated antiquities have been state property since 1936 (Bernhardsson, 2005, pp. 94–197). After the Iraqi occupation of Kuwait in 1990, United Nations Security Council Resolution (UNSCR) 661 placed trade sanctions on any goods exported from Iraq after 6 August, 1990, including cultural objects such as cuneiform tablets. On 22 May, 2003, UNSCR 1483 lifted general trade sanctions but specifically stated that trade in cultural objects had been prohibited since August 1990 and would continue to be so. Despite these national and international prohibitions on export and trade, by the early 2000s it was clear that many previously undocumented (unprovenanced) and presumed illicitly-traded cuneiform tablets had entered private collections outside Iraq and were being studied and published by Assyriologists (Brodie, 2009, p. 43, Table 3.1), though at the time the true scale of the problem was hard to judge. Since then, the study and publication of privately-held unprovenanced tablets has continued. There is now a burgeoning output of scholarly books and papers and it is becoming possible to appreciate just how many unprovenanced cuneiform tablets have entered private collections since the 1990s. It is generally believed, even by the scholars studying and publishing them, that most were looted and illicitly traded (Dalley, 2014; Friberg, 2007, p. 142; George, 2017, p. 95; Maiocchi, 2010, p. 141; Molina, 2020; Monaco, 2016, p. 1; Westenholz, 2010), though that is rarely admitted in print in relation to a specific object.

Scholarly work on unprovenanced, likely-looted antiquities such as cuneiform tablets is controversial, and some academic journals will not publish it. No doubt in reaction to this prohibition, many scholars who do study unprovenanced cuneiform tablets have stated their reasons for doing so. This chapter proceeds with a brief overview of publication policies as they relate to unprovenanced cuneiform tablets. Next, Luc Boltanski and Laurent Thévenot's theory of justification will be used to examine the justificatory statements of Assyriologists and what they reveal about the controversy over study and publication. The chapter will conclude by considering the harms such scholarship might cause to Iraq.

2 Publication Policies and the Cuneiform Exception

During the closing decades of the twentieth century, mounting archaeological concern over the damage caused to archaeological sites and archaeological research by the antiquities trade caused some professional societies to proscribe any involvement of their members. From an archaeological perspective, it was argued that looted antiquities lose much of their scholarly value when their archaeological context is destroyed by unscientific and unrecorded excavation. David Gill and Christopher Chippindale (1993) described the deleterious "material and intellectual consequences" of treating antiquities as collectable art objects, thereby encouraging their looting and illicit trade. At the same time, Ricardo Elia (1993) pointed to the "seductive and troubling work" of scholars working with collectors, and how their collaboration could be construed as stimulating market demand for antiquities and again encouraging their looting and illicit trade.

The potentially problematical nature of scholarly engagement with likely-looted antiquities caused some, but by no means all, academic journals and monograph series to adopt policies prohibiting the first publication of antiquities that could not be shown to have a clear, legitimate provenance (Brodie, 2009; Cherry, 2014; Gerstenblith, 2014). Such policies proved controversial and soon faced accusations of censorship (Boardman, 2009), particularly by scholars working with text-bearing antiquities such as cuneiform tablets (Dalley, 2014; Owen, 2009). They argued that looted and illicitly traded text-bearing antiquities would still be of value to scholarship and a refusal to allow publication would be detrimental to the production of historical knowledge. The large numbers of previously undocumented cuneiform tablets and other cuneiform-inscribed objects appearing in private collections outside Iraq gave added urgency to this objection. For one professional organisation at least, the American Schools of Oriental Research (ASOR), the problem was serious enough to prompt a modification to its previously established publication policy. The modification became known as the *cuneiform exception* (Gerstenblith, 2014).

In 1995, ASOR had adopted a policy prohibiting the publication of any antiquity that could not be documented as having been out of its country of origin before 24 April, 1972 (the date of entry into force of the 1970 UNESCO Convention on the Means of Prohibiting and Preventing the Illicit Import, Export and Transfer of Ownership of Cultural Property) or to have left legally after that date. But the large-scale influx into private collections of unprovenanced cuneiform tablets and other inscribed objects from Iraq caused it to revise its policy in 2004. Henceforth, publication of unprovenanced cuneiform tablets in ASOR journals and monographs would be allowed provided the State Board of Antiquities and Heritage (SBAH) of Iraq gave its consent, the tablets were returned to Iraq and the ownership and custody of the SBAH, and publication included a reference to the fact that the published texts were unprovenanced.

In 2015 the cuneiform exception was revised and broadened in application to include material from other conflict areas and was still in place in January 2021, with the enabling conditions listed as:

> a. The author notes that the text-bearing artifact lacks archaeological provenience in a prominent manner in the text of the publication, in the caption of its illustration, and, if intermixed with objects having archaeological provenience, also in the index or catalog.
>
> b. The author demonstrates that an effort has been made to determine the probable country of origin, which is the location of its final archaeological deposition within a modern nation-state; and prior to publication, the author receives and is willing to transmit to ASOR a written commitment from the owner of the artifact asserting that the artifact will be returned to the Department of Antiquities or equivalent competent authority of the country of origin following any conservation or publication, once permission for its return has been received; or alternatively, that its title has been ceded to the determined country of origin, or to some

other publicly-accessible repository, if return to its country of origin is not feasible (ASOR, 2019).

The cuneiform exception has been weakened since its initial statement. By 2021, there was no longer any requirement for a dispossessed country's antiquities authority, in Iraq's case the SBAH, to approve study and publication. This modified exception is problematical as the scholarly value of a cuneiform tablet resides in its text and not the physical tablet itself. So, as allowed by the 2015 exception, copying and publishing texts without permission while returning the physical tablets themselves can be construed as a mechanism for extracting scholarly value while passing on the long-term curation costs of an exhausted scholarly resource to Iraq (Brodie, 2020).

In reality, publication policies have done little to stop the study and publication of unprovenanced cuneiform tablets. In 2007, for example, the publisher Eisenbrauns, an imprint of Penn State University Press, introduced its series Cornell University Studies in Assyriology and Sumerology (CUSAS). By November 2020, its website listed 41 CUSAS monographs either published or in press. All but five realised the first publication of previously unknown cuneiform tablets from recently formed private collections. The tablets published by CUSAS number in the thousands, and Eisenbrauns is not the only company publishing unprovenanced tablets.

The study and publication of unprovenanced cuneiform tablets has now become commonplace, acknowledged across academia with little adverse comment. Acceptance of study and publication has permeated out into the broader academic ecosystem—universities and public funding bodies are regularly acknowledged in publications for supporting the underlying scholarship. Nevertheless, the existence of publication policies and the continuing international trade embargo on Iraqi cultural objects raise questions about the propriety of engaging with what is generally believed to be looted and illicitly traded material. Many of the Assyriologists publishing these tablets have felt it necessary to defend or justify their actions, either in the publication itself or separately in longer opinion pieces. These justificatory statements imply a sense of moral uncertainty, an understanding that study and publication might be considered wrong or harmful by society at large, or at least some parts of society, and is in need of explanation. There now exists a large number of justificatory statements embedded within publications that can be analysed for what they reveal about the beliefs and moral convictions of Assyriologists who have chosen to study and publish privately-held, unprovenanced cuneiform tablets. Together, they offer the opportunity to make more sense of a debate whose protagonists seem often to be talking past one another, and, standing back, to situate the debate within broader political and sociocultural contexts.

In total, 30 statements by 13 Assyriologists are published here. They are presented as representing the beliefs of "Assyriologists" as a consensual community, though obviously they represent only the beliefs of Assyriologists actually making the statements. Nevertheless, as will be made clear, there are regularities of claims and arguments and it is not unreasonable to suppose that the statements do represent the beliefs of a broad constituency of Assyriologists engaged in publishing unprovenanced cuneiform tablets. It must be remembered though that many Assyriologists do not countenance study and publication of unprovenanced material and their views are not represented by the reproduced statements. The statements are ordered, and their contents examined, using the justification theory of Luc Boltanski and Laurent Thévenot.

3 Justification Theory

Boltanski and Thévenot developed their theory of justification to explore how civil society disputes can develop, proceed and be resolved without recourse to violence (Boltanski & Thévenot, 1999, 2006; Boltanski, 2011). When engaged in a dispute, protagonists are considered to be offering faithful justifications of their beliefs and actions within a cultural frame of reference that is specific to their social group or reality, in this case the scholarly community of Assyriologists, but these justifications are open to misinterpretation or misunderstanding by disputants situated within a different frame of reference. Central to their theory is the idea of the *common good*. Boltanski and Thévenot isolate what they believe to be six different conceptualisations of the common good, which they term in English *polities* or *worlds*, each one drawn from a foundational work of political philosophy. Within the reality of a polity, persons, things, and actions are valued according to cultural understandings that are specific to the polity concerned yet believed by actors within the polity to be universal and constitutive generally of the common good. Four polities are relevant to this discussion:

Market polity (Adam Smith's *Wealth of Nations*). Market worth is created through market competition and measured by price or wealth. Order is maintained through the general demand for scarce resources and the recognition of private property. The market polity is mobilised within academia when scholars are ranked by their success in securing competitive grant awards.

Industrial polity (Henri de Saint-Simon's *L'Industrie*). Industrial worth is created and maintained through efficiency, productivity and long-term growth. It can be measured through demonstrable scales of production, technical proficiency or competence. Order is maintained through rational organisation (and by rational organisations). Examinations and qualifications of merit or achievement are obvious expressions of industrial worth in academia, as are quantitative or qualitative measures of "output", "outcomes" or "deliverables".

Civic polity (Jean-Jacques Rousseau's *Contrat social*). Civic worth inheres within representational political structures promoting or acting in the public or collective interest. Worth is accorded to social collectives rather than individual persons, and worth is derived through representation, accorded to persons acting on behalf of a collective. Order is maintained through agreed laws, rules, and procedures. The civic order finds expression in universities though representative bodies such as committees and senates.

Domestic polity (Jacques-Bénigne Bossuet's *La politique tirée des propres paroles de l'Écriture sainte*). Domestic worth is created and maintained through positioning in an inherited hierarchy or authority structure, analogous to a family. There is a respect for tradition (the natural order of things) and a person cannot be evaluated apart from the inhabited role. Order is maintained through trust and interpersonal relations. Elements of the domestic order can be glimpsed in academia through the convention of collegiality or respect for one's colleagues and the regard accorded to positions: the opinions of tenured faculty and senior professors are considered to carry more weight than those of temporary researchers or assistant faculty.

Within the cultural understanding of a polity, competence has a moral quality—the good way of doing something is the right way of doing something. This moral logic of action underpins justification. Justifications are open and honest defences of actions believed to be good and right, not dissimulations or rationalisations of hidden or dissonant interests. Across polities, objects, persons and actions will be conceptualised and valued differently, sometimes recognised and qualified using different terminologies. Thus, the cultural understandings of a polity cannot be readily apprehended from outside and constructions of the common good might be incommensurable across polities. Seemingly intractable disputes arise when actors find the propriety of their beliefs or actions under criticism or challenge from facts or value judgments exterior to their cultural understandings or moral logics. These disputes cannot be resolved by appeal to a higher authority—there are no higher authorities, only more polities. In practice, disputes range across polities, with composite justifications drawing upon the cultural resources of more than polity. A public dispute can be triggered when events expose the contrivance of omniscience within a polity or highlight a reality gap between polities. Within academia, the sudden appearance and accessibility of large numbers of unprovenanced though likely-looted and illicitly-traded cuneiform tablets proved to be just such an event.

To a large extent, the debate over study and publication of unprovenanced cuneiform tablets can be understood as a dispute between protagonists situated largely within an industrial polity on the one hand (the Assyriologists) and a civic polity on the other (their critics). Assyriologists might bridle at being described as industrialists, but the label does capture the sense of forward-looking professional endeavour that is characteristic of academia, and it is not hard these days to find academia characterised as a "knowledge industry" (Fish, 2014, p. 45; Miyoshi, 2000, p. 24). The civic polity comprises the world of representational organisations such as UNESCO and the United Nations. These organisations are charged with representing the collective interest of the international community in designing policy for cultural heritage protection. Policy is effectuated by a wide-ranging latticework of laws, conventions, regulations, and standards, most relevantly in this cuneiform context the 1954 Hague Convention for the Protection of Cultural Property in the Event of Armed Conflict, the 1970 UNESCO Convention on the Means of Prohibiting and Preventing the Illicit Import, Export and Transfer of Ownership of Cultural Property, and more specifically for Iraq UNSCRs 661 and 1483.

In an industrial polity, "the great persons are the experts" (Boltanski & Thévenot, 1999, p. 373). Defending themselves, it is clear that Assyriologists draw primarily upon their identity as scholarly experts, with the worth of their actions judged and confirmed by the thorough and expeditious study and publication of cuneiform tablets. Publication has a moral quality as a "duty" or a "responsibility":

> I consider it a scholarly duty to assist in publishing whatever can be saved for future generations, whenever an opportunity presents itself (Alster, 2007, p. xi).

> ...Assyriologists, whose duty, as ever, is to make new material available so that it is not lost to posterity (Dalley, 2009, p. ix).

> The undeniable importance of primary sources for the reconstruction of man's past makes it imperative that all cuneiform tablets be published without prejudice (George, 2009, p. xiv).

> I have felt from the outset that it was an obligation of scholars to publish these artifacts before they might disappear (Owen, 2013a, p. xv).

> While aware of the controversy behind the study and publication of these texts, I believe that it is our responsibility to do everything in our power not to lose the precious historical, linguistic and cultural information they convey (Molina, 2020, p. 344).

The process of "publication" should not be underestimated. It includes cleaning, conservation, reconstruction, copying, transcribing and translating. The succession of techniques utilised to bring a freshly excavated tablet to publication does literally constitute a small-scale industrial process (Dalley, 2014). The sheer physical effort involved in achieving publication is impressive. Typically, for a CUSAS monograph, a single scholar will publish anything up to several hundred texts.

Accepting and meeting their burden of publication, Assyriologists are critical of the failures of other scholars to publish and of any obstacles to publication, as broadly conceived:

> It is ironic that in the more than two decades during which fieldwork in Iraq was rendered impossible, few of the many seasons of previous excavations of Iraqi sites have been published. Unfortunately, archaeologists did not utilize this long hiatus to publish their excavations. Instead, many simply moved to Syria, Turkey, or even Iran to initiate new projects, all the while neglecting their responsibilities to publish their previous excavations (Owen, 2010, pp. ix–x).

> If the tablets are left in the hands of poverty-stricken museums or collectors who have neither the knowledge nor the means to conserve them, a good part of them are likely to disintegrate within our lifetime (Westenholz, 2010, p. 258).

> The tens of thousands of unpublished and mostly inaccessible tablets in the Iraq Museum. One wonders if these texts will ever be published (Owen, 2013a, p. xvii).

Assyriologists also deploy a secondary line of justification that Boltanski and Thévenot would recognise as rooted in their domestic polity. The study and publication of looted and illicitly-traded tablets has a long history and therefore the actions of Assyriologists today should be viewed only as the most recent expression of a mature tradition and implicitly as legitimate:

> ... great parts of most collections of non-European cultural heritage ... are unprovenanced texts from the antiquities market or from private collections. ... Now, as then, the task of a serious scholar must be to attempt to make all kinds of texts publicly known and understood ... (Friberg, 2007, p. v).

> Responsibility for publishing tablets that have no archaeological provenance has always been accepted by Assyriologists in the past, to salvage as much as possible from the regrettable ancient and modern practice of looting (Dalley, 2009, p. ix).

> In what is today the state of Iraq, digging for tablets and other ancient artifacts by the local peasants, in order to sell them to Western purchasers, has been carried out almost since the dawn of Assyriology in the Western world (Westenholz, 2010, p. 258).

> Most of the literature on looting emphasizes the negative and tragic destruction of archaeological sites but neglects to mention the enormous contribution to Mesopotamian history and culture that the study and publication of illicitly-excavated inscriptions have provided since the rediscovery of ancient Iraq in the nineteenth century (Owen, 2013a, p. xvi).

> They all come from illicit excavations, which, although carried out by looters since the middle of the nineteenth century, had recently attained, as a consequence of the political situation, an unprecedented level of growth (Monaco, 2016, p. 1).

> Since the early days of Assyriology, only the minority of cuneiform tablets came from archaeological excavations, whereas the lion's share was acquired through the antiquities market (Földi, 2017, p. 8).

An accusation sometimes levelled at Assyriologists is that their engagement with privately-held cuneiform tablets is financially beneficial for the owners and commercially beneficial for the market—the "seductive and troubling work" of Elia (1993). This accusation can be construed as an attempt to situate the work of Assyriologists within the market polity, something they are at pains to resist. Typically, they claim that the trade is supply-led, driven by the poverty of Iraqis who are forced to dig, or that looting is the outcome of a legal regime placing unrealistic controls on what could otherwise be a legitimate trade in legally-excavated tablets:

> It is impossible to undo the disaster that the destruction of the cultural legacy of Iraq, by Iraqis, has created (Owen, 2007, p. vii).

> Recent changes in the law have led to the censorship of scholarly activity and created a black market for the distribution of looted material to dealers and collectors (Dalley, 2009, p. ix).

> The argument that scholarly publications somehow enhance the value of artifacts while glossy, popular, archaeological publications with titles featuring words like "gold" and "treasure" to glamorize discoveries and to attract more funding somehow do not, is ludicrous (Owen, 2009, p. 129).

> ... the plundering of Iraq's rural sites increased dramatically after 1990 as a result of the embargo and the ensuing impoverishment of the rural population and the weakening of Iraq's institutions. In other words, it was dictated by the need to supply rather than by foreign demand (Westenholz, 2010, p. 259, note 9).

> The argument that, by doing so, the Assyriologist increases the market value of the tablet or somehow "launders" it may have some merit as far as the dealer is concerned, but that remains to be proven (Westenholz, 2010, p. 261).

> . . . the root causes that ultimately lie in the country of origin (Owen, 2013a, p. xviii).

> So, to blame museums, collectors, and particularly scholars who publish unprovenanced artifacts and inscriptions for encouraging the looting and destruction of archaeological sites is simply a gross distortion of historical fact. People seeking both precious and utilitarian artifacts pillage archaeological sites regularly (Owen, 2013b, p. 335).

> . . . even members high up in the government, such as Saddam Hussein's son Uday, were instrumental in the looting of their own cultural heritage (Owen, 2013b, p. 335, note 526).

> Did publishing those tablets, and thousands of other unprovenanced tablets, help create a market for cuneiform tablets and thus encourage looting and site destruction? I have seen no well-founded answer to this question, and I can't pretend to know what motivates the small number of serious collectors of these rectangular bits of inscribed mud (Cooper, 2014).

> Especially after the failure of the Iraqi and Syrian states to protect their cultural heritage, a large number of looted cuneiform tablets and other ancient Mesopotamian artefacts have entered the antiquities market and found their way to private collections in the West (Alstola, 2020, p. 39).

Thus, Assyriologists justify their work by positing the scholarly and ultimately public benefit of publication and claiming legitimacy from tradition, while denying that their work has any commercial impact.

Many of the arguments made against the study and publication of unprovenanced cuneiform tablets derive from the international interest in protecting cultural heritage and are founded in Boltanski and Thévenot's civic polity. Assyriologists do seem to recognise this international interest, but rather than acknowledging it as a settled and legitimate consensus they seek instead to misrepresent or demean it as something antithetical to scholarship, as signalled by their use of the term "politics" or its derivatives to describe it. The international consensus is portrayed as a contested domain of conflicting political interests. Scholarship should not be embroiled with politics:

> Those who are not prepared to utilize all sources in their research, including texts available to us through private collections, and certainly those who would presume to limit the access or use in scholarly communications of unprovenienced sources, as has begun to happen with submissions even to such politically neutral editorial boards as those that oversee the publication of papers on the history of mathematics, may want to reconsider the professional choices they have made in their lives (Englund, 2009, p. 6, note 11).

> It is a blatant example of the politicization of scholarship that is taking place particularly in certain British and American universities today (Owen, 2013a, p. xv, note 1).

> I will leave legal arguments about ownership to others; I am making an ethical argument. (Cooper, 2014).

> Scholarship must be separated from political issues and every effort should be made to rescue, record, and publish artifacts without provenance in order to ensure their preservation and publication (Owen, 2015, p. vii).

> In this category I include not only national governments but also international organizations like the U.N. As one would expect of politicians, they appear to be quite convinced that they can change reality simply by writing laws, and their historical consciousness is almost non-existent. The here-and-now is all that matters (Westenholz, 2010, p. 262).

In the course of time, there has been a creeping influence of political correctness. (Westenholz, 2010, p. 262).

In essence, Assyriologist frame the debate over publishing unprovenanced cuneiform tablets as one between scholarship (understood as publication) and politics, with scholarship understood to be apart from or superior to politics.

4 Discussion

It is probably fair to say that publication policies were prompted in the first instance by concerns being voiced in the 1990s about compromised scholarship both caused by and responsible for the destruction of archaeological heritage—the "material and intellectual consequences" of the "seductive and troubling work". Those concerns are still valid and have never been properly addressed. It is notable that Assyriological denials that there work has commercial benefit are never accompanied by any evidential support, and what evidence is available does suggest that scholarly study and publication, as broadly conceived, has commercial value (Brodie, 2011, 2016). Since then, however, understanding has grown of other—political and sociocultural—reasons why the looting and illicit trade of antiquities is considered harmful to a victim country. By the late twentieth century, at the latest, meaningful control over the ownership and management of cultural objects, the principle of cultural self-determination, was recognised internationally as a right among nations (Barkan, 2002). Cultural self-determination is a component of political self-determination and any violation of cultural self-determination is a violation of political self-determination—a violation of sovereignty. Added to that is the more general expectation that each nation will respect the laws and usages of every other nation, what Folarin Shyllon (1998, p. 114) highlighted as the well-established "comity of nations"—mutual respect among nations. Again, any failure to respect a nation's laws is a challenge to its sovereignty. Thus, the absence of any effective international action to stop the unremitting illicit trade of cuneiform tablets must be construed as a failure on the part of the international community to recognise the sovereignty of Iraq and its right to cultural self-determination.

The cycle of violence and foreign interference that has plagued Iraq since 1990 has foregrounded another set of ultimately conflict-related harms. Through the 1990s and early 2000s, bombing and economic sanctions placed a heavy humanitarian toll upon Iraqi civil society. The situation worsened after the 2003 US-led Coalition occupation, when the United States government set about reducing Iraq to the status of a client state (Cockburn, 2016). The plan was predicated upon weakening Iraqi national identity and reducing its sovereignty through the establishment of a power-sharing, sectarian government, with the aim of creating an ethnically, religiously, and politically divided country that would be compliant with United States interests (Kathem, 2020). One of the first actions of the Coalition Provisional Authority after its establishment in May 2003 was to set in motion a process of de-Baathification, ostensibly aimed at dismantling the institutional and military infrastructure of Saddam Hussein's government (Sissons & Al-Saiedi, 2013). But although de-Baathification proceeded as a project of political cleansing, it also entailed a cultural cleansing as academics, museum curators, archaeologists, and media professionals were removed from their jobs (Baker et al., 2010). Many were killed or were forced to flee the country. De-Baathification left an intellectual and cultural capacity gap within Iraq that the country was still struggling to close in 2021 (Nabeel, 2021).

This diminishment of intellectual and cultural capacity has left the study of Iraqi history, and particularly pre-Islamic history, largely in the hands of foreign scholars. Not surprisingly, the work of foreign scholars does not always serve the interests of Iraq or Iraqi civil society. Iraq as a geographical region was known to Islamic geographers as early as the tenth century A.D. (Bahrani, 1998, p. 165), but since the nineteenth century Iraqi cuneiform tablets have been considered the product of "Mesopotamian" culture. Mesopotamia is a signifier as much as it is a place, the anchor point for divisive European narratives of "western" civilisation and "oriental" despotism (Bahrani, 1998). The abstraction of Mesopotamia from the deep history of Iraq hinders any attempts to investigate or establish cultural continuities from the past and cultural commonalities in the present (Kathem, 2020). Although Saddam Hussein had appropriated Mesopotamian monumentality to help forge a collective Iraqi consciousness and legitimise his rule, post-2003, the historical agenda has become increasingly sectarian (Isakhan, 2011; Kathem & Ali, 2020). Iraqi history has become subject to a discontinuity that fails to counter the centrifugal tendencies of sectarianism (Kathem, 2020). To paraphrase Gill and Chippindale, Iraqi scholarship is presently constrained by the material conditions of neo-colonialism and the intellectual conditions of orientalism. Such challenges to scholarship are beginning to be understood and described in relation to "cultural rights" (Matthews et al., 2020; Singh, 1998), by UNESCO recommendations dating back as far as the 1960s, and exemplified since 2009 through the work of the United Nations Human Rights Council (UNHRC). In 2013, the UNHRC published a special report into the writing and teaching of history, emphasising its importance for community building and reconciliation (Shaheed, 2013; see also Barkan, 2009). That is especially true for Iraq (Bernhardsson, 2005).

This emergent understanding and disapproval of compromised sovereignty and violated cultural rights contextualises the work of Assyriologists. Their refusal to seek Iraqi approval of their work or to work cooperatively with Iraqi authorities is at the same time an infringement of Iraqi sovereignty and a missed opportunity to help close the intellectual and cultural capacity gap. This line of argumentation might be regarded as tenuous. Assyriological publication does not embargo Iraqi use of its products and by making transcriptions and translations openly available on online resources such as the Cuneiform Digital Library Initiative (CDLI) Assyriologists would not doubt argue that over the long term they are working for the benefit of Iraqi scholarship and by extension Iraqi civil society. But when Assyriologists claim to be the latest manifestation of a long-established scholarly tradition, they are advertising the persistence of a hybrid cuneiform network that was articulated during the nineteenth century, connecting dollars, collectors, scholars, funders, universities, museums, publishers, dealers, smugglers, diggers, and cuneiform tablets, embedded then as it is now within colonial or neo-colonial relations of political domination. This network acts for the financial, cultural and intellectual benefit of foreigners at the expense of Iraq and Iraqi civil society. Claiming legitimacy from tradition comes perilously close to suspending Iraq within a timeless colonial limbo. Countries that seemingly support the study and publication of unprovenanced cuneiform tablets through funding and institutional acquiescence or assent are the same countries that protect continuing illicit trade through lax law enforcement and that are responsible for the decimation of Iraqi scholarship through military and economic violence. Decomposing this hybrid network into distinct and separate polities or fields of scholarship and politics is what Latour (1993) would consider performative of modernity, acting to disguise or obscure the hidden reality of collective agency. The separation of an industrial polity from a civic polity or of scholarship from politics is a contrivance. Assyriologists maintain it passively with their reductive characterisation of the sovereign and cultural rights of Iraq as politics, but also more actively when they express reluctance to investigate the collecting and trade histories of the tablets they study (Alster, 2007, p. xi; George, 2009, p. iv; Westenholz, 2010, p. 264).

The application of justification theory to the justificatory statements of Assyriologists clarifies the issues at stake when considering the propriety of publishing unprovenanced cuneiform tablets. Assyriological justifications seem trapped within the terms of a debate conducted within ‘western’ academia during the 1990s about interactions among scholars and collectors and the looting of archaeological sites. Concern about these interactions is still salient and although in theory open to empirical resolution the necessary evidence is not always forthcoming. But the justifications take no account of Iraqi grievances arising out of compromised sovereignty and cultural rights violations. When Assyriologists dismiss these grievances as ‘politics’, they betray an anachronistic misunderstanding of what ultimately is considered wrong about their scholarship. They are failing to engage with an emerging international consensus on issues that have been gathered together here as indicative of a civic polity. The segregation of cultural understandings and moral logics into separate industrial and civic polities has stymied meaningful debate and without any common frame of reference has enabled a non-confrontational “business as usual” approach for Assyriologists on the one hand and those arguing in defence of Iraqi sovereignty and cultural rights on the other. Meanwhile, Iraq and Iraqi civil society continue to suffer from the loss of an invaluable cultural and historical resource.

References

Alster, B. (2007). *Sumerian proverbs in the Schøyen collection*. CDL.
Alstola, T. (2020). *Judeans in Babylonia*. Brill.

ASOR. (2019). Policy on professional conduct. *American Society of Overseas Research*. Retrieved June 14, 2021, from https://www.asor.org/about-asor/policies/policy-on-professional-conduct/
Atwood, R. (2003, September/October). Day of the vulture. *Mother Jones*. Retrieved June 14, 2021, from http://motherjones.com/politics/2003/09/day-vulture
Bahrani, Z. (1998). Conjuring Mesopotamia: Imaginative geography and a world past. In L. Meskell (Ed.), *Archaeology under fire* (pp. 159–174). Routledge.
Baker, R. W., Ismael, T., & Ismael, T. Y. (2010). *Cultural cleansing in Iraq*. Pluto.
Barkan, E. (2002). Amending historical injustices: The restitution of cultural property–an overview. In E. Barkan & R. Bush (Eds.), *Claiming the stones/naming the bones: Cultural property and the negotiation of national and ethnic identity* (pp. 16–50). Getty Research Institute.
Barkan, E. (2009). Introduction: Historians and historical reconciliation. *American Historical Review, 114*(4), 899–913.
Bernhardsson, M. (2005). *Reclaiming a plundered past*. University of Texas.
Boardman, J. (2009). Archaeologists, collectors, and museums. In J. Cuno (Ed.), *Whose culture? The promise of museums and the debate over antiquities* (pp. 107–124). Princeton University Press.
Boltanski, L. (2011). *On critique. A sociology of emancipation*. Polity.
Boltanski, L., & Thévenot, L. (1999). The sociology of critical capacity. *European Journal of Social Theory, 2*(3), 359–377.
Boltanski, L., & Thévenot, L. (2006). *On justification: Economies of worth*. Princeton University Press.
Breitkopf, S. (2006, November/December). A reflection of the chaos: Iraq's cultural heritage in crisis. *Museum News*.
Brodie, N. (2006). The plunder of Iraq's archaeological heritage, 1991–2005, and the London antiquities trade. In N. Brodie, M. M. Kersel, C. Luke, & K. W. Tubb (Eds.), *Archaeology, cultural heritage, and the antiquities trade* (pp. 206–226). University Press of Florida.
Brodie, N. (2008a). The western market in Iraqi antiquities. In L. Rothfield (Ed.), *Antiquities under siege: Cultural heritage protection after the Iraq war* (pp. 63–74). AltaMira.
Brodie, N. (2008b). The market background to the April 2003 plunder of the Iraq National Museum. In P. Stone & J. Farchakh Bajjaly (Eds.), *The destruction of cultural heritage in Iraq* (pp. 41–54). Boydell.
Brodie, N. (2009). Consensual relations? Academic involvement in the illegal trade in ancient manuscripts. In P. Green & S. Mackenzie (Eds.), *Criminology and archaeology: Studies in looted antiquities* (pp. 41–58). Hart.
Brodie, N. (2011). Scholarship and insurgency? *The study and trade of Iraqi antiquities*. Unpublished manuscript. Retrieved June 14, 2021, from https://traffickingculture.org/publications/brodie-neil-2011–scholarship-and-insurgency-the-study-and-trade-of-iraqi-antiquities-in-illicit-traffic-of-cultural-objects-law-ethics-and-the-realities-an-institute-of-advanced-studies-works/
Brodie, N. (2016). Scholarly engagement with collections of unprovenanced ancient texts. In K. Almqvist & L. Belfrage (Eds.), *Cultural heritage at risk* (pp. 123–142). Ax:son Johnson Foundation.
Brodie, N. (2020). Restorative justice? Questions arising out of the Hobby Lobby return of cuneiform tablets to Iraq. *Revista Memória em Rede, 12*, 87–109.
Cherry, J. (2014). Publishing undocumented texts: Editorial perspectives. In M. Rutz & M. M. Kersel (Eds.), *Archaeologies of text: Archaeology, technology and ethics* (pp. 227–244). Oxbow.
Cockburn, P. (2016). *Age of Jihad: Islamic State and the Great War for the Middle East*. Verso.
Cooper, J.S. (2014). Cuneiform exceptionalism: An argument for studying and publishing unprovenanced tablets. *The Ancient Near East Today*, 2(2). Retrieved June 14, 2021, from https://www.asor.org/anetoday/2014/02/cuneiform-exceptionalism-an-argument-for-studying-and-publishing-unprovenanced-tablets/
Dalley, S. (2009). *Babylonian tablets from the first sealand dynasty in the Schøyen collection*. CDL.

Dalley, S. (2014, 25 March). Institutions should moderate their rule on looted objects. *National.*
Elia, R. (1993). A seductive and troubling work. *Archaeology, 46*(1), 64–69.
Emberling, G., & Hanson, K. (Eds.). (2008). *Catastrophe! The Looting and Destruction of Iraq's Past*. University of Chicago Press.
Englund, R.K. (2009). The smell of the cage. *Cuneiform Digital Library Journal*, 21, August. Retrieved June 14, 2021, from https://cdli.ucla.edu/files/publications/cdlj2009_004.pdf
Farchakh Bajjaly, J. (2008). Will Mesopotamia survive the war? The continuous destruction of Iraq's archaeological sites. In P. Stone & J. Farchakh Bajjaly (Eds.), *The destruction of cultural heritage in Iraq* (pp. 135–142). Boydell.
Fish, S. (2014). *Versions of academic freedom*. University of Chicago Press.
Földi, Z. (2017). Cuneiform tablets and the antiquities market: The archives from Dūr-Abī-ešuḫ. *Distant Worlds Journal, 2*, 7–27.
Foster, B. R., Foster, K. P., & Gerstenblith, P. (2005). *Iraq beyond the headlines: History, archaeology and war*. World Scientific.
Friberg, J. (2007). *A remarkable collection of Babylonian mathematical texts*. Springer.
George, A. R. (2009). *Babylonian literary texts in the Schøyen collection*. CDL.
George, A. R. (2017). *Assyrian archival texts in the Schøyen collection and other documents from North Mesopotamia and Syria*. CDL.
Gerstenblith, P. (2014). Do restrictions on publication of undocumented texts promote legitimacy? In M. Rutz & M. M. Kersel (Eds.), *Archaeologies of text: Archaeology, technology and ethics* (pp. 214–226). Oxbow.
Gill, D., & Chippindale, C. (1993). Material and intellectual consequences of esteem for Cycladic figures. *American Journal of Archaeology, 97*, 601–659.
Isakhan, B. (2011). Targeting the symbolic dimension of Baathist Iraq: Cultural destruction, historical memory, and national identity. *Middle East Journal of Culture and Communication, 4*, 257–281.
Kathem, M. (2020). Cultural (dis)continuity, political trajectories and the state in post-2003 Iraq. *International Journal of Heritage Studies, 26*(2), 163–177.
Kathem, M., & Ali, D. K. (2020). Decolonising Babylon. *International Journal of Heritage Studies*. https://doi.org/10.1080/13527258.2020.1858140
Latour, B. (1993). *We have never been modern*. Prentice Hall/Harvester.
Maiocchi, M. (2010). The Sargonic "archive" of Me-sag, cup-bearer of Adab. In L. Kogan, N. Koslova, S. Loesov, & S. Tishchenko (Eds.), *City administration in the ancient near east* (pp. 141–152). Eisenbraun.
Matthews, R., Rasheed, Q. H., Palmero Fernández, M., Fobbe, S., Nováček, K., Mohammed-Amin, R., Mühl, S., & Richardson, A. (2020). Heritage and cultural healing: Iraq in a post-Daesh era. *International Journal of Heritage Studies, 26*(2), 120–141.
Miyoshi, M. (2000). Ivory tower in Escrow. *Boundary 2, 27*(1), 7–50.
Molina, M. (2020). The looting of Ur III tablets after the Gulf Wars. In W. Sommerfeld (Ed.), *Dealing with antiquity: Past, present & future* (pp. 323–352). Ugarit.
Monaco, S. F. (2016). *Archaic cuneiform tablets from private collections*. CDL.
Nabeel, G. (2021, 16 February). Fewer young Iraqis choose to study archaeology. *Al-Fanar Media*. February. Retrieved June 14, 2021, from https://www.al-fanarmedia.org/2021/02/fewer-young-iraqis-choose-to-study-archaeology/?fbclid=IwAR1mZMYj52LGrhZ1UloNo662PJeWECW5Tsjoy5ykaL1QfrerOTAJW5K8Z5M
Owen, D. (2007). Preface. In B. Alster (Ed.), *Sumerian proverbs in the Schøyen collection* (p. vii). CDL.
Owen, D. (2009). Censoring knowledge: The case for the publication of unprovenanced cuneiform tablets. In J. Cuno (Ed.), *Whose culture? The promise of museums and the debate over antiquities* (pp. 125–142). Princeton University Press.
Owen, D. (2010). *Garšana Studies*. CDL.
Owen, D. (2013a) *Cuneiform texts primarily from Iri-Saĝrig/Āl-ŠarrĀkī and the history of the Ur III Period. Volume 1: Commentary and indexes*. Bethesda: CDL.

Owen, D. (2013b). To publish or not to publish—That Is the question. In D. Owen (Ed.), *Cuneiform texts primarily from Iri-Saĝrig/Āl-ŠarrĀkī and the history of the Ur III Period. Volume 1: Commentary and indexes* (pp. 335–356). CDL.
Owen, D. (2015). Preface. In F. Pomponio & G. Visicato (Eds.), *Middle sargonic tablets chiefly from Adab in the Cornell University Collections* (p. vii). CDL.
Rothfield, L. (Ed.). (2008). *Antiquities under siege: Cultural heritage protection after the Iraq War*. AltaMira.
Shaheed, F. (2013). *Report of the Special Rapporteur in the Field of Cultural Rights*. United Nations, New York. Retrieved June 14, 21021, from https://undocs.org/en/A/68/296
Shyllon, F. (1998). The right to a cultural past: African viewpoints. In H. Nieć (Ed.), *Cultural rights and wrongs* (pp. 103–119). UNESCO.
Singh, K. (1998). UNESCO and cultural rights. In H. Nieć (Ed.), *Cultural rights and wrongs* (pp. 146–160). UNESCO.
Sissons, M., & Al-Saiedi, A. (2013). *A bitter legacy: Lessons of de-baathification in Iraq*. New York: International Center for Transitional Justice. Retrieved June 14, 2021, from https://www.ictj.org/sites/default/files/ICTJ-Report-Iraq-De-Baathification-2013-ENG.pdf
Stone, E. (2008). Archaeological site looting: The destruction of cultural heritage in southern Iraq. In G. Emberling & K. Hanson (Eds.), *Catastrophe! The looting and destruction of Iraq's past* (pp. 65–80). University of Chicago.
Stone, P., & Farchakh Bajjaly, J. (Eds.). (2008). *The destruction of cultural heritage in Iraq*. Boydell.
Westenholz, A. (2010). Illicit cuneiform tablets. Heirlooms or stolen goods? In A. Kleinerman & J. M. Sasson (Eds.), *Why should someone who knows something conceal it? Cuneiform studies in honor of David I. Owen on his 70th Birthday* (pp. 257–266). CDL.

Crime, Material and Meaning in Art World Desirescapes

How Matter Matters for Art Crime

Donna Yates and Simon Mackenzie

Abstract In this chapter we propose the idea of a 'desirescape', where a spatial array of myriad agentic objects cultivates desire among people to collect, own, possess, and show off artworks. Within this desirescape, people are conceived of as caught in a web of objects that not only generate and manipulate desire, but also disturb reason. Moving away from a human-oriented sociology of art worlds, we explore the object networks of art within market spaces (dealerships, museums, art fairs, auctions) to consider how actor-objects active create a network into which human-subjects are drawn. We then consider how these object-networks might lead to the violation of ethical or social norms or the committing of a crime. While we ultimately advocate for an expansion of object-focused criminological theory, this work has immediate practical implications. Criminologists may benefit from thinking about crime prevention priorities in terms of changing the network properties of these webs of alluring objects, rather than focussing on the more traditional technique of dissuading individuals from committing crime through responding to these allures.

1 Introduction

In criminology and socio-legal studies there has been a groundswell of interest in 'affect'—that is, the emotional influence of things on individuals—leading to a variety of interesting propositions around the 'atmosphere' that places and social arrangements may develop (Fraser & Matthews, 2019), and the affective properties of certain architecture and physical structures that may regulate behaviour (Young,

D. Yates (✉)
Criminal Law and Criminology, Maastricht University, Maastricht, The Netherlands
e-mail: d.yates@maastrichtuniversity.nl

S. Mackenzie
School of Social and Cultural Studies, Te Herenga Waka—Victoria University of Wellington, Wellington, New Zealand
e-mail: simon.mackenzie@vuw.ac.uk

N. Oosterman, D. Yates (eds.), *Crime and Art*, Studies in Art, Heritage, Law and the Market 1, https://doi.org/10.1007/978-3-030-84856-9_8

2021). Encompassing both of these reflections is the idea of a 'lawscape' in which legal rules shape and permeate our social and physical environment entirely, making law 'real' in terms of it being something we actually physically and emotionally encounter in everyday life (Philippopoulos-Mihalopoulos, 2015). This idea that law affects both mind *and body*, through shaping the physical environment, creating atmosphere, and sending affective signals, is a significant extension to most of the extant propositions about why people obey the law. It can be seen for example to be a significant departure from the traditional rational choice theory of law practiced by classical jurists, penal theorists, police, and other criminal justice actors in which advertence to legal rules and norms was taken to be a conscious decision-making process, a weighing up of the pros and cons. It also runs a different path from current interest in procedural justice, in which concerns about legitimacy of decisions, decision-makers, and interactions are paramount to answering questions about legal compliance. These theories are all 'too social', in that they are committed to thinking about human action as choice—as something that is ultimately resolved in the mind—rather than considering people to be bodily participants in a matrix of material things, where ineffable metaphysics like atmospheres and affects play with emotional senses as physical human bodies interact with other material things.

De-centering the human in criminology is therefore a project that is, in some quarters, well underway, and so-called 'art worlds' (Becker, 1982) and the crimes they experience would seem to be a field ripe for this kind of study, since art dealers and collectors have developed a strong and pervasive narrative of the metaphysical meaning and impact of artworks, using terms such as 'aura' and 'spirit'. Art objects are also made more, or sometimes less, attractive to buyers and more ephemeral 'consumers' like museum-goers, with reference to their history. This is another aspect of the atmosphere surrounding an object that has nothing to do with its physical form but is all about the semiotic meaning it radiates: who owned it previously, whether it was part of a tantalising historical scandal, or what it was used for. Where the humanist viewpoint has traditionally seen "objects, things, artefacts and technologies" as essentially "quasi-inert 'in search of meaning' entities" (Caronia & Mortari, 2015), the posthumanist viewpoint which this chapter interrogates is based in what has been called 'the material turn' in the social sciences, which 'has questioned the basic assumption of... the ontological priority of the human subject over any other entity in the sense-making process' (Caronia & Mortari, 2015).

We move away therefore from a view of object agency which, following Gell's (1998) idea of distributed agency, sees cultural objects as being imbued with an extension of the agency of their human creator, user, or observer. A particularly directional version of this view sees cultural objects as being intentionally created by human artists who imbue them with a sense of purpose and a particular identity that renders them agentic as they make their way out into the world, connecting distant artist with users or 'consumers' who, through the object, are exposed to the mediated force of the original purpose or message (e.g., see Hodder, 2003). The object remains "nothing but a passive embodiment of human intentions" (Riggins, 1994, p. 1). Beyond this type of 'original agency' that art objects are given by their creators, we can also see a process of 'secondary agency' in which art objects and their material context generate new patterns of social—and in art markets, commercial—effects. While these meanings may be inscribed onto objects by human actors working to create a certain overall atmosphere for the market (Steiner, 2001), and an affective reach for particular objects, it would be a mistake to only think of these routines as people doing things to, and with, inanimate objects. The actual effect of these market practices is, we argue here, to create an object network that takes on something of a life of its own, created and curated by people but developing organic properties that result in a semi-independence from the forces that made and continue to attempt to manipulate it. This is a further step in the direction of object agency from the now conventional view that "even though from a theoretical point of view human actors encode things with significance, from a methodological point of view it is the things-in-motion that illuminate their human and social context" (Hoskins, 2006).

In this chapter, our proposition is that multi-sited follow-the-thing research (Foster, 2006; Marcus, 1995) and the study of objects in actor networks (Latour, 2005) or assemblages (Deleuze & Guattari, 1987) should be more than just a methodological way to approach the sequencing of research projects that seek to elicit the changing meanings inscribed by humans onto objects as they move or are recontextualised. We are looking for object agency that may reasonably be said to exist, in theory, beyond that methodological approach to the discovery and recording of social construction.

2 The Object Network of Art

Artistic objects exist in a wide network of other objects. While studies of art and the meaning it creates have tended to focus on the obvious objects, the art itself (e.g., Kersel, 2015), we would rather consider the entirety of the complex of objects that provide the context for the presentation of any particular artistic object. This is a move towards 'interobjectivity' (Latour, 1996): a world in which objects are also subjects, enjoying meaningful ties with other material things which influence their function or social meaning.

Becker's work on art worlds drew attention to the wide social networks that exist around the artist. The production of art is not only about individual creative types making wonderful new things, but also about the social, cultural, and economic support network that exists to make such things possible. In other words, art worlds have social context. When we look at an art world through this social context perspective, the artist is somewhat de-centred in favour of a type of realist sociological analysis that takes the creators of any particular artwork as including all of the facilitating people involved: the artist, of course, but also the dealer, the broker, the insurer, the sponsor, the gallery landlord, the paint supplier, and so on.

What happens if instead of looking at the human-oriented sociology of art worlds as Becker did, we were to look at the object-oriented 'thing-ology' of art worlds? How do objects form networks that structure and influence art worlds? These are the questions informing the approach we take in this chapter. And within that, the area of our focus is the thing-ology of a particular aspect of art worlds: crime related to ancient, religious, and so-called 'ethnographic' cultural objects. In respect to the latter, our core area of concern, we might begin by proposing that in most prior studies of trafficking cultural objects (including our own), the objects have been conceived as (a) passive and (b) being drawn into a network of human subjects. What if, to the contrary, we use an object-oriented perspective, considering objects to be (a) active and (b) constituting an object-network into which human subjects are drawn?

We can start with a list of objects that surround and contextualise the central object—the artwork—with the proviso that this is a selective list: simply some other objects of interest rather than an attempt to map the entirety of an object network for art. In no particular order, since this is a network not a hierarchy of influence, we might refer to three key locations in the art market: dealers' spaces, such as galleries and art fairs, auction houses, and museums, and within these, look at a variety of object networks and contexts, including things like the catalogue, the marketing materials, the nameplate and display cabinet write-up, other art objects said to be comparators, the auction gavel, the estimate, and the provenance documents. Let us consider these three locations in turn, along with some of the most relevant objects in each setting.

2.1 *Towards a Thing-ology of Dealers' Spaces*

The gallery cultivates a particular atmosphere somewhere between a museum and a shop, intended to make customers feel that while everything is for sale, this is not crass low-end consumerism but something more like a high-society cultural experience. Various things about the design of art dealership galleries create this impression, from the window displays, the arrangement of the art, the ambient music and lighting, not infrequently the location of the gallery itself in a city's art district (in which the context is set by a mutually reinforcing geographical network of art houses) and/or an affluent district with a prestigious address, and very often the absence of price-tags on the objects for sale. Pedestals may be used to elevate and highlight the art. Spotlighting can deliver a sense of importance, and exclusivity. Glass display cases, where used, bring to mind museum arrangements, implying that the objects for sale should be considered 'museum quality' and priced accordingly.

The art fair, as we have discussed elsewhere (Yates, 2021), is a sort of gallery roadshow, where dealers set up stalls to represent their galleries and to allow human-object intimacy to develop. These fairs can be seen as a site of relationship building, where humans and objects meet and form the kinds of connections that result in bonds that are meaningful to potential buyers, and which inspire sales. Speaking from his own experience as a book collector, philosopher Walter Benjamin wrote that "...for a collector—and I mean a real collector, a collector as he ought to be—ownership is the most intimate relationship that one can have to objects" (Benjamin,

2008, p. 262). Key to the creation of this relationship is the setting in which the objects appear or, more specifically, how those objects are presented within a matrix of other objects that, together, lures a human viewer towards entering into a human-object relationship. Objects appear in settings that are meant to evoke tombs, temples, churches, or museums. Asian pieces are interspersed with orchids or birds-of-paradise flowers, projecting an exotic object landscape that people enter. Each of these factors, and more, involve the use of things, places and spaces to create atmosphere, understanding and ideology.

In galleries and art fairs, the impression created by the assemblage of objects depends on the type of art on display. Asian antiquities may be presented with scented candles, cups of jasmine tea, and tropical jungle themes. Modern art might be set off with avant-garde furniture, large empty box-like white gallery spaces, and jazz music. Whatever the theme, co-ordination of the objects tends to be key to creating a potent object-network, as demonstrated by the rupture we can imagine if we think of an object that is out of place. Things come together to create settings, and these settings or contexts provide the structure within which we perceive the centrepiece objects that are for sale.

2.2 *Towards a Thing-ology of Art Auctions*

Now let us go deeper into the role of objects at art auctions. After all, these are one of the major cornerstones of the art market and aside from museums, possibly its most public face. Art auctions are a useful site of study here since the general unreflective impression of the role of 'things' at auction are simply that they are objects to be sold. Again, we see the standard reversion to a human-centred perspective where objects are passive and manipulated by us, in this case through the construction of trades between buyers and sellers. Our more object-sensitive perspective in this chapter, however, looks for more agency from things and seeks to map and understand the influence of the networks of objects as cross-referential systems of meaning and affect.

On 29 June 2020, Sotheby's New York held their "Contemporary Art Evening Auction". The content of this sale was primarily, as the title suggested, contemporary art with artists such as Lichtenstein, Basquiat, Rothko, Moore, and Bacon represented. Out of 30 lots, 27 sold for more than US$1 million, and the Bacon work sold for US$84,550,000. Notably, due to the COVID-19 pandemic, there was no audience for this auction, and bidding was conducted entirely online or via phone. Yet the object-object networks were still strongly manifest in this sale, their connections and associations influencing the behaviour of potential buyers without physical interactions with them. This is clear from the inclusion of what could be seen as an unexpected piece in this 'contemporary art' sale. Between lot 115,[1] Night

[1] Lots in this sale were numbered 100–130.

Sky #7 by Vija Celmins (1995) and lot 116, an untitled 1985 work by Jean-Michel Basquiat, was a wooden head crafted by an unknown artist in nineteenth century Gabon.

Seen from the perspective we propose, the head is not a non-contemporary intruder into a sale of contemporary art, but rather a node in an object network that creates desire and lures buyers. This 'desire-scape' (discussed further below) is created by associating the ancient object with modern art. Because some of its aesthetics are thought to be comparable to these later great works, the older object is presented as an early point on a continuum that arrives at the famous contemporary artists and their works, which make up most of the sale catalogue. That is, the object context in which the wooden head is presented gives it a particular resonance in terms of its artistic relevance that it would not otherwise have had.

Note, when and under what circumstance this head left Gabon is not presented in the text. Its first appearance the market is in the 1930s. It is possible that theft, criminality, or colonial domination led to the presence of the head in this catalogue, something that should always be emphasised about unprovenanced cultural objects.

Within initial photographs, the head is not alone. It stands on a chipped and worn pedestal which at once both recalls the setting of museum display and thus value, and also the 'auction block': the head is for sale. Scrolling downward in the digital catalogue, the viewer is presented with a series of associations: a provenance history that includes humans, but also two other sales events where the head appeared at auction. Next the viewer sees a list of seven physical books and five museum exhibitions that the head has appeared within. In both cases, the presence of the head among other objects in the museums and in the books (the museums and books themselves being material things that the head interacted with, part of the wider network) lends legitimacy to the piece, asserting value from association, and creating desire within potential buyers.

Scrolling further down, a viewer reaches the most tangible representation of the object-object network that may provoke buyer response. The Catalogue Note, which traditionally contained a simple one-line description of the object for sale, has grown to over 1000 words, 11 images of other objects, and a dramatic one-minute video. Through this presentation, buyers have no choice but to look beyond the head in question to a series of object-object relationships that they, the buyers, find meaningful, with that meaning then inspiring their behaviour.

Within the video, the head spins around on the pedestal, with dramatic lighting and music. Words such as "Before Modigliani" and "Before Basquiat" flash across the screen, connecting the head not to those men, but rather to their art objects, emphasising an association that appears to rest outside of human control. Indeed, while the writing in the Catalogue Note clearly identifies the collected network of African art as "a direct inspiration, propelling the formal ideas of the Western artists", an assertion that fits our model of human response to object networks, it is the seemingly more indirect object-object associations presented in this sale that reveal more of the landscape of desire that people enter into when they interact with art object worlds.

The viewer of this nineteenth century head from Gabon within a Contemporary (meaning inevitably European and American) art auction is presented with photographs of the famous Nike of Samothrace (Greek, 200 B.C.), a Bronze Age Cycladic figurine head (Greek, 2500 B.C.), and undated Bodhisattva sculpture from a temple in Kyoto. The text says that the head "recalls" the "forward energy" of the Nike of Samothrace, the "simple gravity" of the Cycladic figurine, and the "sublime expression" of the Bodhisattva. The viewer then sees a Picasso sculpture and painting and a sculpture by Brancusi, followed by five additional photographs of other African sculptural heads, and one older photo of the head for sale. With this, multiple object networks become connected to each other through the node of the African head for sale, with all of their further object associations and meanings converging to create what might be an irresistible web of value for the viewer. Effectively it would seem: the head sold for US$3,530,000.

While the large number of pictures of other objects present alongside the previously discussed head serve to make some of the desire-provoking object networks at play obvious, even objects that appear at auction without an immediately present web of connection to draw value from attract through the object networks that they are part of. At times these object connections can be quite disturbing, luring via a network of objects that reflect unsettling manifestations of dominance, control, and crime.

Take for example lot 49 of Sotheby's May 2017 "Art of Africa, Oceania, and the Americas" sale. The piece in question is presented as being a "Flesh Fork" from Fiji. Again, the circumstances under which this object was taken from Fiji are not presented and, as an unprovenanced piece, it is possible that it appears in this sale due to crime, violence, or colonial control. The Catalogue Note states:

> Few objects draw such macabre fascination as the flesh forks of Fiji, which have long had the popular name of 'cannibal forks' due to the mistaken notion that human flesh was so special that none dared touch it with their fingers. Whilst cannibalism was practiced in Fiji, the notoriety of these objects owes a good deal to Victorian sensationalism and the European fascination with anthropophagy.

Prior to this sale, Sotheby's and its rival Christie's had always referred to these objects as 'cannibal forks', and in the 22 prior sales we found of this type of object across the two houses, no mention was made of the problematic nature of the identification or name.

To some degree, the reflection on the market notoriety of these pieces and the name change, from 'cannibal forks' to 'flesh forks', is a manifestation of contemporary societal trends which sees the gross exoticisation and commodification of the material manifestations of colonialism as being something that a culturally respectful buyer cannot openly take part in. However, in repeated reference to the 'cannibal forks' of past, 'European fascination', and three paragraphs of text that emphasise the association of these objects with human flesh made into an object via cannibalism, we find suggestive evidence that troubling but alluring object networks are influencing buyers. "History is exactly the currency that things trade in" (Brown, 2004, p. 13), and this is a 'cannibal fork' for a buyer who has been caught by the overwhelming narrative of those colonial object associations, an object network radiating from racism and domination. Again, as in the case with the head, these networks appear to be extremely effective at luring buyers. The 'cannibal fork' that is not a 'cannibal fork' sold for US$16,250, much higher than its estimated price of US$3000–6000.

2.3 *Towards a Thing-ology of the Museum*

In her ethnography of so-called "Tribal Art" at auction (Geismar, 2001, p. 32) noted that "the museum collection [is] the ultimate reference point by which objects are judged, defining criteria of rarity, authenticity and desirability". The objects in museums, then, become the touchstone against which all other objects are considered, and the network of object relationships that radiate out from museums are the ultimate source of validity within the antiquities market. This is particularly the case with so-called unprovenanced or looted antiquities: antiquities removed from their original archaeological context without being documented and in a situation that was likely illegal (Mackenzie et al., 2019). In this circumstance, which is thought to represent the vast majority of antiquities on the market, validity cannot come from an object network formed from shared archaeological context. Instead, museums, as respected cultural institutions and, more so, as repositories for objects and object relationships, form a nexus point where object networks are maintained and preserved.

Both the dealers and the auction houses discussed above respond to the power that museum-based object networks have over consumers. As noted previously, within gallery and art fair settings, many objects are presented in a pseudo-museum setting. Object labels, pedestals and stands, even the lighting of stalls mimic the physicality of the museum space. Within auction catalogues, objects such as the head from Gabon are photographed on a museum-style block, pedestal or mount, and are again labelled with museum-style information. In both circumstances, associations that the object for sale has with museums, such as prior placement among 'real' museum objects in an exhibition or even just a physical resemblance to a museum piece, are featured prominently.

Consider, the term 'Tribal Art' itself, used by Geismar above and applied to both the African and the Oceanic objects discussed in the previous section. The controversial term, along with its equally racist synonyms 'Ethnographic Art' and 'Primitive Art', sees cultural objects from Africa, Oceania, and the Native cultures of the Americas as comprising the same category of art.[2] On the market they are presented

[2] Even individually "African", "Oceanic", and "Native American" are not accurate terms as they crudely lump together cultural traditions which usually have no relationship with each other beyond externally-defined geographic boundaries. That the market, and we authors if reluctantly, lump them speaks to the influence undesirable objects networks have on people.

together in the same auction catalogues, sold together by the same dealers, and collected by the same collectors. Thus, the term 'Tribal Art', itself, can be seen as a manifestation of complicated object networks that effectively lure white humans to form connections and make purchases. Yet these objects have no relationship with each other in their original cultural contexts: a 150-year-old wooden sculpture from Papua New Guinea has no cultural connection to a 700-year-old brass plaque from Benin, which in turn has no cultural connection to a 3000-year-old jade mask from Mexico. Their association, and the origin of the networks that bind these objects together, is enshrined in the museum.

The history and controversial nature of 'ethnographic museums', a particular type of European museum that emerged from the spoils of imperial and colonial domination and control, is beyond the scope of this chapter. Suffice to say, however, that with these museums, objects form connections with other objects: relationships that could never occur in their original context. When arranged by 'type', a Zulu iwisa, or ceremonial club-like walking stick, is placed next to a club from the Solomon Islands, a Kwakwaka'wakw mask from Vancouver Island is placed next to a mask from the Sepik River region of Papua New Guinea, and the physical boundaries between them begin to blur. New associations form and, from them, object networks that permeate the market.

In this respect, the social lives of archaeological objects as brought together in museum collections are gatherings of 'strangers': objects effectively unknown to each other, unrelated in culture and unconnected in history. These gatherings of strangers then, through the relationship between the museum collection and the art market, create group categories of artefacts that take on a referential function of their own, coming together as sections of the art market—'Tribal', 'Primitive', and so on—and pulling collectors into their orbit, becoming coherent as a network of objects where previously they were not, through this process of gathering, labelling and institutionalising.

3 Object Networks and Art Crime

Moving then into how object networks might inspire a form of lure or desire that could eventually lead to the violation of ethical or social norms or the committing of a crime, we can consider a case that we have discussed at length in prior publications (Mackenzie & Davis, 2014a, 2014b): that of a stolen Cambodian statue that was offered for sale at Sotheby's in 2011. While a complete retelling of this case unnecessary, some aspects of it appear to fit the framing we discuss here. The statue in question, as well as several others, once formed a battle scene within a temple at the site of Koh Ker. Stolen sometime in the 1970s, by the 2000s all of the statues had ended up in the United States and in the possession of various public and private museums, and at Sotheby's and Christie's auction houses. Documents released by Sotheby's during a suit for the statue's return to Cambodia revealed that auction house employees were aware that the piece did come from Koh Ker as the feet of the statue in question and some of the others had been located still at the site.

Rather than the presence of the feet within the physical temple grounds signalling evidence of crime, the object network of the feet—connected to the temple, connected to the Sotheby's statue, connected to the other statues within the United States—became interwoven with desire on the part of Sotheby's (and, presumably buyers). Sotheby's employees experienced this object network as proof that the statue was authentic, rather than as proof that the statue was stolen, increasing the statue's value. Desire to sell into and buy into the authenticity created by that object network, then, could be seen as leading auction house employees towards actions that, in this case, resulted in a lawsuit and a repatriation.

In our fieldwork, we have become aware of the occasional practice of more dubious dealers showing prospective buyers photos of objects at the point of being looted (see for example Yates, 2015). This achieves a similar effect to the proof of authenticity the remnant feet had in the case of the statue from Koh Ker. Where a buyer knows, as most do, that the antiquities trade is full of fakes, a photograph showing an object being pulled from the ground seems like the ultimate proof of authenticity, as well as criminality. The object here is the centrepiece of a network connecting and contextualised by other objects like the photo, the shovel, the hole, the various atmospheric paraphernalia of the dealer's back room where the customer has been ushered to view this illicit photographic proof, other looted objects known in the market and displayed/legitimised in museums, and so on. All of these objects create a web of reference that creates the meaning of the moment: the illicit chance to acquire a real find, something ancient, something hitherto unknown, something valuable.

Such is the known power of tricks of the trade like the 'act of looting' photo that they are reported by insiders to have become scams in which fake antiquities are dropped in the hole before the photo is taken and then 'excavated' in front of the camera as apparent proof of their new discovery, and thus authenticity. This is a kind of semiotic gerrymandering where the meaning of objects—in this case the photo—becomes confused beyond repair, so that now nobody really knows what to make of the 'proof of looting' photo: it may indicate authenticity, or it may very well not.

Another interesting aspect of the sales tactics employed by Sotheby's in marketing the Cambodian statue was the transformation of the idea of the object in a gallery to the idea of the object in a home. The auction house employed an expert to give a publicity talk ahead of the auction to raise interest in the statue, and this talk was accompanied by a slideshow that was made publicly available as an item of evidence in the subsequent lawsuit between Cambodia and Sotheby's. After covering the historical importance of the object, the slideshow ends with an attempt to transform an ancient statue from a temple in a far-flung jungle into a work of art to be displayed in a private residence. Accompanied by a picture of the statue in such a new private setting, the slideshow says it would be 'easy to live with' and suggests to prospective buyers that they should 'buy it and turn the light on'. This recontextualisation of a statue from a faraway archaeological outdoors context into a closer to home, artistic, indoors context is a strategy that uses the power of object networks to create suggestive scenes in order to make the process of commodification and marketisation complete. It brings the statue into a relationship of reference to other surrounding objects both explicit, like the light, and implicit, like other items imagined to be in such a living room setting. These contextualising objects are a material network that generates meaning, connecting with and influencing the emotional dispositions of the consumer through the impression of an imagined desirable future. Everyone can enjoy these object effects, including the creative individuals who have built the imagined scene. The reason creatives know that such object network creations will have the desired tempting effects on consumers is that they can feel them too, so they know they have got it right when they can themselves feel the power of the scene they have created.

3.1 The Social Lives of Objects or the Objectification of Social Life?

Appadurai, in the introductory chapter of his famous collection *The Social Life of Things* (1986), observed along with his contributors that commodities are 'thoroughly socialised things' (p. 6). In this, they have meaning ascribed to them by the humans trading them, and for the time of their commodification the most important thing about their 'social life' is their exchangeability (p. 13). Humans defining objects as commodities, thereby influencing their social life, is one way of looking at trade. It seems quite a conceited anthropomorphic view: as if the most important thing about objects is what we make of them, their lives being understood as social, like ours. If we return to our earlier consideration of the view that the agency of objects is mainly a feature of their original purposeful creation, then the subsequent affective properties of emergent object assemblages which rework, amplify, dilute, or pervert that 'original agency', as we have called it, seems adequately to be caught in the notion of the social life of things. Beyond their original purpose, things develop a social life as they interact over time with other objects and people.

However, in keeping with our contrarian view of human-object relations in this chapter, perhaps we should ask not how the objects appear from the human perspective, but how the humans appear from the object perspective. Rather than think of objects as being social, can we think of the social as being objectified? That is, to what extent does an object-oriented viewpoint deplete the sense of subjectivity in human agents, and present instead a persuasive picture of objectified humans, directed by object networks? If it sounds overly deterministic, our orientation towards the forces of affect in this chapter should help us distinguish determinism from the softer tones of *influence*, which humans feel in their 'object lives'.

We also draw attention here to the recursiveness we consider to be present in the human-object relations in actor networks. Latour (1993) said, "it is the same task to define the artefact tying together the various groups or the groups tying together one artefact". From which we take the suggestion that moving one's analytical perspective from that of the humans to that of the objects should not be as vexing to sociology or criminology as it might seem. It is affronting to move from talking about the social lives of objects towards talking about the object life of society, but as we explore the empirical research we have conducted over the years on art worlds and their societies it is hard to resist the sense that some art world denizens are indeed living 'object lives' and that the social structures that have grown up around the trade and collection of art are the shadows cast by the object networks and the acquisitive and appreciative emotions they engender, more than they are free-standing social institutions calculated to exploit objects to the benefit of social life.

To say, following Kopytoff (1986), that objects should be regarded as having 'life histories' and that one should therefore be able to write up 'object biographies' may be appealing to sociologists and anthropologists as it plays to their temptation to anthropomorphise the material world, explaining it through the same lens they have used to analyse the social. This anthropomorphism is sometimes implicit, but also sometimes explicit, performed as a particular thought exercise to elicit object biographies that may reveal aspects of the social lives of objects that might not have otherwise been noticed (e.g., Meskell, 2004). Either way, whether explicit or implied, object biographies are socially constructed vehicles for the encapsulation, explanation and exploitation of commodified art. As well as object biographies compiled by academics as a methodological tool applied for research purposes, less rigorously interpreted object biographies are created by the market as part of the attempts that people make to engage with objects, to array them, to profit from them, and to acquire them. These attempts themselves become 'objectified' in the form of plinth labels, catalogue write-ups, prior sales data, collections that aggregate objects for comparison and display, and so on. These are the structures through which the so-called 'social lives' of objects are constructed and lived. They are the social effects (and affects) of objects returned to those objects through a process of meaning-making; a social construction of objects that is a process itself captured by the power of the objects themselves; a recursive and difficult-to-separate ongoing dialogue of human and object agency.

4 Conclusion: Desirescapes

The nature of the thing-networks we have described here is to create desire for artistic objects. Why not simply consider the whole process to be a contemporary manifestation of consumer capitalism, in which sellers use clever sales techniques to influence prospective buyers to want their objects, and leave it at that? The kind of straightforward instrumentalism involved in a 'sociology of consumption' approach, or a 'marketing and communications' approach, or any other current disciplinary framework for dissecting contemporary sales practices, seems too reductionist in light of the observations we have made about the power of objects and the complex networks they create, amplifying affect through the internal references the networks generate. Just as the 'lawscape' is conceived as an intersection of space and the law

(Philippopoulos-Mihalopoulos, 2015), it may help to think of art worlds as *desirescapes* where a spatial array of myriad objects cultivates desire among individuals to collect, own, possess, and show off the things at the centre of the network, the art.

We arrive at a picture of people caught up in a web of objects that are affecting to the point that they not only generate and manipulate desire, but they disturb reason. Collectors of art regularly report this sensation: the feeling that they must have an object at all costs: 'it just spoke to me', 'the connection was overwhelming'. Belk, in his research on the psychology of collecting, interprets these sentiments as occurring when collectors "have gone beyond mere passion and are *possessed* by the objects of their desire" [emphasis added] (1995, p. 80).[3] Art sales defy standard economic analysis, as seemingly wild and crazy prices are sometimes paid for objects that are the focus of a hot and competitive desire among frenzied bidders. There is a well-acknowledged circumvention of reason in the processes of buying some art, especially high-end and absurdly priced art.

That is not meant to sound pejorative for this temporary abandonment of rational engagement with the world is the wonderful, celebrated effect of the art experience and considered proof, tautologically, that the experience is indeed real. 'It must be true: it caused me to lose my mind!' In our studies of trafficking ancient cultural objects, overwhelming desire such as this is one of the key criminogenic factors at work. Respondents in our research have described it in various ways, using words like temptation and lure. Buying or selling an illicit cultural object knowing or suspecting that it was looted is a legal infraction that seems to be quite well explained in terms of humans (more passive than they are usually taken to be) being ensnared in an affective and alluring network of objects (more active than they are usually taken to be). All of those objects have themselves been made by humans, you say, and quite so. Our answer recalls Geertz on culture:

> Believing, with Max Weber, that man is an animal suspended in webs of significance he himself has spun: I take culture to be those webs, and the analysis of it to be therefore not an experimental science in search of law but an interpretive one in search of meaning. (Geertz, 1973, p. 5)

So it is with affective object networks. People create culture and their culture creates them in return. Likewise, and of course connected to and part of the manifestation of culture, people create objects and those objects also create them in return. Material *desirescapes* are made by, and make, choices and behaviour.

The next step in this line of thinking for the practical, rather than the theoretical, interests of criminology might be to think about crime prevention priorities in terms

[3] Although Belk does not consider objects to have agency in their own right, rather favours the idea of objects as "fetishes", with agentic qualities existing entirely in the mind of the beholder (Belk, 1995, p. 146). This use of "fetish" follows from Marx's use of the term, implying a misrecognition of the object on the part of the beholder (Sansi Roca, 2015). We do not consider the idea of collectors misinterpreting some idea of objective reality to be particularly useful to our current discussion.

of changing the network properties of these webs of alluring objects, rather than focussing on the more traditional technique of dissuading individuals from committing crime through responding to these allures. The law governing this space currently establishes, as is normal, penalties for dealing in looted cultural property but does little to destabilise the atmosphere of art worlds which are conducive to criminal activity. So many of the 'atmospheric' attributes of the field can be traced around the things that make up the material aspects of the networks. These atmospheres include things like: the norms of privacy; an assumed legitimacy attributed to sellers absent overwhelming evidence to the contrary (and sometimes even in that case); the high social status and economic power of some of the key participants; the vested financial interests of the major institutional actors like the auction houses; the culture of trading that instils in buyers a reluctance to ask piercing questions about provenance whether through feelings of naivety or wanting to keep a dealer onside so as not to lose out on future opportunities to buy; and the depth of the systemic production of allure by the inter-lacing of objects.

The conclusion for future research on art crime is straightforward but also challenging: as well as the *people* involved we should look more closely at the *things* that make up art worlds.

Acknowledgements The funding for this research was provided by the European Research Council (ERC) under the European Union's Horizon 2020 research and innovation programme (grant agreement n° 804851) and from European Commission EAC/06/2017 "Improving Knowledge on Illicit Trade in Cultural Goods in the EU".

References

Appadurai, A. (1986). Introduction; commodities and the politics of value. In A. Appadurai (Ed.), *The social life of things: Commodities in cultural perspective* (pp. 64–91). Cambridge University Press.

Becker, H. S. (1982). *Art worlds*. University of California Press.

Belk, R. W. (1995). *Collecting in a consumer society*. Routledge.

Benjamin, W. (2008). Unpacking my library: A talk about book collecting. In F. Candlin & R. Guins (Eds.), *The object reader*. Routledge.

Brown, B. (2004). Thing theory. In B. Brown (Ed.), *Things* (pp. 1–22). University of Chicago Press.

Caronia, L., & Mortari, L. (2015). The agency of things: How spaces and artefacts organize the moral order of an intensive care unit. *Social Semiotics, 25*(4), 401–422.

Deleuze, G., & Guattari, F. (1987). *A thousand plateaus*. Athlone Press.

Foster, R. J. (2006). Tracking globalization: Commodities and value in motion. In C. Tilley, W. Keane, S. Küchler, M. Rowlands, & P. Spyer (Eds.), *Handbook of material culture* (pp. 285–302). Sage.

Fraser, A., & Matthews, D. (2019). Towards a criminology of atmospheres: Law, affect and the codes of the street. *Criminology & Criminal Justice*. https://doi.org/10.1177/1748895819874853

Geertz, C. (1973). *The interpretation of cultures*. Basic Books.

Geismar, H. (2001). What's in a price? An ethnography of tribal art at auction. *Journal of Material Culture, 6*(1), 25–47.

Gell, A. (1998). *Art and agency: An anthropological theory*. Oxford University Press.

Hodder, I. (2003). The 'Social' in archaeological theory: An historical and contemporary perspective. In L. Meskell & R. Pruecel (Eds.), *A companion to social archaeology* (pp. 23–42). Blackwell.
Hoskins, J. (2006). Agency, biography and objects. In C. Tilley, W. Keane, S. Küchler, M. Rowlands, & P. Spyer (Eds.), *Handbook of material culture* (pp. 74–84). Sage.
Kersel, M. M. (2015). The lure of the artefact? The effects of acquiring eastern Mediterranean material culture. In A. B. Knapp & P. Van Dommelen (Eds.), *The Cambridge prehistory of the bronze and iron age Mediterranean*. Cambridge University Press.
Kopytoff, I. (1986). The cultural biography of things. In A. Appadurai (Ed.), *The social life of things: Commodities in cultural perspective* (pp. 64–91). Cambridge University Press.
Latour, B. (1993). Ethnography of a 'high-tech' case: About Aramis. In P. Lemonnier (Ed.), *Technological choices: Transformation in material cultures since the neolithic* (pp. 372–398). Routledge.
Latour, B. (1996). On interobjectivity. *Mind, Culture and Activity, 3*(4), 228–245.
Latour, B. (2005). *Reassembling the social: An introduction to actor-network theory*. Oxford University Press.
Mackenzie, S., & Davis, T. (2014a). Cambodian statue trafficking networks: An empirical report from regional case study fieldwork. In S. Manacorda & A. Visconti (Eds.), *Protecting cultural heritage as a common good of humanity: A challenge for criminal justice*. ISPAC.
Mackenzie, S., & Davis, T. (2014b). Temple looting in Cambodia: Anatomy of a statue trafficking network. *British Journal of Criminology, 54*(5), 722–740.
Mackenzie, S., Brodie, N., Yates, D., & Tsirogiannis, C. (2019). *Trafficking culture: New directions in researching the global market in illicit antiquities*. Routledge.
Marcus, G. E. (1995). Ethnography in/of the world system: The emergence of multi-sited ethnography. *Annual Review of Anthropology, 24*, 95–117.
Meskell, L. (2004). *Object worlds in ancient Egypt: Material biographies past and present*. Berg.
Philippopoulos-Mihalopoulos, A. (2015). *Spatial justice: Body, lawscape, atmosphere*. Routledge.
Riggins, S. H. (1994). Introduction. In S. H. Riggins (Ed.), *The socialness of things: Essays on the socio-semiotics of objects* (pp. 1–6). Mouton de Gruyter.
Sansi Roca, R. (2015). Fetishism. In J. D. Wright (Ed.), *International encyclopedia of the social & behavioral sciences* (pp. 105–110). Elsevier.
Steiner, C. (2001). Rights of passage: On the liminal identity of art in the border zone. In F. Myers (Ed.), *The empire of things: Regimes of value and material culture* (pp. 207–231). School of American Research Press.
Yates, D. (Forthcoming, 2021). Crime and its objects: Human/object relationships and the market for illicit Latin American antiquities. In *Expolio: le realidad que deja objetos huerfanos de context*. Dossier Débat. Mélange de la Casa de Velázquez.
Yates, D. (2015). Photographs of the looting of Placeres, Mexico. *Trafficking Culture Website*. Retrieved March 10, 2021, from https://traffickingculture.org/data/placeres/
Young, A. (2021). Architecture as affective law enforcement: Theorising the Japanese Koban. *Crime, Media, Culture*. https://doi.org/10.1177/1741659021993527

Authentically Exotic and Authentically Beautiful

Constructing the Authenticity of Peruvian Antiquities at Sotheby's and eBay

Federica Villa

Abstract Influenced by many cultural, economic and historic factors, the antiquities market of Andean archaeological artefacts is a complex issue. Authenticity is one of the most important aspects upon which the attribution of value within the antiquities trade depends. On the one hand, a theoretical discourse around the concept of 'constructed authenticity' inevitably derives from the contradiction generated between the almost total absence of data regarding archaeological provenience and the value assigned to these commodified antiquities. On the other, like beauty and culture, the opposition between true and false is also culturally constructed and changes throughout an object's biography. I argue that authenticity can be polysemic and Peruvian antiquities that cannot be authenticated archaeologically can be perceived as authentic differently: authentically exotic or authentically beautiful. Even though e-commerce and in-person auction houses have many divergences, a comparison allows for a focus on the cross issues connected to authenticity. Indeed, a juxtaposition of two listings offering similar items on sale in eBay and Sotheby's allows a discussion on how those artefacts are perceived outside of the national borders where they were collected, and how this perception impacts on selling techniques and venues.

1 Introduction

The first time I had contact with Andean pre-Columbian pottery was in a European ethnographic museum. I was fascinated enough by it that the next time I observed that kind of object was in the field, during an archaeological excavation in Peru. I also found pre-Columbian vessels again in small local museums in Peruvian provinces and in big museums in the capital. In these museums' shops, replica vessels were on sale. Moreover, ancient pottery souvenirs were sold in local shops, which I visited as a tourist. Later in Lima, I met craftspeople who celebrate the origins by

F. Villa (✉)
Mudec—Museum of Cultures, Milano, Italy

N. Oosterman, D. Yates (eds.), *Crime and Art*, Studies in Art, Heritage, Law and the Market 1, https://doi.org/10.1007/978-3-030-84856-9_9

making their own pottery art through ancient iconography and ancient techniques. Finally, I came across Peruvian pre-Columbian pottery in Europe again, while working as an intern in a Museum of Cultures and when I was studying for my master's degree in a research centre on world cultures. After so many different encounters with Andean pottery over the years, in different places and I being in different positions myself, I started to question how I experienced their authenticity in relation to the contexts in which they were inserted: how were these various Peruvian vessels contextualised according to their perceived authenticity?

Authenticity is defined as "the quality of being real or true" by the Cambridge Dictionary. However, it is rarely so simple to define it, especially when referring to objects such as pre-Columbian antiquities. While it can be straightforward to designate an antiquity as authentic when it can be clearly associated to a specific authorship, time frame, and geographical origin, it is indeed quite hard to grasp the significance of such a notion when analysing how it is affirmed within the context of the grey market of antiquities.[1]

When an archaeological artefact from Peru enters the market, it becomes a commodity, which means that it undergoes a "cognitive process" (Kopitoff, 1986, p. 9) of attribution of market value, thus price, in order to be traded. In the antiquities market, authenticity is possibly the most important element to attribute value, it is in other words the "deal-breaker" (Yates, 2015). An object considered to be of highest quality, rarity, or beauty can lose its market value when its connection to the past is torn apart by doubt.

Because authenticity is the focus of this analysis, the phenomenon of fakes cannot be disregarded. The forgery problem within the pre-Columbian market has largely been recognised and discussed in academia (see e.g., Boone, 1982; Bruhns & Kelker, 2010; Sease, 2007). However, it is a continuing mutable phenomenon that needs constant investigation.

Following some political changes that occurred in the end of the 1960s and the foundation of the *Istituto de Cultura* in 1972, the risks connected to looting activity[2] were increasing but market demand for Peruvian antiquities was not diminishing. By consequence, forgery production that had already started from the second half of the nineteenth century, improved in style and technique in order to supply the demand from European and North American museums, tourists, and private collectors (Gänger, 2014, pp. 83–91; Sonin, 1982, p. 23). Forgers were well aware that they needed to appeal to European or North American collectors' taste. As Pasztory (2002, p. 162) argued: "Sometimes forgeries are better than real because they fit our ideas better". Fakes are thus the expression of our projection of pre-Columbian

[1] The expression 'grey market' refers to the opacity of the market of antiquities, to the complexity of its legal and illegal, public and private dynamics, to the "moral ambiguity" of taking part in it and to the impossibility to separate the legal and illegal markets (Mackenzie & Yates, 2017).

[2] Which existed since the Conquest and deeply damaged many archaeological sites in Peru (see Alva, 2001).

cultures and looking at their evolution through history is an action of acknowledging our perception of the "beyond in time and space" (Pasztory, 2002).

Their appeal in the art market has resulted in their spread to the point where Bruhns and Kelker asserted that at least 40% of pieces presented in art sales, displayed in museums, or described in catalogues and books, are fakes (2010, p. 192). The presence of fakes is certainly problematic as undetected forgeries have an "accumulative effect" that can alter our understanding of ancient styles (see Sawyer, 1982). Therefore, in order to persuade buyers to acquire antiquities within such a risky market, proof of authenticity should be clearly stated during any kind of transaction, especially when referring to objects that are frequently looted or faked. How is authenticity affirmed in online and in-person transactions according to the contexts where they take place?

As it would not be possible in this chapter to look into all the frameworks in which these antiquities might be traded and claimed as authentic, I focus on in-person and online market venues. Many have investigated the articulated on-line world and the mundane sphere of auction houses using different approaches (see e.g., Brodie, 2014a, 2015; Chippindale & Gill, 2000, 2001; Fay, 2011, 2013; Yates, 2006). This chapter will compare Sotheby's and eBay listings to identify the variations in the definition of authenticity that occur when Peruvian antiquities, specifically pre-Columbian ceramics, enter the market.

To deliver this qualitative analysis I will use the lens of constructivism, which states that authenticity is not a fixed attribute of an item but is instead negotiable. This allows us to understand that the definition of authentic Peruvian antiquities on the market fluctuates depending on sellers' selection of authenticity markers. Therefore, I argue that Peruvian antiquities' identity is not static nor is their attribution of authenticity.

2 Variation in Authenticity: A Constructivist Approach

Debates around authenticity are primarily philosophical. Specifically, heritage authenticity has been long discussed by experts in different fields, therefore with many different approaches of analysis.[3] In terms of interpreting Peruvian antiquities' authenticity within the market, I distance myself from the materialist approach, which is typical of heritage conservation and management and points out that authenticity is an objective and intrinsic characteristic depending on material, design, production, and use. I have instead applied a constructivist approach, that is based on the idea that authenticity is a cultural construct. The authentication process is considered a multi-sided negotiation generated in the relationship between people, things, and context and, in some way, even objects' materiality (see Jones, 2010; Holtorf, 2013). In general, things' genuineness depends on mutable elements

[3] See Jones (2010) for a comprehensive bibliography and a history of approaches to authenticity.

such as the beholders' judgment and interpretation, personal expectations and beliefs, or historical and power dynamics (Reisinger & Steiner, 2006). I will thus consider that the biography of an artefact influences its perception as authentic, and that simultaneously its authenticity depends on the current social and cultural context as well as on the concurrent setting and interpersonal relationship between dealers and buyers.

Peruvian antiquities are complex and are themselves located within the complex and perpetually changing system of art and culture. As the system itself has not reached an ultimate form, none of the art or culture objects that constitute it are stationary (Clifford, 1988, p. 226) and the values and meanings associated with and given to collectibles change over context and history. These views have also influenced contemporary attitudes towards them. From the Spaniards' 'gold fever' and 'idolatry extirpation', through the antiquarian interest and fascination for the 'exotic other', to the first professional archaeological approaches, ethnographic pedagogical studies, and interest from the avant-garde, the same objects have been defined as ethnographic artefact, archaeological data, or full-fledged 'Work of Art', depending on non-indigenous conceptions and expectations. Throughout these centuries, European and North American appreciation of different categories of indigenous objects have determined, and still determine how Peruvian antiquities are valued in the modern globalised world. As these objects have lost their original functions, their meaning has come to depend on the subjective point of view. In this case, as the market direction is mainly toward higher income countries in the global north, European and North American perceptions of objects is still fundamental in how their value is defined within a specific collection and within the market.

Looking at objects as entities with specific biographies, we accept that their 'identity'—namely their meaning and value—depend on human perceptions of it. Moreover, when cultural heritage enters the market, it changes its trajectory and undergoes what Appadurai calls a "tournament of value" (1986, p. 21): it enters the world of commodities and a price is attributed to it. We define 'price' as the monetary amount that the market assigns to an object, while 'value' is the "set of judgments surrounding the assignment of price that are established in a multiplicity of ways—social, political and so on" (Geismar, 2001, p. 28).

Many factors contribute to determining an item's price. Context, trends, appeal of specific categories, provenance, recent discoveries, and rarity are among the circumstantial definers of value. Furthermore, historical relevance or artistic qualities obviously influence an item's value and have historically dominated the interest in Peruvian antiquities of academic research and the market. The duality of aesthetic appreciation and historicity is still relevant today (see Ortiz, 2006, p. 15, 21).

The art-artefact debate is complex and cannot be comprehensively analysed here. However, considering the theoretic frame of Clifford's (1988) art-culture system scheme I believe that archaeological objects are not necessarily just fixed entities. In my opinion, authentic antiquities fluctuate between two semantic zones, authentic artefacts or authentic masterpieces, and their prevalent meaning is attributed by the observer. Moreover, I believe that another semantic layer exists when non-European antiquities enter the scheme: the 'authentic exotic' or 'authentic primitive'. The feeling of ‘curiosity’ for the ‘Other’, which characterised the encyclopaedic cabinet of curiosities from the sixteenth to the eighteenth century, is a mindset that persists in some market settings of Peruvian antiquities.

Peruvian antiquities are multifaceted and complex entities *per se*, and they embed a diverse spectrum of authenticity interpretation depending on their position within personal or commercial interrelations. An ancient pre-Columbian ceramic pot on sale in the market, within a North American or European context as I am considering here, is in the first place a commodity. Secondly it can be considered having the intrinsic characteristics of an *interesting* archaeological object, a *primitive/curious* ethnographic artefact and a *beautiful* piece of art. Indeed, they are listed among “American antiquities” on eBay and along with Oceanic and African Art at Sotheby’s. Given their peculiar status as commodities, Peruvian antiquities have many different internalised identities originating from their complex biographies. Thus, the representation of an authentic commodified archaeological-ethnographic-artistic object is strategic and not necessarily coherent, as it takes advantage of the selective exploit of a specific identity out of the object’s history (see Geismar, 2001, p. 26).

While historical relevance of Peruvian antiquities is something that cannot be disregarded, the archaeological perspective based on scientific data or excavation documentation seems to have a secondary role for the specific analysis that I present with this chapter. What seems to matter more is what Holtorf describe as “pastness”, namely the “quality of being of the past” which is “the result of a particular perception or experience and as such it is firmly situated in a given cultural context” (2013, p. 430). The perception of an archaeological object “pastness” depends on different factors such as material clues, plausible stories that connect the objects to the past and the observer’s prejudices to be met (Holtorf, 2013, pp. 430–435).

As demand is what drives the market, buyer expectations must be considered as one of the most important factors in this specific authenticity negotiation: sellers have to choose markers and set up attractive settings to present their items in specific ways in order to lure the buyer and meet what they believe authenticity to be. If a museum label can convince the visitor that an artefact is authentic (Holtorf, 2013, p. 431), a dealer’s listing can do the same. To accomplish that, Sotheby’s and dealers on eBay have to select which strategies to apply. I believe they focus on ideas of time-depth, aesthetic appreciation and otherness.

Indeed, in this analysis, concepts of ’primitive/other’ (ethnographic/curiosity) and ’beautiful’ (aesthetic appreciation), significantly interact and overlap to construct and affirm an antiquity’s authenticity, confirming its worth of being on the market and associated with a monetary value.

3 eBay and Sotheby's: Fakes and Authenticity

As previously discussed, contexts and counterparts are both fundamental influencers of authenticity variations. Both eBay and Sotheby's host buy-and-sell dynamics, yet they operate in completely different ways. Brodie (2014a) argues that Sotheby's in-person auctions and eBay online transactions are located at the two ends of the complex spectrum of the market of Pre-Columbian antiquities.

Sotheby's tradition of a biannual public auction of pre-Columbian antiquities started in 1978 in New York (Yates, 2006). Sotheby's impression of openness is only apparent as bidders and sellers are offered anonymity if they please, bids can be placed by phone, and the auction house does not disclose buyers' identity. The whole auction system is complex and composed of many different stages, from the catalogue to the viewing and champagne opening. While each of these stages can be accessed by anyone, dealers, buyers, collectors, and museum experts are all part of a "closed self-conscious community" (Geismar, 2001, p. 39).

The online auction site eBay was founded in 1995 and from that moment it expanded until it was launched worldwide. It is now the biggest auction website—although not the only one—and it was predictable that it would be used for the sale of antiquities as well (see Fay, 2011). Nowadays, anyone with a debit card, an email address, and access to the internet can create an account.

Both Sotheby's and eBay pose some complications by being part of an ambiguous market. Indeed, they both have been involved in the illicit traffic of antiquities and art.[4] In terms of the legal status of the objects that are sold within their platforms, neither Sotheby's nor eBay assume full responsibility. Indeed, eBay sellers and Sotheby's property owners are considered fully responsible for the legal status of their items (eBay, 2020a; Sotheby's, 2020)

The circulation of fakes is another issue connected to both Sotheby's and eBay's policies. On the "Sell with Sotheby's" page it is declared that:

> Sotheby's does not authenticate objects or artworks [. . .] Sotheby's gives no representation, warranty or guarantee with respect to an item's origin, provenance, attribution, condition, date, age or authenticity." (Sotheby's, 2020).

On the other hand, the debate about the effects of fakes in the online market has continued for years and it is probably impossible to get a fixed estimation of the number of fakes that are sold online or a clear idea of the dynamics behind a continuously mutable phenomenon (see Bohem, 2009; Stanish, 2009). In eBay's policies, fakes are banned, and it is mandatory for replicas to be declared as such or to be listed in the category "Reproduction or Fantasy" (eBay, 2020a). Even though the platform is based on 'neoliberal ideas', and the 'community' is expected to police itself and build trust from the inside (Jarret, 2006), some expert dealers noted that, around 2010, they were given authority to remove those items and sellers they considered fraudulent (personal communication; see Fay, 2011, p. 459).

---

[4] See Watson (1997) and Brodie (2014c) for Sotheby's, and ICE (2012, 2014) for eBay.

4 eBay and Sotheby's: Defining Contexts.

While objects in a museum catalogue have already reached their final validation, meaning that "museum collection being the ultimate reference point by which objects are judged" (Geismar, 2001, p. 32), antiquities offered on the market are being subjected to a "tournament of value" (Appadurai, 1986, p. 21), so they emanate a different tension toward authenticity.

Both eBay's and Sotheby's listings are a form of 'marketing'. On the one hand, as Geismar puts it, auction catalogues are the first instrument to lure the buyer using both written words and images (2001, pp. 35–36). On the other, eBay listing can be considered as "a form of advertising" (Fay, 2013, p. 46). In both cases, the auction house or the online vendor make decisions about the most convenient ways to present their items in order for them to be sold. Nevertheless, there are significant differences in auction mechanisms that need to be considered. These differences clearly reflect on different strategies and methods that are used to reaffirm authenticity, depending on the sale context.

Sotheby's specialists oversee all sale phases and ensure they respect the venue norms and standards. They have the responsibility of inspecting items integrity, do provenance and historical research, and provide a value estimation. Both the property owner and the buyer pay respectively a commission and a buyer's premium for the sale to be staged properly. All the collected information is then organised in the catalogue following a specific editorial line. Moreover, as previously said, even though the identity of the previous collector might be relevant in the evaluating and selling process, Sotheby's frequently respects owners wishes to not disclose their information. Thus, the auction house's reputation, the auctioneer, and the 'knowledgeable experts' must provide buyers with a good level of reassurance about objects authenticity to justify their price. However, in their "Conditions of sale" (Sotheby's, 2020b) Sotheby's states that the auction house is not responsible and make no warranties for any mistakes or omissions in the catalogue.

On the other side, eBay has a completely different structure as the auction website is not a part of the transaction. The online platform does not have any involvement in buyer-seller dynamics, and it only provide the web-based venue for the sale to happen. eBay is a facilitator that does not play the role of the 'illustrious' intermediary as Sotheby's does. Vendors are fully in charge of their own showcase and they are responsible of their own selling strategies. Indeed, vendors on eBay must take care not only of photographing, researching, and in general presenting the object, but also of packaging and posting it. Likewise, the lack of an intermediary and of structured information results in uneven and discontinuous levels of reliability, which means that buyers have a higher need to inspect objects and check if their declared value is real.

In short, eBay sellers have to independently build their own credibility. In order to do that, they frequently provide their background in the item description, but with a lot of variability in terms of expertise. 'Feedback', namely clients' assessments on the transaction, does not always appear as an effective way to check sellers' reliability. On the one hand, sellers often offer on sale items of completely different categories. On the other hand, buyers' satisfaction depends on their expectations as well as their expertise.

5 Moche Vessels on eBay and at Sotheby's

To identify sellers' systems to produce and state their objects' authenticity, thus assign value to them, I consider here an eBay and a Sotheby's listing offering similar antiquities: Moche fine-line stirrup vessels. I offer a qualitative comparison of those elements that are of more relevance to underline differences between Peruvian antiquities' representation within the two auctioning contexts.

Moche[5] vessels decorated with fine-line paintings have long attracted looters to the point where 95 percent of these objects in museums and private collections do not have archaeological documentation (Donnan & McClelland, 1999, p. 18). They are still being trafficked, as evidenced by the repatriation of one of these vessels to Peru in 2017. Their high appeal in the market is confirmed by the early tradition of manufacturing high-quality fakes (Donnan, 1982) and by the ongoing improvement of faking techniques (Bruhns & Kelker, 2010, pp. 100–103).

In 2018, on eBay, a Moche fine-line vessel was on sale and its price was much higher than the other items on sale in the same period among Peruvian antiquities ($1825 USD). In the Sotheby's catalogue for the 2014 auction for African, Oceanic and Pre-Columbian Art (2014: p. 13), the estimated price of a similar item was $4000–$6000 USD and it sold for $9375 USD. The vessel is now part of the Yale University Art Gallery collection.[6] Looking at their prices, both these objects were very saleable. Figure 1 and 2 respectively show the eBay and Sotheby's listings for the considered Moche vessels.

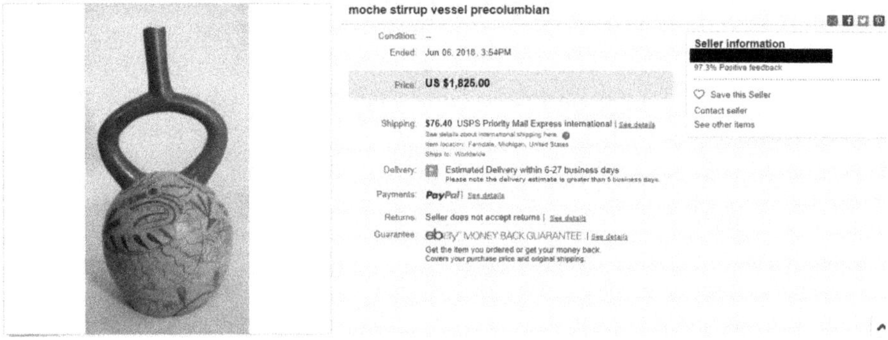

Fig. 1 eBay listing of a Moche fine-line stirrup vessel in 2018

[5]Moche, or Mochica, culture developed in the coast of northern Peru between the first and seventh century A.D.

[6]See at https://artgallery.yale.edu/collections/objects/193707.

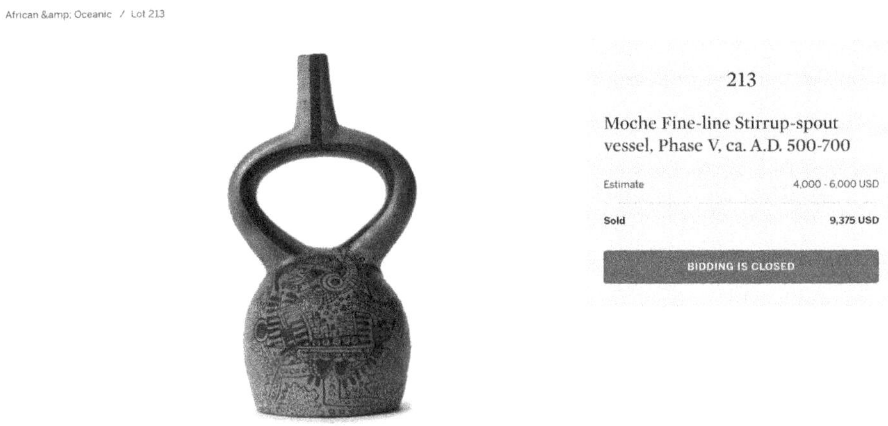

Fig. 2 Sotheby's listing of a Moche fine-line stirrup vessel in 2014

5.1 Authenticity Markers: Images

Images in both Sotheby's catalogues and eBay listings are a fundamental part of the staged sale. Indeed, on the one hand pictures allow vendors to frame the object and highlight specific characteristics; on the other, they allow buyers to get a first, and for eBay the only possible, look at the item on sale. However, comparing images in Sotheby's catalogues and in eBay listings makes it visually clear that buyers get completely different general impressions. On one side, leafing through a Sotheby's catalogue gives the impression of walking into a 'fine art' gallery; on the other, eBay has been defined by Trodd (2006, p. 79) as a "cabinet of curiosities".

For Sotheby's, photographs are professionally taken with attention to aesthetic values of the object to enhance its material qualities and present it as both a piece of art, seen through a 'primitivist' filter, and a commodity. The parallels between an auction catalogue and a magazine have already been used to highlight how much of an impact this kind of photographic representation has in delineating a piece's identity (Geismar, 2001, p. 35). At the same time, the conformity of these photos contrast with the impression of uniqueness that this style of picture gives. This paradox is connected to the ironic construction of a piece's authenticity namely the fact that the object's authenticity depends on its relationships with similar ones or with people (2001, pp. 36–37).

Browsing eBay listings of Peruvian antiquities gives a completely different impression. Each object normally has more than one picture and even though eBay provides some "photo tips" (eBay, 2021), the impact is one of inhomogeneity as each vendor has a different style, and possibly different intentions: along with high quality professional pictures, blurry and badly lit ones are frequent. I believe that surfing the eBay list, the buyer gets the impression of a bazaar or a flea market. Backgrounds are often improvised: items are sometimes laid on the floor or against a bright cloth, or even held by sellers themselves. However, photos are perceived as fundamental by vendors because the buyer will not have the possibility to look closely at the item in person.

5.2 Authenticity Markers: Listings

In short, both Sotheby's and eBay listings aim to sell the item they depict. However, even similar objects such as the Moche fine-line stirrup vessels I am considering in this paper, are presented with different techniques and through different lenses. Besides the title and non-discursive entries (provenance, literature, exhibition, etc.), narratives play a central role in how sellers present the object authenticity within the specific context and according to it. Narratives are discourses about different aspects of an object biography, and they are crucial to the authentication process as they reinforce both the items and the dealer's credibility. Indeed, they are aimed to define objects' value through the validation of aspects that are believed to appeal to the buyer (Fay, 2013, pp. 229–252). While most narratives in Sotheby's sales possibly take place during the in-person events like viewings and at auction, on eBay the situation is completely different. Listings are usually less structured and uniform as eBay does not provide a specific guidance, and narratives are generally more abundant possibly because histories are necessary to minimise the impossibility of personally viewing the object (Trodd, 2006, pp. 82–83). Therefore, the information selected by sellers to describe their pieces is that considered the most relevant to define that object's biography and Sotheby's and eBay vendors apply quite different strategies to formulate narratives.

Provenance and provenience information are important indicators of "pastness" (Holtorf, 2013) as they provide a connection between the object's origin and its contemporary context. Indeed, they play significant role within the market of antiquities as they "recontextualise" the object and are fundamental to assert authenticity and define market value. Coggins (1998, p. 57) defined provenience as "the original context" of an object while provenance is the "ownership history" of it. Thus, provenience information is based on the object re-location from its original context which still define them, and provenance data on its de-location within the market dynamics that are now a fundamental part of its biography (see Fay, 2013, pp. 228–229, 236, and Geismar, 2001, p. 26).

If authenticity is the most relevant definer of an object's cultural value and price, then provenience is the strongest way to confirm authenticity for an archaeological piece. Yet provenience is very rarely provided within transactions in the antiquities market and, when the originating context of an antiquity is provided, it is not usually more precise than broad regions or even nations.

Neither the Moche vessel at Sotheby's nor the one on eBay are provided with specific archaeological provenience (namely the find spot), nor region or country of origin, but they both are identified through cultural reference. This approach has been widely accepted as archaeological collections displayed in museums have normally been authenticated this way by archaeologists. However, Chippindale and Gill (2000, pp. 468–470) already identified this problematic practice based on stylistic affiliation which over-simplifies cultures' complexities and all the displacements that an object might have been subjected to before being interred.[7] Moreover, it can be risky especially when applied to categories that are affected by a large fake production like Pre-Columbian antiquities (see Boone, 1982; Bruhns & Kelker, 2010).

At Sotheby's, the 'authorship' guarantee (that is, period, culture, or origin) can be, to some extent, associated to the concept of authenticity. In the "Conditions of Sale" (2020b), it is stated that only bold or capitalised cultural attribution is guaranteed. If authorship is in capital letters, the piece could be refunded (within 5 years) if Sotheby's agrees that the conditions are satisfied. The Moche stirrup vessel I am considering was not listed in capitalised or bold letters.

On eBay, more than one cultural attribution is frequently mentioned, to the extent that is fair to state that in some cases this might be a technique to attract more buyers who look for antiquities by searching in the "Search for anything" bar. In other cases, like the one considered, I believe there is a predominant attention to the association with a general pre-Columbian past than to the historical or archaeological value of a piece. Moreover, on eBay claims of authenticity are discontinuous as any other element of antiquities listings. Often vendors explicitly claim the genuineness of their artefacts, some even provide a certificate or thermoluminescence documents upon request, some offer the possibility to return the object (often within a noticeably short time) or a 'lifetime guarantee'.[8] On the other side, some sellers simply admit they are not sure about the item's authenticity, or even do not feel the need to directly affirm authenticity nor provide any kind of guarantee. This is the case for the considered Moche vessel on sale.

Narratives about the original context of the object's creation and use are related to provenience. While provenience narratives at Sotheby's usually consists of historical context, original use details and technical notions (frequently well referenced with academic bibliography), on eBay they often consist of a varied balance between accurate notions and catching curiosities—frequently connected to rituals—resulting in the creation of "origin myths" (Geismar, 2001, p. 26). To confirm the relevance of these narratives in defining antiquities value on eBay, it must be noticed that the Moche vessel listed on eBay in 2018 is presented through provenience narratives only:

> moche stirrup vessel pre-columbian
>
> Pre-Columbian vessel This vessel, dating from 200bc to 150ad, was used for storing essential fluids for rituals. would have been owned by a high ranking shaman.

---

[7] Scholars are discouraged from taking part in the identification of unprovenienced objects and, more generally, in any activity which can enhance the market value of potentially illegally excavated antiquities (ICOM, 2004; SAA, 1996).

[8] I am talking here about additional guarantees other than the "Money Back Guaranty" (eBay, 2020b)

This kind of narrative, which is more commonly associated with ethnographic objects, focuses on the idea of sacred, esoteric, powerful and somehow 'exotic' and 'primitive', involving shamans. The fact that the seller chose to present the object's authenticity and its value through this specific piece of information about the antiquity's biography and decide to emphasise 'primitivising' aspects reflects the seller convictions about buyer's expectations.

Regardless the importance of provenience to define authenticity, it is more frequent that an antiquity on the market is provided with provenance information. The effects of provenance within the market have been discussed from different perspectives (see Brodie, 2014a, 2014b) but I believe it cannot be estimated unconditionally to what extent provenance has a role in the attribution of authenticity. However, surely ownership history means that the piece has been validated as valuable by many different individuals. Previous owners' prominence also contributes to the negotiation of authenticity and value, and as Geismar said (2001: p. 36) objects are somehow personified and incorporated "into real family trees". The fact that a well know collector or scholar believe the object to be authentic, legitimises the antiquity in terms of acculturated appreciation. The same mechanism happens when an unprovenienced antiquity is published and literature is cited in market listings. While the Moche vessel listed on eBay does not have any provenance specification, the one at Sotheby's (2014) has passed through three different collections and surfaced, namely first appeared on sale, in 1970.

Narratives about antiquities collecting underline the importance of ownership history, namely provenance, as they narrate the seller's personal connection to the object's biography. At Sotheby's, narratives about collecting mainly consists of mentioning owners' collecting practices and standards. Indeed, Sotheby's tends to underline the association of pre-Columbian antiquities and Western art in the collectors' taste. This narrative technique automatically "promotes to fine art", as Clifford would say (1988, p. 224), not just the items owned by the famous collector, but all the antiquities associated to them within the auction. This is what happened with the Moche stirrup vessel considered. In eBay, the connection between the items and the vendor's collecting habit is as variable as any other element of online listings. While it frequently lays in 'treasure hunting' discourses, in my eBay case I note that the seller, who had more pre-Columbian pots on sale in 2018, frequently referred to their wide Pre-Columbian collection, once referred to Sotheby's, once to a general Manhattan estate, and most times did not mention any collecting narrative. This summarises the diversity among eBay listings narratives about collecting.

Physical description of the piece is also significant, especially on eBay as buyers cannot personally inspect the object. Physical descriptions of the items are indeed frequently (but not always) present in eBay listings, and the antiquity of the piece is frequently referred to, usually by descriptions of physical damage such as scratches, patinas, mineral/manganese deposits, root marks derived from use, or archaeological provenience. Physical imperfections are usually presented as positive characteristics that add value to a piece as they are "pastness" indicators (Holtorf, 2013). Also, in eBay listings, statements such as "museum masterpiece", "museum quality", and "museum-grade" are quite frequent.

On the other hand, Sotheby's listings provide a description of the object materiality that focuses on completely different bases. These notes are frequently dominant and tend to focus mainly on rarity, artistic value and technical ability, style and iconography. They consist in a short physical description of each piece and a scholar's note that usually praises the item's quality. This discursive information frequently demonstrates the object to be rare or unique, but not entirely. This recalls again Geismar's (2001, p. 37) idea of "ironic authenticity". The considered Moche vessel offered on Sotheby's is described as such:

> Moche Fine-line Stirrup-spout vessel, Phase V, ca. A.D. 500–700
>
> depicting battle scenes by the Doering Painter on each side, distinguished by the large crescentic nose ornaments with dangles, the larger warrior holding his club low across his waist, his opponent facing down and spear pointed at the warrior's knees, each with elaborate clothing, the dusty landscape indicated by dotted outlined areas. [...]
>
> CATALOGUE NOTE The Doering painter is one of the few identified artists from the Phase V corpus of fine-line vessels. The style is noted for the fine jewelry, elaborate clothing and the particularly animated and fierce combat scenes."

In this listing, the vessel is described exclusively through an art-historical language and is associated to a painter's identity, identified exclusively on stylistic and subject basis (see Donnan & McClelland, 1999, pp. 266–268), a process typical of Western history of art.

As previously stated, narratives are fundamental for the vendor to outline an object's value within the specific context in which it is offered on sale. Therefore, focusing on how dominant narratives are used to describe and make similar objects appealable within different market venue allows us to understand how authenticity is stated and constructed according to those contexts.

The objects' connection to the past is relevant in both the considered cases: regardless the concerns about this practice, cultural affiliations, which automatically implies geographical setting and a chronological span, are mentioned in the beginning of both listings. Lowenthal argues (1985, pp. 240–242) that we perceive the 'ancient' according to different cultural, environmental, historical and personal factors. Therefore, once the preconception of how a specific object should express 'pastness' is satisfied, then the assumption of antiquity matters more than the actual proof that archaeological documentation and scientific tests could provide (see Holtorf, 2013, p. 433). Meanwhile, Sotheby's and the eBay seller focused on different preeminent narratives. What is relevant for the vessel on eBay refers to its origin myth while Sotheby's focused on the object material aspect.

In this example, possibly with the aim of meeting buyers' expectation of authenticity, at Sotheby's, it is all about the aesthetic value of the object. The idea of 'work of the genius' fits perfectly in a Western stylistic analysis of Peruvian antiquities in a post-Modernist manner. On the contrary, what gives value to the vessel on eBay is the fact that it meets the idea of 'exotic', 'sacred', and 'primitive' ethnographic object. In both cases, the perspective is clearly that of Europeans and North Americans whose expectations regarding the authenticity of Peruvian archaeology are met in two different ways and within two different market contexts. Consequently, both objects are presented as authentic, differently: authentically exotic and authentically beautiful.

6 Conclusions

Like all Peruvian antiquities, ceramic vessels have complex, articulated, and mutable biographies. Their entrance into the market implies one or more "tournaments of value" (Appadurai, 1986, p. 21) that make them simultaneously cultural heritage and commodity. This multifaceted condition inherently carries a holistic approach into analysis.

Within the two market fields I investigated, I considered Moche vessels as culturally constructed entities that fall into specific culturally constructed categories. These categories are fundamental to understand and interpret the past and its material culture.

Vendors' intention of persuading buyers about the authenticity of Moche vessels are enacted in two different ways and within two different venues. Consequently, objects' authenticity on eBay and at Sotheby's are stated differently: Moche fine-line stirrup vessels are suggested to be authentically primitive and authentically beautiful. From a materialist perspective it would be difficult to accept the claimed authenticity of an artefact without a finding context or without scientific testing being performed. However, within the market system, authenticity detaches from its exclusive objective definition, being assessed in ways that lie outside of the archaeological materialist perception. The object's connection to the past is fundamental and it is clearly stated in the considered listings, but expectations of what an authentic Moche piece should be are relevant as well. Narratives that are made to guide buyers' perceived authenticity highlight different layers of these antiquities' social life and are developed according to two different cultural categories.

In conclusion, authenticity is culturally constructed and historically influenced but also depends on the object materiality to some extent. As we accept that the archaeological authenticity of an object can be untied from its material substance (Holtorf, 2013, p. 431), we also embrace the possibility that the perception of an object's genuineness depends on the beholder's eyes and on their ability to create a connection to that specific object biography and materiality (Jones, 2010, p. 199). To facilitate this connection, dealers select specific fragments of the item's complexity with the aim of persuading the buyer of the object's truthfulness. In this case, authenticity seems to acquire polysemic meanings related to objects' physical and intrinsic properties, connected to how they are presented and how they are perceived and depending on "settings" and "individuals". Indeed, as vendors decide to deliver two different but specific narratives of Moche vessels, namely their material artistic qualities and biographical 'otherness', the objects seem to assume authentic properties differently.

Acknowledgements I would like to thank Dr. Lau and Professor Hooper for supporting me with the research for my MA dissertation at the SRU–University of East Anglia, UK as the present contribution is based on those investigations.

References

Alva, W. (2001). The destruction, looting and traffic of the archaeological heritage of Peru. In N. Brodie, J. Doole, & C. Renfrew (Eds.), *Trade in illicit antiquities: The destruction of the World's Archaeological Heritage* (pp. 89–96). McDonald Institute Monographs.

Appadurai, A. (1986). Introduction: Commodities and the politics of value. In A. Appadurai (Ed.), *The social life of things: Commodities in cultural perspectives* (pp. 3–63). Cambridge University Press.

Bohem, M. (2009, May 29). Relic sellers are faking it on EBay. *Los Angeles Times*. Retrieved December 23, 2020, from http://articles.latimes.com/2009/may/29/entertainment/et-ebayfakes29

Boone, E. H. (Ed.). (1982). *Falsifications and Misreconstructions of Pre-Columbian Art: A Conference at Dumbarton Oaks, October 14th and 16th, 1978*. Dumbarton Oaks, Trustees for Harvard University.

Brodie, N. (2014a). The internet market of pre-columbian antiquities. In J. D. Kila & M. Balcells (Eds.), *Cultural property crime: An overview and analysis of contemporary perspectives and trends* (pp. 237–262). Brill.

Brodie, N. (2014b). The antiquities market: It's all in a price. *Heritage and Society, 7*(1), 32–46.

Brodie, N. (2014c). Auction houses and the antiquities trade. In S. Choulia-Kapeloni (Ed.), *3rd international conference of experts on the return of cultural property* (pp. 71–82). Archaeological Receipts Fund.

Brodie, N. (2015). The internet market in antiquities. In F. Desmarais (Ed.), *Countering illicit traffic in cultural goods: The global challenge of protecting the world's heritage* (pp. 11–20). ICOM.

Bruhns, K. O., & Kelker, N. L. (2010). *Faking the ancient Andes*. Left Coast Press.

Chippindale, C., & Gill, D. W. J. (2000). Material consequences of contemporary classical collecting. *American Journal of Archaeology, 104*(3), 463–511.

Chippindale, C., & Gill, D. W. J. (2001). On-line auctions: A new venue for the antiquities market. *Culture Without Context, 9*, 4–12.

Clifford, J. (1988). *The predicament of culture: Twentieth-century ethnography, literature and art*. Harvard University Press.

Coggins, C. (1998). United States cultural property legislation: Observation of a combatant. *International Journal of Cultural Property, 7*(1), 52–68.

Donnan, B. C. (1982). The identification of a Moche Fake through iconographic analysis. In E. H. Boone (Ed.), *Falsification and misreconstructions of pre-columbian art: A conference at Dumbarton Oaks, October 14th and 16th, 1978* (pp. 37–50). Dumbarton Oaks, Trustees for Harvard University.

Donnan, B. C., & McClelland, D. (1999). *Moche fineline painting: Its evolution and its artists*. UCLA Fowler Museum of Cultural History.

eBay (2020a). *Artifatcs and cave formations policy*. Retrieved December 20, 2020, from https://www.ebay.com/help/policies/prohibited-restricted-items/artifacts-cultural-heritage-graverelated-items-policy?id=4282#section1

eBay (2020b). *Money Back Guarantee Policy*. Retrieved January 27, 2021, from https://www.ebay.com/help/policies/ebay-money-back-guarantee-policy/ebay-money-back-guarantee-policy?id=4210

eBay (2021). *Photo Tips*. Retrieved January 27, 2021, from https://pages.ebay.com/seller-center/listing-and-marketing/photo-tips.html

Fay, E. V. (2011). Virtual artifacts: eBay, antiquities and authenticity. *Journal of Contemporary Criminal Justice, 27*(4), 449–464.

Fay, E. V. (2013). *Trading in antiquities on eBay: The changing face of the illicit trade in antiquities* (Unpublished doctoral dissertation). Newcastle: Keele University.

Gänger, S. (2014). *Relics of the past: Collecting and study of Pre-Columbian antiquities in Peru and Chile, 1837–1911*. Oxford University Press.

Geismar, H. (2001). What's in a price? An ethnography of tribal art at auction. *Journal of Material Culture, 6*(1), 25–47.
Holtorf, C. (2013). On pastness: A reconsideration of materiality in archaeological object authenticity. *Anthropological Quarterly, 86*(2), 427–443.
ICE (2012). *ICE returns stolen and looted art and antiquities to Peru.* Retrieved February 19, 2021, from https://www.ice.gov/news/releases/ice-returns-stolen-and-looted-art-and-antiquities-peru
ICE (2014). *25 Peruvian cultural treasures returned to the government of Peru.* Retrieved February 19, 2021, from https://www.ice.gov/news/releases/25-peruvian-cultural-treasures-returned-government-peru
ICOM. (2013[2004]). *Code of Ethics for Museums. Resource document.* Retrieved January 25, 2021, from http://musei.beniculturali.it/wp-content/uploads/2016/05/ICOM-Code-of-Ethics-for-Museums.pdf
Jarret, K. (2006). The perfect community: Disciplining the eBay used. In K. Hillis, M. Petit, & N. S. Epley (Eds.), *Everyday eBay. Culture, collecting, and desire* (pp. 107–122). Routledge.
Jones, S. (2010). Negotiating authentic objects and authentic selves: Beyond the deconstruction of authenticity. *Journal of Material Culture, 15*(2), 181–203.
Kopitoff, I. (1986). The cultural biography of things: Commoditization as process. In A. Appadurai (Ed.), *The social life of things: Commodities in cultural perspective* (pp. 64–94). Cambridge University Press.
Lowenthal, D. (1985). *The past is a foreign country.* Cambridge University Press.
Mackenzie, S., & Yates, D. (2017). What is grey about the "Grey Market" in antiquities? In J. Beckert & M. Dewey (Eds.), *The architecture of illegal markets: Toward an economic sociology of illegality in the economy* (pp. 70–86). Oxford University Press.
Ortiz, G. (2006). Overview and assessment after fifty years of collecting in a changing world. In E. Robson, L. Treadwell, & C. Gosden (Eds.), *Who owns objects? The ethics and politics of collecting cultural artefacts* (pp. 15–32). Oxbow book.
Pasztory, E. (2002). Truth in forgery. *Anthropology and Aesthetics, 42*, 159–165.
Reisinger, Y., & Steiner, C. (2006). Reconceptualizing object authenticity. *Annals of Tourism Research, 33*(1), 65–86.
SAA (1996). Principle for Archaeological Ethics. *Resource document.* Retrieved January 30, 2021, from https://documents.saa.org/container/docs/default-source/doc-careerpractice/saa_ethics.pdf?sfvrsn=75f1b83b_4
Sawyer, A. R. (1982). The falsification of ancient Peruvian slip-decorated ceramics. In E. H. Boone (Ed.), *Falsifications and misreconstructions of Pre-Columbian Art: A Conference at Dumbarton Oaks, October 14th and 16th, 1978* (pp. 19–36). Dumbarton Oaks, Trustees for Harvard University.
Sease, C. (2007). Faking pre-Columbian artefacts. *Objects Speciality Group Postprints, 14*, 146–160.
Sonin, R. (1982). The art historian's Dilemma: With remarks upon the state of art falsification in the Central and North Andean Region. In E. H. Boone (Ed.), *Falsifications and Misreconstructions of Pre-Columbian Art: A Conference at Dumbarton Oaks, October 14th and 16th, 1978* (pp. 1–18). Dumbarton Oaks, Trustees for Harvard University.
Sotheby's. (2014). *African, Oceanic and Pre-Columbian Art. 16th May. Auction catalog.* Sotheby's.
Sotheby's. (2020). *Sell with Sotheby's.*. Retrieved December 20, 2020, from https://www.sothebys.com/en/sell
Sotheby's. (2020b). *Condition of sale.* Retrieved December 22, 2020, from https://www.sothebys.com/content/dam/sothebys/PDFs/cob/N09502-COS.pdf
Stanish, C. (2009). Forging ahead: Or, How I Learned to Stop Worrying and Love eBay. *Archaeology*, 62(3). Retrieved March 5, 2021, from https://archive.archaeology.org/0905/etc/insider.html

Trodd, Z. (2006). Reading eBay: Hidden Stores, Subjective Stories, and a People's History of the Archive. In K. Hillis, M. Petit, & N. Scott Epley (Eds.), *Everyday eBay. Culture, collecting, and desire* (pp. 77–90). Routledge.

Watson, P. (1997). *Sotheby's: The inside story*. Random House.

Yates, D. (2006). *South America on the Block: The Changing Face of Pre-Columbian Antiquities Auctions in Response to International Law* (Unpublished MPhil Dissertation). Cambridge: University of Cambridge.

Yates, D. (2015). Value and doubt: The persuasive power of "authenticity" in the antiquities market. *PARSE, 2*, 71–84.

"Blitzkrieg Against Black Magic"

The Collection of Afrobrazilian Sacred Items of the Civil Police Museum Between Repression and Restitution

Rodrigo Christofoletti and Vitória dos Santos Acerbi

Abstract This article discusses the distinct perceptions of crime, justice and heritage concerning the collection of Afrobrazilian sacred items during their constitution, patrimonialisation, restitution dispute, and final restitution, which is a case of heritage return within a State. The collection belongs to the Civil Police Museum in Rio de Janeiro and was recently transferred to the Museum of the Republic, in a State reparation towards the Afrobrazilian religions. Based on criminology, decolonial studies, and heritage studies, this text analyses the values attributed to the collection across time and how their changes help to explain the collection's trajectory: from an initial juridical perspective of crime present in the objects, that were crime proofs, to a final perspective of crime based on the deviance and social injury in the State institutional racism, and of breach of law in the State heritage negligence; from colonial justice, where descendants of the colonisers criminalise the objects and practices of descendants of the colonised and enslaved, to decolonial justice, which acknowledges and repairs this oppression; from an understanding of heritage anchored in property to one that stems from cultural value and rights. The article concludes that these shifts in understanding made restitution possible, when they were translated into an institutional language, pointing to a significant State legalism in this internal heritage return.

1 Introduction

> The son asked the father/ "Where is my grandfather? [...]/
>
> The father asked the grandfather/ "Where is my great-grandfather? [...]/
>
> The grandfather asked the great-grandfather/ "Where is my great-great-grandfather?[...]/
>
> Great-great-grandfather, great-grandfather, grandfather/

R. Christofoletti (✉) · V. dos Santos Acerbi
Universidade Federal de Juiz de Fora–UFJF, Juiz de Fora, Brazil

Universidad de Salamanca, Salamanca, Spain

N. Oosterman, D. Yates (eds.), *Crime and Art*, Studies in Art, Heritage, Law and the Market 1, https://doi.org/10.1007/978-3-030-84856-9_10

Father Xangô, Aganju/Long live egum, babá Alapalá!

(Babá Alapalá, Gilberto Gil, 1977)

Gilberto Gil is an Afrobrazilian singer and songwriter who was forced into exile during the civic-military dictatorship (1967–1985) and was later a Minister of Culture (2003–2008) who promoted social inclusion and development through culture. His lyrics match the social realism of the Brazilian writer Jorge Amado, also forced into exile, but in the 1940s. In Amado's novel *Tenda dos Milagres* (1969), the main character, Pedro Archanjo, is a *Ojuobá*, a Yoruba word meaning 'the eyes of the King'. He is part of the cult of Orixá Xangô, God of justice, evoked in Gil's song to help the people who want to know about their ancestry. In this religion, the character Archanjo is an *Oyê*, a high priest in the cult of Xangô, in Africa, or Candomblé, This character personifies the pluri-symbolic dimension of the cultural, social and legal struggle analysed in this text. The novel *Tenda dos Milagres* tells the history of the systematic persecution of Afrobrazilian people, objects, practices, and places through the law, science, and public opinion in the twentieth century, centred in the story of Pedro Archanjo, a poor, self-taught Afrobrazilian man from the periphery who writes books about the life and customs of his people, wishing to fight, through this officially recognisable means, the racism that was installed in society at that time. The novel combines social criticism with the portrayal of the daily life of black people in Salvador, the capital of Bahia, capturing simultaneously the powerful symbolism of Afrobrazilian religions and its brutal criminalisation by the State, illustrating how the material objects of the former were violated and stolen by the latter in a context of systemic discrimination.

Five decades after the launch of Jorge Amado's novel, on 21 September 2020, in a ceremony with public authorities and religious leaders, 523 Afrobrazilian sacred objects were transferred from the Civil Police Museum of Rio de Janeiro to the Museum of the Republic. The transfer was celebrated as the "freeing of the apprehended" objects (Mota, 2020), or the "recovery of the confiscated" artworks (Alves, 2020). It fulfilled the provisions of the transfer term, signed on 7 August 2020 between the state of Rio, and the Museum of the Republic (Diário Oficial dá União, 2020), as a result of three years of negotiations and three decades of mobilisation.

This collection originated from the enforcement of articles n° 157, n° 158, and n° 159 of the 1890s Brazilian Criminal Code, which criminalised the practices of "Medicine, Magic and Charlatanism". Under these categories, Afro-Brazilian religions were stigmatised: the police were entitled to break into their worship spaces and apprehend proof of these crimes (Valle, 2017, 2018, 2020). These apprehensions formed the "Collection of Black Magic", part of the Civil Police Museum, founded in 1912.[1] The collection was turned into the "Black Magic Museum" and recognised as National Heritage in 1938 as the first *Archaeological and Ethnographic Brazilian*

[1] Other similar collections exist across Brazil, having been the object of studies and restitutions, although without such a public notoriety. See Valle (2018, 2020) and Gama (2018).

Heritage. The items declared heritage (158 in total) were joined by other similar objects apprehended in subsequent raids and the collection, which is not recognised as a national heritage in its entirety, grew to be currently composed of 523 items. It was kept in the Civil Police Museum until the transfer, though restitution[2] requests started in the 1970s.

This article analyses the trajectory of this collection through the prisms of crime, justice, and cultural heritage. We examine its processes of constitution (end of nineteenth century to the beginning of the twentieth century), patrimonialisation (1930s–1980s), restitution disputes (starting in the 1980s, and gaining intensity from the 2000s), and restitution (2020) to determine the values underlying the perspectives of the three aforementioned concepts that the distinct actors held at different moments.

The attribution of value is inherent to any heritage action or policy (Viladevall i Guasch, 2003: p.17) and diverging 'valuational' criteria regarding heritage are often a point of discord between the parties in a return dispute (Bieńkowski, 2014, p. 2; Warren, 1999, p. 5). Hence, understanding the changes of values over time and between actors is key to explain decisions concerning cultural heritage and to shed light on the broader socio-political, cultural, legal context in which they are made. Our framework to examine understandings of crime comes from Hutchings and La Salle (2017), based on Michalowski (2010, p. 17), "who outlines three ways to view crime itself: juridical, where a law is broken; deviance, where the activity violates social norms; and social injury, where the action results in harm of a gravity to be on par with crime" (Hutchings & La Salle, 2017, p. 71).

Our compass to examine justice is the abyss between colonial and decolonial justice (Maldonado, 2007). 'Colonial justice' can be understood—in the context of formally independent states as was Brazil throughout the period here analysed—as the use of legal order to perpetuate in social and mental structures the economic, political, cultural, ethnic hierarchies of colonisation. Conversely, 'decolonial justice' not only reverses this oppression, establishing *de facto* equalities and horizontal dialogues, but also provides reparation for the multidimensional damage of such oppression.

According to decolonial theories, the colonial matrix of power is a multi-layered structure that originated in modernity (roughly the colonial epoch, sixteenth to nineteenth century) and remains very much present in the contemporary world (from nineteenth century to the present time), where distinct levels of control are intertwined in the political, economic, social, cultural, and natural spheres as well as

---

[2]Return, recovery, recuperation, restitution are used here following Prott (2009, pp. xxi–xxiv), to whom 'return' is a neutral term, that slightly focuses on the action of the requested party, 'recovery' is also relatively value-free, although highlighting the view of the requesting party, 'recuperation' frames the issue from the requesting party's view as well, albeit more strongly imbued with justice/injustice values, and 'restitution' is the most contentious term, with different meaning according to the legal system in question, but generally evoking the idea of restoration to the proper owner or reparation for an injury, mixing issues of legitimacy and legality, justice and ownership, usually grounding/favouring the requesters' claim.

in matters of gender, sexuality, and individual subjectivity (Mignolo, 2008). It articulates the peripheral-central places of the international division of labour with the ethnical-racial global divide (as well as the above-mentioned forms of control) and constitutes a continuity of colonial power and knowledge systems that did not end with the political colonial administrations. (Acerbi & Lima, 2020: p.36)

Thus, beyond the characterisation of justice itself, when a legal text, an action of the State, or a perceived value is henceforth referred to as 'colonial', or in a frame of 'coloniality', we indicate the continuity, in the present, of such complex colonial matrix of power that hierarchically defines and classifies people—their social place, possibilities and value—according to their ethno-racial ascendance, creating multidimensional privileges for those of European origins (the former colonisers) and multifaceted oppressions for those of non-European origins (the former colonised and enslaved). Conversely, when regulations, statements, critiques or criteria are hereafter described as 'decolonial', or in a frame of 'decoloniality', we suggest that they aim to, in the present, deconstruct and repair such historical oppression and the asymmetries derived thereof—in terms of, among others, cultural value, social acceptance and relations, legal framework, and political actions.

Finally, for heritage, we verify oscillations between what we name a restrictive, *legalistic* perspective, grounded in property, ownership, and possession, the legitimacy and authority of certain groups concerning the objects deriving from the relations these concepts engender (Brown, 2004); and another frame of analysis that we call extensive, 'culturalist' perspective of heritage, built on a notion of (human cultural) rights, on identity and social well-being, the legitimacy and authority of groups regarding it being thereto related and to the belonging these notions foster (Blake, 2011).

This case may be paradigmatic as it is one of heritage return internal to a state, a topic that seems to be less explored in literature than inter-state ones (Prott, 2009), which hence allows for a different set of considerations about what heritage crime consists of, who perpetrates it, why, and how it can be resolved, to a certain extent. Furthermore, the case is complex because it comprises the intersection of issues such as heritage confiscation, negligent care and return, law and criminology, religious and cultural (societal and institutional) racism, and coloniality. Hence, it is at the crossroad between heritage studies (Harrison, 2013), heritage crime studies (Grove, 2013; Grove & Thomas, 2014), decoloniality (Ballestrin, 2014), and cultural heritage return (Prott, 2009).

On the one hand, mainly, but not exclusively, in the phases of constitution and recognition of the collection as national cultural heritage, the case embodies state internal coloniality, its (heritage) crimes, the instrumentalisation of criminology by the State to legitimise its own oppressive and repressive practices based on colonial social and ethnic classifications and hierarchies. The concepts of crime, justice, and cultural heritage were, in this sense, socially constructed, legally defined, and applied to legalise, socially normalise, and culturally value the practices and property of the dominant groups—mainly composed of people of European descent—and to criminalise, socially subordinate, and culturally devalue the practices and property of the marginal groups—in this case, and to a great extent at the national level, of African descent.

On the other hand, predominantly during restitution disputes and final restitution, the case represents decoloniality, in the empowerment of marginalised communities, the public claim for reparation to the Afro-Brazilian religious communities through restitution. Consequently, the concepts of crime, justice and cultural heritage slowly but surely underwent a shift. Firstly and more prominently in public discourse, recognising the value of this heritage in its cultural significance as representative of an elaborate cosmology and rich cultural tradition, acknowledging the social injury that the Afrobrazilian community suffered in the apprehension of their sacred objects, which is a crime that the State committed, administering colonial justice, a crime that was renewed in time as the State continuously kept the collection away from the descendants of the original owners, the Afrobrazilians. Secondly and more timidly, in State action, coinciding in the cultural heritage perception described above, but diverging as for the crime and justice perceived in the case, the crucial crime formally leading to restitution being the negligent care of the civil police regarding the items, which are part of national heritage, and the justice carried out being the reversion of this inadequate maintenance and the opening of the possibility of access of the Brazilian people, widely speaking, to the items.

2 Constitution: "Blitzkrieg Against Black Magic" and the Confiscation of Crime Proofs (1891–1938)

> The holy war of the police [. . .] lasted for years and bit by bit the tenacious resistance of the religious leaders began to give way [. . .] Smaller communities [. . .] disappeared for good. [. . .] Only a few persisted [. . .] On celebration days, the percussion called the saints and the people faced police raids, prison, beatings. (Amado, 2009: p. 235. Our translation)

The Brazilian Empire ended in 1889 with a military coup that inaugurated the republic. A year earlier, after years of abolitionist movements, slavery was ended with a law that set millions of people free overnight but did not make any provisions on how to include them in society. Both processes involved many distinct actors but were predominantly driven by a couple of core ideas, ideologies, and projects, such as positivism, social evolutionism and an obsession for modernisation. Politically, modernisation meant abandoning monarchies for republics, a view inspired by the French example, and preferably in a federal model, following the North American blueprint. Economically, it involved moving from an agricultural to an industrial economy, and towards a fully capitalist system, where workers were salary earners and consumers, not slaves. Socially, it entailed promoting policies to have a population as white(ned) as possible. Philosophy, anthropology, biology, medicine, Christianism, international exhibitions, economics, and politics were presumably proving the superiority of white people over all others (Novais & Sevcenko, 1998; Schwarcz, 1993).

Culturally, consequently, modernisation was synonymous with Europeanisation. The elites leading Brazil perceived an imperative need to define the new-born republic as close as possible to the centres of high culture, at the time considered to be England and France. This entailed redesigning cities to look more European in style, and forcing former slaves to their peripheries, far away from the public eye. Likewise, it meant promoting, in education, in the press, in the arts, and in sports, the social practices, images, and expressions that were of European descent. Forcefully, it also required the opposite attitude, of abandoning, hiding, and oppressing those objects, places, and practices that were in the way of this modernisation or that were considered as its exact opposite, being of non-European origin and character. This process and period came to be known as the *Tropical Belle Époque* (Novais & Sevcenko, 1998).

It is against this backdrop that the 1891 Brazilian criminal code was written and entered into force. Informed by the notions and the intellectual background discussed above, the articles n° 157, n° 158, n° 159 typified the crimes of black magic, charlatanism and illegal medicine. Equally influenced and shaped by this context, the police of the time acted to comply with these articles when they raided ceremonies of Afrobrazilian religions, apprehended their objects, beat and arrested participants, legally criminalising and socially delegitimising the practice and its practitioners.

In Rio de Janeiro, the new civil police academy (1912) instituted a museum that was simultaneously a place to store the objects collected and a laboratory to teach the apprentices of the academy to identify crime. This is how the "Black Magic collection" was constituted—objects were apprehended in police raids in Afrobrazilian religious spaces and ceremonies as crime proofs, and then used as teaching materials for police in training and, later, also for citizens, in public exhibitions (Corrêa, 2005, 2014; Pereira, 2017).

Hence, the heritage values present in the collection's constitution are mainly legal and pedagogical: legal, since they are the property of the police, confiscated in the exercise of their work of enforcing law and order and applying the criminal code. In this perspective, the objects are the evidence of police work correctly done, and hence, they legitimately belong to the police. Pedagogical, as they are a teaching resource on the crimes of black magic, charlatanism and illegal medicine. Thus, they are objects of study for police in training and, years afterwards, for citizens, visitors of the museum of crime.

Thus, the crime perspective present in the collection is both one of juridical nature, as proofs of the abovementioned crimes, typified in the articles n° 157, n° 158, n° 159 of the criminal code, and one of socially deviant nature, as material evidence of behaviour that violates the social norm of adequacy to European standards or 'civilisation' process following the European blueprint. The objects were, for one thing, the material proof that these illegal spells, magic and dishonesty existed (Melo, 2020) and, for another, a demonstration that there was social resistance to the civilisation project of the elite, in the continuity and vitality of the Afrobrazilian culture that was considered shameful and disgusting, barbaric, and primitive.

Finally, the notion of justice present in this collection's constitution could not be of a more colonial nature: the Brazilian State officially commits itself to exclude from the public space and imagination all those representations of African descent and Afrobrazilian belonging. The apprehensions of objects were not accompanied by any procedure of listing and description of them, or of a report of the context, exact place, time, and date for the registers of the police or criminal process. Hence, the present-day Federal Prosecutor's Office (MPF, Portuguese acronym of *Ministério Público Federal*) affirms that even according to the legal regulations at the time, they were not entirely regular, not completely lawful (Jornal O Globo, 2019). The apprehension of these objects was arbitrary and went unregistered, done without any reporting, which made it impossible for anyone to hold the police accountable. And the police, the State force operating such justice, was much acclaimed, applauded, and thanked by the elite public opinion then, as newspapers of the time show us (Valle, 2017, 2018). The operations of apprehension of Afrobrazilian sacred objects that resulted in this collection were baptised as "the blitzkrieg against black magic", in a reference to the kind of quick war the Nazi waged against their enemies. The intellectual, social, and economic elite who held the pen to write the dominating social narratives, vehiculated in the press, welcomed such blitzkrieg, such fight against this black religious, social and medical threat in a largely positive tone, as a great service of the police to society, and as a show of their moral fibre, value, and bravery (Valle, 2017, 2018).

3 Patrimonialisation: Social Evolutionism and Institutional Racism (1938–1980s)

> Disgrace on this country if we assimilate such barbarities [. . .] Listen: all this bullshit from Africa, we will sweep it away from the life and culture of the country, even if it is necessary to use violence.—It has already been used, Professor. (Amado, 2009, p. 136. Our translation)

In 1938, on the initiative of the one-year-old National Institute of Historical and Artistic Heritage (IPHAN), the collection became the first inscription in the book of Ethnological and Anthropological National Heritage (Corrêa, 2005, 2014; Melo, 2020). In an unusual process, if we examine the pattern of heritage protection and official recognition at the time, those selected as national heritage were almost exclusively objects and places that had European origins, roots, and style.

There is a line of continuity, although with some important nuances of change, with the context abovementioned, of the turn between the nineteenth and twentieth century. In the 1930s, the Brazilian institutions and intellectuals were trying to build a national identity, from above, in a project to define what it meant, culturally, to be Brazilian. The dominant conception was that Brazil was made of a mixture of three races: the Amerindian, the African, and the European. Thus, the image more often deployed was that *Brazilianness* was a river made of the confluence of these three affluents that were not, however, supposed to coexist in the nation's future. Rather, their influence was perceived in an evolutionary logic that gave origins and horizons to the nation: Amerindians were the distant past, the founding of the nation; the Africans were part of a recent one, the nation's maturation; giving way to the European legacy, the present, and future (Schwarcz, 1993, 2006).

Hence, in the general efforts of visual artists, writers, musicians, and institutions writing the history of the country and promoting national education and culture, the elements of the past (Amerindians and Africans) were present, involved in an aura of heroism, curiosity, folklore, and otherness. They were not supposed to be part of the nation's present. Conversely, the rightful elements of the present (European) were officially equated with Brazilianness and were the object of official recognition, protection, and systematic studies. Thus, specifically in most of the first works of IPHAN, the cultural heritage that was publicly highlighted, officially registered, and protected were of a Latin character, above all colonial architecture and Luso-Brazilian arts (Corrêa 2005).

Consequently, the inscription of the Black Magic Museum as the first Ethnological and Anthropological National Heritage can seem incoherent at first, although it is clarified with the exam of its trajectory. This patrimonialisation[3] seems to have been made with the goal to preserve for posterity a tradition that was going to disappear—or, if needed, was going to be directly annihilated by the State. Thus, the patrimonialisation of the collection aimed to conserve traces of a primitive cultural matrix that was bound for elimination—in the evolution of the nation towards a civilised Brazilianness of European character—but was part of Brazilian national history nonetheless, in its past period of constitution and maturation, and thus had to be protected. In this sense, the police seemed to be a suitable actor for this 'protection', since they lawfully confiscated the items and were, by doing so, rendering the nation a service, acting as a key promoter of this intended elimination of Afrobrazilian religions as a living culture that composed Brazilian society. This hypothesis is supported by the inscription of the collection in the national list as *ethnological and archaeological heritage*. The first category was reserved at the time for the scientific study of cultures that were considered primitive or isolated from modern civilisation, and the second was a reference to items that are material vestiges allowing to study past human activities (Corrêa 2005).

The collection was inscribed in the heritage list as a "criminal museum", with the objects kept alongside "toxic and narcotic items" (Melo, 2020, p. 49) and dividing space with categories such as "Games, Narcotic Drugs and Subversive Activities; Counterfeiting of Banknotes and Coins; Mystifications, Documentary, Library" in the 1950s (Melo, 2020, p. 50) and "Meele Weapons, Toxicology; Gambling; Magic Objects" (Corrêa 2014, p. 38), and more concretely, for instance, with Nazi flags and objects. The collection received only marginal attention from cultural authorities,

[3]We use the term patrimonialisation since it seems the most appropriate translation of the concept *patrimonialização*, in Portuguese, which refers not only to the process of inscription of certain objects, places or practices in the national heritage list, but also to their insertion in national narrative and, within the long-term, ongoing process of nation-building.

with the complete inventory not made until 1940 (Melo, 2020, p. 49), two years after its official nomination as national heritage, in 1938. Furthermore, its inscription in the annual book of heritage, a compilation of all Brazilian cultural heritage recognised as such by IPHAN, was only made in 1984 (Corrêa 2005).

The framing of the objects in the museum and annual heritage book were made in disregard to their original context and cultural background, showing the projection of European narratives and symbols to interpret those of African descent, through, for instance, the description of a statuette of Exu, a deity that is the messenger between humans and divinities, as Mephistopheles, the incarnation of evil in European traditions (Corrêa 2005, 2014). The exhibition of the items included a museography with a *mise-en-scène* that underlined the evil which the objects represented (Maggie, 2007; Melo, 2020).

All this allows us to affirm that the heritage' ethnological value present in the patrimonialisation, of the collection was based on the historical narratives and scientific parameters of the time, anchored in social evolutionism and institutional racism. Of a heavy colonial nature was the notion of justice reflected in this act that framed African culture as crime, evil, objects from which one should keep a distance but to which one could nurture curiosity, as they were bound to disappear. Finally, as much as the items that referred or paid tribute to Nazism, drugs, and weapons, the Afrobrazilian sacred objects were considered, officially registered, kept, and displayed as crime proofs. Thus, the crime is present in the objects in a legal perspective, since they are proof of the codified crimes of black magic, charlatanism, and illegal medicine, and in a deviant perspective, as they are the material evidence of the violation of the social norm of *Europeanness*. This norm made objects, places or practices all the more socially suitable, acceptable and laudable, the closer they were to European culture and heritage, and the more socially inappropriate, unacceptable and despicable, the closer they were to African and Amerindian culture and heritage.

4 Restitution Requests and Disputes: State Crime and Heritage Crime (1980s–2020)

> Cultural enrichment acquires the importance of a true miracle that only the mixture of cultures explains and enables (Amado, 2009, p. 227).

In 1978, students of the Fluminense Federal University (UFF) and parts of the Black movement asked for the return of the objects to their rightful owners, which would at the time likely be impossible (Maggie, 2007; Pereira, 2017, p. 52). The negative stigma of Afrobrazilian religions was still so strong at this point in time that the communities themselves were not willing to have their objects returned, in order not to be further associated with objects that were considered as proof of sorcery and source of evil, shunned and marginalised by wider Brazilian society. The legal and social scenario changed significantly after the civic-military dictatorship

(1964–1985). The 1988 constitution recognised the country's racial-ethnic diversity and thereafter social movements for the valorisation of Afrobrazilian culture became increasingly institutionalised and visible. In 1984, a *terreiro* (Afrobrazilian worship space) was first declared national heritage and the advent of the official recognition of intangible heritage, in 2001, has ever since been an important instrument of valorisation of Afrobrazilian cultural heritage (Pereira, 2017, pp. 52–53). Furthermore, since the 1980s' transition from the civic-military dictatorship to democracy, demands and disputes for the return heritage of Indigenous and African nature have become more potent, visible, and numerous (Christofoletti & Acerbi, 2021). However, mobilisations for the return of this collection specifically remained punctual and proved to no avail, consisting of restitution requests of the Afrobrazilian communities to the police and authorities of the state of Rio, that encountered deaf ears.

This changed in 2013, when the case of the collection of Afrobrazilian sacred objects gained public notoriety, which engendered an approximation of activists, researchers, and other State institutions towards the Afrobrazilian religious leaders in order to raise public awareness on the subject and articulate multi-stakeholder requests to restitution. This happened as a consequence of the then ongoing—and highly under the public eye and in the public debate—investigations of the Commission of Truth, an organism of transitional justice.

In May 2012, the National Commission of Truth was established, following law n° 12.528/2011, with the mandate to investigate human right violations during the period 1946–1988, in particular of the civic-military dictatorship (1964–1985). The national commission at the federal level was complemented by state commissions, among them the state Commission of Truth of Rio de Janeiro (CEV-RJ, acronym in Portuguese for *Comissão Estadual da Verdade do Rio de Janeiro).* Due to the fact that during the dictatorship, the Civil Police Museum building had become the state headquarters of the DOPS (Department of Social and Political Order), a body of political repression, it was studied by the Rio Commission. The collection of Afrobrazilian sacred items was mentioned in the organism's final report, released in 2015, as follows:

> evidence of *police action, which in that period criminalised habits typical of the black culture*. [...] Interpreting the practice of umbanda, candomblé and other religious and cultural expressions as acts of 'spiritism, black magic and its spells", typified as crimes by the criminal law at that time, *the police persecuted the Afrobrazilian population,* made arrests and accumulated a series of objects, later recognised of ethnographic value (CEV-Rio, 2015, p. 298. Our translation and emphasis).

This signals a change of perspective in an official document of a State-commissioned body. It denotes an understanding of the production of the crime by the police through a biased interpretation of the law, discriminating and persecuting Afrobrazilian people and practices. Likewise, it comments on the State attribution of ethnographic-heritage value to the objects, a value not intrinsic to them. In the wake of the articulation process above mentioned between different sectors of society, in May 2017, Members of Parliament (MPs), activists of the Black movement, researchers, Umbanda and Candomblé (Afrobrazilian religion) leaders officially founded the campaign *Free Our Sacred*[4] to raise public awareness and to press the authorities for restitution. In the documentary *Free Our Sacred* (Sousa, 2017), the campaign articulates the history and the desired future of the objects from their viewpoint and show us the values they attribute to it:

> The orixás [..] aren't meant to be imprisoned. [. . .] they were being held in a place where people had been tortured. [. . .]. To think objects which would have been used to appease pain were apprehended by police officers, removed in an authoritarian manner. [. . .] To think of all those objects, of all the religious leaders who lost them and the suffering they endured for having lost them [. . .] Just to think someone could take one of my sacred symbols away . . . it would be torture to me, endless, comparable to death. [. . .] most of those people aren't around anymore and they died with the sadness of knowing that their holy objects [. . .] were apprehended by the police and didn't have a single right [. . .] to claim them again. That's absurd. So, we must. . . society must demand the rights of these people (Luizinha de Nanã, human rights defender, as cited by Sousa, 2017).

This statement emphasises *the prevailing religious value of the items* to those seeking restitution. They see the objects' original purpose and their restitution as reparation, *in memoriam,* to those from whom they were stolen. The items are representations of deities. As the items are imprisoned, so are the deities. Regarding the perception of crime, they consider that the apprehensions were authoritarian. In a similar way to the people that were tortured in the same building for political reasons, these objects were forbidden by the State to socially exist. On the victims' side, these apprehensions constituted a loss, perpetrated by the State. Hence, the violation of their rights must be compensated. Mãe Meninazinha de Ogum, the religious leader heading the campaign, reinforces this:

> Our objects kidnapped. Our objects are our wealth, our gold, our sacred, worth to us much more than gold, it has a lot of value. But not for the police (Pereira, 2017, p. 51, our translation).
>
> Things that came from Africa, ours, religious. Sacred. In the police? How do I feel? Like my ancestors, grandmother and others felt [. . .] when the house was invaded, robbed. [. . .]. It is as if my people and I were imprisoned there. As long as it doesn't get out of there, I won't feel free. Ours, it is ours. It belongs to us (Pereira, 2017, pp. 53–54, our translation).
>
> It's theft! [. . .] If it were me, it would be theft. [. . .] And we want what is ours. What was the crime we committed? [. . .] Being black? Our religion coming from Africa? Worshipping Orixá? If we were Catholic, this would never have happened (Pereira, 2017, pp. 83–84, our translation).

According to her, beyond the original crime of removal of the objects from their original owners and contexts, the State also commits a crime in the present, causing damage to the living Afrobrazilian people, by keeping this collection away from them, given their relationship with the Gods the objects represent. Since the deities, embodied in the sacred items, are imprisoned, the people spiritually connected to them are imprisoned too. Both religious leaders that were quoted above see the State crime primarily due to the social injury this action caused. They refer to this crime as

[4]Their Facebook page is: https://www.facebook.com/libertenossosagrado/.

one which is not legally considered as such, since it is not recognised as a breach of the law, that in this case favours the powerful, Christian people of European descent, but is psychologically, socially, and culturally harmful to their communities (Hutchings & La Salle, 2017, pp. 71–72). Furthermore, they make a decolonial critique to the State, that does not equalise people of different cultures, but rather criminalises, dehumanises, and denies rights to those who are descendants of the enslaved people (Maldonado, 2007). However, the social injury approach is not the only perspective of crime present in the claims:

> This is part of a very strong cultural process of religious institutional racism and devaluing the culture of black people. Regarding international human rights, genocides against a specific people and cultural extermination can only be effectively overcome through a process of transitional justice. It's crucial [. . .] to reclaim the memory and culture of black people [. . .] to remove objects [. . .] apprehended as products of a crime but actually holy to African religions (Lívia Casseres, public defender, as cited by Sousa, 2017).

> We need a human rights museum of memory, freedom and justice in the DOPs building and we need the items [. . .] to be returned as a symbolic gesture. Both are part of a movement where the Brazilian State acknowledges that, [. . .] it used violence, it committed acts which we now condemn (Flavio Serafini, congressman, as cited by Sousa, 2017).

These statements condemn the State crime in a juridical approach: a breach of human rights standards, in the institutionalised religious racism, in the persecution of black people, in the non-reparation after this centuries-long massive violation of rights. Declarations about the future envisaged for the collection reveal the heritage values associated with the collection and those of justice, with its restitution.

> Reclaiming those items represents a historical reparation from a moment when this country made it official and legal to persecute African religious traditions. To have those objects and display them [. . .] to show Brazil's crimes of religious intolerance is to reclaim that memory for our children and teach them that it can't happen again (Mãe Flavia Pinto, religious leader, as cited by Sousa, 2017).

> It is important to take care of these holy objects not just for historical responsibility but for our need to learn about who we are [. . .] and also to recognise that these are knowledges, ways to see the world and elaborate life, highly sophisticated aesthetic experiences [. . .] If we don't realise how sophisticated [. . .] this legacy is not just for Brazil [..] but for mankind, [. . .] that perspective will be lost (Luiz Antonio Simas, historian, as cited by Sousa, 2017).

Other than their *sacred value*, after having been violently removed from this original context, the pieces have also become a testimony of Brazilian history of State racism and oppression. Returned as a reparation, they can become an example of, and apology for, what should not have happened and shall never happen again. Thus, they have a *historical/pedagogical valu*e. Finally, they have a *cultural/artistic value,* not only to their group of origins but to humanity as they represent a religion and knowledge system, and thus broaden our collective repertoire of ways to relate to the spiritual world. Both their historical and cultural values should be, thus, publicly emphasised. Furthermore, the claimants' decolonial notion of justice is explicit: the restitution would be an acknowledgement of the crimes committed in the past and a recognition of the full equal humanity of this 'Other' of African descent—until then denied.

Finally, the case comprises another State crime, this one officially codified[5] and as such in the end recognised by the State, that is not central in the claimants' public campaign for return but that must have been included in the formal requests directed to authorities since it was key to the resolution of this case. The negligent care of the police towards the collection of Afrobrazilian objects was a heritage crime[6], and resulted in damage to the objects. The building of the Civil Police Museum, that had been converted in the headquarters of an organism of political police during the dictatorship (1964–1985), caught fire in 1989. In this fire, more than 40 items, amongst which were some that had been recognised as national heritage, were completely destroyed (Corrêa, 2014, p. 38). Since then, the collection had been kept in boxes appropriate only for short term transport (Pereira, 2017, p. 61) and was no longer exhibited or accessible to the public in any way (Corrêa 2014, p. 36; Gama, 2018, p. 30; Pereira, 2017, p. 61).

Between 2013 and 2019, investigations of the MPF on the case of return of the Afrobrazilian collections were carried out. Their studies included a report commissioned by IPHAN, which concluded that the collection was not maintained adequately in the Civil Police Museum and should be transferred immediately (Mota, 2020; Valle, 2020). In 2017, this finding triggered the start of the official negotiations for restitution and the consequent search for a new institution to host the objects, despite protests of the Civil Police Museum, which claimed intentions to in due course give the objects proper treatment and even promote future exhibitions (Alves, 2019).

Two aspects stand out in the negotiations, meetings, public hearings, and efforts of the working group set up to tackle the issue, made of MPs, religious leaders, the MPF, Civil Police, and federal and regional public bodies working on culture. One is how the heritage crime, in the legal sense, reported by the Brazilian national authority for heritage triggered the restitution. The State crime of religious intolerance and racism constituting a social injury to the Afrobrazilian communities, in particular, and to Brazilian society, in general, was not recognised by the Police as such and did not lead them to agree to restitution. However, the heritage crime, a breach of codified law signalled by a State institution concerning the action and

[5]Cultural heritage is recognised as a legal good, since it is one of the cultural rights the Brazilian 1988 constitution provides for. More specifically, it is contained in the Title VIII–Social Order, Chapter III–Education, Culture and Sports, Section II–Of Culture, in arts. n^0 215 and 216. The law that provides for heritage crimes in the Brazilian legal order is the law of environmental crimes, n^0 9.605/98, between the articles n^0 32 and 65, that lists as a crime against heritage any action or omission that destroys, renders useless and deteriorates any item of Brazilian cultural heritage, as defined in the article n^0 216 of the constitution. Almost identical provisions were in place before these dates also, stemming from regulations passed in the 1940s, when the protection of heritage was first being set up in the country. For more on the definition of crimes against cultural heritage in the Brazilian legal order see Prado et al. (2006).

[6]Independently of the Brazilian law, if we understand heritage crime as "any offence which harms the value of [a country's] heritage assets and their settings to this and future generations" (English Heritage, 2011), neglect is unquestionably one. For further discussion on heritage crime, see Grove (2013) and Grove & Thomas (2014).

omission of another, did. This shows that the decolonial perspective of the claim does not resonate with the police, who are more prone to recognise a crime on their part as a legal fact involving technicalities than as a social fact of persecution based on prejudices.

Another aspect worthy to note is the agreement of the police to restitution only if it was to another State institution, and not directly to the people. Neither the return of the objects to religious communities nor to their community museums were accepted as alternatives for restitution (Pereira, 2017, pp. 55–59). Instead, they agreed to the restitution only as long as the pieces left their museum for another (State) one (Pereira, 2017, p. 57), and many were contacted by the working group for this purpose.

This viewpoint of the police points to their non-recognition of Afrobrazilians as people who they oppressed and are thus entitled to reparation from their part.[7] It highlights also their perception of the *official heritage* value of the collection, anchored in a legalistic view of it which is overly strict, reflecting a rigid adherence to the codified law that they were applying, although it was brutally colonial, when the collection was constituted through the confiscations. This legalistic perspective of the police concerning heritage privileges a technical interpretation of regulations in place at the time when apprehensions happened over an analysis of the broader historical, cultural, and social context, and of the colonial, violent, and racist basis in which this law was grounded. Hence, this interpretation, in their view, rightfully entitles them as owners and custodians of the objects, which were legally confiscated initially, and subsequently, while in their care, formally recognised as ethnological heritage by the State, thus bound to be in an institution that can custody them as such.

5 Final Restitution: Reparation and Decolonial Justice? (2020)

> Race hatred cannot be successful in the Brazilian climate, no wall of prejudice resists the impetus of the people (Amado, 2009, p. 228. Our translation).

The transfer of the collection of Afrobrazilian sacred items from the Police Museum to the Museum of the Republic was first decided in September 2019, signed in August 2020, and concretised in September 2020. The Museum of the Republic was neither one of the first museums contacted by the repatriation movement in 2017 nor a volunteer candidate to receive the objects (Alves, 2019; Mota,

[7]It seems relevant to underline that this treatment is not exclusive to the Afrobrazilians, since the State has been resistant to recognise the legitimacy of, and concretely allow or carry out, direct heritage reparations to indigenous groups as well. However, it can be said that societal and State oppression (in terms of past stigma and criminalisation and present heritage retention) have historically been harsher concerning Afrobrazilians than Amerindian descendants (Schwarcz, 1993, 2006). For further discussion on disputes involving Brazilian indigenous heritage see Christofoletti & Acerbi (2021).

2020; Pereira, 2017; Valle, 2020). What seems to have motivated the repatriation movement's first contact with the museum in November 2018 is the symbolic meaning inherent in it receiving the objects (Alves, 2019; Mota, 2020): as the former Presidential Palace, the museum building strongly represents the State that endorsed the persecution of Afrobrazilian religions. Accepting the objects would symbolically show the acceptance and full integration of Afrobrazilian culture into the Brazilian State, in a frame of acknowledgement of an injustice and recognition of its cultural value. Furthermore, what seems to have motivated the movement to prefer this museum to any other is the approach proposed by its director, Mário Chagas, to this restitution (Alves, 2019; Valle, 2020): "a gesture of reparation of the Museum of the Republic, a State institution" (Rede TVT, 2020). He also agreed to the "shared custody and management" of these objects, in horizontal dialogue and cooperation with the religious leaders, respecting "the ecology of knowledge" (Rede TVT, 2020). This already happens in the process of research and restoration of the objects and in the planning of the exhibition to open on the Black Consciousness Day of 2021—all done in collaboration with the religious leaders (Alves, 2020).

In this management of the restituted objects in the press and official notes (Alves, 2020; Ascom, 2020; Mota, 2020; MPF, 2020), the decolonial justice demanded by the restitution claimants has prevailed. The requesters' view of the State crime of religious intolerance and racism present in the history of the collection has also publicly come to the fore. Much more so than the State heritage crime of negligent care that officially justified the restitution. Finally, the extensive culturalist notion of heritage of the requesting parties perceived in the collection has also become the predominant one in the public debate and in the public discourse of authorities. The sacred value of the collection is recognised, respected in the research, maintenance, and display of the items in the museum, and is the basis of the request that is currently under the analysis of the IPHAN to change the name of the collection from "Collection of Black Magic" to "Afrobrazilian Sacred Collection" (MPF, 2020). Simultaneously, the historical and pedagogical role of the collection, as a testimony of past oppression and token of reparation, as well as its cultural value, as objects issuing from a sophisticated Brazilian cultural matrix like any other, are acknowledged. This can be seen in the IPHAN consideration to make national heritage the 397 pieces of the collection not yet recognised as such (Amado, 2021), and in Chagas' declarations that the collection is of interest not only to people of Afrobrazilian religions but to all who defend religious freedom and are interested in Brazilian culture and history (Rede TVT, 2020).

These perspectives, however, if predominant, are not unanimous. They prevail in the public sphere but not backstage in the binding agreements that were signed to shape the conclusion of the case. From a strictly legal point of view, the signed transfer act does not affect the ownership of the collection that remains with the police, as it is a non-onerous cession of use for two years. The MPF declared it to be a temporary act, as the final donation will be agreed upon in the near future (MPF, 2020). This legal aspect of the transfer is a direct contradiction to the public statement of the police of Rio concerning the return. It affirmed that the items had been only "under the[ir] tutelage" and that they were "carrying out the spontaneous return of the items to whom they always belonged" (Ascom, 2020), neither of which is true. Furthermore, the resolution of the case points to a significant State legalism in the handling of the dispute, as the determined crime that gave rise to restitution was based not on the social injury that the State itself had caused in the past but on the breach of its law. Similarly, the agreed solution for the transfer of the collection from the police involved a State public institution, not the communities' proposed spaces. The terms, to trigger the process of return and to condition how to finalise it, were dictated, in the end, by the State's legal texts (laws on crimes against heritage) and bodies (the police, the MPF, the state of Rio).

Finally, this coexistence of legalistic and 'culturalist' perceptions of heritage, colonial and decolonial forces is evidence of how restrictive legalistic perspectives continue to exist, mediating the resolution of heritage return disputes like this one but no longer preventing it completely, which proves that the debate is no longer incarcerated around binary notions of European, property, possession, legality, rights. Rather, this monopoly has been broken. Cultural and ethical frames of reference have been incorporated. The resolution of this case is a compromise and as such does not fulfil all the wishes of the claimants. Yet, to a large extent, it is their victory, a feat of the multi-stakeholder working group and the Free our Sacred campaign. And it involves alternative parameters such as shared heritage, rights of use, multiple appropriations, inclusive and participative models of management (König et al., 2018, p. 61). Therefore, we agree with the director of the Museum of Republic when he says that this case will become "exemplary", not only in terms of historical reparation, but because "it brings a set of innovative theoretical and practical questions, so the collection transfer means a contribution of innovations" (Jornal O Globo, 2019).

6 Final Considerations

> Listen, my friend, one day the orixas will be dancing on the stage (Amado, 2009, p. 248. Our translation).

This study has sought to analyse the historical trajectory of the Afrobrazilian sacred collection, through the changes in attribution of value of different actors to it across time, through the conceptual lens of crime, justice, and heritage. Firstly, the collections' constitution, through the confiscations of Afro-Brazilian sacred religious items as crime proofs, to begin with, and their pedagogical use, as teaching resources regarding the crimes of black magic, charlatanism, and illegal medicine in the police academy, subsequently, show how State law was used in a discriminatory, religious racist manner. Secondly, the patrimonialisation of the collection, its inscription as national heritage evidence how State actors projected European categories to evaluate objects of a non-European background, following social evolutionist and racist historical narratives and scientific theories to decide how to label, expose or hide them. Finally, the long mobilisation for restitution and its final concretisation show

how culture is a vector for empowerment and decoloniality, how much social resistance and campaigning has shifted the pendulum of interpretation of legality and heritage from a mono-cultural imposition to another more plural perception, respecting the right to culture, memory, ancestry, and reparation.

This *parcours,* the study of the oscillations of values present in the perceptions of the collection and the actions that were taken towards this set of objects allows us to conclude that the struggle in the arena of intellectual and social narratives, representations and images is complemented with one in the political-legal sphere. The criminalisation of Afrobrazilian religions that originated the collection was preceded by centuries of international and Brazilian racist and social evolutionist studies and images legitimising social relations, representations, the narrative of Brazilian history itself and its teleological projections. Likewise, the final restitution, concluded in the transfer from the Police Museum to the Museum of the Republic, embodies the decriminalisation of these religions and the recognition of their value as Brazilian culture and history. It is important to understand that it was preceded by decades of decolonial studies, social movements, and cultural policies valuing the African and Afrobrazilian legacy.

However, the State and society are not homogeneous, unified actors, but rather fragmented in sectors that were partisans of the restitution and reparation, informed by decolonial perspectives, and others that were resistant to it, and share a broader view of the world still based on racist, sexist, patriarchal, and socially hierarchical notions. And the State, when dictating resolutions to disputes, given such divisions, seems to abide by, primarily, the letter of its law. Consequently, restitution did not happen as a consequence of the claims that articulated their demand in terms of reparation for a social injury, requesting concretisation of decolonial justice through the recognition of cultural rights. Rather, it was a viewpoint centred in a legally codified—and thus, arguably, formally unquestionable—technical State heritage crime, recognised by a State authority in the actions of another, that triggered agreement upon and concretisation of restitution.

In short, this case reflects the example of the musician Gilberto Gil and the writer Jorge Amado. The first became Minister of Culture and promoted social inclusion through it, the second was an MP in the 1940s and fought against what he denounced in his novels by proposing constitutional amendments for religious tolerance and freedom. Following their example, the multi-stakeholder movement, championed by Afrobrazilian religious leaders, to revert past oppressions through the restitution of this collection allied two pathways of fight. On the one hand, it promoted communication and actions provoking shifts in public perceptions regarding crime, justice, and heritage. On the other hand, it undertook an official struggle in the political, administrative, and bureaucratic structure of the State, in the fields of human rights, public history, historical memory, and legal regulations of cultural heritage management. The combat in the first battlefield has proven to be fundamental, shaping the understanding that led to the articulation between different sectors around the campaign and the public discourse that seems to be today predominant. However, it was not enough, without a strategic position in the second one, to change the course of the restitution dispute and bring about return and reparation, which points to a State legalism in the heritage dispute in question.

Nevertheless, it is for this two-fold struggle that the questions asked by the son to the father, by the father to the grandfather and by the great-grandfather to the great-great-grandfather, in the quest to find their ancestry, evoked in Gilberto Gil's lyrics, will henceforth be openly asked and hopefully answered, in the research on and shared management of the Afrobrazilian religious collection that was restituted.

References

Acerbi, V. S., & Lima, F. C. (2020). Non-Universal Human Rights: Western and Latin American contributions for the formation of a more complete human being. *Cadernos de Pesquisa Direito Internacional sem Fronteiras, 2*(2), 2–49.

Alves, L. (2020). Rio museum recovers Afro-Brazilian art works confiscated more than a century ago as black magic. Resource document. *The Art Newspaper*. Retrieved January 10, 2021, from https://www.theartnewspaper.com/news/rio-museum-recovers-afro-brazilian-art-works-confiscated-more-than-a-century-ago-as-black-magic?fbclid=IwAR3fDMg4Tfu2RVcXPGXoY7hvXMKhSe1aNY6fP_8JgGxa3LnmKd0sfF4paZ0

Alves, L. G. (2019). A situação da "Coleção Magia Negra" e o cenário dos processos de restituição dos objetos. In M. A. Vilela (Ed.), *30° Simpósio Nacional de História da Anpuh. História e o futuro da educação no Brasil*. Associação Nacional de História. https://www.snh2019.anpuh.org/resources/anais/8/1565059462_ARQUIVO_trabalhoANPUH.pdf

Amado, G. (2021). Iphan avalia tombar outros 394 itens do acervo do museu de magia negra. Resource document. *Época*. Retrieved January 3, 2021, fromhttps://epoca.globo.com/guilherme-amado/iphan-avalia-tombar-outros-394-itens-do-acervo-do-museu-de-magia-negra-1-24818425

Amado, J. (2009). *Tenda dos milagres*. Companhia das Letras.

ASCOM. (2020). SEPOL é a primeira polícia do Brasil a devolver acervo de religiões de matriz africana. Resource document. *Polícia Civil do Estado do Rio de Janeiro*. Retrieved January 13, 2021, from http://www.policiacivilrj.net.br/noticias.php?id=7884

Ballestrin, L. M. A. (2014). *Teoria Política da Decolonização: uma perspectiva latino-americana*. IX Encontro ABCP—1964–2014: autoritarismo, democracia e direitos humanos. Brasília. Retrieved January 16, 2021, from https://cienciapolitica.org.br/system/files/documentos/eventos/2017/04/teoria-politica-descolonizacao-perspectiva-latino-americana.pdf

Bieńkowski, P. (2014). Authority and the power of place: exploring the legitimacy of authorised and alternative voices in the restitution discourse. In L. Tythacott & L. Arvanitis (Eds.), *Museums and restitution. New practices, new approaches* (pp. 37–52). Ashgate Publishing Limited.

Blake, J. (2011). Taking a human rights approach to cultural heritage protection. *Heritage & Society, 4*(2), 199–238.

Brown, M. F. (2004). Heritage as property. In K. Verdery & C. Humphrey (Eds.), *Property in question: value transformation in the global economy* (pp. 49–68). Berg.

CEV-RIO. (2015). *Relatório Final da Comissão Estadual da Verdade do Rio de Janeiro*. Comissão Estadual da Verdade do Rio de Janeiro.

Christofoletti, R., & Acerbi, V. S. (2021). Brazil on the Circuit of International Cultural Relations: Return and Devolution of Ethnographic Goods. In R. Christofoletti & M. Olender (Eds.), *World Heritage Patinas. The Latin American Studies Book Series*. Springer. https://doi.org/10.1007/978-3-030-64815-2_14

Corrêa, A. F. (2005). A coleção museu de magia negra do Rio de Janeiro: O primeiro patrimônio etnográfico do Brasil. *Mneme-Revista de Humanidades, 7*(18), 404–438.
Corrêa, A. F. (2014). Um museu mefistofélico: museologização da magia negra no primeiro tombamento etnográfico no Brasil. *Textos escolhidos de cultura e arte populares, 11*(1), 33–51.
Diário Oficial da União. (2020). Extrato da Cessão Não Onerosa de Uso de Bem móvel. *Diário Oficial da União,* 159(3), 96. Retrieved January 12, 2021, from https://www.in.gov.br/web/dou/-/extrato-de-cessao-nao-onerosa-de-uso-de-bem-movel-273012038
English Heritage. (2011). Heritage crime. Resource document. *English Heritage*. Retrieved January 23, 2021, from http://www.english-heritage.org.uk/professional/advice/advice-by-topic/heritage-crime
Gama, E. C. (2018). *Lugares de memórias do povo-de-santo: patrimônio cultural entre museus e terreiros* (Unpublished Doctoral Dissertation). Universidade Federal Fluminense.
Grove, L. (2013). Heritocide? Defining and exploring heritage crime. *Public Archaeology, 12*(4), 242–254. https://doi.org/10.1179/1465518714Z.00000000046
Grove, L., & Thomas, S. (2014). *Heritage crime: Progress, prospects and prevention*. Palgrave Macmillan.
Harrison, R. (2013). *Heritage: critical approaches*. Routledge.
Hutchings, R. M., & La Salle, M. (2017). Archaeology as state heritage crime. *Archaeologies, 13* (1), 66–87.
Jornal O Globo (2019, December 10). *Os objetos religiosos apreendidos, há um século, pelo Estado brasileiro.* [Video] Youtube. Retrieved January 10, 2021, from https://www.youtube.com/watch?v=lT_OVy5hOwU
König, V., L'Estoile, B. D., López Caballero, P., Négri, V., Perrin, A., Rinçon, L., & Bosc-Tiessé, C. (2018). Les collections muséales d'art «non-occidental»: constitution et restitution aujourd'hui. *Perspective. Actualité en histoire de l'art, 1*, 37–70.
Maldonado, N. (2007). On the coloniality of being. *Cultural Studies, 21*(2), 240–270.
Melo, S. F. (2020). A coleção de 'Magia Negra' e o Terreiro da Casa Branca: cultura (i) material, patrimônio e decolonialidade. *Museion, 35*, 47–56. https://doi.org/10.18316/mouseion.v0i35.6424
Michalowski, R. (2010). In search of 'state and crime' in state crime studies. In Chambliss, J. William, R. Michalowski, & R. Kramer (Eds.), *State crime in global age* (pp. 13–30). Willan.
Mignolo, W. (2008). Desobediência epistêmica: a opção descolonial e o significado de identidade em política. *Cadernos de Letras da UFF–Dossiê: Literatura, língua e identidade, 34*, 287–324.
Mota, C. V. (2020). Os objetos sagrados de religiões afrobrasileiras 'libertados' mais de 100 anos após serem apreendidos. Resource document. *BBC News Brasil*. Retrieved January 12, 2021, from https://www.bbc.com/portuguese/brasil-55018196
MPF. (2020). MPF acompanha entrega de acervo de religiões de matriz afrobrasileira ao museu da república. *Resource Document*. Retrieved January 15, 2021, from http://www.mpf.mp.br/rj/sala-de-imprensa/noticias-rj/mpf-acompanha-entrega-de-acervo-de-religioes-de-matriz-afrobrasileira-ao-museu-da-república
Novais, F. A., & Sevcenko, N. (1998). *História da vida privada no Brasil 3: República da Belle Époque à era do rádio*. Companhia das Letras.
Pereira, P. O. (2017). *Novos olhares sobre a coleção de objetos sagrados afro-brasileiros sob a guarda do museu da polícia: da repressão à repatriação* (Unpublished MA Dissertation). University of the State of Rio de Janeiro.
Prado, L. R., de Carvalho, É. M., & Armelin, P. K. (2006). Crimes contra o patrimônio cultural. *Revista dos Tribunais Online, 4*, 1–17.
Prott, L. V. (2009). *Witnesses to History: a compendium of documents and writings on the return of cultural objects*. Unesco.
Rede TVT. (2020, November 25) Artigos religiosos finalmente chegam a um museu. [Video] *YouTube*. Retrieved January 12, 2021, from https://www.youtube.com/watch?app=desktop&feature=youtu.be&v=SralYTuA07Q&fbclid=IwAR1jyzi5MBmLE53w0ReJjiSEtZSQddKVBAPO-pLpXaC159P5ES0XyM2pSMM

Schwarcz, L. M. (1993). *O espetáculo das raças: cientistas, instituições e questão racial no Brasil do século XIX*. Companhia das Letras.
Schwarcz, L. M. (2006). A Mestizo and tropical country: The creation of the official image of independent Brazil. *European Review of Latin American and Caribbean Studies, 80*, 25–42.
Sousa, F. (Director). (2017). *Nosso sagrado*. Quiprocó filmes.
Valle, A. (2017). No mundo dos feitiços: cultura material religiosa afro-brasileira em artigos na Gazeta de Notícias do Rio de Janeiro, 1904-1905. *Revista Nós. Cultura, Estética e Linguagens, 2*(2), 59–80.
Valle, A. (2018). O sagrado em exílio: objetos afrobrasileiros em degredos institucionais. In M. J. Neto & M. Malta (Eds.), *Coleções de Arte em Portugal e Brasil nos séculos XIX e XX–Coleções em Exílio* (pp. 263–278). Lisboa.
Valle, A. (2020). Coleções de objetos religiosos afrobrasileiros: confisco, conservação, "repatriação". In *4° Simpósio Científico do ICOMOS Brasil /1° Simpósio Científico ICOMOS-LAC*. Rio de Janeiro. www.even3.com.br/Anais/simposioicomos2020/241275-COLECOES-DE-OBJETOS-RELIGIOSOS-AFROBRASILEIROS%2D%2DCONFISCO-CONSERVACAO-REPATRIACAO
Viladevall i Guasch, M. (2003). *Gestión del patrimonio cultural: Realidades y retos*. Benemérita Universidad Autónoma de Puebla.
Warren, K. (1999). Introduction. In P. M. Messenger (Ed.), *The ethics of collecting cultural property* (pp. 1–26). University of New Mexico Press.

Art Crime and the Myth of Violence

Foundational Questions for a Critical Analysis of Art Policing

Fiona Greenland

Abstract Why did site protection and conservation become the natural purview of uniformed police or military? What forms of art policing are warranted today? What are the effects of this authority structure on our perception of the value and purpose of artworks and archaeological materials? These questions are central to contemporary debates about the place of state violence in the governance of cultural objects. To answer them, I begin with an analysis of the deep cultural codes that shape collective interpretations of art crime. Next, I trace the manifestation of these codes in the Italian Art Squad. Founded in 1969, Italy's Art Squad (Comando Carabinieri per la Tutela del Patrimonio Culturale) is the most influential and visible armed unit dedicated to enforcing cultural heritage laws. In the third section, I use art crime data from the FBI and Interpol to show that the majority of art crime is non-violent, and that the myth of violence has broader effects that should concern us. I will argue that the spread of heritage policing is symptomatic of a longer-term trend toward increased state reliance on violence to solve social problems.

1 Introduction

In February 2016, UNESCO announced a new partnership with the Italian Carabinieri: The Emergency Task Force for Culture, which is part of a wider effort by UNESCO to build multilateral support for cultural heritage policing. Calling it "a major and innovative step," UNESCO General-Director Irina Bokova highlighted Italy's expertise in fighting the illicit traffic in cultural objects. Most importantly, she suggested, the Carabinieri's specialised art crime agents would do more than investigate active cases. By combining cultural heritage expertise with law enforcement, the task force "will enhance our capacity to respond to future emergencies" (UNESCO, 2016). If cultural heritage has a future, police power will be integral to how it is imagined and experienced.

F. Greenland (✉)
Department of Sociology, University of Virginia, Charlottesville, VA, USA
e-mail: fargreenland@virginia.edu

N. Oosterman, D. Yates (eds.), *Crime and Art*, Studies in Art, Heritage, Law and the Market 1, https://doi.org/10.1007/978-3-030-84856-9_11

Cultural heritage and state power have a long history (Meskell, 2018). Scholarly work on this history has emphasised the relationship between archaeologists and the military—a nexus of associations referred to as the "military-archaeology complex" (Hamilakis, 2009, pp. 48–53). Building on this fruitful area of work, in this paper I consider a less-discussed aspect of the relationship between cultural heritage and state power: the reliance on armed police officers to enforce laws concerning art, archaeology, and other cultural objects (Block, 2011). The Emergency Task Force for Culture presents the Italian Carabinieri as the logical source of authority over cultural objects, and yet this authority had to be developed over time. This was done in part through language and symbols, which in turn draw on deep cultural codes about violence, mortal existence, and hidden enemies. I will argue that an unwarranted emphasis on art crime as violent crime has misdirected attention from what it really means to 'protect and preserve' cultural heritage.

To bring this critique into conversation with art and crime, I build on prior work in criminology, sociology, and critical heritage studies. I pose three fundamental questions for a critical history of cultural patrimony policing. First, why did site protection and conservation become the natural purview of uniformed police agents? Second, what forms of archaeological policing are warranted today? Finally, what are the effects of this authority structure on our perception of the value and purpose of archaeological materials and, more broadly, on cultural heritage practices? These questions are of central importance to studies of art and crime. I address them as problems of societies and communities, and use ideas from sociology and cultural studies to analyse the effects on social relationships of art policing.

By 'art policing,' I refer to law enforcement units that have specific authority over artworks, archaeological sites, and archaeological artefacts. In any given polity, multiple law enforcement units may technically have jurisdiction over those sites and materials (Block, 2011; Gerstenblith, 2019; Oosterman & Yates, 2020). Art policing takes this a step further by combining specific training, techniques, and knowledge to enforce cultural property protection laws (Rush & Benedettini Millington, 2015). While these units are typically small in relation to the non-specialist ranks of law enforcement, they enjoy outsize visibility for the work that they do. This visibility is often positive, driven by a celebratory narrative, and impacts public thinking about what kind of a community resource art and archaeological materials constitute (Kersel, 2012). Intentional violence against artworks and archaeological sites and materials is a painful fact and an ongoing threat. But it is important to contextualise it alongside other threats to cultural heritage. Archaeological sites are at significant risk of destruction and material loss by urbanisation, agricultural and industrial development, and climate change (Erlandson, 2012; Hambrecht & Rockman, 2017; UNESCO, 2008). My argument, therefore, is that the creation and deployment of law enforcement units to enforce cultural property law must be mindful of the competing needs and interests of the public, scholars, and archaeological materials and their sites of origin. I support the argument with data from the Federal Bureau of Investigation's (FBI) National Stolen Art File (NSAF) and the Interpol PSYCHE database (Protecting System for Cultural Heritage). To be clear, I do not oppose the application of law enforcement resources to ensure compliance with cultural heritage protection laws. I offer, instead, a critical analysis of the logic of relying on the military to solve problems that were once the domain of archaeologists and local residents.

2 Theorising Art Crime and Violence: The Work of Deep Cultural Codes

Art crime, like many other forms of crime, straddles multiple interpretive domains. As a subject of law and public policy, but also popular entertainment, it carries and reflects a range of meanings (Amore & Mashberg, 2011; Atwood, 2004). Because 'art crime' is an umbrella term that contains a number of quite different forms of action—property theft, forgery, vandalism, money laundering, smuggling, and wire fraud—these meanings are flexible and expansive. At the same time, these meanings are persistent, arising as they do from deep cultural codes. Such codes, Jeffrey C. Alexander reminds us, are "critically important in constituting the very sense of society for those who are within and without it" (Alexander, 2006, p. 54). They supply categories of purity and impurity into which every person—and, in the case of art crime, every cultural object—can be fit. Significantly for cultural heritage studies, they also contribute to boundary-making work that shapes national and ethnic categories of belonging (Sciortino, 2012). Through these codes, deviance—expressions of power, evil, and sacrality—overlap and intersect in ways intentional and inadvertent (Smith, 2008). This symbolic structure varies across time and place. In the prevailing system of global cultural governance, artworks are seen to have the capacity to convey human experience. Because of this, they are given specialised resources for preservation and protection. These regimes seek to stave off pollution, decay, and impurity (Domínguez Rubio, 2020). In light of this, intentional injuries to artworks take on an almost eschatological significance, hence the moral outrage often directed at perpetrators of certain kinds of art crime (Fine & Shatin, 1985).

Artworks and artefacts are ideal 'victims' because they cannot speak, err, or stand accused of hypocrisy. We animate them with stories and interpretations, and imbue them with near-human characteristics, and yet they are unblemished by the imperfections of actual humanity. In this way, we construct them as *charismatic mega artefacts*. I take this term from the concept of *charismatic megafauna*, those iconic, exotic mammals that populate the public-facing imagery of conservation efforts, and whose beguiling features compel people to support species protection. Charismatic megafauna secure public attention and sympathy, because they offer compelling images and stories. But they also detract from some of the less compelling, less glamorous aspects of nature conservation and habitat protection (Lorimer, 2006; Monsarrat & Kerley, 2018). I suggest that something similar is going on in the world of art and archaeology crime. The iconic and singular artworks that are photographed for art crime studies and media reports have "nonhuman charisma" (Lorimer, 2007, pp. 915–916). Without saying a word, they generate persuasive associations between art crime and the beautiful objects that everybody can agree should be protected. In dramaturgical terms, the muteness of charismatic mega artefacts makes them the perfect 'stage' on which to play out aggregated clusters of meaning (Turner, 1980). High-profile art crime cases—the handful that grab international media headlines or generate novels and films—are plays, with civilising, moral messages about fairness, social coherence, and the public good. They emphasise that the loss of an artwork is about something much bigger than one painting or statue; it is a loss to the community, to the abstraction of 'universal culture' and the socio-cultural identities that stem from it (Matthes, 2015). With temporal finitude, morality, human mortality, and community identity at stake, it is easy to understand why, in the public imagination, art and artefacts require for their protection nothing less than military power. The threats as we conceive of them merit punishment that will both purge the cultural object of its pollutant (the thief, vandal, or hustler), and restore the object to its rightful place in society—namely, as a relational tie (Smith, 2008). Uniformed officers are a singularly powerful symbol of the lines between sacred and profane, licit and illicit, and truthful and deceitful. Such binary oppositions permeate every instance of art crime (cf. Alexander, 2006: 56–67 on binary discourse).

For an example of this, consider a parallel development to the UNESCO Emergency Task Force: the creation of a formal partnership between the United States Army Civil Affairs & Psychological Operations Command (Airborne) and the Smithsonian Cultural Rescue Initiative (CRI). The partnership trains combat soldiers to recognise and avoid damaging culturally significant materials in mission zones. It is noteworthy that when the agreement was signed, media outlets explicitly likened the partnership to the World War II Monuments, Fine Arts, and Archives (MFAA) section of the Civil Affairs and Military Government Sections of the Allied Armies (Wolfe, 2019). The 'Monuments Men,' as they were known, were 345 specialists from fourteen countries who worked during and after the war to locate and secure highly vulnerable artworks and other cultural heritage objects (Edsel, 2009; Nicholas, 1994). The work of the MFAA has been celebrated with official recognition and in popular culture. It is an appealing comparison because the MFAA story is redolent with powerful and recurring myths. It features heroes, villains, innocent victims, and a dramatic backdrop. Significantly, the heroes (MFAA personnel) fight the Nazi villains for possession of iconic artworks that symbolise civility and humanity itself.

I am suggesting that the MFAA has a particular kind of symbolic power because of its grounding in deep cultural codes. The meanings that come from these codes merit interpretation and analysis as independent socio-cultural elements. The military capacity of the Monuments Men and Women is read as the natural solution for 'art threats' writ large, but this reading conflates the relevant issues. The MFAA worked in a period of formal war and its aftermath, during which there was a clearly delineated enemy and a discrete list of target objects. Today's threats to cultural heritage are asymmetric and diffuse, and cultural heritage itself goes well beyond iconic objects to include archaeological materials of diverse typology and size. Wartime anti-Nazi protections and contemporary archaeological site protections are easily elided in public discussions, but these two endeavours are distinct from each other in their structure, operation, and interface with the public.

Another example of the deep cultural codes of art crime come from media coverage of a foiled plot in 2020 to steal artworks from the palace of Fontainebleau (López-Fonseca & Ayuso, 2020). The alleged offender, Juan Maria Gordillo Plaza, was described as a 'Spanish thug' nicknamed 'Juan the kid.' The European Observatory of Crimes and Society (EU-OCS) dramatically recounted the botched plan:

> There, acting on shadowy orders from the Chinese triads, they plotted to steal priceless artworks. It sounds like a saga worthy of a Hollywood film script, but French and Spanish authorities recently foiled this exact stratagem, sweeping in the wee hours the very day the house was supposed to occur to arrest the would-be robbers (EU-OCS, 2020).

This characterisation of art crime is not representative of the majority of art crime cases. But 'thug,' 'shadowy orders,' and 'the Chinese underworld' are highly evocative terms that deliberately cue organised crime and violence. They mark the accused perpetrators as threats to the civil sphere whose putative art theft would have destabilised the fragile material links between people and the past. To the concept of the charismatic mega artefact, then, we can add another construct: the charismatic mega crook. This is the bad actor, the villain, who lurks in the dim underbelly of the art and antiquities illicit market. The charismatic mega crook is construed as a specialist art or antiquities thief who does his work for the love of art and the thrill of the chase. This stereotyped figure was shown by Mackenzie (2005) to be a fiction. But this is how we think about art and archaeology crime because the anecdotes of armed gangs and insurgents confirm what the deep cultural codes are telling us about risk, danger, and threat.

Deep cultural codes are always in play, shaping our interpretations of the social world. Art crime dramaturgy may be effective for commanding public attention and distilling moral lessons, but simplistic invocations of villains and heroes obscure the complexities of the market and community ecosystems in which artefacts and artworks are stolen, damaged, or otherwise transgressed. Prior scholarship has greatly illuminated our understanding of these ecosystems by exploring the horizons of affect, meaning, and need in which such actions take place (Greenland, 2021; Hollowell-Zimmer, 2003; Kersel, 2013; Stone, 2009). Building on the discussions generated by this body of work, I will focus on the emergence of specialist art policing as a specific response to a specific perceived threat. The emergence has multiple possible starting points. Local, national, and ecclesiastical authorities took different steps to enforce archaeological protection laws prior to World War II, but it is in the post-war period that we can point to the formation of the modern archaeological policing apparatus. The 1954 Hague Convention included a recommendation that Convention signatories take steps to raise heritage awareness among their armed forces personnel, and introduce new regulations or instructions to ensure armed forces' observation of the Convention's cultural property mission.[1] In addition, Article 7.2 made the following recommendation:

[1] The literature on the 1954 Hague Convention is vast, and it is beyond the scope of this paper to do it justice. Recent contributions to the discussion include Fox and Cunliffe (2018) and Gerstenblith (2019).

> The High Contracting Parties undertake to plan or establish in peace-time, within their armed forces, services or specialist personnel whose purpose will be to secure respect for cultural property and to cooperate with the civilian authorities responsible for safeguarding it.

The Convention left it to the States Parties to decide what form the 'services or specialist personnel' would take. This and other recommendations were subject to a range of interpretations (Gerstenblith, 2019). Article 7.2 does not specify that it should be a uniformed police unit, but it is this organisational form that became dominant. Domestic politics, socio-economic shifts, and cultural anxieties were major factors behind this development, and help explain why it took root and flourished in the Italian Carabinieri.

3 Archaeology as the Domain of Police Power

After World War II, Italy underwent a period of rapid economic growth characterised by urban population increase, rising household income levels, rising industrial manufacture, and an expanded private sector (Crafts & Toniolo, 1996; Ginsborg, 2003). The economic miracle brought a number of positive changes to the average working-class family. It also triggered anxieties about the state of Italy's cultural heritage. Urban population growth demanded new housing projects, which sometimes entailed the loss of historic structures and culturally sensitive sites. Agricultural production, similarly, swallowed up archaeological sites and historic natural features. Electrification and the accessibility of popular culture through television, film, and radio were interpreted as threats to traditional regional dialects, religious practices, and cultural identities (Forgacs & Gundle, 2007). And mass tourism brought foreigners to Italy in record numbers (Hom, 2015). Many of those tourists had an appetite for Etruscan and Roman souvenirs, and some enterprising individuals fed that appetite by illegally digging up and selling archaeological materials. All of this contributed to a widespread fear that Italy's cultural traditions were under assault.

To address these concerns, the national government created a series of commissions to study the administration and organisation of Italy's cultural goods and sites. The first, the Franceschini Commission (1964–1967)—named after its chairman—comprised experts in art history, archaeology, law, and library science, in addition to elected members of parliament. The commission was asked to revise the nation's cultural heritage administrative framework and identify funding needs and delivery mechanisms to support the framework. During its three-year period of activity, the Franceschini Commission produced nine key recommendations (Lambert, 2019; Pallottino, 1987). They included conservation administration measures, such as the creation of a systematic inventory of culturally significant moveable and immoveable objects and supporting scientific training for conservation professionals. The recommendations also called for a moratorium on development projects that threatened archaeological sites of interest, and programs to increase public awareness of the importance of respecting archaeological and other culturally sensitive sites. Finally, the Franceschini Commission called for a security service focused on cultural heritage protection. This, the commission stressed, was the most urgent of its recommendations, and they defined it as follows: "[The] Superintendents [of archaeology] will avail themselves of a security service of administrative autonomy, with the powers necessary to carry out their prescribed functions" (Franceschini, 1967, pp. 4–5).[2] Unable to agree on the best course of action, the government set in motion yet another official assessment of the country's cultural property. This effort resulted in the Papaldo I (1968) and Papaldo II (1970) Commissions. They, too, generated a range of recommendations on what the national government and its regional arms should do to protect Italian cultural patrimony (Pavone, 2013).

The results of these commissions were inconclusive (Condemi, 2003). After the presentations of the recommendations to parliament, they failed to gain traction (Lambert, 2019). There are several reasons for this, including governmental preoccupation with civil unrest, and a lack of a critical mass of elected officials willing to champion the comprehensive reforms called for by Franceschini (Zanardi, 1999). The urgent call for a security service was heeded, however, and plans were put in place for the Italian Art Squad, founded in May 1969 as the Nucleo Tutela Patrimonio Artistico (NTPA). Initially staffed with just three full-time employees, the NTPA reported to the Ministry of Education and was constituted as a unit of the Carabinieri. During the Fourteenth UNESCO General Conference in Paris during October and November 1970, Italian officials presented the NTPA model to the general assembly. The model was received with enthusiasm, and Italy was heralded as an exemplar of national investment in cultural property protection. The official origin story, as told by the Carabinieri today, nods toward this event and sets the unit's creation in the context of rampant looting across Italy:

> The 1960s, while marked by an important economic recovery, was also, on the other hand, characterized by an intensification of clandestine exports of culturally significant items, stolen or illegally excavated, for enriching museums and private collections all over the world (Comando Carabinieri Tutela Patrimonio Culturale, 2008).

Italian journalist Fabio Isman has referred to the 1960s and 1970s as 'the great raid' in recognition of a vast increase in the number and impact of tomb robbers in Italy (Isman, 2009). These are difficult claims to corroborate because reliable, comparable numbers are non-existent, though archaeologist Carlo Lerici reported—and attempted to quantify—looters' pits at Etruscan sites (Lerici, 1962). Criminologist Marc Balcells argues, further, that it was in the 1960s and 1970s that tomb robbers professionalised their skill set and network specialisation (Balcells, 2018).

What we can establish is that the Italian government's articulation of tomb robbing as a particular kind of problem changed in this period (Greenland, 2021).

[2] Original: "Per i provvedimenti d' ufficio e per l'esecuzione dei propri provvedimenti, il Soprintendente si avvale del Servizio di Sicurezza dell'Amministrazione autonoma, provvedendo con propri ordini di servizio ad impartire le prescrizioni opportune," Declaration 16, pp. 4–5.

It became a problem of public order and security. The art market, long criticised by Italian officials for draining cultural treasures from the country, was no longer (merely) a powerful external network of buyers and pricing mechanisms. It was now internal to Italy, being diffuse, opaque, and amoral, with Italians themselves feeding the market by willingly looting their own patrimony. The antiquities market took on its own characterisation outside of the art market, stigmatised as the 'dark side' of art buying and presumptively guilty of theft. This way of thinking about the trade in antiquities required a tailored strategy for defending Italian national culture. The 'strategy of tension' involved inciting alarm about the nation's cultural materials (i.e., 'our heritage is disappearing' or 'the foreign museums are taking everything'), and pointing to the Carabinieri as the logical, and only effective, solution.[3]

Since 1969, the Art Squad has steadily grown in size and institutional stature. In 1992, the Ministry for Internal Affairs designated the NTPA as a Special Force of the Carabinieri, at which point its functions and duties were formalised under the name of Comando Carabinieri Tutela Patrimonio Artistico (TPA). By the end of 1994 the Carabinieri TPA had 145 staff members. Just four years later the unit size had nearly doubled and the TPA, now known as the Tutela Patrimonio Culturale (TPC, or Art Squad), became the largest specialist law enforcement unit for the protection and recovery of national culture. By 2018 there were 300 agents spread across the Italian peninsula. Its recoveries are said to total nearly a million artefacts, worth hundreds of millions of euros. The Art Squad's headquarters are located in central Rome, though the unit describes itself as a force without a single head but with a capillary presence—spread thin but everywhere, even in the *privi di strade* (impenetrable) spaces of the country. Uniformed and plainclothes officers patrol Italy from the sky and under sea, giving them hypothetical presence everywhere. This policing model is symbolised by the Art Squad's coat of arms, which features a dragon looming over the ancient Pantheon in central Rome. The dragon's tail snakes around the piazza in front of the building, as if to show the extent of its reach in public life.

When the unit makes a public presentation of the artefacts and artworks that it recovered, it displays them the way narcotics units make a show of their intercepted cocaine bricks: in stacks and rows designed to impress the audience with mass and value. This, too, is a conscious performance of police power. From its origins as a small state office, the Art Squad has become the most visible manifestation of the state's protection of national cultural property. Its expertise is sought by other nations' governments, as when it sent officers to Iraq to train local specialists in cultural protection techniques (Foradori, 2017; Rush & Benedettini Millington, 2015).

At this point I can offer a preliminary answer to my foundational question—why did archaeological protection become the natural purview of law enforcement? As a response to acute anxieties about the loss of Italian culture in the post-war economic boom, commissioned experts recommended significant investments in object

[3]The idea of the 'strategy of tension' in the context of Italian policing and public violence is developed by Ferraresi (1995).

conservation, archaeological training and site management, and scientific training; new regulations to stop unchecked urban and agricultural development; public awareness-raising; and a dedicated security service. The government made modest investments in some of these areas, and supported the formation of the security service. Precisely when Italy was struggling to redeem itself on the international stage, cultural property policing emerged as a key arena of inter-state negotiation and cooperation. To be a legitimate state actor in this arena required recognition of states' cultural sovereignty, and a shift from museum-building to technical and scientific expertise in managing artefacts *in situ* (Matthes, 2015; Meskell, 2018). The language of safeguarding became associated with state intervention. Heritage took on new value as a security threat that required armed protection. With positive publicity and exemplification by UNESCO, the NTPA served as more than a model for archaeological policing. It symbolised a national approach to cultural heritage protection. The conservation and site management tasks that were once the ambit of archaeologists and art historians were normatively supplanted by policing expertise. When the government did make investments in the regional archaeological superintendencies, the sensibility and organisational protocols of policing were embedded in the operational procedures. In the next section, I will ask whether circumstances today continue to justify this arrangement.

4 Rethinking Archaeological Policing Today

Perhaps the most salient current argument for the necessity of archaeological policing stems from the Islamic State's (IS) atrocities during the Syrian war. Those atrocities included the torture, enslavement, and murder of thousands of children, women, and men. Deliberate destructions of archaeological sites, structures, and artefacts were also part of the toll (Casana & Laugier, 2017; Casana & Panahipour, 2014; Greenland, 2020). Wartime disruptions to social and civic institutions put archaeological sites at unusual risk, and to protect sites from harm would have required increased levels of military or police presence (Cunliffe, 2014). IS, moreover, did not attempt to conceal its actions but rather broadcast its 'performative violence' (Danti, 2015, p. 138). Terrorism thrives on publicity. Recent work demonstrates that terrorist threats to cultural sites are not limited to Syria. In a study of museum sector security, Atkinson et al. (2020) used data from security professionals, police departments, and museum management offices to establish that a range of museums in Britain had received terrorism threats. Museums are attractive targets for terrorism both because they are potentially casualty-rich and because they are keepers of symbolically valuable artefacts. Counter-terrorism is a complex area of public governance, the authors remind us, involving multiple strategies of which policing is only one. Given the expressly violent intent of terrorist attacks, which are by definition aimed at destruction and disruption, policing can be an important strategy for countering them.

With terrorism as the extreme example, let us consider the more quotidian dynamics of archaeological materials' movement through social networks. In their study of the One Belt, One Road initiative in China, Mackenzie and Yates (2020) found three categories of threat to artefacts: infrastructure development that infringes on the physical integrity of cultural heritage sites, increased opportunities for the efficient movement of illicit artefacts from site to buyers, and new narratives available to market actors to explain and justify their own participation in the illicit antiquities trade. The findings are an important reminder that archaeological materials are imperilled by changes and disturbances that are readily subsumed under 'development' and justifiable on economic grounds.

Another way to rethink archaeological policing is to ask whether art and archaeological crimes are violent to a degree that requires military-police power. The FBI's Art Crimes team is grouped in the Violent Crimes division, suggesting that the crimes themselves involve bodily harm to persons (or credible risks thereof). The information included in the public-facing version of the National Stolen Art File (NSAF) is of insufficient granularity to identify co-occurrences of violence (FBI UCR). The most frequent incident type is "Stolen," with no details of the circumstances. The FBI's Uniform Crime Reports (UCR) are no more helpful. The UCR is a database of crime reports that are submitted annually by state and local law enforcement units. It constitutes the most comprehensive source of crime information in the United States, and is used by criminologists to establish trends in felonies and misdemeanours. Although the UCR provides multi-level classifications for several categories of crime, art crime is not one of them. Instead, thefts of artworks and antiquities are lumped with other types of property theft under a category called 'Miscellaneous.' As a result, it is difficult to distil descriptive statistics of art crime, much less establish trends over time.

In one of the first comprehensive analyses of UCR and NSAF data, Kate Burmon (2017) showed that 77.2 percent of art theft reports indicated that the theft occurred in an empty building. No person was present, in other words, except the thief or thieves. In 64.5 percent of the reports, there was no forced entry. The data show a notable *absence* of violence from art crime. In many cases, Burmon (2017) argues, the offender knew the owners of the artwork and was familiar with the premises from which it was stolen. Similar patterns are present in the art crime data collected by Interpol through the PSYCHE project (Protecting System for Cultural Heritage). According to its website, PSYCHE is 'the only database at the international level with certified police information on stolen and missing objects of art' (Interpol 2021). The database contains more than 52,000 unique reports of stolen cultural property. Most of the cases involve cultural property removed from private residences by breaking and entering (Brown, 2018). The National Stolen Art File and PSYCHE data together suggest a picture of art crime that is far from the image presented in media and popular culture, with its dramatic elements of violence and criminal masterminds.

In sum, is art crime violent? Statistically speaking, no. The majority of incidents are property theft without altercation. Just as any other form of property crime, local authorities need to have appropriate tools to apprehend law breakers, recover stolen property, and prevent future crimes. Insurgent looting and violent gangs are responsible for a small fraction of global art crime. We need tools and measures to deal with those cases, but we also need narratives that realistically frame the market.

5 Broader Implications: The Effects of Police Power on Art and Artefacts

What are the effects of police power on our perception of the value and purpose of archaeological materials and, more broadly, on cultural heritage practices? One of the most critical responses to this question is the thesis of the military-archaeology complex. Hamilakis (2009) defines the military-archaeology complex as formal, professionalised links between archaeology and the military. It can include archaeologists providing no-strike lists; archaeologists working at sites under military authorisation (but without local consent); training active duty personnel to recognise culturally sensitive materials and sites; and providing maps, surveys, and images related to archaeological sites and materials in conflict or occupation zones. As he puts it, archaeologists no doubt see this as the right thing to do in the interest of 'protecting and preserving' material culture. They may conclude that if they do not offer training or assistance, the consequences will be far worse. But Hamilakis argues that the longer-term outcomes are problematic. Military power becomes the "naturalised state of world affairs" (Hamilakis, 2009, p. 50). Military conceptions of cultural worth are imposed through battle plans and occupation governance. The cooperation of archaeologists can be interpreted (indeed, claimed as) an endorsement of war, which depoliticises war itself. These types of military-archaeology links after the invasion of Iraq in 2003, "set the foundations, un-intentionally perhaps, for a new militarised archaeology, a military-archaeology complex" (Hamilakis, 2009, p. 51). Hamilakis turns the military-archaeology complex into an interrogation of the ontology of archaeology. The discipline's primary responsibility is to living people, he reminds us, in dynamic communities with changing relationships to cultural materials.

Militarisation is the process through which ever expanding categories of human behaviour are turned into a problem to be solved by the armed forces. By this logic, armed soldiers and police officers are not only provided with the equipment to address the phenomenon of art crime, they also become the optimal actors to do so because of the implied dangerous nature of looters and smugglers. Recent scholarship confirms that danger is a 'ubiquitous cultural theme' in policing (Crank, 2014, p. 140, as cited by Sierra-Arévalo, 2021, p. 72). Michael Sierra Arévalo advances the concept of the *danger imperative* to explain this. In his words, the danger imperative is a cultural frame that emphasises the high potential for any suspect to respond with violence. The necessity of proceeding as though every encounter could turn violent is a pervasive philosophy that is reinforced at all levels of the police organisation. To avoid this in art policing requires careful coordination of local and intra-regional enforcement of art and archaeology protection laws—a topic that scholars have recently begun to analyse comparatively (Oosterman & Yates, 2020). Past work has demonstrated that people *do* desire law enforcement support to protect cultural treasures, provided that support is sensitive to local needs (Yates, 2014). Without that sensitivity, including careful calibration of violent response, archaeological policing might exacerbate situations that could be handled through peaceful and unarmed civilian interventions.

Closely related is the assertion that looters should be shot on site (Kennedy, 2003). To my knowledge, such a policy has never been implemented by the police forces under discussion here. But what are the effects of this way of thinking and talking about the use of state force to control human-artefact relations? The general policy direction could lead to pre-emptive uses of force seen as necessary to ensure control of a site, before there is physical resistance from a subject. The question here is not whether looting is illegal, since in many cases it is. The question is whether pre-emptive use of force is accomplishing the desired goals of protection and conservation. The reputation of an archaeological police force for aggressive and antagonistic behaviour can create interactions that reinforce perceptions of distrust and fear, jeopardising the entire project of protecting cultural property for the benefit of local people. When we focus on the potential for violence, and on mythical mega crooks or violent insurgents, we stop thinking about other kinds of people involved, including white-collar fraudsters in North America and Europe who exploit artworks for money laundering (Bowley, 2020; Tijhuis, 2011). This is not the way we want to think about art and archaeology crime because the anecdotes of armed gangs and insurgents confirm other, powerful stereotypes about geography, ethnicity, and class.

For all that art police are compelling cultural figures that bring valuable capacities to a subset of art crime, the most effective means of countering the illicit trade in cultural objects is market regulation, devaluation of unprovenanced objects, and other buyer-end mechanisms (Mackenzie, 2011; Yates, 2015). Because art crime is largely driven by market demand, by addressing dealer and collector activities cultural property officials stand a better chance of preventing archaeological site disruptions in the first place. Data from the Italian Carabinieri indicate that the number of reported thefts of archaeological materials dropped after the Italian government changed its investigatory approach.[4] The head of the Art Squad attributed this drop both to increased pressure on international museums not to acquire unprovenanced antiquities and to closer collaborations between police forces, the judiciary, foreign embassies, and cultural institutions (Demuro, 2004, p. 124). Collectors and museum directors wished to avoid the stigma of repatriation lawsuits and potential criminal charges. Uniformed police were only one of several types of state authority involved in this work. In protecting artefacts and artwork for the common

[4]In 1997, there were 2120 thefts reported for 23,513 objects taken, in 1998, 2032 thefts reported for 24,058 objects taken, 1999 showed 2168 reported thefts, and for 2000 the figure was 2136 reported archaeological thefts for over 30,000 objects taken. Data from 2001 onward indicate a reversal of the tendency: the number diminished to 1784 thefts for 21,316 objects taken (Demuro, 2004, pp. 124–125).

good, then, we must attend to the resonant meanings of art crime but also move beyond the traditional models of police authority to connect with broader communities of people.

To be sure, the Italian Carabinieri and other specialist art police have made important inroads into illicit cultural markets and the networks that feed them. But the proliferation of such units may be crowding out other approaches to protecting archaeological sites and materials. Recall the Franceschini Commission's recommendation that an art police unit be only one component of a multi-faceted approach to cultural heritage custodianship. Archaeologists, anthropologists, and materials conservators were also meant to lead the effort. Policing art was not inevitable, and the role of the art police must be the object of continued critical analysis.

Acknowledgements The author thanks the volume editors as well as audiences at the American Sociological Association and the Neubauer Collegium for Culture and Society at the University of Chicago for helpful comments on earlier versions of this paper.

References

Alexander, J. C. (2006). *The civil sphere*. Oxford University Press.

Amore, A. M., & Mashberg, T. (2011). *Stealing rembrandts: The untold stories of notorious art heists*. Palgrave Macmillan.

Atkinson, C., Yates, D., & Brooke, N. (2020). 'Now that you mention it, museums probably are a target': Museums, terrorism and security in the United Kingdom. *Museum Management and Curatorship, 35*(2), 109–124.

Atwood, R. (2004). *Stealing history: Tomb raiders, smugglers, and the looting of the ancient world*. St. Martin's Press.

Balcells, M. (2018). *Contemporary archaeological looting: A criminological analysis of Italian tomb robbers*. Unpublished Doctoral Dissertation. CUNY Graduate School.

Block, L. (2011). European police cooperation on art crime: A comparative overview. *Journal of Art Crime, 4*(1), 13–25.

Bowley, G. (2020, July 29). Senate Report: Opaque Art Market Helped Oligarchs Evade Sanctions. *New York Times*. https://www.nytimes.com/2020/07/29/arts/design/senate-report-art-market-russia-oligarchs-sanctions.html

Brown, K. (2018, April 6). Art thieves prefer sculpture over paintings and 4 other revelations from Interpol's Art Theft Database. *Artnet News*. https://news.artnet.com/market/art-theft-interpol-database-1261133

Burmon, K. (2017). *Patterns of fine art theft in the United States*. Unpublished Doctoral Dissertation. Northeastern University.

Casana, J., & Laugier, E. J. (2017). Satellite imagery-based monitoring of archaeological site damage in the Syrian civil war. *PLoS ONE, 12*. https://doi.org/10.1371/journal.pone.0188589

Casana, J., & Panahipour, M. (2014). Satellite-based monitoring of looting and damage to archaeological sites in Syria. *Journal of Eastern Mediterranean Archaeology & Heritage Studies, 2*, 128–151.

Comando Carabinieri Tutela Patrimonio Culturale: Origini, funzioni e articolazioni (Rome: CCTPC, 2008), Part 5, "Il Comando Carabinieri Tutela Patrimonio Culturale," 10.

Condemi, S. (2003). *La salvaguardia dei beni culturali. Lineamenti di storia della tutela*. Palazzo Spinelli.

Crafts, N., & Toniolo, G. (1996). *Economic growth in Europe since 1945*. Cambridge University Press.
Crank, J. P. (2014). *Understanding police culture*. Routledge.
Cunliffe, E. (2014). Archaeological site damage in the cycle of war and peace: A Syrian case study. *Journal of Eastern Mediterranean Archaeology and Heritage Studies, 2*(3), 229–247.
Danti, M. (2015). Ground-based observations of cultural heritage incidents in Syria and Iraq. *Near Eastern Archaeology, 78*(3), 132–141, Special Issue: The Cultural Heritage Crisis in the Middle East.
Demuro, G. P. (2004). *Beni culturali e tecniche di tutela penale*. Giuffrè.
Domínguez Rubio, F. (2020). *Still life: Ecologies of the modern imagination at the art museum*. University of Chicago Press.
Edsel, R. M. (2009). *Monuments men: Allied heroes, Nazi thieves and the greatest treasure hunt in history*. Preface Publishing.
Erlandson, J. M. (2012). As the world warms: Rising seas, coastal archaeology, and the erosion of maritime history. *Journal of Island Conservation, 16*, 137–142.
EU-OCS. (2020, February 7). Bungled Fontainebleau theft shines a spotlight on organised crime in the art world. *European Observatory for Crimes and Society*. https://eu-ocs.com/bungled-fontainebleau-theft-shines-a-spotlight-on-organised-crime-in-the-art-world/
FBI UCR. https://www.fbi.gov/investigate/violent-crime/art-theft/national-stolen-art-file?q=&Subject=
Ferraresi, F. (1995). *Minacce alla democrazia. La Destra radicale e la strategia della tensione in Italia nel dopoguerra*. Feltrinelli.
Fine, G. A., & Shatin, D. (1985). Crimes against art: Social meanings and symbolic attacks. *Empirical Studies of the Arts, 3*(2), 135–152.
Foradori, P. (2017). Protecting cultural heritage during armed conflict: The Italian contribution to 'cultural peacekeeping'. *Modern Italy, 22*(1), 1–17. https://doi.org/10.1017/mit.2016.57
Forgacs, D., & Gundle, S. (2007). *Mass culture and Italian society from fascism to the cold war*. Indiana University Press.
Fox, P., & Cunliffe, E. (2018). *UK implementation of the 1954 Hague Convention for the protection of cultural property in the event of armed conflict*. Position Paper I. Newcastle-upon-Tyne: UK Blue Shield.
Franceschini. (1967). *Atti della Commissione d'indagine per la tutela e la valorizzazione del patrimonio storico, archeologico, artistico e del paesaggio* 1967, Republic of Italy.
Gerstenblith, P. (2019). *Art, cultural heritage, and the law: Cases and materials*. Carolina Academic Press.
Ginsborg, P. (2003). *A history of contemporary Italy*. Palgrave Macmillan.
Greenland, F. R. (2020). The art of destruction: Theorizing ontological violence in the Islamic State. In F. R. Greenland & F. M. Göçek (Eds.), *Cultural violence and the destruction of human communities: New theoretical perspectives* (pp. 116–140). Routledge.
Greenland, F. R. (2021). *Ruling culture: Art police, tomb robbers, and the rise of cultural power in Italy*. University of Chicago Press.
Hambrecht, G., & Rockman, M. (2017). International approaches to climate change and cultural heritage. *American Antiquity, 82*(4), 627–641.
Hamilakis, Y. (2009). The "war on terror" and the military-archaeology complex: Iraq, ethics, and neo-colonialism. *Archaeologies, 5*(1), 39–65.
Hollowell-Zimmer, J. (2003). Digging in the dirt: Ethics and "low-end looting". In L. J. Zimmerman, K. D. Vitelli, & J. Hollowell-Zimmer (Eds.), *Ethical issues in archaeology* (pp. 45–56). Rowman & Littlefield Publishers.
Hom, S. M. (2015). *The beautiful country: Tourism and the impossible state of destination Italy*. University of Toronto Press.
Interpol. (2021). *Stolen works of art database*. Retrieved May 26, 2021, from https://www.interpol.int/Crimes/Cultural-heritage-crime/Stolen-Works-of-Art-Database
Isman, F. (2009). *I predatori dell'arte perduta. Il saccheggio dell'archaeologia in Italia*. Skira.

Kennedy, M. (2003, July 9). Kill looters, urges archaeologist. *The Guardian*. https://www.theguardian.com/uk/2003/jul/09/iraq.internationaleducationnews
Kersel, M. (2012). The power of the press: The effects of press releases and popular magazines on the antiquities trade. In E. Meyers & C. Meyers (Eds.), *Archaeology, bible, politics and the media: Proceedings of the Duke University Conference, April 23–24, 2009* (pp. 73–83). Eisenbrauns.
Kersel, M. (2013). Looting. *The Oxford companion to archaeology, 3*, 232–234.
Lambert, S. (2019). Italy and the history of preventive conservation. *CeROArt, 1*. https://doi.org/10.4000/ceroart.1707
Lerici, C. (1962). *Italia Sepolta*. Lerici editori.
López-Fonseca, Ó., & Ayuso, S. (2020, January 10). Chinese mafia suspected of hiring Spanish thieves for heist in French palace. *El País*. https://english.elpais.com/elpais/2020/01/10/inenglish/1578653299_635283.html
Lorimer, J. (2006). Non-human charisma: Which species trigger our emotions and why? *Ecos, 27* (1), 20–27.
Lorimer, J. (2007). Nonhuman charisma. *Environment and Planning D: Society and Space, 25*(5), 911–932.
Mackenzie, S. (2005). Criminal and victim profiles in art theft: Motive, opportunity and repeat victimisation. *Art, Antiquity and Law, 10*(4), 353–369.
Mackenzie, S. (2011). Illicit deals in cultural objects as crimes of the powerful. *Crime, Law and Social Change, 56*, 133–153.
Mackenzie, S., & Yates, D. (2020). Crime, corruption, and collateral damage: Large infrastructure projects as a threat to cultural heritage. In T. Wing Lo, D. Siegel, & S. I. Kwok (Eds.), *Organized crime and corruption across borders exploring the belt and road initiative*. Routledge.
Matthes, E. H. (2015). Impersonal value, universal value, and the scope of cultural heritage. *Ethics, 125*(4), 999–1027.
Meskell, L. (2018). *A future in ruins. UNESCO, world heritage, and the dream of peace*. Oxford University Press.
Monsarrat, S., & Kerley, G. I. H. (2018). Charismatic species of the past: Biases in reporting of large mammals in historical written sources. *Biological Conservation, 223*, 68–75.
Nicholas, L. H. (1994). *The rape of Europa: The fate of Europe's treasures in the Third Reich and the Second World War*. Vintage.
Oosterman, N., & Yates, D. (2020). Policing heritage crime in Latin America. *Revista de Direito Internacional, 17*(3), 275–290. https://doi.org/10.5102/rdi.v17i3.7030
Pallottino, M. (1987). La stagione della Commissione Franceschini. In M. Pallottino (Ed.), *Memorabilia: il futuro della memoria. Beni ambientali architettonici artistici e storici in Italia. 1. Tutela e valorizzazione oggi* (pp. 7–11). Editori Laterza.
Pavone, C. (2013). La commissione Papaldo. *Parolechiave*, January–June, 175–182.
Rush, L., & Benedettini Millington, L. (2015). *The Carabinieri Command for the protection of cultural property: Saving the world's heritage*. Boydell & Brewer.
Sciortino, G. (2012). Ethnicity, race, nationhood, foreignness, and many other things: Prolegomena to a cultural sociology of difference-based interactions. In J. C. Alexander, R. N. Jacobs, & P. Smith (Eds.), *The Oxford handbook of cultural sociology* (pp. 365–389). Oxford University Press.
Sierra-Arévalo, M. (2021). American policing and the danger imperative. *Law and Society Review, 55*(1), 70–103.
Smith, P. (2008). *Punishment and culture*. University of Chicago Press.
Stone, E. (2009). Patterns of looting in Southern Iraq. *Antiquity, 82*(315), 125–138.

Tijhuis, A. J. G. (2011). Trafficking in cultural artifacts. In M. Tonry (Ed.), *The Oxford handbook of crime and public policy*. Oxford University Press. https://doi.org/10.1093/oxfordhb/9780199844654.013.0019

Turner, V. (1980). Social dramas and stories about them. *Critical Inquiry, 7*(1), 141–168.

UNESCO. (2016, February 16). Italy creates a UNESCO Emergency Task Force for Culture. UNESCO World Heritage Convention press release. http://whc.unesco.org/en/news/1436/

Wolfe, J. (Lt. Col.) (2019, October 22). USACAPOC, Smithsonian to train the next generation of Monuments Men. *Army Reserve News*. https://www.usar.army.mil/News/Article/1995754/usacapoc-smithsonian-to-train-the-next-generation-of-monuments-men/

World Heritage Commission UNESCO. (2008). *Policy document on the impacts of climate change on world heritage properties*. http://whc.unesco.org/en/climatechange/

Yates, D. (2014). Church theft, insecurity, and community justice: The reality of source-end regulation of the market for illicit Bolivian cultural objects. *European Journal on Criminal Policy Research*. https://doi.org/10.1007/s10610-014-9232-z

Yates, D. (2015). Value and doubt: The persuasive power of "authenticity" in the antiquities market. *PARSE, 2*, 71–84.

Zanardi, B. (1999). Introduzione. Le attività di tutela dopo il 1963. In B. Zanardi (Ed.), *Conservazione, restauro e tutela. 24 dialoghi* (pp. 9–52). Skira.

Part III
Data Applications

Small Museums, Big Problems

Failure to Comply with the American Alliance of Museums' Policies on Archaeological Materials and Ancient Art

Erin Thompson and Mackenzie Priest

Abstract Despite being issued by one of the two main professional associations for museums in the United States, the efficacy and limitations of the American Alliance of Museums' (AAM) "Standards Regarding Archaeological Material and Ancient Art" remain largely unstudied. Issued in 2008, the AAM's guidelines establish mechanisms for public accountability: (1) museums should maintain a publicly available collection policy; (2) if a museum acquires an object that does not comply with the guidelines, it should be transparent about why the museum has deemed it appropriate to do so; and (3) museums should make all ownership information for archaeological and ancient material accessible to the public. Over the course of a year, we contacted 67 AAM member museums to survey whether they complied with each mechanism and to what extent. The responses showed that compliance with the AAM's guidelines is significantly lacking, and transparency is—alarmingly, though unsurprisingly—not a priority in small museums. Using the David Owsley Museum of Art as a case study, this chapter will discuss our findings and the dangers unregulated acquisitions in small museums can pose to cultural heritage preservation and art market integrity.

1 Introduction

Among the many barriers to the efficient protection of cultural heritage are the gaps between promise and execution in various international treaties, national laws, and codes of ethics. The limitations of international treaties, even those that have been ratified into law, are substantial and well documented. The most pertinent example is the 1970 Convention on the Means of Prohibiting and Preventing the Illicit Import,

E. Thompson (✉)
City University of New York, New York City, NY, USA
e-mail: ethompson@jjay.cuny.edu

M. Priest
Fordham Law School, New York, NY, USA

N. Oosterman, D. Yates (eds.), *Crime and Art*, Studies in Art, Heritage, Law and the Market 1, https://doi.org/10.1007/978-3-030-84856-9_12

Export and Transfer of Ownership of Cultural Property, administered through the United Nations Educational, Scientific and Cultural Organization (UNESCO, 1970). The 1970 UNESCO Convention is perhaps the most widely cited international treaty addressing cultural property crimes. Despite its sweeping title, it has very little in the way of binding requirements on its signatories to prohibit or prevent any of its namesake activities (Beltrametti, 2013; Fisman & Wei, 2009). Similarly, national laws might be strict on their face but are lax in their enforcement, due to differing prosecutorial priorities, a lack of official resources, or other local situations (Carducci, 2006; Cunning, 2004; Gerstenblith, 2015, 2016; McAlee, 1981, 1983; Nafziger, 1998; Orenstein, 2020; Vrdoljak, 2006).

Less attention has been paid to the similar issues within the implementation of codes of ethics created by interested parties within the world of cultural heritage. Museums, dealers, scholars, and even collectors have developed a variety of ethical codes or guidelines about the acquisition and retention of various forms of cultural property. On the surface, these codes and guidelines appear to compensate for the limitations of laws and treaties. But a closer look shows that their success is severely limited by a lack of accountability mechanisms.

Both of the main associations for museums in America, the American Alliance of Museums (AAM) and the Association of Art Museum Directors (AAMD), have issued guidelines for their member museums on the acquiring and holding of antiquities (Thompson, 2014).[1] These guidelines are especially important because, although the United States government does use a variety of legal mechanisms for combatting the illegal trade in cultural property, there are no directly relevant statues setting out American museums' responsibilities for their antiquities collections or acquisitions by donation or purchase (Cunning, 2004; Gerstenblith, 2015, 2016; McAlee, 1981, 1983; Nafziger, 1998; Orenstein, 2020). Thus, while American museums, like any other entity, are responsible for following the law, it is not always very clear what this law might be when it comes to the patchwork of relevant state and federal laws about antiquities. Additionally, unlike the state-run museums that occupy much of the rest of the world, United States museums are typically private entities and are not overseen by any specific governmental regulatory agency.

The AAMD and AAM issued their antiquities guidelines in, respectively, 2006 and 2008, to clarify museums' legal responsibilities and add certain ethical guidelines which sometimes go beyond the law but have been widely agreed to, in principle at least, by the American museum community (AAM Board of Directors, 2008; AAMD, 2006). Of the two sets of guidelines, those of the AAMD have

[1]The AAM, founded in 1906, currently represents around 4000 institutions and offers professional network opportunities as well as training for various museum departments (AAM, 2021a). As discussed further below, the AAM issued guidelines for the ethical acquisition and possession of antiquities in 2008 (AAM Board of Directors, 2008). The AAMD, founded in 1916, currently has 227-member museum directors, split among museums in the United States, Canada, and Mexico (AAMD, 2021). The AAMD has promulgated a Code of Ethics as well as standards on topics such as deaccessioning art from museum collections, the use of intellectual property in museums' digital initiatives, and the relationship between museums and corporate sponsors (AAMD, 2006).

received the most attention (Gerstenblith, 2019; Thompson, 2014; Tsirogiannis, 2017). This is unsurprising, since it is AAMD member museums, such as the Metropolitan Museum of Art, Museum of Fine Arts, Boston, and Brooklyn Museum, that hold America's largest collections of antiquities. By contrast, the AAM's guidelines have received relatively little scholarly attention.

While some museums with antiquities in their collections belong to both organisations and generally follow the AAMD's more detailed guidelines, we found nearly 70 collections of antiquities held by American museums that are members of the AAM but not the AAMD. None of these collections approach the scale of the Metropolitan Museum. But even small museums can cause big problems if they acquire or accept donations of unprovenanced antiquities.[2] Every antiquity sold without provenance documentation is an encouragement to participants in the marketplace for illicit antiquities. Even if the antiquity itself was legally exported, the willingness of a collector or museum to acquire it without knowing its full history tells looters and intermediaries that they can sell the antiquities they uncover without having to provide provenance information. When a museum buys an unprovenanced antiquity, it directly participates in creating these incentives. When it acquires an unprovenanced antiquity as a donation, it also rewards buyers with tax deductions and social capital for purchasing a potentially looted or forged antiquity (Thompson, 2010).

Action by American museums is especially crucial, since America is one of the largest markets for antiquities. The looting of archaeological sites will slow only if museums, collectors, and dealers became reluctant to buy antiquities without documentation of their provenance to show that they were legally excavated and exported from their countries of origin (Adams et al., 1995; Brodie & Tubb, 2001; Chase et al., 2006; Lynott, 1997; Vitelli, 1979). Ideally, museums would have a complete record of provenance for every object in its collection including, the names of each owner; when, where, and from whom each owner acquired it; where each owner possessed it; transportation records (including import and export documents for international transactions); and its entire exhibition and publication history. Ideally, this information would allow researchers to determine if an antiquity was legally exported from its country of origin and legally imported into the United States. The challenges in compiling and maintaining comprehensive provenance documentation for every object are numerous, ranging from decades of lax acquisition standards to the decay of living memory and privatisation of the art market. While the AAM guidelines recognise the difficulty of this task, they also advise that, at the very minimum, museums should make serious efforts to seek out this information.

Museums become AAM members in one of two ways. A museum may purchase a tier-based membership, which primarily offers professional development

[2]Provenance is the detailed ownership history of a work of art or artefact, ideally starting at the time of the object's creation, but usually beginning with the time of recovery from an archaeological site, or earliest known existence (possession) of the item, to present (Bankoff, 2012). Unprovenanced antiquities are archaeological objects that do not have a documented record of discovery, export, and ownership.

opportunities for museum staff (AAM, 2021c). Alternately, museums may seek AAM accreditation. Accreditation is based on the AAM's Core Standards for Museums and involves a self-study and peer review process every ten years. The accreditation process involves a review of the applying institution's core documents, including their Code of Ethics and Collections Management Policy (AAM, 2021b). While museums purchasing a tier-based membership must agree to the AAM's Code of Ethics upon application, they are not required to undergo a review process as are museums seeking accreditation. Regardless of whether a museum is a tier-based or an accredited member, there is no penalty from the AAM for ignoring the antiquities guidelines altogether. The AAM's guidelines are just that—guidelines. And while the AAM strongly recommends that all museums utilise their guidelines, compliance is not required to maintain association with the AAM at any membership level.

The opening line of the AAM's antiquities guidelines states that their purpose is to "promote public trust and accountability for U.S. museums" (AAM Board of Directors, 2008). Although the AAM is a self-regulatory organisation, it posits that its member museums are accountable to—if no one else—the general public. The guidelines assert three mechanisms through which institutions may achieve public accountability: adoption of a publicly available collections policy, transparency in reasoning behind any non-policy-compliant acquisitions, and publication of all known ownership information. We decided to survey museums with antiquities collections governed by the AAM guidelines to measure compliance with these three mechanisms.

2 Summary of the AAM Antiquities Guidelines' Accountability Mechanisms

First, and most clearly, the guidelines specify that museums "should have a publicly available collections policy setting out the institution's standards for provenance concerning new acquisitions of archaeological material and ancient art" (AAM Board of Directors, 2008).

The guidelines recommend that museums do not acquire antiquities without documentation that said antiquities were out of their probable country of modern discovery by 17 November 1970, the date on which the 1970 UNESCO Convention was signed. The second accountability mechanism appears in the guidelines' discussion about permitted exceptions to this limitation on acquisition. The guidelines state that if a museum acquires antiquities "when there is substantial but not full documentation" about their provenance, the museum "should be transparent about why this is an appropriate decision in alignment with the institution's collections policy and applicable ethical codes" (AAM Board of Directors, 2008). The language is less clear here than for the first mechanism, but it is reasonable to read this requirement of transparency as meaning that a member of the public should be able to ascertain when a museum has made a post-July 2008 antiquities acquisition without full provenance documentation as well as the grounds on which the museum justified this decision.

The third accountability mechanism is again clearly written: "museums should make available the known ownership history of archaeological material and ancient art in their collections, and make serious efforts to allocate time and funding to conduct research on objects where provenance is incomplete or uncertain" (AAM Board of Directors, 2008). This guideline applies to all a museum's antiquities, regardless of acquisition date (AAM Board of Directors, 2008). Of course, this mechanism could be very burdensome. Smaller American museums have limited staff and funding. Provenance research often takes time, training, and expertise in a particular area of art history or archaeology. Small museums often do not have the resources to hire staffers or outside researchers with this expertise.

3 Methodology

Our goal was to survey all the United States museums with antiquities in their collections who are AAM members but not AAMD members to assess those institutions' compliance with each of the AAM's three mechanisms for public accountability. The quality of public information about provenance information was foreshadowed by the difficulty of merely ascertaining which museums had antiquities in their collections at all. This is often not at all obvious from their websites' descriptions of their collections, and so we might have missed some relevant museums. In the end, we surveyed a total of 67 relevant museums (Appendix). We thank the staffs of these museums for the generosity with which they offered their time to reply to our inquiries.

Since the purpose of the AAM guidelines is to promote public trust, we decided to make inquiries as an interested member of the public might, by using the most readily available contact email visible on a museum's website. If there was no general email address available, we searched within the website to find the email address of either the museum's curator responsible for antiquities or its director. We then sent an email with the subject line "inquiry about your ancient art holdings," asking three main questions:

1. Do you have a publicly available collections policy setting out your institution's standards for provenance concerning new acquisitions of archaeological material and ancient art originating outside the United States?
2. Have you acquired any archaeological material and ancient art originating outside the United States since the AAM guidelines were approved in July 2008? If so, could you direct me to information about these acquisitions?
3. Has your institution made available the known ownership history of all archaeological material and ancient art in its collections, even if acquired before July 2008?

The email also contained a short description of our research project as well as a reminder that institutions were required to provide this information by the AAM guidelines.

The AAM's guidelines do not explicitly state what it means to be "publicly available". Given the guideline's above-stated purpose, however, we believe that, at the very least, any information that the guidelines call to be "public" should easily be made available to any individual or organisation that requests it. For the purposes of our study, institutions that provided us with access to their entire collections policy or the appropriate passage addressing archaeological material and ancient art, whether it was provided via email or posted on their website, are categorised as having a publicly available collections policy.

Each institution was given three opportunities to respond. Only 22 of the 67 museums responded to our first email. Given the unfolding COVID-19 pandemic beginning in early 2020, we waited eleven months (from January 2020 to December 2020) to send a second round of emails. While most American museums had resumed remote administrative operations by the time we resumed our inquiries, it is possible that museums that did not respond were unable to do so because of pandemic staffing issues.

For those institutions that did not initially respond, we tried to locate alternate contact addresses on the museums' websites and sent a follow-up email with the same questions. Where we had emailed a general email address in the first round, we tried to locate a specific email address for curators or directors. Where we had emailed specific individuals in the first round, we tried to locate contact information for different curators or directors. The process was repeated a third time for non-responsive institutions.[3] A further 26 museums responded after the second and third rounds of attempted communications, leaving 19 museums that did not acknowledge our inquiries. A response does not indicate that a museum answered our questions, since some museums replied wanting to know more about the project, including with whom the collected information would be shared, asked for time to respond, or indicated that they were forwarding our request to another staffer, but ultimately did not provide the requested information.

4 Results

4.1 Collections Policies

Eleven museums told us they did not have a publicly available antiquities collection policy. Two of these museums explained that they had no plans to acquire antiquities

[3]For six of the non-responsive institutions, we were unable to locate a different email address for a relevant staff member. In those instances, we called the museums to attempt to speak directly with staff. We did not receive a response from those institutions.

in the future, but seven of these museums indicated that they were currently working on creating an antiquities collection policy. These responses came to our later rounds of contact attempts, hinting that some museums may have been spurred by our initial contact to begin working on bringing themselves into compliance with the AAM guidelines.

A total of 29 museums simply never answered our question about whether they had an antiquities collection policy.[4] We could not locate a relevant policy on their websites. Thus, while we cannot rule out the possibility that these institutions have an internal collection policy, it cannot be said to be easily accessible by any member of the general public. For our purposes, we have categorised these institutions as not having a public collections policy.

Twenty-seven museums stated that they had a publicly available antiquities collection policy and provided us with access to it. Only six of these had proactively made that policy available to the public by posting it on their website. The other 21 museums made their policies available only on request. However, only nine of these 'on request' museums responded to our first email, and four of them responded only to our third attempts to contact them. Thus, obtaining this policy, even where it does exist, is not necessarily easy.

4.2 *Information on Antiquities Acquisitions*

It was even more difficult to obtain confirmation of whether the museums had acquired any archaeological material and ancient art originating outside the United States since the AAM guidelines were approved. Eleven museums told us they had not. Twenty-four museums either replied to our inquiry saying that they had made such acquisitions or had information indicating relevant acquisitions on their websites. The remaining 32 museums did not respond to either our inquiries as a whole or to this question in particular, and it was not possible to search their collections online in a manner that ruled out relevant acquisitions.

In question 2, we requested provenance information about post-July 2008 acquisitions. We asked both whether museums would be able to provide this information if requested and whether they could actually provide it to us. Some museums replied to us claiming that their website's existing collections pages provided provenance information. However, these pages generally provided information only about the donors who gave the antiquities to the museum, without a complete ownership history. Only three museums responded with comprehensive lists of the antiquities they had acquired since July 2008. However, none of these lists included complete provenance information or justifications for why the museum acquired these objects

[4]Of the 29 museums that did not answer our question about whether or not they had an antiquities collection policy, 21 museums did not answer our inquiry at all. The remaining eight museums responded but did not address this question specifically.

without sufficient provenance information. Thus, they were not in compliance with the AAM's transparency guidelines.

The results were much the same for museums' obligation to provide information on the ownership history of all archaeological material and ancient art in their collections, even if acquired before July 2008. Around the same number of museums indicated they could provide relevant information as for post-July 2008 acquisitions, although in the same insufficient forms. A few museums even volunteered that they would find this information impossible to provide, as they either had little provenance information about their antiquities or had not catalogued the information they did have.

Seventeen of the museums either told us or indicated on their websites that they would provide information on the provenance of specific antiquities acquisitions upon request. Several of these museums also specified that they would accommodate only the requests of scholars or 'serious students'. Some museums posted this qualification requirement on their website, creating a barrier that may discourage curious inquiries altogether. However, even a scholar would not find all doors open. One of the museums responded that they would simply not act on a 'bulk' request such as ours. Another directed us to fill out their information request form, only to ignore our completed form when we submitted it. The assertion that ownership information would be made available upon request was thus too often an unfulfilled promise.

Additionally, making provenance information available on request is meaningless if there is no means for a researcher to know which antiquities might be of interest. It is understandable that a small, underfunded museum might not want to devote the necessary resources to maintaining a comprehensive collections website. But it does not seem reasonable to think that a museum is satisfying the AAM guidelines' demand for publicly available provenance information if a researcher must visit the museum to read gallery labels to discover which objects are post-July 2008 acquisitions. This is all the more true since this route is only open to objects on display. Most museums only display a small portion of the objects in their permanent collections at one time, rotating them out for various curated exhibitions or conservation needs. Objects not on display are typically housed in a storage facility accessible only by staff of the curatorial and registrar departments. If a museum has not published their entire collection, either in a publicly-available catalogue or website, and an object goes into storage, what member of the public will know to look for it?

Even were it reasonable to require researchers interested in the provenance of museum holdings to travel to museums to read gallery labels, this would satisfy the AAM's requirement of public transparency only if these labels did indeed provide all relevant provenance information. But most often they do not. Gallery labels generally record the year the museum acquired the object and, perhaps, the name of its donor. Thus, even if a visitor did determine that they were interested in the provenance of an object, this visitor would still then need to overcome the hurdle of submitting an inquiry to and receiving a response from the institution for more complete provenance information.

5 Case Study: Owsley Museum

The collections of the David Owsley Museum of Art (DOMA) at Ball State University in Muncie, Indiana can serve as a case study for what happens when AAM member museums do not rigorously adhere to their antiquities guidelines. In recent years, this museum has acquired hundreds of unprovenanced antiquities from all over the globe, due, it seems, to a combination of lack of curatorial expertise about antiquities and pressure to maintain positive donor relations (Yates & Smith, in press).

We wish to emphasise that we are able to comprehend the scope of DOMA's problem with unprovenanced antiquities precisely because it does a better job than most museums adhering to the AAM's call for transparency. Most of DOMA's collections are included in an open, online database run through Ball State's library system. These listings contain most, but not all, of the provenance information the museum has for its collections. We discuss DOMA not to point it out as having a uniquely bad habit of acquiring unprovenanced antiquities; instead, we discuss it as a uniquely and admirably transparent example of what we believe is a widespread, but generally much better hidden, problem among smaller American museums.

An examination of DOMA's collections database reveals around 200 donations of antiquities by a single donor, David Owsley. These artefacts originate from Afghanistan, Africa (with some further specified as originating in Burkina Faso, Mali, Nigeria, Sierra Leone, and Timur), China, Egypt, Fiji, Greece, India, Indonesia, Iran, Iraq, Italy, Mongolia, Nepal, New Zealand, Russia, Syria, Thailand, Tibet, and Turkey. There are also general "Pre-Columbian" and "Roman" categorisations. All of these are regions or contemporary countries with known recent looting of archaeological sites as well as prohibitions on exporting the types of antiquities that ended up in DOMA.

Owsley donated these antiquities between 1964 and 2014. Of these 200 donations, 120 have no provenance information included in their publicly available record, aside from listing their donation by Owsley. The remaining 80 artefacts have some provenance information, but this is almost always merely a note about Owsley's purchase of the artefact at an auction or through a dealer. Sometimes these entries are quite vague, reading, for example, simply "New York art market." Only half of these 80 records contain any dates in their provenance information. Of the donations, whose provenance entries do contain dates for previous transactions, only four record a pre-1970 provenance history.

Seventy of Owsley's antiquities were donated after 2008 and are thus covered by the AAM's guidelines for "New Acquisitions" (AAM Board of Directors, 2008). The remainder are covered by the AAM's guidelines for "Existing Collections" (AAM Board of Directors, 2008). According to a 2019 testimonial written by then DOMA Director of Education, Tania Said, and published on the AAM's website, DOMA has been participating in AAM assessments since at least 2008 (Said, 2019). Yet, DOMA has shown little effort to gather provenance information beyond, it seems, accepting whatever limited information Owsley provided upon donation.

While DOMA has been transparent in providing the provenance information they possess, it has not been transparent about why its wholescale and continued acceptance of unprovenanced antiquities donations from Owsley is in the public's interest, or what, if any, collections policy or ethical codes it is following when deciding to accept or reject his donations. Given the limited provenance information DOMA seems to have about these donations, it may well be acquisitioning looted, even very recently looted, antiquities—and doing so at the expense of American taxpayers, since donations to DOMA entitle the donor to claim a tax deduction (Thompson, 2010, 2019). Additionally, failing to do rigorous provenance research leaves the museum open to acquiring fakes. To our sceptical eyes, the authenticity of a number of these thinly provenanced donations is questionable.

An explanation for why DOMA is not adhering to its AAM responsibilities to scrutinise antiquities donations may lie in its name. In 2011, Ball State changed the name of its museum from the Ball State University Museum of Art to the David Owsley Museum of Art "in honour of [Owsley's] generous gifts" (DOMA, 2021). At the time, the university issued a news story stating that Owsley intended to "bequeath $5 million to the museum as an endowment together with his bequest of about 90 percent of the works in his extensive art collection" (Ransford, 2011). The university's president is quoted in this story, praising Owsley "for his tireless work to build the university's collection of art that benefits students and faculty as well as visitors to campus." DOMA's director thanks Owsley for allowing the museum to transform its collection from "very narrow. . .to one that ranges the full scope of art on a worldwide basis." In turn, Owsley describes his "productive relationships" with the museum's directors: "they have been very receptive to my ideas, and I've worked with them to build upon their ideas. It has [sic] an extremely fruitful partnership that I can see continuing for many years" (Ransford, 2011).

Owsley is the grandson of Frank C. Ball, one of the founders of a glass manufacturing company. The Ball Corporation, founded in 1880 and headquartered in Muncie, Indiana, produced all sorts of food and beverage containers, but is best known for their home canning jars. The company made its founders wealthy enough that they also purchased a failing local private school and donated it to the state of Indiana. This would become Ball State University, and the Ball family continued to be generous to the institution. Frank C. Ball contributed heavily to the construction of the campus museum in the 1930's. He and other members of the family donated many artworks to the museum.

Owsley's donations continue his family tradition—as he puts it, "I just felt it was my obligation and my pleasure to create something and to continue what my grandparents had started" (Brookey & Dresch, 2015). As of 2011, Owsley had donated more than 2300 artworks to DOMA—many more than just the unprovenanced antiquities (Ransford, 2011). In a documentary made by DOMA to honour Owsley, the museum's associate director explains that he sometimes thinks of Owsley as a *bodhisattva*, a category of beings in Buddhism who have achieved enlightenment but who have decided to remain on earth in order to help humans, "because he has remained here and made it sort of his own mission to help us become enlightened in a certain way" (Brookey & Dresch, 2015).

Owsley and his family made and continue to re-make Ball State and DOMA. Few universities or museums would care to question the source of so many donations, both monetary and in kind, even if some of these donations might seem to violate ethical guidelines.

6 Conclusion

The results of our survey are easy to summarise. Only 40 percent of the museums in our study provided us with access to their collections policy for the acquisition and maintenance of archaeological material and ancient art, even though the creation and dissemination of a collections policy is the least burdensome of the AAM's antiquities guidelines. Creating a collection policy could be as simple as copying and pasting the AAM guidelines into an internal document, as many compliant museums who responded to our study have done.

While 36 percent of the museums studied have acquired antiquities since the guidelines came into effect in 2008, not a single one provided full provenance information in response to question number two of our inquiry. While 33 percent of museums studied indicated that provenance information is publicly available in some format (i.e., on the institution's website, on in-gallery text labels, or upon request), 25 percent indicated that we could have this provenance information only if we asked for it on an object-by-object basis—which would require knowing which artefacts to ask about. And these museums did not always follow up on their promised availability of information (e.g., those museums that ignored our completed information request form or stated they would not provide information on a 'bulk' request).

We would conclude that not a single museum in our survey is as transparent as is envisioned by the AAM guidelines. In the case of the third, most burdensome requirement, this is not surprising. Making provenance information available for all a museum's antiquities is perhaps an even harder task for a smaller museum than a larger one. Most small museums lack expertise and funding. They simply do not have the staff and time prioritise making ownership information available when they are also charged with all other operational tasks. Moreover, when working to publish known ownership information on older acquisitions, curators are plagued by their predecessors' lax standards of due diligence and document preservation. An even greater challenge is the expectation that institutions not only publicise known ownership information, but also diligently work to fill in any informational gaps for existing collections. But there are fewer excuses for failure to comply with the first and second mechanisms. True, to do so takes some work; but member museums have had more than a decade to do so.

Several museums did not respond to our inquiries in detail; instead, they gave a general response stating that they were aware of their legal and ethical guidelines for acquiring antiquities and would not violate them. They were asking us to trust them—but without providing any means for us to check if our trust was justified.

Much of the information that museums classified as 'provenance' in response to our inquiry included only one or two steps back in an ownership chain. This information generally included the name of the piece's donor and, sometimes, the dealer, auction house, or collection from which the donor obtained it. But this information is not usually enough to answer the question of when the antiquity entered the United States, when it left its country of origin, and whether it did so legally.

There are other gaps in publicly available provenance information. For instance, although one institution admirably created a webpage specifically listing objects that do not have a known provenance history, its general online database of objects in its permanent collection is largely void of provenance information. That museum also did not specify whether an object's provenance information would be made available if specifically requested. Another institution provided objects' countries of modern discovery on their webpage but neglected to include the year in which those objects were removed from those countries. The gap between what many institutions classify as publicly available ownership information and what is adequate for the public (not only for scholars and students) to conduct research is severely lacking.

The guidelines are an attempt by the museum sector to govern itself; but, as one of us argued in a previous publication, such self-regulatory regimes are effective only when external pressure can be brought to bear by the government, press, private interest organisations, and other members of the public (Thompson, 2014). The AAM issued their antiquities guidelines for a reason: the antiquities market is largely unregulated, secretive, and stocked at least in part with objects that were illegally exported from their countries of origin or are otherwise fraudulent (Day, 2014). As it currently stands, the AAM does not impose penalties on museums that ignore its suggested guidelines. It is not surprising, then, that many museums are not even motivated to take on the simplest of the AAM's suggestions, let alone the more complex and resource-draining ones. Since the AAM treats their guidelines as merely suggestions, it is up to the public to put pressure on institutions to take those steps. Transparency is crucial to assure that self-regulatory guidelines function.

Compliance with the AAM's guidelines is not only for the public's benefit. Compliance with the guidelines and proactive provenance research could protect museum staff from prosecution. In most jurisdictions, charges associated with the possession and sale of stolen property require prosecutors to prove that the defendant knew of the property's illegality. Prosecutors may prove knowledge indirectly by, for example, arguing that a defendant actively avoided compromising information (Grenig et al., 2019; Orenstein, 2020).

It is also worth noting that the AAM's guidelines oblige members of the board, staff, and volunteers involved with acquisitions and collections management "to be knowledgeable concerning legal compliance requirements and ethical standards" regarding antiquities (AAM Board of Directors, 2008). At the very least, museum staff who practice compliance with the AAM's guidelines could argue that they did in fact take proper steps to uncover compromising information and none arose. While the circumstances of having acquired a stolen object regardless of those efforts are unfortunate, the provable culpability of an individual staff member may be lessened. Proactive provenance research of existing collections would also likely bring to light any problematic objects and present a museum with the opportunity to resolve an ownership dispute before law enforcement even need get involved.

But currently, the benefits of complying with the AAM guidelines seem to be outweighed by the downsides of doing so in the decision-making of the staff of smaller museums. Such museums, with their smaller pool of donors, have perhaps even more reasons for not wanting to reject a donation than larger museums. As larger American museums more and more refuse to accept donations of unprovenanced antiquities, spurned donors are going to more and more test smaller museums' willingness to take these donations so they can claim their tax deductions (Blumenthal & Mashberg, 2012). As it stands, the AAM's guidelines and accountability mechanisms do little to tangibly prevent museums from succumbing to the pressures of donors and allure of acquiring rare but possibly looted objects. If the public cannot access the information to establish that a museum's acquisition is or is not in compliance with both the AAM's guidelines and the law, the public cannot scrutinise such acquisitions. Our study has shown that not only are many AAM member museums unprepared or unwilling to address such inquires, but that when they do the information is often incomplete or misleading.

We urge AAM member museums to follow their organisation's guidelines and refuse to acquire unprovenanced antiquities. But we also urge them to follow the AAM guidelines' requirements for transparency, so we can all help to hold them accountable if they fail. For without this transparency, the AAM guidelines do little to prevent small museums from becoming havens for looted artefacts.

Appendix

For this study, we contacted the following 67 museums that are members of the AAM (but not the AAMD) and have antiquities in their permanent collection.

Alice C. Sabatini Gallery, Topeka & Shawnee County Public Library
Allen Memorial Art Museum, Oberlin [1]College; Amarillo Museum of Art
American Museum of Ceramic Art
Appleton Museum, College of Central Florida
Arnot Art Gallery; Art Complex Museum
Art Museum of the University of Memphis
Asia Society Museum, New York
Doris Ullman Galleries, Berea College
Drexel Collection; Fairfield University Museum
Fine Arts Collection at UC Davis; Fitchburg Art Museum
Fleming Museum, University of Vermont
Frances Lehman Loeb Art Center, Vassar College
Fred Jones Jr. Museum of Art
Fresno Art Museum; Glencairn Museum

Bates Museum of Art; Binghamton University Art Museum	Godwin-Ternbach Museum, Queens College
Colorado College Fine Arts Center	Hallie Ford Museum of Art, Willamette University
Colorado State University Museum	Hispanic Society
Crow Museum of Asian Art, University of Texas at Dallas	Hofstra University Museum of Art
Cummer Museum	Huntington Museum of Art (West Virginia)
David Owsley Museum of Art, Ball State University	Hyde Collection
Davis Museum, Wellesley	James E Lewis Museum of Art
Denison Museum	Krannert Art Museum
DePauw Art Collection	Kruizenga Art Museum, Hope College
La Salle University Art Museum	Pomona College Museum of Art
Longwood Center for the Visual Arts, Longwood University	Robert and Frances Fullerton Museum of Art
Louisiana State University Museum of Art	Ruth and Elmer Wellin Museum at Hamilton College
Mandeville Gallery, Union College	Ruth Chandler Williamson Gallery of Scripps College
Maridon Museum	Samuel Dorsky Museum of Art State University of New York at New Paltz
Mead Art Museum at Amherst College	Sherwin Miller Museum of Jewish Art, Tulsa; Snite Museum of Art, University of Notre Dame
Miami University Art Museum	Staten Island Museum
Middlebury College Museum of Art	Taubman Museum of Art
Mount Holyoke College Art Museum	Trout Gallery, Dickinson College
Museum of Indian Arts & Culture (Museum of New Mexico)	Tucson Museum of Art
National Museum of Mexican Art	University of Colorado Boulder Art Museum
Newcomb Museum of Tulane	University of Southern California Pacific Asia Museum
Palmer Museum of Art, Pennsylvania State University	University of Wyoming Art Museum
Picker Art Gallery, Colgate University	
Polk Museum of Art, Florida Southern College	

We initially contacted nine additional museums, but removed them from the study after learning that the AAM guidelines were not relevant to them for various reasons, including that they had not collected antiquities from outside the United States.

References

Adams, R., Beaudry, M., Brown, J., & Murphy, L. (1995). Commercialization: Beyond the law or above it? Ethics and the selling of the archaeological record. In M. Lynott & A. Wylie (Eds.), *Ethics in American Archaeology: Challenges for the 1990s* (pp. 38–41). Society for American Archaeology.

American Alliance of Museums. (2021a). About AAM–American Alliance of Museums. Retrieved February 22, 2021, from http://www.aam-us.org/about-us

American Alliance of Museums. (2021b). Accreditation. Retrieved May 30, 2021, from https://www.aam-us.org/programs/accreditation-excellence-programs/accreditation/

American Alliance of Museums. (2021c). Museum Membership. Retrieved May 30, 2021, from https://www.aam-us.org/programs/membership/museum-membership/

American Alliance of Museums Board of Directors. (2008). Standards Regarding Archaeological Material and Ancient Art. Resource Document. American Alliance of Museums. Retrieved February 22, 2021, from https://www.aam-us.org/programs/ethics-standards-and-professional-practices/archaeological-material-and-ancient-art/

Association of Art Museum Directors. (2006). Standards and Practices. Retrieved February 22, 2021, from https://aamd.org/standards-and-practices

Association of Art Museum Directors. (2021). Membership. In Association of Art Museum Directors. Retrieved February 22, 2021, from https://aamd.org/about/membership

Bankoff, A. (2012). Context. http://depthome.brooklyn.cuny.edu/anthro/SCP50/archaeology/context.html. Online source consulted 13 August 2007 (no longer available) in Joyce, R. (2012). From place to place: Provenience, provenance, and archaeology. In G. Feigenbaum & I. Reist (Eds.), *Provenance: An alternate history of art* (pp. 48–60). Getty Research Institute.

Beltrametti, S. (2013). Museum strategies: Leasing antiquities. *Columbia Journal of Law and Arts, 36*(2), 203.

Blumenthal, R., & Mashberg, T. (2012, July 12). The curse of the outcast artifact. *The New York Times*. Retrieved May 30, 2021, from https://www.nytimes.com/2012/07/15/arts/design/antiquity-market-grapples-with-stricter-guidelines-for-gifts.html

Brodie, N., & Tubb, K. (2001). From museum to mantelpiece: The antiquities trade in the United Kingdom. In R. Layton, P. Stone, & J. Thomas (Eds.), *The destruction and conservation of cultural property* (pp. 102–116). Routledge.

Brookey, R., & Dresch, M. (2015). Gift of David T. Owsley. Retrieved February 22, 2021, from https://dmr.bsu.edu/digital/collection/WIPBVid/id/3/rec/2

Carducci, G. (2006). The growing complexity of international art law: Conflict of laws, uniform law, mandatory rules, UNSC resolutions and EU regulations. In B. Hoffman (Ed.), *Art and cultural heritage: Law, policy, and practice* (pp. 68–86). Cambridge University Press.

Chase, A., Chase, D., & Topsey, H. (2006). Archaeology and the ethics of collecting. In K. Vitelli & C. Colwell-Chanthaphonh (Eds.), *Archaeological ethics* (pp. 16–26). Altamira Press.

Cunning, A. (2004). U.S. policy on the enforcement of foreign export restrictions on cultural property & destructive aspects of retention schemes. *Houston Journal of International Law, 26*(3), 449–506.

David Owsley Museum of Art. (2021). History of the David Owsley Museum of Art. Retrieved February 22, 2021, from https://www.bsu.edu/web/museumofart/about/history

Day, G. (2014). Explaining the art market's thefts, frauds, and forgeries (and why the art market does not seem to care). *Vanderbilt Journal of Entertainment and Technology Law, 16*(3), 457–495.

Fisman, R., & Wei, S. (2009). The smuggling of art, and the art of smuggling: Uncovering the illicit trade in cultural property and antiques. *American Economic Journal: Applied Economics, 1*, 82–96. https://doi.org/10.1257/app.1.3.82
Gerstenblith, P. (2015). For better or for worse: The evolution of cultural property policy and law in the United States. *International Law Journal of Cultural Property, 22*, 357–378.
Gerstenblith, P. (2016). The legal framework for the prosecution of crimes involving archaeological objects. *U.S. Attorney's Bulletin, 64*, 5–17.
Gerstenblith, P. (2019). Provenances: Real, fake, and questionable. *International Journal of Cultural Property, 26*(3), 285–304.
Grenig, J., Lee, W., & O'Malley, K. (2019). Deliberate ignorance—Explained. *Federal Jury Practice and Instructions,* §17:09.
Lynott, M. (1997). Ethical principles and archaeological practice: Development of an ethics policy. *American Antiquity, 62*(4), 589–599.
McAlee, J. (1981). From the Boston Raphael to Peruvian Pots: Limitations on the importation of art into the United States. *Dickinson Law Review, 85*, 565–585.
McAlee, J. (1983). The McClain case, customs, and congress. *New York University Journal of International Law and Politics, 15*, 813–838.
Nafziger, J. (1998). Seizure and forfeiture of cultural property by the United States. *Villanova Sports and Entertainment Law Journal, 5*, 19–30.
Orenstein, K. (2020). Risking criminal liability in cultural property transactions. *North Carolina Journal of International Law and Commercial Regulation, 45*(2), 527–548.
Ransford, M. (2011). Longtime benefactor David Owsley honored for expanding university's cultural horizons. Ball State University: David Owsley Museum of Art. Retrieved February 22, 2021, from https://www.bsu.edu/news/press-center/archives/2011/10/longtime-benefactor-david-owsley-honored-for-expanding-universitys-cultural-horizons
Said, T. (2019). Time to reassess: A university art museum plans its next chapter with the MAP program. American Alliance of Museums. Retrieved February 22, 2021, from https://www.aam-us.org/2019/09/27/time-to-reassess-a-university-art-museum-plans-its-next-chapter-with-the-map-program/https://www.aam-us.org/2019/09/27/time-to-reassess-a-university-art-museum-plans-its-next-chapter-with-the-map-program/
Thompson, E. (2010). The relationship between tax deductions and the market for unprovenanced antiquities. *Columbia Journal of Law and Arts, 33*, 241–265.
Thompson, E. (2014). Successes and failures of self-regulatory regimes governing museum holdings of Nazi looted art and looted antiques. *Columbia Journal of Law and Arts, 37*(3), 379–404. https://doi.org/10.7916/jla.v37i3.2139
Thompson, E. (2019). 'Official fakes': The consequences of governmental treatment of forged antiquities as genuine during seizures, prosecutions, and repatriations. *Albany Law Review, 82* (2), 407–447.
Tsirogiannis, C. (2017). Unethical actions, inactions and reactions by the museum and market community to the seizure of the Met's Python Krater. *Nekyia Journal of Art Crime, 18*, 65–68.
UNESCO. (1970). Convention on the means of prohibiting and preventing the illicit import, export and transfer of ownership of cultural property. Resource Document. UNESCO. Retrieved May 30, 2021, from http://portal.unesco.org/en/ev.php-URL_ID=13039&URL_DO=DO_TOPIC&URL_SECTION=201.html
Vitelli, K. (1979). The antiquities market. *Journal of Field Archaeology, 6*(4), 471–488.
Vrdoljak, A. (2006). *International law, museums and the return of cultural objects.* Cambridge University Press.
Yates, D., & Smith, E. (in press). Illicit antiquities and museums. In A. Stevenson (Ed.), Handbook of museum archaeology. : Oxford University Press.

Guardians in the Antiquities Market

The Role of Specialised Law Enforcement Units in Disrupting the Illicit Antiquities Trade

Anya Eber

Abstract This chapter examines how specialised Art, Antiquities, and Cultural Property (AACP) units, in the United Kingdom and the United States, police the illicit antiquities trade and operate as guardians within the antiquities market. The field of cultural property protection has considered several ways to disrupt the illicit antiquities trade, but more attention needs to be devoted to the role that specialised law enforcement units can play in this effort. This chapter considers how AACP units assert guardianship within the UK and the US antiquities market, and how these units increase and enhance security efforts across the antiquities trade. Drawing upon concepts from Routine Activity Theory, Nodal Governance, and Third Party Policing, this chapter examines how AACP units contribute to a networked system of guardianship in the antiquities market. This chapter argues that AACP units are an important guardianship entity within the UK and the US antiquities market, that not only assert guardianship in their own right, but also strengthen the wider guardianship network by mobilising other sectors to take on guardianship tasks and responsibilities. To examine the role that AACP units play in disrupting the illicit antiquities trade, this study collected qualitative data from law enforcement units including the United States Federal Bureau of Investigation (FBI) Art Crime Team, United States Homeland Security Investigations (HSI) Cultural Property, Art and Antiquities Program (CPAA Program), and from a sample of current and past members of the United Kingdom Metropolitan Police's Art and Antiques Unit, as well as several other guardianship sectors across the antiquities market.

1 Introduction

The looting of archaeological sites, and the trafficking and sale of illicit antiquities, and cultural property, can cause irreparable harm to cultures and communities worldwide. This form of transnational crime has been shown to deplete a

A. Eber (✉)
Centre for Criminology, The University of Oxford, Oxford, UK
e-mail: anya.eber@crim.ox.ac.uk

N. Oosterman, D. Yates (eds.), *Crime and Art*, Studies in Art, Heritage, Law and the Market 1, https://doi.org/10.1007/978-3-030-84856-9_13

non-renewable cultural resource (Gerstenblith, 2007, p. 172), impact our ability to understand the past (Gerstenblith, 2007, pp. 170–174), and destabilise economic, social, and political infrastructures in several regions (see Brodie, 2010, pp. 261–264; Brodie et al., 2000, pp. 13–14; Luke, 2012, p. 177). In some cases, the trafficking of illicit antiquities and cultural property has also been found to be interconnected with other illicit trades and transnational crimes (Bowman, 2008, pp. 230–231; Luke, 2012, p. 177). New means of disrupting and preventing the illicit antiquities trade should increasingly be considered at several stages of the trafficking chain.

This chapter uses the theoretical framework of Routine Activity Theory (RAT) (Cohen & Felson, 1979) to examine how formal guardians, such as specialised Art, Antiquities, and Cultural Property units (hereafter AACP units), in the UK and the US, can help disrupt the illicit antiquities trade. In their development of RAT Cohen and Felson (1979) suggest that guardians could help disrupt criminal activities in several environments, and this premise should be explored within the antiquities market. An examination of the guardianship network that exists within the UK and the US antiquities market, and how AACP units operate as guardians, could advance our understanding of how to disrupt the illicit antiquities trade, and assist with crime reduction efforts in this field.

2 Routine Activity Theory and Its Application for the Illicit Antiquities Trade

The concept of 'risk versus reward' decision making forms the basis of several theoretical models of human behaviour and is the foundational premise of Rational Choice Theory (RCT). Paternoster et al. (2017, p. 848) suggest that for the most part "criminologists understand RCT theory simply to imply that offending is based upon a self-interested appraisal of the costs and benefits of alternative courses of action, with the action taken being the one with the greatest perceived utility." Routine Activity Theory (RAT) forms a subset of RCT and is predicated upon RCT's premise that offenders calculate the risks and rewards of criminal activity (see Hollis et al., 2013, p. 66). RAT, however, shifts the analytical focus toward criminal events and activities—wherein offenders are one variable within a larger criminal equation (see Cohen & Felson, 1979, p. 590; Felson & Cohen, 1980, p. 392; Madero-Hernandez & Fisher, 2012, pp. 515–516; Williams, 2016, p. 23). In their development of RAT, Cohen and Felson (1979, p. 590) considered, "the circumstances under which crime can thrive" and by extension how these circumstances could be disrupted to prevent criminal activity. Cohen and Felson (1979, p. 589) propose that:

> structural changes in routine activity patterns can influence crime rates by affecting the convergence in space and time of the three minimal elements of direct-contact predatory violations: (1) motivated offenders, (2) suitable targets, and (3) the absence of capable guardians against a violation

The theoretical framework of RAT suggests that if the motivation of offenders, the suitability of targets, or the presence of guardianship, is altered within different environments then the potential for criminal activity in these spheres could be increased or decreased (Tilley et al., 2015, p. 59).

RAT has been used to analyse several aspects of the illicit antiquities trade (e.g., Fabiani, 2018; Ojedokun, 2012). Further, several bodies of work in the field of cultural property protection have built upon concepts within RAT without necessarily referencing this criminological theory. Gerstenblith (2007, pp. 173–174) for example, advocates that "[w]hile it is obviously important that looting at sites be interdicted, the law in market countries should also impose detrimental consequences on sellers and purchasers in order to reduce demand and the incentive to loot archaeological sites." Gerstenblith's (2007) argument for increased regulation and legal deterrents in the antiquities market connects with RCT and crime control strategies that seek to increase the risks and decrease the rewards of criminal activity. These arguments, however, can also be understood through RAT as an effort to disrupt criminal activity by altering the suitability of antiquities as targets and the motivation of various actors to loot, traffic, and sell illicit antiquities. In several ways, the field of cultural property protection has drawn upon concepts within RAT to consider how to disrupt the illicit antiquities trade by altering both the suitability of targets and the motivations of offenders. What has received less attention in this field, however, is RAT's guardianship construct.

One of the key contributions of RAT is that this framework opens up lines of inquiry into variables of the criminal equation beyond offenders. Hollis et al. (2013, p. 66) note that within RAT "offender motivation is often assumed—the theory is based on a rational choice perspective. The two key elements of the theory are, therefore, the suitable target and capable guardianship dimensions." In several environments and spheres of criminal activity, however, RAT's guardianship construct, has yet to be fully examined as a tool for crime control. Hollis-Peel et al. (2011, p. 67) argue that "guardianship is currently an under-researched component of routine activity theory" and that there is a need "for a theoretical elaboration of what the guardianship process entails and how exactly guardianship occurs" (see also Reynald, 2009). Research on guardianship and the way it manifests in different environments, however, can be difficult to produce as successful guardianship is often less visible than an absence of guardianship. Cohen and Felson (1979, p. 590) acknowledge "[t]hough guardianship is implicit in everyday life, it usually is marked by the absence of violations; hence it is easy to overlook." Research into RAT's guardianship construct needs to be developed, as it could advance our understanding of how to disrupt criminal activities in several environments and markets—including the antiquities trade.

3 Guardianship

Guardians are a key component of Routine Activity Theory. Reynald (2009, 1) argues that in their development of RAT, Cohen and Felson "singled out the capable guardian as the only actor within the crime event who has the power to prevent a crime from being executed." Cohen and Felson (1979, p. 590) suggest in RAT that the presence of guardians can prevent motivated offenders from pursuing suitable targets, and that the absence of guardians could produce opportunities for crime (see also Reynald, 2010, p. 359). Indeed, Felson (1995, p. 53) argues:

> A case can be made that the offender is not the most important actor for explaining crime. From the perspective of the routine activity approach those who interfere with offenders, however inadvertently, play an even more central role in crime and its prevention.

Precisely which actors operate as guardians and how guardianship is defined, however, has been interpreted in several different ways (Hollis-Peel et al., 2011, p. 55). Cohen and Felson's (1979) original construction of RAT, defined guardians by their function. Felson (1995, p. 53) later elaborated on the guardianship concept, defining guardians as agents that serve "by simple presence to prevent crime, and by absence to make crime more likely." These interpretations allow for a variety of agents, both formal and informal, to be conceptualised as guardians, and suggest that law enforcement units, members of museums, auction houses, dealers, academics, government agencies, collectors, conservators, collectors, NGOs, and private companies could all be conceptualised as guardians within the antiquities trade.

Since 1979, however, research on guardianship has increasingly focused more narrowly on informal guardians and those that specifically protect targets. Felson and Boba (2010, p. 28) argue that guardians "should not be mistaken for police officers or security guards, who are very unlikely to be on the spot when a crime occurs." The role of informal guardians should be examined as a tool for crime control, but to develop a full understanding of guardianship, so too should the role of formal guardians such as the police, and even hybrid models of guardianship (see Felson, 1995). Hollis-Peel et al. (2011, p. 54) suggest that defining guardians around their ability to protect targets is too limited and propose instead that guardians could be defined as "the physical or symbolic presence of an individual (or group of individuals) that acts (either intentionally or unintentionally) to deter a potential criminal event." This study draws upon this definition and RAT's original construction of guardianship to consider the role of formal guardians such as specialised AACP units in the antiquities market.

Guardianship can be asserted by informal guardians, but in most environments the responsibility for crime control and guardianship activities are also taken up, in some form, by law enforcement agents. Specialised units with assigned mandates to monitor specific spheres of criminal activity, embody many of the foundational elements of RAT's guardianship concept (see related discussion in Felson, 1995, p. 62). This chapter considers how specialised AACP units, in the United Kingdom and the United States, assert guardianship and prevent criminal activity within the antiquities market.

Guardianship can be asserted in numerous ways but one of the key ways that guardians are understood to disrupt criminal activity is by monitoring spheres of potential criminal activity. Several attempts to deconstruct and analyse the guardianship process have centred around the availability, monitoring, supervisory, and interventionist capacity of guardians (see Hollis & Wilson, 2014; Reynald, 2019; Reynald, 2016; Reynald, 2010; Reynald, 2009). Reynald (2010, pp. 358–359; 2009, p. 4) conducted a study on residential guardians in the Netherlands which found that there are three critical dimensions to capable guardianship within "micro-places: (1) the willingness to supervise, (2) the ability to detect potential offenders, and (3) the willingness to intervene when necessary." This connects with Hollis-Peel et al.'s (2011) argument that within RAT, two of the core features of guardianship are availability and monitoring. Hollis-Peel et al. (2011, p. 55) argue that, "it is the idea that someone is watching and could detect untoward behaviors that deters the likely offender from committing a criminal act." Building upon previous scholarship, and research into RAT's guardianship construct, this chapter presents research findings on the proactive capacity of specialised AACP units, in the United Kingdom and the United States, to monitor and detect criminal activity in the antiquities market. Monitoring is only one aspect of guardianship but an examination of how, and to what extent, AACP units and other guardians monitor the antiquities trade contributes to our understanding of how guardianship is asserted in this market.

4 Methods

Semi-structured interviews for this study were conducted between 2018 and 2021 with law enforcement agents in the United States Federal Bureau of Investigation (FBI) Art Crime Team, the United States Homeland Security Investigations (HSI) Cultural Property, Art and Antiquities Program (CPAA Program), and from a sample of current and past members of the United Kingdom Metropolitan Police's Art and Antiques Unit (hereafter the Met sample pool).[1] Law enforcement agents were the primary focus of the study, but in order to consider wider systems of guardianship within the antiquities market interviews were also collected from several other sectors with guardianship potential in the United Kingdom and the United States. In addition to law enforcement agents, individuals working in the antiquities trade and within museums, auction houses, government agencies, academic institutions, and private organisations were included in the project. The data pool included more than 30 interviews. Participants in this study were assigned anonymous numeric codes and a thematic analysis was applied to investigate various police strategies and aspects of police work in relation to the illicit antiquities trade. This chapter presents

[1]This chapter presents data from a larger doctoral study, at the University of Oxford, which examined how the illicit antiquities trade is policed in the United Kingdom and the United States, and the role of AACP units in cultural heritage protection.

research findings from the larger study related to crime detection and proactive systems of crime control. Given the scope of the study, the term AACP units and the research outputs presented in this chapter refer specifically to United States and United Kingdom units unless otherwise noted.

5 Proactive Crime Control in the Antiquities Market

In most environments, crime comes to the attention of law enforcement agents through two detection systems: (1) crime detection through victim/witness reports: reactive crime control, or (2) crime detection by law enforcement agents: proactive crime control. Guardianship in the form of detecting and monitoring criminal activity connects with several aspects of proactive police work and crime control. Crank (2015, p. 296) outlines that in proactive systems of crime control, the police "acting on their own initiative, develop information about crime and strategies for its suppression." Reactive crime control in contrast orients the police to focus on responding to calls-for-service and investigating reported crime (National Academies of Sciences, Engineering, and Medicine, 2018, p. 20; Black & Reiss, 1967, p. 3).

During this study, AACP units were asked about their proactive capacity, to monitor the antiquities market and detect looted or stolen antiquities. Not all AACP units, focus resources on this task, but in the United States Department of Homeland Security, the Homeland Security Investigations (HSI) Cultural Property, Art and Antiquities Program (hereafter CPAA Program) in collaboration with United States Customs and Border Protection (CBP), outlined a substantial proactive screening capacity. In the US, CBP and HSI have unique search authorities that enable them to monitor and investigate illegal trade activities. Antiquities, like many goods, that are moved into or out of the United States are subject to screening by Customs and Border Protection Officers (CBP) and when CBP Officers encounter suspicious antiquities in their searches, they notify HSI. Within HSI the CPAA Program trains and supports HSI agents in CPAA investigations. This study identified that together HSI and CBP have a clear guardianship capacity to monitor and investigate the antiquities trade at US borders and ports of entry.

In terms of proactive screening efforts, CBP Officers are in an important position to monitor the antiquities trade.[2] Like many of the curators, dealers, auction houses, or conservators that handle and examine antiquities in the market, CBP Officers operate in a front-line position inspecting artefacts for signs of an illicit origin. Reynald (2010, p. 361) suggests that one of the important functions of both formal and informal guardians is that they detect "suspicious behaviour based on cues that

[2] In the UK, Border Force agents may operate in a similar capacity, but did not participate in this study.

are out of the ordinary." CBP officers provide this guardianship function during their examination of shipments, customs declarations, and provenance documents.

Members of the HSI CPAA Program outlined several cases in which CBP officers had identified illicit antiquities and notified HSI. Not always because CBP had identified illicit antiquities, but often because they had detected suspicious activity and referred that to the HSI CPAA Program. CBP Agricultural Specialists, for example, have helped intercept cases of illicit antiquities, during their screening efforts. One member of the HSI CPAA Management Team, noted:

> If [CBP] are looking at wood products, they are concerned about bugs that may be in the wood, but the wood may be something like a sarcophagus, or a statue from a different part of the world. So, yes, that does catch their attention. So we've been making an effort to get CBP Agricultural Specialists to know, "OK, maybe you didn't find any Boll weevils, in this cotton, but it is a textile that you [should] raise concerns about.

The more information that is shared between CBP and HSI, the more antiquities can be detected in CBP searches and investigated by HSI agents. HSI's CPAA Program facilitates this information exchange and guardianship capacity with efforts such as a yearly training program for HSI agents at the Smithsonian Museum which CBP Officers are invited to. CBP and HSI's collaborative efforts represent a visible guardianship presence and monitoring/investigative capacity that can help disrupt the illicit antiquities trade at United States borders and ports of entry.

Monitoring the antiquities trade, however, is not something all AACP units focus resources on. For several reasons, including time, expertise, and resources, proactive screening efforts were not reported as a focus for either the Metropolitan Police's Art and Antiques Unit nor the FBI Art Crime Team. In the antiquities trade, as with numerous other trafficking crimes, including diamonds, arms, and wildlife products, the illicit origins of antiquities are laundered and obscured the further antiquities move within trafficking chains (Mackenzie & Yates, 2017, p. 82). Within the antiquities market, illicit antiquities can be difficult to identify without archaeological expertise or extensive research into provenance documents (Brodie, 2006, p. 53; Proulx, 2011, p. 4). In a conversation with a participant from the Met sample pool, I asked about screening efforts.

> AE: Did you ever screen the market?
>
> Member of the Met sample pool: No. We would have done I think had we had the right numbers of personnel [but] we constantly said to the art market, even if we look within the art market we aren't going to have these things leap out at us because we haven't got the training.
>
> AE: So most of the work was responding to intelligence?
>
> Member of the Met sample pool: Yeah, we would have liked to have done more proactivity but we just didn't get the time for it. Occasionally we would walk around the markets.

Physical law enforcement searches provide one means of detecting illicit antiquities in the market, but cases can also be identified through remote research and surveillance of auction catalogues, collections, and online platforms.

In the United States, a few agents discussed cases in which they had proactively generated their own investigative leads through such efforts. Agents in the FBI Art Crime Team and HSI CPAA Program reported that agents in these units (particularly senior agents), have a capacity to identify criminogenic patterns, false provenance, and anomalies within the market. One HSI agent, explained:

> One area that I think, is underappreciated is that once you [as an agent] start to develop a knack for cultural property cases, you can start generating your own investigative leads. So you'll see something come onto the market or you'll read something about something somewhere or you'll notice, an anomaly in something. And then you go down a route and realise you might have a case there I've done that a lot, that took a while to get there. Another [HSI CPAA Agent], X would read a book written by an art dealer or collector and then be able to generate leads right off of that so, the more knowledge you get and the more understanding you get of cultural property and the bigger network of people that you come in contact with, the more chance that you're going to get leads.

This conversation highlights the guardianship capacity of AACP agents that receive training and experience working on cultural property cases. Reynald's, (2010, p. 383) study on residential guardians found that monitoring guardians "reinforce their own capability by acquiring contextual knowledge and information through the act of monitoring itself." A process which also appears to be true for formal guardians.

Several United States AACP agents reported a capacity to identify anomalies in the market but agents in the United States FBI Art Crime Team and members of the United Kingdom Met sample pool also raised concerns about the time and resources that monitoring efforts require. One FBI agent from the Art Crime Team explained:

> It's just time and resources for us. We don't really have the time to go and scour all that [the market] and make those determinations. People come to us when there's a problem and then we'll try to solve it.

Increased proactivity and intrusive screening efforts could also have potential consequences for AACP units. One member of the Met sample pool, suggested that there are specific reasons the Met does not focus on proactively screening the London art market:

> If it became common knowledge that [the unit] were routinely doing that [screening the market], then auction houses or galleries would say, "It's been reviewed by the Metropolitan Police." It would give some sort of credence. So [the unit] would never, ever say officially, "we are looking at auction houses catalogues" because [the market] would use that. They would say, "Well if we haven't been contacted by the police, it must be fine." and then members of the public would say "Oh it's been looked over by the police." So that's the reason [the unit] would never. [The unit] wait until [they] are approached in the form of academics, saying this is suspicious! Or [the Unit] would identify something because of a financial report, and then look at that.

Financial reports indicate yet another form of proactivity and monitoring which can be undertaken separately from antiquities and art as objects, particularly for the Met, in connection with the implementation of the Fifth Money Laundering

Directive.[3] All increased proactivity in the form of research and monitoring capabilities, however, costs time and resources to implement. Several agents in this study challenged the notion that expertise or an ability to identify illicit antiquities was a problem for agents but highlighted the resource that are needed for proactive efforts. On the topic of screening one FBI agent in the Art Crime Team stated:

> We don't do it often. We don't have time. We just don't have the bandwidth for that. I won't say that no one is doing it in their respective AOR's but it's not a program requirement. It's not something that we manage. If [agents] are doing it, they are doing it on their own time. We just don't have time for it.
>
> AE: What about the expertise to identify that material?
>
> FBI Agent: Well if we don't possess it organically we rely heavily on a network of folks for that right. So that's not really the struggle, identifying the pieces. I mean most of the agents on the team, particularly the senior ones, have enough knowledge and experience to take a first blush at something and to say that doesn't quite look right, and then we'll dig into it. Then we start reaching out to the experts and say, 'Hey take a look at this for me.' So I feel pretty comfortable with that.
>
> It's just that we don't have time for it. And you know some countries do. Some countries have units that spend a lot of time scouring the internet looking for their patrimony, and some of those countries are our typical usual customers. They are the ones that [send us] the most MLA [Mutual Legal Assistance] requests. "We saw this or we saw that."

Given the various guardianship activities that AACP units, in the United Kingdom and the United States, are involved in, an important question emerges as to whether other actors in the market could help monitor the market and report cases to AACP units.

In this study, AACP agents reported that they receive information and leads about antiquities from several sources including: foreign and domestic law enforcement partners, academics, museums, auction houses, government agencies, private companies, NGOs, dealers, and members of the public. How these sectors assert guardianship and work with AACP units needs to be considered to understand the larger system of guardianship within the antiquities market.

6 Guardians Within the Antiquities Market

In the antiquities trade, there are several guardianship sectors that could help monitor the market or operate as place managers (Eck, 1994). Hollis & Wilson (2014, pg. 171) argue that, within RAT (Cohen and Felson, 1979) guardians are described as agents that carry out "important supervisory activities as they proceed through their daily routines." In the antiquities market, several individuals at auction houses, museums, academic institutions, and within the antiquities trade, are, by

[3] See HM Treasury Transposition of the Fifth Money Laundering Directive: Consultation (2019).

their employment, in guardianship positions which allow them to examine antiquities that circulate within the market. Specialists in specific artefact types or archaeological sites are not only in positions to encounter illicit antiquities through their routine activities, they also have the expertise to identify suspicious activity.

This potential for 'monitoring guardianship' was acknowledged and brought up during interviews with several individuals in the antiquities market. In a conversation with a participant from the auction house sector, I asked:

> Do you think that auction houses play a role in preventing the illicit antiquities trade at market, and if so how?
>
> Auction house participant: Well I do think we do, because if you're a policeman on the border you have to be very lucky to catch something, you've got to be opening the right suitcase, stopping the right person at the border, going into the right lorry/truck or whatever. What, happens with [. . .] any auction house dealing with antiquities is that we get a huge number of things coming in and shown to us, which means it's less about luck, it's more about vigilance. And so, there's more of a chance that you will spot things that are problematic at that point I think what's interesting is that until now I don't think the people who are opposed to the illicit antiquities trade, quite rightly, have realised that auction houses can actually play an enormous part in fighting their fight for them or with them.

AACP units reported a capacity to monitor the antiquities market, provided they are equipped with time and resources, but individuals in other sectors of the antiquities market may already be in positions to assist with this form of guardianship. Certain individuals in the antiquities trade arguably have routine activities that expose them to more activity than law enforcement agents may be able to gain access to (see related discussions in Black & Reiss, 1967, p. 3). Hollis et al. (2013, p. 72) argue that Felson and Boba's (2010) elaborations on guardianship suggest the original theoretical intent of guardianship is to involve "those individuals who are present and can deter untoward behaviors rather than police officers or other informal social control attempts where the *goal* of the involved parties is to actively prevent or control those behaviors." Indeed, Felson and Boba (2010, p. 30) argue that place managers could contribute significantly to guardianship efforts as, "they control the physical environment, set and enforce rules, oversee behavior, and thus influence crime." A combined monitoring effort between several guardians, such as AACP units and localised place managers (Eck, 1994), however, could potentially provide the strongest potential for crime control. Felson (1995, p. 57) indicates that hybrid models of guardianship and responsability for crime control can exist, observing that "employees with strategic jobs [can] act in an unpaid auxiliary role, assisting police with information to prevent crime. Thus, they combine general [guardianship] responsibilities with employee status." Examples, of collaborative forms of guardianship are evident in several past cases, where individuals in the antiquities market identified suspicious activity and brought cases to the attention of AACP units for investigation.

Envisioning groups within the art market as guardians or place managers (Eck, 1994), however, might require a paradigm shift and run counter to much of the current academic discourse. Brodie et al. (2000) and Mackenzie and Yates (2017) have raised concerns about relying on individuals within the antiquities market to report crime and monitor the antiquities market. Mackenzie and Yates (2017, p. 78) argue that at present, "the antiquities trade relies on self-regulation of participants, which clearly does not work as there is no financial or social motivation for them to self-regulate." Returning to Reynald's (2010) three elements of guardianship, the main critique that emerges within the micro-environment of the antiquities trade revolves primarily around the willingness of several sectors to supervise and to intervene when necessary. Law enforcement agents largely accept guardianship responsibilities as part of their duty, but for other actors in the antiquities trade monitoring and guardianship activities may not come naturally. Instead of dismissing localised guardianship sectors in the antiquities market, however, the question is: what factors might prevent capable guardianship in this market and how could these be altered?

In the antiquities trade, there are several reasons that some of the groups with guardianship potential, beyond AACP units, may not present as reliable guardians. Felson (1995, p. 57) notes, "in general, one's tendency to discourage crime will vary with the primacy of responsibility." At the market stage of the illicit antiquities trade, very few actors are compelled by personal responsibility as might motivate a guardian to take care of their own home or belongings. Instead, guardianship sectors in the antiquities market primarily operate under what Felson (1995, p. 57) terms assigned, diffuse, or general levels of responsibility. This suggests that in the antiquities trade, several actors with guardianship potential might not have a clear motivation or incentive to monitor the market beyond what is required of them. Hollis-Peel et al. (2011, p. 62) observe that for many place managers "who perform a guardianship function by virtue of their position of employment the task of guardianship for these employees is secondary to other job duties." Further, even among the groups that are motivated to take on monitoring activities in the antiquities market, not all guardians necessarily have the resources or time to operate as capable guardians (Reynald, 2009, p. 7). The same concerns about resources and time that AACP units voiced, are evident across several sectors of this market.

Academics, for example, represent a guardianship sector with a capacity to detect illicit antiquities and monitor the antiquities trade during the course of their routine activities. Without the foundational support, encouragement, or funding of the universities or institutions in which academics are embedded, however, academics may not operate as guardians or take up additional work monitoring the trade and reporting cases to AACP units. At best, guardianship from the academic sector will manifest in an inconsistent and unreliable form based upon the personal motivations and drive of individuals.

Members of the museum community similarly have a clear capacity to identify illicit antiquities and contribute to guardianship efforts, as evidenced in projects such as the British Museum's Circulating Artefact Project.[4] Experts watching and monitoring material within their fields of expertise could assert a powerful guardianship

[4] See: https://www.britishmuseum.org/our-work/departments/egypt-and-sudan/circulating-artefacts.

effect on this market and bring information and cases to AACP units, but these efforts are also contingent upon resources.

Finally, members of the antiquities trade itself are in prime positions to monitor the market through their routine activities. Indeed, several participants from the auction house sector and dealers in this study outlined that they have increasingly dedicated time to provenance research for antiquities sales. If monitoring tasks require too many resources or become financially unviable for businesses, however, an absence of guardianship is likely to emerge in these sectors as well. Reynald, (2009, p. 7) cautions that, "only when a guardian is available and has the resources that make him capable, is he able to take action through monitoring and intervention." In the antiquities market, several groups could operate as guardians, and many are even taking on guardianship tasks, but without resources reliable consistent forms of guardianship may prove difficult to sustain in several areas of this market.

7 Collaborative Systems of Guardianship and Crime Control

In the antiquities trade, as in several other spheres, there is a question as to whether crime control should be the domain of the state, outsourced to external actors, or composed of hybrid partnership models (see: Loader, 2000; Wood et al., 2011; Zedner, 2006). If guardianship is too heavy a burden to impose on the market or for any one sector to take up, one solution is to build collaborative systems of crime control. Burris et al. (2005, p. 38) propose that governance, can be understood through a framework in which, "governance takes place through a multiplicity of nodes." If such a nodal governance framework is accepted, then guardianship in the antiquities market could be envisioned as a system in which security is co-produced between a network of guardians. Shearing (2001, p. 261) suggests that the act of policing could be conceptualised as "a regulated network of participatory 'nodes'—each with authority, capacity and knowledge that together provide for the governance security." In the antiquities trade, several groups have guardianship capabilities which, in isolation, may not be sufficient to deter criminal activity but as a network may prove far stronger.

Law enforcement agents might operate as one entity in this networked system of guardianship, but that does not mean that AACP units are not still a crucial part of the guardianship process. Burris et al. (2005, p. 14) observe, "all nodes are not created equal. Nodes vary in their accessibility, their efficacy, the other nodes they can influence and how that influence is exerted." This study draws upon this notion and proposes that AACP units form an important component of the guardianship network, not necessarily because of their individual monitoring capabilities, though agencies such as HSI and CBP do play an important role in this task, but because AACP units have a capacity to mobilise and encourage other guardianship sectors to participate in a collaborative crime control agenda.

8 Re-Envisioning Proactive Crime Control in the Antiquities Market

In this study, few AACP units, aside from HSI/CBP, discussed an emphasis on proactive crime control in the form of law enforcement screening or monitoring. All AACP units, however, referenced an important form of proactivity connected with what this study terms 'guardianship mobilisation' or the activation of third parties. Mazerolle and Ransley (2005, p. 193) propose that "[in] third party policing, the police *create* or *enhance* crime control guardians in locations or situations where crime control guardianship was previously absent or non-effective." Guardianship may not be entirely absent or non-effective in sectors of the antiquities trade but a third-party policing concept in which AACP units enhance and encourage guardianship within the antiquities market is applicable. Rather than monitoring the market themselves, or waiting passively for crime reports to be received, AACP units, in the United Kingdom and the United States, discussed strategies in which they encourage other guardianship sectors to monitor the market and report cases to them. Proactive strategies which encourage other guardians and place managers to monitor the antiquities market increase guardianship in the antiquities market, preserve unit resources, and deliver AACP units a feedback loop on crime for reactive strategies.

In this study, several AACP agents outlined proactive strategies in which they encouraged reporting from third parties, including academics, museums, and members of the art and antiquities markets. In the United States, HSI agents and agents in the FBI Art Crime Team, specifically identified the cultivation of information networks and outreach efforts as a form of proactive crime control. During a conversation about unit strategy one FBI Art Crime Team agent explained:

> Our strategy is obviously to be proactive, and to do the best work that we can and to develop and expand our relationships with other law enforcement partners, with the private sector, with the public sector too. We are always going to have a proactive stance.

This FBI agent outlined that within regional assignments agents are involved in outreach efforts and even recruit intelligence from local auction houses, galleries, and museums:

> Every Art Crime agent goes out and we do a lot of outreach. I think I'm really good at going out and doing outreach to galleries and museums and institutions to say look "this is who I am, these are the cases that I work, I hope to God you never need me but if you do, if you have a theft or you learn about something and you want the FBI Art Crime Team to know about it and do something about it, here's my business card—call me" so we drum up case work by doing local outreach here in the United States.

This strategy of "drumming up case work" also emerged in conversations with members in the HSI CPAA Program. Members of the HSI CPAA Program also discussed proactive efforts to develop crime control networks and encourage reporting from groups in the antiquities market. One member of the HSI CPAA Management Team explained:

> We are trying to be more proactive, and not just wait for things to come to us. So New Orleans, I think was a great example. We had a Special Agent, who had gone to our Smithsonian training, who reached out to us and said, "I'd like to do more here in New Orleans." So when we went down, we [visited academic institutions]. We went and physically visited [several museums]. We tried to make the rounds to introduce ourselves, and to, build relationships so they're not so intimidated, [and] if they've got a question they can call us.
>
> With New Orleans, I think it was highly unusual, because, we had people literally walking the streets. Our, Intel Analyst had identified all of the different galleries and auction houses and museums in New Orleans, and [HSI agents went and visited them].
>
> We would like to do that more. We've talked about doing that in a couple of other places, in fact we had something that we were planning [...] it was going to be a much larger effort, to try to reach out to individuals who not only sell art, but then also some of the collectors, making some of the collectors aware.

For sectors of the antiquities market that are already motivated to monitor the market and report cases, outreach efforts by law enforcement agents provide points of contact and help organise crime control efforts. In other sectors, however, these efforts could raise awareness, encourage vigilance, and even act as a visible deterrent. Proactive mobilisation efforts on the part of AACP units could, therefore, both increase guardianship and deter criminal activity by signalling an active guardianship presence within the antiquities market.

Outreach efforts by AACP units also ensure that guardianship capabilities from several sectors of the antiquities market are drawn upon to disrupt the illicit antiquities trade. Several AACP agents, acknowledged the capacity of other actors and experts to identify anomalies within the market and a number of AACP agents outlined the importance of working with other actors to police the illicit antiquities. In the United Kingdom, one member of the Met sample pool stated:

> I think you can't solve a crime in a vacuum, I think with all criminality not just with the art market. You have to go out, you have to talk to people. The trade know what's normal and what's not normal. [The Police do not know]. The Police do not know if someone's level of information is reasonable.
>
> And I think it's really important to have a feel of what's going on, the issues that are facing them. Just on a very practical perspective, you know? They understand the market better than [the Police]; it's their livelihood. So, I do think it's important [to reach out to the market], but I also think it's important to reach out to museums. I also think it's important to engage with, people in educational institutions. I think the police are there to be helpful, neutral and enforce the law and I think there's no section that [the police shouldn't] engage with.

Within the larger regulatory network, AACP units are a node which can mobilise and bring together guardians with different capabilities to combat the illicit antiquities trade. AACP units also increase guardianship efforts by facilitating information exchanges across several sectors of the antiquities trade.

Law enforcement agents rarely spoke of location as an aspect of strategy, but each unit's focus on art market locations indicates a form of proactive crime control which ensures that AACP units can monitor art market hotspots and work with other guardianship sectors. Mazerolle and Ransley (2005, p. 51) argue that in third party policing, "the public police intersect with willing, mandated and/ or unwilling partners (including regulatory "nodes") to control and prevent crime problems." Location is a primary step in asserting this type of influence and form of proactive crime control.

In the United Kingdom, the Metropolitan Police's Art and Antiques Unit, by its remit, is focused on London, establishing a law enforcement presence in the largest United Kingdom art market and a crucial art market globally. In the United States, the FBI Art Crime Team manages cultural property cases across the country but has strategically positioned agents to manage specific art market locations. Members of the HSI CPAA Program also discussed a similar proactive approach focused on art market locations including New York and Miami. In New York, members of the HSI CPAA Program reported that a Cultural Property Group of roughly six agents work about 90 percent of the time on CPAA cases. The strategic distribution of AACP agents in key art markets embeds agents in locations where they can connect with cultural property networks for leads, information, and support on cases. The presence of AACP agents in key art market locations also ensures AACP units are in a position to work with and exchange information with several other guardianship sectors. In several ways, specialised AACP units encourage, enhance, and facilitate crime reporting from the communities they police in the United Kingdom and the United States. From a nodal governance perspective, AACP units are a guardianship entity which helps enhance and increase security efforts throughout the art and antiquities market.

9 Conclusion

AACP units play an important role within the guardianship network in the antiquities market in the United Kingdom and the United States. Several AACP units have a capacity, provided they are equipped with time and resources, to assert guardianship by identifying anomalies and criminal activity in the antiquities market. HSI and CBP, for example, assert guardianship at United States borders and ports of entry by monitoring the antiquities trade and detecting trafficking activities. FBI and HSI agents also reported that they can detect suspicious activity within the antiquities market and generate their own investigative leads for cases. Law enforcement agents, however, are not the only guardians capable of, or responsible for, monitoring the antiquities market. Analysing guardianship through a nodal governance framework, suggests that several sectors of the antiquities market could assist AACP units by monitoring and reporting cases of illicit antiquities. Indeed, given the resources and expertise that are required to monitor the antiquities trade, collaborative forms of crime control may provide the strongest potential for guardianship in this market.

One of the key ways that AACP units can help disrupt the illicit antiquities trade, therefore, is by mobilising guardianship sectors within this market to participate in a collaborative crime control agenda. In the antiquities market, AACP units not only operate as guardians in their own right, these units encourage other actors to take on guardianship responsibilities—thereby reinforcing and preventing an absence of guardianship in several sectors of the market. AACP units are an important category of guardians, that enhance and strengthen the foundational structure of the guardianship network within the antiquities market in the United Kingdom and the United States.

References

Bowman, B. A. (2008). Transnational crimes against culture: Looting at archaeological sites and the "grey" market in antiquities. *Journal of Contemporary Criminal Justice, 24*(3), 225–242. https://doi.org/10.1177/1043986208318210

Brodie, N. (2006). An archaeologist's view of the trade in unprovenanced antiquities. In B. Hoffman (Ed.), *Art and cultural heritage: Law, policy and practice* (pp. 52–63). Cambridge University Press.

Brodie, N. (2010). Archaeological looting and economic justice. In P. M. Messenger & G. S. Smith (Eds.), *Cultural heritage management: A global perspective* (pp. 261–278). University Press of Florida. https://doi.org/10.5744/florida/9780813034607.003.0021

Brodie, N., Doole, J., & Watson, P. (2000). *Stealing history: The illicit trade in cultural material.* McDonald Institute for Archaeological Research.

Burris, S., Drahos, P., & Shearing, C. (2005a). Nodal governance. *Australian Journal of Legal Philosophy, 30*, 1–43. Retrieved August 27, 2021, from https://ssrn.com/abstract=760928

Circulating Artefacts (CircArt). (2021). *The British Museum.* Retrieved June 1, 2021, from https://www.britishmuseum.org/our-work/departments/egypt-and-sudan/circulating-artefacts

Cohen, L. E., & Felson, M. (1979). Social change and crime rate trends: A routine activity approach. *American Sociological Review, 44*(4), 588–608. https://doi.org/10.2307/2094589

Crank, J. (2015). *Understanding police culture*. Ebook Central, Routledge. Retrieved August 30, 2021, from https://ebookcentral.proquest.com/lib/oxford/detail.action?docID=1798337

Eck, J. E. (1994). Drug markets and drug places: A case-control study of the spatial structure of illicit drug dealing. University of Maryland College Park: ProQuest Dissertations & Theses Global.

Fabiani, M. D. (2018). Disentangling strategic and opportunistic looting: The relationship between antiquities looting and armed conflict in Egypt. *Arts (Basel), 7*(2), 1–26. https://doi.org/10.3390/arts7020022

Felson, M. (1995). Those who discourage crime. In J. E. Eck & D. Weisburd (Eds.), *Crime and place. Crime prevention studies* (Vol. 4, pp. 53–66). Criminal Justice Press.

Felson, M., & Boba, R. L. (2010). *Crime and everyday life*. Sage Publications. https://doi.org/10.4135/9781483349299

Felson, M., & Cohen, L. E. (1980). Human ecology and crime: A routine activity approach. *Human Ecology, 8*(4), 389–406. https://doi.org/10.1007/BF01561001

Gerstenblith, P. (2007). Controlling the international market in antiquities: Reducing the harm, preserving the past. *Chicago Journal of International Law, 8*(1), 169–195. https://ezproxy-prd.bodleian.ox.ac.uk:2090/scholarly-journals/controlling-international-market-antiquities/docview/237217976/se-2?accountid=13042

HM Treasury. (2019). *Transposition of the Fifth Money Laundering Directive: Consultation.* Retrieved August 30, 2021, from https://assets.publishing.service.gov.uk/government/uploads/system/uploads/attachment_data/file/795670/20190415_Consultation_on_the_Transposition_of_5MLD__web.pdf

Hollis, M. E., Felson, M., & Welsh, B. C. (2013). The capable guardian in routine activities theory: A theoretical and conceptual reappraisal. *Crime Prevention and Community Safety, 15*(1), 65–79. https://doi.org/10.1057/cpcs.2012.14

Hollis, M. E., & Wilson, J. (2014). Who are the guardians in product counterfeiting? A theoretical application of routine activities theory. *Crime Prevention and Community Safety, 16*(3), 169–188. https://doi.org/10.1057/cpcs.2014.6

Hollis-Peel, M. E., Reynald, D. M., van Bavel, M., Elffers, H., & Welsh, B. C. (2011). Guardianship for crime prevention: A critical review of the literature. *Crime, Law and Social Change, 56* (1), 53–70. https://doi.org/10.1007/s10611-011-9309-2

Loader, I. (2000). Plural policing and democratic governance. *Social & Legal Studies, 9*(3), 323–345. https://doi.org/10.1177/096466390000900301

Luke, C. (2012). U.S. policy, cultural heritage, and U.S. borders. *International Journal of Cultural Property, 19*(2), 175–196. https://doi.org/10.1017/S094073911200015X

Mackenzie, S., & Yates, D. (2017). What is grey about the "grey market" in antiquities? In J. Beckert & M. Dewey (Eds.), *The architecture of illegal markets: Towards an economic sociology of illegality in the economy*. Oxford University Press. https://doi.org/10.1093/oso/9780198794974.003.0004

Madero-Hernandez, A., & Fisher, B. S. (2012). Routine activity theory. In F. T. Cullen & P. Wilcox (Eds.), *The Oxford handbook of criminological theory* (pp. 513–536). Oxford University Press. https://doi.org/10.1093/oxfordhb/9780199747238.013.0027

Mazerolle, L., & Ransley, J. (2005). *Third party policing*. Cambridge University Press.

National Academies of Sciences, Engineering, & Medicine. (2018). *Proactive policing: Effects on crime and communities*. The National Academies Press. https://doi.org/10.17226/24928

Ojedokun, U. A. (2012). Trafficking in Nigerian cultural antiquities: A criminological perspective. *African Journal of Criminology and Justice Studies, 6*(1–2), 163–176.

Paternoster, R., Jaynes, C. M., & Wilson, T. (2017). Rational choice theory and interest in the "fortune of others.". *The Journal of Research in Crime and Delinquency, 54*(6), 847–868. https://doi.org/10.1177/0022427817707240

Proulx, B. B. (2011). Organized criminal involvement in the illicit antiquities trade. *Trends in Organized Crime, 14*(1), 1–29. https://doi.org/10.1007/s12117-010-9115-8

Black, D. J., & Reiss, A. J. (1967). Studies in crime and law enforcement in major metropolitan areas. Volume 2. Field surveys III. A Report of a Research Study Submitted to The President's Commission on Law Enforcement and Administration of Justice. U.S. Government Printing Office. Retrieved August 27, 2021, from https://hdl.handle.net/2027/uiug.30112004744113

Reynald, D. M. (2009). Guardianship in action: Developing a new tool for measurement. *Crime Prevention and Community Safety, 11*(1), 1–20. https://doi.org/10.1057/cpcs.2008.19

Reynald, D. M. (2010). Guardians on guardianship: Factors affecting the willingness to supervise, the ability to detect potential offenders, and the willingness to intervene. *The Journal of Research in Crime and Delinquency, 47*(3), 358–390. https://doi.org/10.1177/0022427810365904

Reynald, D. M. (2016). *Guarding against crime: Measuring guardianship within routine activity theory*. Routledge.

Reynald, D. M. (2019). Guardianship in the digital age. *Criminal Justice Review, 44*(1), 11–24. https://doi.org/10.1177/0734016818813693

Shearing, C. (2001). A nodal conception of governance: Thoughts on a policing commission. *Policing and Society, 11*, 259–272. https://doi.org/10.1080/10439463.2001.9964866

Tilley, N., Farrell, G., & Clarke, R. V. (2015). Target suitability and the crime drop. In M. A. Andresen & G. Farrell (Eds.), *The criminal act: The role and influence of routine activity theory* (pp. 59–76). Palgrave Macmillan. https://doi.org/10.1057/9781137391322_5

Williams, M. L. (2016). Guardians upon high: An application of routine activities theory to online identity theft in Europe at the country and individual level. *British Journal of Criminology, 56* (1), 21–48. https://doi.org/10.1093/bjc/azv011

Wood, J., Shearing, C., & Froestad, J. (2011). Restorative justice and nodal governance. *International Journal of Comparative and Applied Criminal Justice, 35*(1), 1–18. https://doi.org/10.1080/01924036.2011.535686

Zedner, L. (2006). Policing before and after the police. *The British Journal of Criminology, 46*(1), 78–96. https://doi.org/10.1093/bjc/azi043

More Than Just Money

Human-Object Relationships in Low-End Collecting

Diāna Bērziņa

Abstract Art crime often is viewed in terms of being profit driven. Although it is the case in many contexts, it is hard to fully justify this viewpoint in the low-end antiquities trade. The focus on high financial value portrays an art crime as a clear-cut issue, however alternative engagement spaces such as online forums provide the hint that art crime is more than just about money. This chapter presents data that was gathered during a cross-sectional analysis of Russian treasure hunting forums and discusses the main trends observed from the data and offers a glimpse into the low-value antiquities trade that takes place in these spaces. It is argued that in the low-value antiquities trade, potentially even in the wider market, financial value is intertwined with other values, it is possible to witness emergence of human-object relationships, and make a case that an object should not be only viewed as a passive thing with a price tag.

1 Introduction

Cultural heritage consists of both tangible and intangible heritage. 'Cultural heritage' itself, consisting of 'culture' and 'heritage', is a complex term to define (for a more detailed discussion see Blake, 2000). Each component of the term is not neutral and at times they have been embroiled in conflicts resulting from different meanings attached to them. For instance, in the past, 'culture' was viewed in the terms of European culture, and therefore indigenous peoples encountered by Europeans were viewed as "inferior" as they were viewed as not having culture in "a European understanding of that term" (Koehler, 2007, p. 105). Similarly, heritage can be argued to be "an ideological construct" (Anico, 2008, p. 67) and its meaning and importance is multi-layered and can represent different things to different people. While this chapter is not about semantics, it is important to note that even these commonly used terms are laden with different, sometimes competing values and

D. Bērziņa (✉)
Faculty of Law, Maastricht University, Maastricht, The Netherlands
e-mail: d.berzina@maastrichtuniversity.nl

N. Oosterman, D. Yates (eds.), *Crime and Art*, Studies in Art, Heritage, Law and the Market 1, https://doi.org/10.1007/978-3-030-84856-9_14

interests. This study almost exclusively discusses tangible cultural heritage, more precisely archaeological objects, but it is recognised that the tangible and the intangible are interlinked in a "symbiotic relationship" so that objects are evidence of "underlying norms and values" (Bouchenaki, 2003, p. 1).

When it comes to tangible cultural heritage, the high financial value[1] of looted, stolen, or trafficked objects of cultural heritage are often discussed in the media. From movies, like Entrapment (1999) to headlines like 'Million-dollar Art Heist', art crime conjures a particular image in the public mind—one of a gentleman art thief who steals high value paintings. However, art crime can involve anything from coins, paintings, antiquities, to even vintage cars and watches (Korner, 2016). Similarly, the crime itself can involve anything from theft, vandalism, smuggling of antiquities, to white-collar crime, such as art fraud (Durney & Proulx, 2011). In other words, art crime is as broad and varied as the values we attach to art (Durney & Proulx, 2011). For instance, heritage professionals underline cultural, heritage, scientific, and educational values of public art collections, however, these collections also must be evaluated in terms of monetary value when it comes to financial reporting purposes (Ferri et al., 2021).

In the case of art crime, the *financial* value seems to be emphasised more often than not. Phillips (2016, p. 217) argues that the mass media has two main ways in which it focuses on art: a "scandalous controversy" and/or "a luxury good". In the media, titles like "Gentleman thief poses as art lover before stealing £40,000 statue" (Evans, 2015) or "American Authorities Have Returned 10 Looted Antiquities Worth a Combined $1.2 Million Back to India" (Kinsella, 2020) are not uncommon. However, media outlets are not the only ones using financial values to create an effect. The emphasis on the monetary value also has been used by people in the heritage sector, as Durney (2013, p. 221) argues that the monetary value is used "heavily (. . .) in order to impress upon the public the scope of the problem as well as to generate support" for the protection of cultural heritage. Similarly, the financial values are used to address art-related financial crimes. In Europe, the fifth Anti-Money Laundering Directive[2] targets money laundering in the art market. Article 1 (c) brought into the scope of the new directive art traders in cases where the value of the transaction or a series of linked transactions amounts to 10,000 EUR or more. When such values are involved, traders must undertake customer due diligence by verifying the identity of the customer, obtaining the information on the source of funds and by examining the purpose of all transactions.

By focusing mostly on high value objects, we overlook a section of art market that potentially functions in a different way than the high value one. The engagements with objects and structure of the low-value market can look very different than perhaps the high value art market where only best of the best, or described as such, is

[1] In this chapter, 'financial values' are used interchangeably with 'price'.

[2] Directive (EU) 2018/843 of the European Parliament and of the Council of 30 May 2018 amending Directive (EU) 2015/849 on the prevention of the use of the financial system for the purposes of money laundering or terrorist financing, and amending Directives 2009/138/EC and 2013/36/EU.

being sold for high prices. This major area of the art market goes largely unmonitored, admittedly not helped by the lack of funding for law enforcement agencies and their ability to fund this type of work (see Brodie et al., 2019), and there is a significant number of actions taking place that involve smaller quantities or financial values that still affect our cultural heritage.

To emphasise the above point and counter the narrative that every art crime is 'all about the money', this research will discuss data gathered during a snapshot analysis of Russian treasure hunting forums. This is used to look at low-end collecting of archaeological objects. This research does not imply that all archaeological objects discussed here were collected by treasure hunters who broke the law, nor does it suggest that the forums surveyed and its participants, have been involved in illicit trade. It also does not argue against treasure hunting hobbies. It advocates for a more nuanced view when it comes to low-value archaeological objects.[3] We might define them as low (financial) value antiquities and instead choose to turn our intention to high value antiquities, but that would be a mistake considering the high volume of these smaller, lower value objects. Brodie (2017) argues that the Internet market can be highly damaging based on the number of objects traded when compared to the traditional, smaller physical market. The theories, policies, and outreach activities cannot hope to be successful if they exclude these alternative engagement spaces, and interactions with low-value objects.

2 Russia and Treasure Hunting

This research focuses on Russia for a number of reasons. Despite the large amount of people who allegedly participate in treasure hunting in the region (see Zubacheva, 2017), Russia is nearly absent from research on the global antiquities trade and Russia, and post-Soviet countries, have lacked a more in-depth focus in criminology (see Slade & Light, 2015). This is changing now with, for example, research done by Hardy (2016) who has carried out quantitative research on metal detecting in Eastern Europe but there is still a lot to explore about this region.

To provide a brief legal context, Russian Federal Law of 23rd of July 2013 (N245-FZ,[4] as amended on 28 December 2017) introduced into the Criminal Code of the Russian Federation several changes. It introduced article 243.2 "Illegal search and (or) removal of archaeological objects from the places of occurrence" which

[3]The term 'archaeological objects' was used here as that is the term used in the Russian Federal Law. However, the term 'antiquities' will also be used as it is more commonly used term when talking about the trade. Here 'antiquities' and 'archaeological objects' will be used interchangeably without a reference to the object's age.

[4]Федеральный закон от 23 июля 2013 г. N 245-ФЗ "О внесении изменений в отдельные законодательные акты Российской Федерации в части пресечения незаконной деятельности в области археологии" ["On Amendments to Certain Legislative Acts of the Russian Federation Concerning the Suppression of Illegal Activities in the Field of Archaeology"].

among other things specifies that the use of special technical means with a goal to find archaeological objects is allowed only when carrying out an archaeological fieldwork. In this law, the special technical means are understood to mean metal detectors, radars, magnetic devices, and any other equipment that could determine the presence of archaeological objects. In order to carry out archaeological field-work, an individual must apply for a permit, and to get it they must meet very strict requirements making it challenging to receive it. Search or removal of archaeological objects resulting in damage or destruction of a cultural layer without a permit is punishable. In this law, a cultural layer is defined as a layer in the earth or in the water that has preserved traces of human life which are more than a 100 years old. As such, the law protects objects which are found in a cultural layer that are older than 100 years old. This law also added to administrative offenses the illegal circulation of archaeological objects. However, certain objects such as weapons which are under 100 years old are governed by other laws such as article 222 of the Criminal Code of the Russian Federation.

3 Snapshot Analysis

The snapshot analysis was carried out as part of a European Commission-funded study into the illicit trade in cultural goods (Brodie et al., 2019). It is a cross-sectional analysis—in this case it is an analysis of objects offered on a specific website over a certain time period. Cross-sectional analysis has been used by several studies in the past to observe trade in specific objects and/or to observe trade on a specific marketplace. For instance, Brodie (2014) used a sampling methodology to conduct a study of the Internet market in pre-Columbian antiquities over a 3-year period (2011–2013) and establish baseline estimates for the volume of the trade. Elkins (2008) tracked listings on the 'Ancient Coins' section on the United States eBay site and concluded that this market in "undocumented coins" in the United States and Canada alone is "a multi-million-dollar industry" (Elkins, 2008, p. 4). As such a snapshot analysis is a useful tool to gain an overview of what is happening in a subset of the antiquities market during a specific period, for example, to record what type of objects are available on a particular platform and observe possible correlations that could then be explored by a further research.

This snapshot analysis focused on treasure hunting forums to get an insight into the Russian metal detecting[5] hobby. The usefulness of forums for data gathering has been noted in many studies related to as varied topics as sentiment analysis to better understand propaganda dissemination (Abbasi et al., 2007), e-crime market

[5]Metal detectors as they are known today originated in the setting of WWII where they were essential for locating land mines (Stine & Shumate, 2015), however soon after WWII metal detecting was picked up as a recreational hobby (Thomas & Stone, 2009)—looking both for valuables such as lost jewellery and archaeological objects.

(Motoyama et al., 2011), and social psychological research (Holtz et al., 2012). When it comes to research related to archaeological objects, metal detecting forums give us a chance to see the types of objects that have been found recently, the prices they are being sold for, and the number of objects offered. Additionally, in some cases we can find out what happens to these objects such as they are being added to personal collections or sold to a fellow forum user. The goal of the snapshot was to get a glimpse into types of objects that are being found by metal detectorists in Russia.

4 Main Observations

An Internet search was conducted to find relevant forums. This involved looking for treasure hunting forums and finds with metal detectors. Multiple forums were identified but it was decided to focus on one main one and two smaller ones, one of these was just a single subsection dedicated to metal detecting finds on a forum dedicated to various electric equipment. The majority of the analysed posts (122) came from a forum that seems to be the largest online forum of treasure hunters who metal detect as a hobby in Russia; in November 2020 it had almost 89,000 registered users. Only open, publicly available posts were analysed. The snapshot focused on metal objects, more specifically, the items which looked like they could have been found by a metal detector. As the posts were analysed manually and the allocated time to carry out the data gathering was limited, it was decided to focus on a 3-day time span. A 3-day time span was chosen to ensure that all subpages of the selected forums could be analysed as certain sections such as numismatics had a large number of posts therefore if longer time span would have been chosen it had a potential to skew the number of object categories that were analysed. All told, 127 publicly available posts were analysed, which were posted in the time span of first to third July 2018. The majority of the posts described just a single object however few of them listed multiple objects (e.g., two posts described finding large hoards of coins consisting of 600 and 7199 coins respectively). The posts were in Russian and the sites analysed had a Russian domain name.

As one would expect when carrying out a study of online social media platforms, this study comes with some limitations. Some posts on these forums were locked for unregistered users. As this study only looked at posts that were available for anyone to look at, it potentially can have an error in the number of finds per object category. However, it is believed that it provided a good estimate of the variety of categories (see Fig. 1 for object categories).

As mentioned at the start, although high-value archaeological objects make the headlines in popular media and some view them as "the hottest investment" (Baugh, 2007), a large proportion of the trafficked antiquities are in fact small, low-value objects such as coins and figurines (Alder & Polk, 2002; Elkins, 2008). Small metal objects are usually located with the assistance of a metal detector, at times in violation of the law (Elkins, 2008; Valdés, 2015). This pattern was also evident

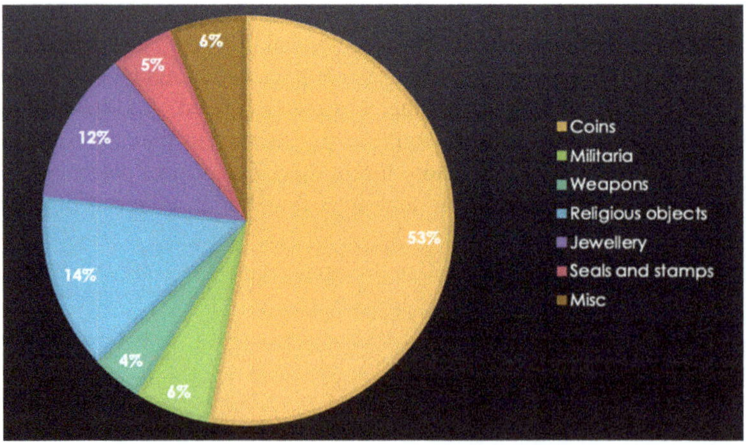

Fig. 1 Object categories by percentage

during the snapshot analysis. The archaeological objects appearing on these treasure hunting forums were small, low-value objects. However, the volume of these objects is high as the Internet in general has contributed to the shift towards low-value, high-volume antiquities (Brodie, 2017). As a way of example, the numismatics section on one of the forums in July 2018 had 3987 pages. There were 19–30 pages per post, which potentially amounts to an estimated 75,000 finds. In January 2021 the number of pages in that one section had increased to 4746.

4.1 Estimated Financial Value of Finds

One hundred and five of the 127 posts were users looking for evaluations or gauging interest whether anyone would be interested in a particular object. Sixty-six of these were given evaluations at the time of the snapshot (see Fig. 2). From these 66 posts, 11 objects were moved to the auction part of the forum, while seven objects were described as for sale but did not indicate how they were being sold. From 66 evaluations provided by forum users, 52 objects were evaluated as being worth less than 2500 rubles (€28).[6] This, in combination with the potential amount of finds as discussed earlier, conforms to an idea expressed by Brodie (2015, p.11) that the Internet market makes it "financially viable to trade in low-value and potentially high-volume material".

Although one can speculate about the cumulative financial value of the objects on these forums, there is a need to move beyond financial values as will be discussed later. However, as a brief example, we could consider a hypothetical scenario, where

[6]Conversion rate used 1 RUB = 0.0112324 EUR as on 3 June 2021.

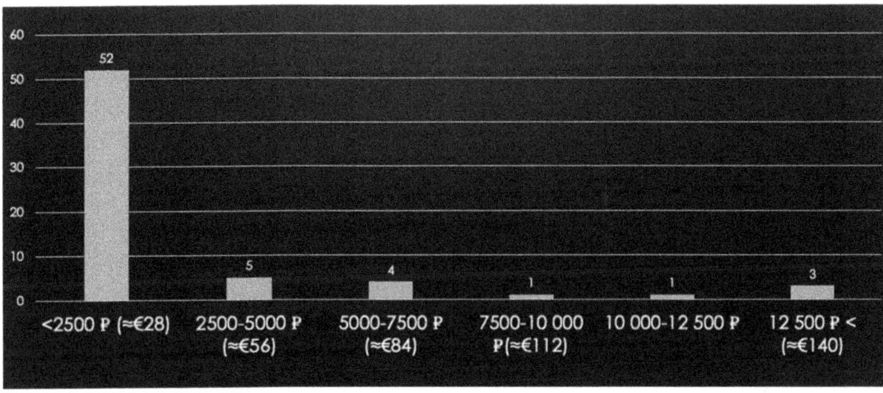

Fig. 2 The number of finds by the estimated value

a person has decided to look for archaeological objects without a permit using a metal detector. If we crudely summarise a rational choice perspective in criminology, crime will be committed if the benefits outweigh the costs (see Gül, 2009 for a summary on the use of the rational choice theories in criminology). In the case of Russia, the previously mentioned law (N245-FZ) sets out the financial penalty for the unauthorised search and/or removal of archaeological objects from the places of occurrence using the metal detector as high as one million rubles (over €11,000). If we consider that the majority of finds are worth less than €28, it is unlikely that the financial values are the main motivators for metal detectorists to break the law. Of course, this example is just hypothetical, and one could argue that in a large country such as Russia law enforcement agencies would struggle to enforce the law. However, it seems unlikely that someone would spend a considerable amount of money, time, and other resources to look for something that financially is not worth a lot if they were primarily driven by money. Metal detectorists argue that they spend a lot of financial resources on the hobby while the return is not as high, for instance, in the Heritage Journal's discussion section (Swift, 2012), one metal detectorist, with the username Andrew, claimed that he has been metal detecting for over 40 years and has spent over £100,000 on the hobby.

Regarding the evaluations, the object financial values were estimates rather than the actual price the objects were sold for. However, some evaluations were confirmed to be accurate. For example, a 10 rubles coin was evaluated by forum users to be worth 22,000 rubles ($\approx$ €247), a same type of coin was found to be sold for that price earlier, but with other evaluations it is impossible to tell due to the shortness of the time span that this snapshot analysis used.

4.2 *Quality of Finds*

An interesting point to note is the varied quality of finds. The online marketplaces have created a phenomenon called 'the vacuum cleaner effect'—antiquities which previously had very little material value are being sold to an ever-growing audience (Hollowell-Zimmer, 2003). This is something that Brodie (2017) has talked about as well—that archaeological objects sold on the Internet are generally of poorer quality than you would usually see in auction houses or dealerships. This 'vacuum cleaner effect' is evident in this snapshot analysis of Russian metal detecting forums. A portion of the finds posted were of quite poor quality but there were still people interested in them. For instance, in one of the posts on the forum, the finder of a heavily corroded bayonet knife of a Mauser 98k asked whether anyone would be interested in the knife in the current state of corrosion, and they were told that there would be people interested in buying it to restore it. Similarly, a heavily corroded, almost fully illegible coin from 1756 was evaluated to be worth 200–300 rubles (€2.24–3.36), a small amount but not nothing.

Of course, not all finds were of low quality, other finds such as a 1 ruble coin from 1724, or a ring potentially from the sixteenth or seventeenth century, were found in good quality or were cleaned up before being posted for evaluation. This also potentially suggests a different skill level of the finder, but it is something one could only speculate about. One thing is clear the quality of finds covers a wide spectrum rather than having a consistency and good standard of quality.

5 Engagement with Low-Value Objects

In criminology, research tends to focus on social aspects of the crime, and it has been argued that "criminal conduct is predominantly a social behaviour" (Warr, 2002, p. 3). As such trafficking research also tends to focus on social and criminal networks. While drug trafficking and human trafficking have been widely researched from a criminological perspective, antiquities trafficking, especially low-end antiquities trafficking has been less so. Furthermore, what is generally missing from this research is the role that objects potentially play in these networks. Objects are largely viewed as passive, and as accumulating increased financial value as they exchange hands. However, while objects accumulate financial value, they also accumulate histories. Kopytoff (1986) suggests the idea that one can write a biography about an object, the same way as one would write a biography about a person. These object biographies then can reveal relationships between people and objects, and how meaning and values are accumulated and transformed (Gosden & Marshall, 1999). While this approach has been taken up and explored in archaeological research (e.g., Marshall & Gosden, 1999), this is not a widely explored perspective in criminological research. Even cultural criminology which gives a chance to research crime in terms of "subcultural behaviour (. . .) organised around networks of symbol, ritual, and shared meaning" (Ferrell, 1999, p. 403), has been criticised for being "extraordinarily anthropocentric" (Schuilenburg et al., 2018, p. 268) and "privileg[ing] human experience" (Natali & McClanahan, 2017, p. 201), and as such if non-human actors are mentioned then their role is passive and instrumental.

The data discussed here is just a single snapshot coming from a region that could be argued to be on the fringe of art crime research. However, even this small dataset encourages more questions about engagements with low-value objects that move beyond anthropocentric view. Considering the number of finds, low-values, and sometimes poor quality of objects, it is hard to simply characterise this part of an art market as being purely profit-driven. Although it might not quite confirm to the idea of luxurious art market, it is still a part of it, a part that often falls outside our theorisation attempts.

Focus on only high-value objects and financial values has a number of drawbacks. On a theoretical level, objects are viewed in a passive way, as things with a price tag ascribed by people. On a public outreach level, focus on financial values excludes the range of motivations and beliefs for engaging with archaeological objects, therefore, making outreach activities potentially less successful and alienating some groups.

5.1 Are Objects Just Vessels for Financial Value?

There are many observations made in different contexts where illegal removal of objects from archaeological sites or looting has taken place or increased due to financial motivations such as economic downturn, war, or poverty (Gill, 2013; Parcak et al., 2016; Yahya, 2008). Similarly, studies have shown that in large scale trafficking networks, participants in the first stage of this activity, i.e., involving theft, might be willing to participate if presented with a profitable opportunity (Campbell, 2013). Additionally, it could be hard to entertain the idea that certain cases might be more than just about the money, especially when the financial value of the object increases at every stage of its journey.[7] All of these activities could be considered to be under the umbrella of art crime. However, the focus on financial values creates a very specific clear-cut image of what art crime is. Certain themes such as idea of the gentleman art thief or huge financial values emphasised in the media, reduce art crime to being purely profit-driven which alienates and distances art crime from day-to-day life. Values shape and inform policy decisions (Avrami et al., 2000). By over-emphasising certain values such as financial value, policy is shaped in a way that can exclude certain motivations, actions, and beliefs. The danger of emphasising one value over another or over-simplifying issue at hand has been noted before. Ellwood and Greenwood (2016) have hypothesised that heritage valuation in terms of economic value might alter the perceived cultural value of it, while EmBree and Scott (2015) argue that if we distance ourselves from

[7]This was the case with Dancing Shiva Statue, which was sold by Subhash Kapoor, New York based art dealer, to National Gallery of Australia for US$5 million. In comparison, Kapoor paid the local dealer at the source only US$30,000, while the thieves who stole the statue from the temple received even less (see Boland, 2019 for more details on the case).

the notion that art crime is driven by only profit, we can better understand subtleties in art forgery.

What we can see from the snapshot analysis is that, yes, there are many posts gauging interest or asking for an object's evaluation (to be more precise, 105 out of 127), however, that is just one aspect of the relationships between people and objects. Appadurai (1986) suggests that a commodity is a thing in a particular situation, this situation can be applicable to any object at different stages of its life. Kopytoff (1986, p. 73) argues that commoditisation should be viewed as "a process of becoming rather than as an all-or-none state of being". As such it could be argued that commodities have social lives the same way humans do (Appadurai, 1986; Kopytoff, 1986). At the commodity stage of an object the most important feature of it is its exchangeability (Appadurai, 1986). During the snapshot, this is the stage that we can observe in majority of cases, however, by focusing on just this part of it, and on materialistic values, we overlook the other side of these relationships.

As mentioned earlier, the quality of finds covers a wide spectrum, so for instance the finder of a bayonet knife of a Mauser 98k was told that someone would still buy it and restore it even though it was in a heavily eroded state, so the object's life would continue. What makes someone buy an object in such a poor state? On the flip side, what makes someone keep a find that is in such a bad state? Why not discard it? In this situation it is hard to argue that it is all about the money, if a potential financial gain is less than €28. By reducing these relationships between humans and objects to only one aspect (in majority of cases to financial motivations or greed), we are shutting off potential avenues for further research, including research that would grant objects a degree of agency in the low-end antiquities trade. This idea might at first seem absurd, but this perception lies in "the Western opposition between 'objects' and 'subjects'" (Jones & Boivin, 2010, p. 334).

I am not suggesting that, by having agency, an object physically makes us do something, but following Latour (2005, p. 71) it is possible to extend an agency to anything that "modifies a state of affairs by making a difference". In this snapshot analysis, for instance, some objects were put on the forum, but they were not for sale even though they were described as rare and as such could be more financially valuable. One such object was an oxidised lead Berdan or Minié bullet which was decided to be kept as a souvenir as it is rare for the region where it was found. Arguably an object made a difference—it modified a state of affairs and influenced a more rational decision that would be to sell it as it is rare, but instead it was kept.

Even in the cases involving high financial value objects, monetary value is not always the most important one. For instance, in an interview, Jean Paul Barbier-Mueller, the Swiss collector and museum founder, stated that he is happy after he has completed a collection for it to be sold and find a new owner. As he put it "It is not a question of price, I do not need money, it is a question of how you will treat it, how you will show it" (Barbier-Mueller, as cited by Moore, 2017). In the interview, he stated that he works "in the shadows" so that "the unknown people" who created objects that he owns are connected to the people who come to see them, and he hopes that "that these encounters will be a revelation—and in the dark the authors of these works are smiling in silence and probably happy to see that the objects that they did not make as works of art are important" (Barbier-Mueller, as cited by Moore, 2017). Similarly, Lawrence Fleischman, a gallery owner, art dealer, and collector, argued that when you start adding "a price tag" to your collection, "you dilute that experience" of engaging with the works of art (Fleischman, 1994). Both Barbier-Mueller (see Ruiz Romero, 2020) and Fleischman (see Watson & Todeschini, 2007) have been accused of buying and/or selling illicit antiquities, but we can begin to question if their motivation to do so was purely financial.

What both the snapshot analysis and the above interview excerpts show is that an engagement with the objects is more than just about money. As mentioned earlier, there are instances of art crime when it is motivated by economic gains, however, there is a spectrum of other engagements that are not all about the financial gains, and where objects are not passive things with a price tag. What would happen if we moved away from this notion of an object being passive? The answer to this question could have important implications for how we attempt to regulate antiquities buyer behaviour. It is something that further research could and should explore.

5.2 *Burning or Building Bridges: Greed or Love for History?*

The commodification of cultural heritage[8] in many instances is criticised, and this focus on financial value is used as a key divider that separates 'good' treasure hunters from the 'bad'. For instance, the motivation of metal detectorists seems to be an important consideration when deciding who is worthy of official collaboration with professional archaeologists. Stine and Shumate (2015, p. 291) emphasise that those "avocationalists who do not dig in order to buy or sell artifacts can serve as important partners in historic-site archaeology projects". However, this makes the issue rather clear-cut. As mentioned earlier, commoditisation is just a phase in an object's life, a phase that object can move in and out of. By focusing just on this stage, when the exchangeability and financial value of the object is the most important, we dismiss relationships and values before and after it. We take a human-centred approach, where the sale of the object is the most important act, not the object itself. The focus on social and criminal networks, or more generally networks just involving people, has not brought the desired results to reduce antiquities looting at source (e.g., Mackenzie, 2013; Yates, 2014). This would suggest that different approach is required.

Animosity between metal detectorists and archaeologists has been discussed elsewhere (e.g., Karl, 2016; Lecroere, 2016), however it is worth mentioning that realistically speaking, even just based on the snapshot discussed here, there are a lot more of treasure hunters who engage with archaeological objects than there are archaeologists. There is a need for finding a way where these human-objects

[8]By that it is meant that the cultural heritage is viewed primarily in terms of its financial, exchange value and transformed into commodities that can be bought and sold.

relationships can be explored. As this snapshot shows, these engagements with low-value archaeological objects are happening and are happening at quite a large scale. It is hard to justify these engagements as being purely profit-driven, so what is it then about engaging with these objects, that make people sometimes commit a crime? What is the nature of the influence and pull these objects have that make people spend time, resources, and effort to look for them, care for them, and sometimes cross the line and break the law? The case discussed here cannot answer these questions, but it hints at more complicated, intertwined values that are more than just about money.

6 Conclusion and Further Research

The snapshot discussed in this chapter can be viewed as a gateway into an alternative engagement space, a space where relationships between humans and objects are created, reinforced, and changed. This snapshot analysis covered only a 3-day period; however, it showed the high number of low-value objects that are available on treasure hunting forums. This was seen as a hint that low-end treasure hunting and collecting is more than just about money. Qualitative, in-depth research is required that explores these relationships with low-value objects. These relationships, focusing on objects, have a potential to reveal more effective points of intervention that could be applied to the illegal antiquities trade. A single archaeological object might not seem like a big deal or worth mentioning but if everyone removed these our cultural heritage would be quickly depleted. We can focus on large financial values, but it is the persistence of smaller activities that over time can cause a significant damage. The question is, what we can do to prevent this or change the nature of the damage? There is a need to acknowledge an alternative engagement spaces and interactions that have been discussed in this chapter. It is time to include things in our theorisation attempts. The heavily corroded bayonet knife of a Mauser 98k is not just a thing with a price tag, it had a story (or a life), before appearing on the forum, and it will have a life after. Whether its life contributes to creation of alternative frameworks of crime and influences a committal of crime is something that needs consideration.

Acknowledgements The funding for this research was provided by the European Research Council (ERC) under the European Union's Horizon 2020 research and innovation programme (grant agreement n° 804851) and from European Commission EAC/06/2017 "Improving Knowledge on Illicit Trade in Cultural Goods in the EU".

References

Abbasi, A., Chen, H., & Salem, A. (2007). Sentiment analysis in multiple languages: Feature selection for opinion classification in Web forums. *ACM Transactions on Information Systems, 26*(3), Article 12.

Alder, C., & Polk, K. (2002). Stopping this awful business: The illicit traffic in antiquities examined as a criminal market. *Art, Antiquity and Law, 7*(1), 35–53.

Anico, M. (2008). Representing identities at local municipal museums: Cultural forums or identity bunkers. In M. Anico & E. Peralta (Eds.), *Heritage and identity: Engagement and demission in the contemporary world* (pp. 63–75). Routledge.

Appadurai, A. (1986). Introduction: Commodities and the politics of value. The cultural biography of things: Commoditization as process. In A. Appadurai (Ed.), *The social life of things: Commodities in cultural perspective* (pp. 3–63). Cambridge University Press.

Avrami, E., Mason, R., & de la Torre, M. (2000). *Values and heritage conservation.* The Getty Conservation Institute.

Baugh, M. (2007). Antiquities: The hottest investment. *Time* [online], 12 July. Retrieved May 10, 2021, from http://content.time.com/time/business/article/0,8599,1693792,00.html

Blake, J. (2000). On defining the cultural heritage. *The International and Comparative Law Quarterly, 49*(1), 61–85.

Boland, M. (2019). The Kapoor case including the stolen Shiva. In S. Hufnagel & D. Chappell (Eds.), *The Palgrave handbook of art crime* (pp. 463–482). Palgrave Macmillan.

Bouchenaki, M. (2003). The interdependency of the tangible and intangible cultural heritage. In: 14th ICOMOS General Assembly and International Symposium: 'Place, memory, meaning: preserving intangible values in monuments and sites', 27–31 October, Victoria Falls, Zimbabwe.

Brodie, N. (2014). The Internet market in Precolumbian antiquities. In J. Kila & M. Balcells (Eds.), *Cultural property crime: An overview and analysis on contemporary perspectives and trends* (pp. 237–262). Brill.

Brodie, N. (2015). The internet market in antiquities. In F. Desmarais (Ed.), *Countering illicit traffic in cultural goods: The global challenge of protecting the world's heritage* (pp. 11–20). ICOM.

Brodie, N. (2017). Virtually gone! The Internet market in antiquities. In *Proceedings of the 6th International Conference of Experts on the Return of Cultural Property* (pp. 190–204). Overseas Korean Cultural Heritage Foundation.

Brodie, N., Yates, D., Slot, B., Batura, O., van Wanrooij, N., & op 't Hoog, G. (2019). Illicit trade in cultural goods in Europe: Characteristics, criminal justice responses and an analysis of the applicability of technologies in the combat against the trade. Report. Directorate-General for Education, Youth, Sport and Culture, European Commission. Retrieved from https://op.europa.eu/en/publication-detail/-/publication/d79a105a-a6aa-11e9-9d01-01aa75ed71a1

Campbell, P. B. (2013). The illicit antiquities trade as a transnational criminal network: Characterizing and anticipating trafficking of cultural heritage. *International Journal of Cultural Property, 20*, 113–153.

Durney, M. (2013). Reevaluating art crime's famous figures. *International Journal of Cultural Property, 20*, 221–232.

Durney, M., & Proulx, B. (2011). Art crime: A brief introduction. *Crime, Law and Social Change, 56*, 115–132.

Elkins, N. T. (2008). Survey of the material and intellectual consequences of trading in undocumented ancient coins: A case study on the North American Trade. *Frankfurter elektronische Rundschau zur Altertumskunde* [online], 7, 1–13. Retrieved from http://s145739614.online.de/fera/ausgabe7/Elkins.pdf

Ellwood, S., & Greenwood, M. (2016). Accounting for heritage assets: Does measuring economic value 'kill the cat'? *Critical Perspectives on Accounting, 38*, 1–13.

EmBree, C., & Scott, D. A. (2015). The multifarious nature of art forgery in France: Four case studies of Belle Epoque fakes and forgeries. *The Journal of Art Crime, 13*, 3–16.

Evans, M. (2015). Gentleman thief poses as art lover before stealing £40,000 statue. *The Telegraph* [online], 8 July. Retrieved May 14, 2021, from http://www.telegraph.co.uk/news/uknews/crime/11726895/Gentleman-thief-poses-as-art-lover-before-stealing-40000-statue.html

Ferrell, J. (1999). Cultural criminology. *Annual Review of Sociology, 25*, 395–418.

Ferri, P., Sidaway, S. I. L., & Carnegie, G. D. (2021). The paradox of accounting for cultural heritage: A longitudinal study on the financial reporting of heritage assets of major Australian public cultural institutions (1992–2019). *Accounting, Auditing & Accountability Journal, 34*(4), 983–1012.

Fleischman, L. A. (1994) Oral history interview with Lawrence A. Fleischman, 18 April. *Archives of American Art, Smithsonian Institution.* Retrieved from https://www.aaa.si.edu/collections/interviews/oral-history-interview-lawrence-fleischman-12955#overview

Gill, D. W. (2013). Cultural tourism in Greece at a time of economic crisis. *Journal of Eastern Mediterranean Archaeology and Heritage Studies, 1*(3), 233–242.

Gosden, C., & Marshall, Y. (1999). The cultural biography of objects. *World Archaeology, 31*(2), 169–178.

Gül, S. K. (2009). An evaluation of the rational choice theory in criminology. *GAU Journal of Social and Applied Science, 4*(8), 36–44.

Hardy, S. A. (2016). 'Black Archaeology' in Eastern Europe: Metal detecting, illicit trafficking of cultural objects, and 'Legal Nihilism' in Belarus, Poland, Russia, and Ukraine. *Public Archaeology, 15*(4), 214–237.

Hollowell-Zimmer, J. (2003). Digging in the dirt: Ethics and "Low-End" looting. In L. J. Zimmerman, K. D. Vitelli, & J. Hollowell-Zimmer (Eds.), *Ethical issues in archaeology.* Walnut Creek, CA.

Holtz, P., Kronberger, N., & Wagner, W. (2012). Analyzing internet forums: A practical guide. *Journal of Media Psychology, 24*(2), 55–66.

Jones, A., & Boivin, N. (2010). The malice of inanimate objects: Material agency. In *Oxford handbook of material culture studies* (pp. 333–351).

Karl, R. (2016). More tales from heritage hell: Law, policy and practice of archaeological heritage protection in Austria. *The Historic Environment: Policy & Practice, 7*(4), 283–300.

Kinsella, E. (2020). American authorities have returned 10 looted antiquities worth a combined $1.2 million back to India. *artnet news* [online], 20 August. Retrieved May 14, 2021, from https://news.artnet.com/art-world/us-government-returns-seized-artifacts-india-1903220

Koehler, E. M. (2007). Repatriation of cultural objects to indigenous peoples: A comparative analysis of U.S and Canadian law. *The International Lawyer, 41*(1), 103–126.

Kopytoff, I. (1986). The cultural biography of things: Commoditization as process. In A. Appadurai (Ed.), *The social life of things: Commodities in cultural perspective* (pp. 64–91). Cambridge University Press.

Korner, W. (2016). Article: The reality of art crime. *The Art Loss Register* [online]. Retrieved May 14, 2021, from https://www.academia.edu/25582807/The_Reality_of_Art_Crime

Latour, B. (2005). *Reassembling the social: An introduction to actor-network theory*. Oxford University Press.

Lecroere, T. (2016). "There is None So Blind as Those Who Won't See": Metal detecting and archaeology in France. *Open Archaeology, 2*(1), 182–193.

Mackenzie, S. (2013). Conditions for guilt-free consumption in a transnational criminal market. *European Journal on Criminal Policy and Research, 20*, 503–515.

Marshall, Y., & Gosden, C. (Eds.). (1999). The cultural biography of objects. *World Archaeology, 31*(2), 169–320.

Moore, S. (2017). Jean Paul Barbier-Mueller (1930–2016). Apollo, 4 January. Retrieved May 26, 2021, from https://www.apollo-magazine.com/interview-with-jean-paul-barbier-mueller/

Motoyama, M., McCoy, D., Levchenko, K., Savage, S., & Voelker, G. M. (2011). An analysis of underground forums. *IMC'11–Proceedings of the 2011 ACM SIGCOMM Internet Measurement Conference*, pp. 71–79.

Natali, L., & McClanahan, B. (2017). Perceiving and communication environmental contamination and change: Towards a green cultural criminology with images. *Critical Criminology, 25*, 199–214.

Parcak, S., Gathings, D., Childs, C., Mumford, G., & Cline, E. (2016). Satellite evidence of archaeological site looting in Egypt: 2002–2013. *Antiquity, 90*(349), 188–205.

Phillips, L. (2016). Examine your own limits. *Social Research: An International Quarterly, 8*(1), 217–221.

Ruiz Romero, Z. (2020). Lawfulness and ethics around cultural property auctions: The case of the Barbier-Mueller pre-Columbian collection. *International Journal of Cultural Property, 27*, 397–416.

Schuilenburg, M., Staring, R., & van Swaaningen, R. (2018). Cultural criminology going Dutch. In K. Hayward (Ed.), *Cultural criminology* (pp. 252–272). Routledge.

Slade, G., & Light, M. (2015). Crime and criminal justice after communism: Why study the post-Soviet region? *Theoretical Criminology, 19*(2), 147–158.

Stine, L. F., & Shumate, D. L. (2015). Metal detecting: An effective tool for archaeological research and community engagement. *North American Archaeologist, 36*(4), 289–323.

Swift, N. (2012). Metal detecting: A landowners' guide to "Finds Agreements"– Part 2. *The Heritage Journal* [online], 14 October. Retrieved June 2, 2021, from https://web.archive.org/web/20210602120541/https://heritageaction.wordpress.com/2012/10/14/metal-detecting-a-landowners-guide-to-finds-agreements-part-2/

Thomas, S., & Stone, P. G. (2009). *Metal detecting and archaeology*. The Boydell Press.

Valdés, A. R. (2015). Fighting against the archaeological looting and the illicit trade of antiquities in Spain. *International Journal of Cultural Property, 22*, 111–130.

Warr, M. (2002). *Companions in crime: The social aspects of criminal conduct*. Cambridge University Press.

Watson, P., & Todeschini, C. (2007). *The Medici conspiracy*. Public Affairs.

Yahya, A. H. (2008). Managing heritage in a war zone. *Journal of the World Archaeological Congress, 4*(3), 495–505.

Yates, D. (2014). Church theft, insecurity, and community justice: The reality of source-end regulation of the market for illicit Bolivian cultural objects. *European Journal on Criminal Policy and Research, 20*(4), 445–457.

Zubacheva, K. (2017). How to find hidden treasures in Russia. *Russia Beyond* [online], May 17. Retrieved May 12, 2021, from https://www.rbth.com/arts/2017/05/17/how-to-find-hidden-treasures-in-russia-and-not-get-thrown-into-prison_764761

Offender Motivations and Expectations of Data in Antiquities Looting

Michelle D. Fabiani

Abstract Understanding offender motivation is key to developing effective crime reduction policies. Criminological theories seeking to explain offender motivations are plentiful—some argue for a pure utilitarian agenda driven by opportunity (rational choice), others for the influence of socially constructed standards of behavior (strain, learning), and still others argue for accounting for multiple layers of influence (crime pattern theory). Though these theories have been used to explain the presence of antiquities looting, few have sought to examine offender motivations specifically due to a lack of data. But what kind of data should those interested in offender motivations be looking for? How does this align with possible underlying theoretical motivations? This study speaks to these questions by first considering how criminological theoretical paradigms account for antiquities looter motivations. Then, it traces how to approach examining looting motivation by identifying the types of evidence and data needed to test theoretical predictions and which methodologies would be appropriate for such an analysis. Finally, this study demonstrates this approach using case study featuring a newly collected spatiotemporal dataset on antiquities looting in Egypt. Looking from 2015 to 2017, this study will determine what can be learned about possible offender motivations in Egypt at this time.

1 Introduction

Understanding offender motivation is key to being able to develop effective policies to proactively reduce crime. Within criminology, theories seeking to explain offender motivations are plentiful (see below for detailed discussions of each). Some argue for a pure utilitarian agenda driven by opportunity (rational choice) while others argue for the influence of socially constructed standards of behaviour (strain, learning), and still others argue for the need to account for multiple layers of influence (crime pattern theory). Several of these theories have been used to examine antiquities looting, often as a component of the broader process of trafficking

M. D. Fabiani (✉)
Department of Criminal Justice, University of New Haven, New Haven, CT, USA

N. Oosterman, D. Yates (eds.), *Crime and Art*, Studies in Art, Heritage, Law and the Market 1, https://doi.org/10.1007/978-3-030-84856-9_15

antiquities (Alder & Polk, 2002; Mackenzie & Green, 2009; Mackenzie & Yates, 2016). When considering antiquities looting on its own, theories focusing on situational elements are more common. Routine activities theory (RAT, see below) is the most often applied given its focus on the combination of capable guardianship, assumed motivated offender, and a suitable target (Casey, 2006; Fabiani, 2018, 2019). Situational crime prevention is a more recent, promising application (Weirich, 2019).

However, few have sought to examine offender motivations in antiquities looting specifically due to a *perceived* lack of data (Balestrieri, 2018). The notable exception is Balcells Magrans (2018), who applies social learning theory and differential association to explore the structure and participation of *tombaroli* in antiquities looting in Italy through interviews. Despite increasing availability on looting events through satellite imagery (Fabiani, 2019), news reports (Fabiani, 2018), social media (Al-Azm & Paul, 2019), and intelligence reports (Cuneo & Danti, 2019), information on the offender remain elusive. This is due both to the retroactive nature of most data collection on antiquities and the areas of interest. Even if a looting event is reported the same day by a local observer, few reports capture the would-be looter *in situ*. Similarly, known offenders who loot are less interested in being interviewed by academics (see Balcells Magrans, 2018 for exception). Moreover, many of the areas of greatest focus are on countries where crime statistics are not consistently available (UN, 2017).[1] These limitations significantly restrict analyses seeking to move beyond current often-times mutually exclusive characterisations of looters as 'looter-victims' or 'looter-criminals' (Balestrieri, 2018). As a result, studies gravitate towards theories that assume the motivated offender (e.g., RAT), omitting the need for data on offenders.[2] Though much can be learned about the circumstances in which looting occurs using routine activity theory, any efforts to design preventative measures without accounting for offender motivation will treat the symptoms rather than the underlying cause of the problem.

This study seeks to facilitate future research in this area by first reviewing how offenders and motivations are discussed in the literature on antiquities looting. It then presents a criminological theoretical framework for looking at antiquities

[1] Accessing international crime statistics that are consistently available for multiple time periods (e.g., for longitudinal analysis) is a well-established issue. The United Nations has dedicated projects around the world to establish reliable methodologies and standards for international crime statistics (UN, 2017). Though availability of statistics has improved overall, there remains inconsistent availability longitudinally and the types of statistics available are country dependent. Countries with a history of or actively involved in conflict tend to have the least availability for crime statistics. This is mirrored in data available from other sources like the World Bank.

[2] Criminological theories are more commonly applied to explain behavior within the art market, including techniques of neutralisation (Conklin, 1994; Mackenzie & Yates, 2016) and routine activity theory (Mackenzie & Green, 2009). These studies are able to access more varied data sources with a focus on how assumptions of offender motivations across theories can serve to improve preventative measures (e.g., through deterrence). This study focuses on how criminological theory can assist in understanding offender motivation specifically in the area of antiquities looting.

looting by integrating the extant literature's conceptualisations of looters with theoretical views of offender motivation. Then, it traces how one could approach a theoretically grounded examination of antiquities looting offender motivation by identifying the types of evidence and data needed and which methodologies would be appropriate for such an analysis. Finally, this approach is demonstrated using a case study featuring a newly collected spatiotemporal dataset on antiquities looting in Lower Egypt from 2015 to 2017. The chapter ends with a discussion of implications for future research.

2 Offenders, Motivations, and Antiquities Looting

Within the extant literature on antiquities looting, multiple groupings of potential offenders are common—looter-victims' (or 'subsistence' looters), 'cultural' looters, 'professional' looters, "looter-criminals,' and 'resistance' looters.[3] 'Looter-victims' are motivated by need, often resulting from socio-economic factors beyond their control (Balestrieri, 2018; Borodkin, 1995; Matsuda, 1998). In this view, 'looter-victims' have little agency of their own (Balestrieri, 2018).

'Cultural' looters see the objects they dig up as part of their cultural legacy and may be part of an intergenerational tradition of looting. They may or may not be impoverished, but the distinguishing feature is that looting is a trade that is learned or culturally viewed as acceptable (Alderman, 2012; Kersel, 2007; Matsuda, 1998; Paredes Maury, 1999; Patel, 2009). For example, some see looting as part of the same tradition of exploiting the natural environment that their ancestors engaged in, a culturally passed down norm that is similarly reflected in the looting folklore of the area (Paredes Maury, 1999, pp. 13, 15–30). Similarly, "cultural" looting encompasses looting as a 'leisure' activity, where skill and expertise are involved but the motivation is enjoyment rather than economic need (Kersel, 2007, pp. 87–90).

Relatedly, the term 'professional' looter is used to describe individuals for whom looting is a form of gainful employment, a learned profession or vocation. They may have motivations tied to cultural norms that view looting as just another job, potentially lucrative and dangerous (Kersel, 2007, p. 87; Paredes Maury, 1999, p. 20). They may or may not be impoverished, but often are described as having intention and agency in their decision to loot, while at the same time failing to see looting as illegal. 'Looter-criminals' by contrast are motivated by greed and may have connections to organised crime, syndicates, or insurgent financing activities (Alderman, 2012; Bernick, 1998; Cuneo & Danti, 2019; McCalister, 2005). They are aware of the illegality of their acts and choose to operate within a 'criminal' space.

[3] Other conceptualisations have also been offered in the literature. Fabiani (2018) offers 'opportunistic' and 'strategic' looters as a means of bypassing the implied mutual exclusivity between victim, criminal, and professional. Mac Ginty (2004) offered a typology of looting from a political science perspective, rejecting the premise that looting can be considered from a criminological lens since the crime of theft ignores important socio-political contexts.

Finally, 'resistance' looters have increasingly been documented and recognised as a unique group of offenders with a distinct motivation (Kersel, 2007, pp. 91–94; Lowenthal, 2005). They engage in deliberate destruction and targeting of archaeological sites as a form of protest a government or opposing group. Kersel's (2007, p. 92) study focused on looters who prioritised the destruction of Israeli or Jewish heritage while preserving Palestinian heritage. These looters may be motivated by macro-level and cultural factors (e.g., socio-political dynamics, cultural conflict) and act with agency.

All these groupings make assumptions about the offender, their motivations, and their ability to act with agency despite little concrete data as evidence (Balestrieri, 2018; see Kersel, 2007 for exception). Rather, they are often tied to archaeologists' perceptions of and reactions to looting behaviour at the sites they study. As such, they are inherently tied to issues of archaeological ethics and subjective views of what *should* or *should not* be a crime (Alderman, 2012; Balestrieri, 2018) and how looting relates to broader social and political contexts (Devine, 2016). Discussions of ethics and the utility of sanctions for looting are worthwhile; however, conflating these conversations with arguments of offender motivation are counterproductive and can lead to flawed analyses or policy initiatives. Indeed, when considering the diversity of possible looter groupings represented in the literature, it is difficult to discern a single policy approach that could adequately address all the potential motivations, degrees of assumed agency, and macro-level contextual factors.

This study argues that when viewing antiquities looting from a criminological perspective, the question of offender motivation should be theoretically grounded and rooted in less value-laden language (e.g., 'offender' vs 'looter'). Such an approach allows for more flexibility in considering offender motivation in the context of antiquities looting. Rather than picking a subjectively defined motivation and fitting theory, data, and methods to it, scholars can examine what unit of analysis they intend (or are able) to study and match their theoretical assumptions with the research questions of interest, their data, and methods.

3 A Criminological Framework for Offender Motivation in Antiquities Looting

3.1 Motivations for Offending in Criminological Theory

Criminological theories have a wide range of explanations for why crime occurs. The degree to which offender motivations are considered—either explicitly or implicitly—also varies considerably. It depends on at minimum the unit of analysis (micro, community, or macro), assumptions of human behaviour (rational, social, utilitarian), and the role of the environment. Figure 1 is a heuristic guide to conceptualising how offender motivation may be examined in criminological theory

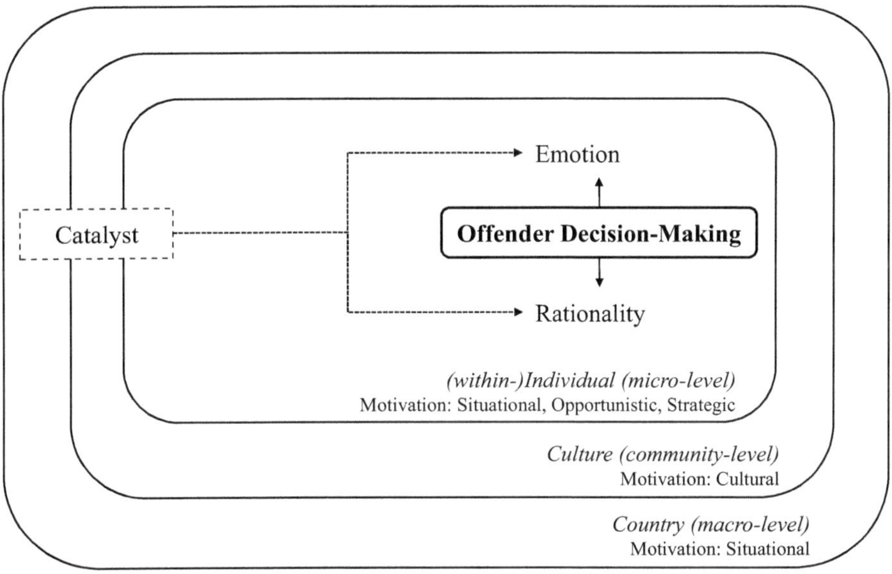

Fig. 1 A heuristic for offender motivations in criminological theory

based on the location of the influence and the assumed motivation.[4] In any given situation where crime may occur, an offender will be motivated by a catalyst and their decision-making process will be a tension between acting based on emotion or on rationality. The catalyst in this heuristic is the source of offender motivation and can come from any combination of country (macro-level), cultural (community-level), or (within-) individual (micro-level) factors. Offender motivations may be multifaceted and layered.

Country (macro-level) catalysts are those societal factors that can create situations conducive to criminal conduct and exert influence on individuals. Criminological theories looking at offender motivation from a country level specifically focus on the influence of the environment on the individual. Both crime pattern theory (Brantingham & Brantingham, 1993, 2013) and classic strain theory (Merton, 1938) view offender motivation as rooted in this macro-level *situational* approach. Catalysts at the community-level are localised, cultural influences that shape an individual's normative perceptions of crime. Central to these theories the argument that crime is learned through interaction with others like any occupation (Sutherland, 1937). Specific mechanisms of learning can influence individual motivation. Social learning theories in criminology focus explicitly on these mechanisms and are heavily influenced by studies of behavioral responses to stimuli (Akers, 1985).

[4]This heuristic is based on my analysis of offender motivation in criminological theory. The presentation is informed Coyne and Eck's (2014) representation of the differing levels of influence of situational choice in offender decision-making.

Offender motivation originates from a *cultural* location tied to interaction with community and norms favorable to specific crimes.

Micro-level catalysts can occur both at the individual level and the within-individual level. A plethora of criminological theories examine these catalysts, including general strain theories, opportunity theories, and social control theories. These approaches differ in their assumption so human agency and the assumed mechanisms of offender motivation (situational, strategic, or opportunistic). Individual-level *situational* motivations can be derived either from within the offender or local situational factors. General strain theory (Agnew, 1992, 2006) views motivation originating from a combination of negative emotions, the type of strain experienced and the type of coping mechanism (Agnew, 1992, 2006). Crime pattern theory's (Brantingham & Brantingham, 1993, 2013) specific offender adaptations and Clarke's (1999) CRAVED (Concealable, Removable, Available, Valuable, Enjoyable, and Disposable) principles focus motivation deriving from local situational factors.

These same criminological approaches allow for *strategic* motivations depending on the individual adaptation. A decision to pursue criminal behavior based on characteristics of the target and the situation are encompassed in both Agnew's (1992, 2006) general strain theory and Brantingham's (2012) offender targeting behaviors in crime pattern theory. Some applications of opportunity theories like rational choice theory (Cornish & Clarke, 1986) and thoughtfully reflective decision-making (Paternoster & Pogarsky, 2009) also suggest a *strategic* motivation for offending grounded in the assumption that individuals are naturally self-interested and hedonistic (Bentham, 1789).

Finally, the role of *opportunity* around and within an individual can influence offender motivation. Both opportunity theories and social control theories broadly assume that humans are naturally self-interested, hedonistic (Bentham, 1789), and employ rational decision-making. If committing a crime will result in a positive outcome that outweighs the cost, then crime is more likely to occur (Becker, 1968). Individual rationality is bounded by limited time and information available in their decision-making process (Simon, 1979). Where they differ is that opportunity theories argue that the *opportunity* to commit a crime is key in determining whether that motivation translates to concrete action. By contrast, social control theories focus on what prevents individuals from committing crime. Often these explanations include the strength of social bonds (Hirschi, 1969) and low self-control (Gottfredson & Hirschi, 1990). Though offender motivation is broadly assumed, these theories implicitly discuss the nuances of motivation through the consideration of individual qualities like self-control (Hirschi, 2004). These qualities determine an individual's inclination to take advantage of an *opportunity* should one be present.

Figure 2 describes how each location of influence (catalyst) relates to analytical units of analysis, offender motivations, and criminological theories. The characteristics of offending associated with catalysts and theories also have implications for the role of human agency—an individual's conscious decision-making while considering whether to act. Situational catalysts at the macro- or micro-level can either allow for agency on the part of the potential offender or relegate them to victims of

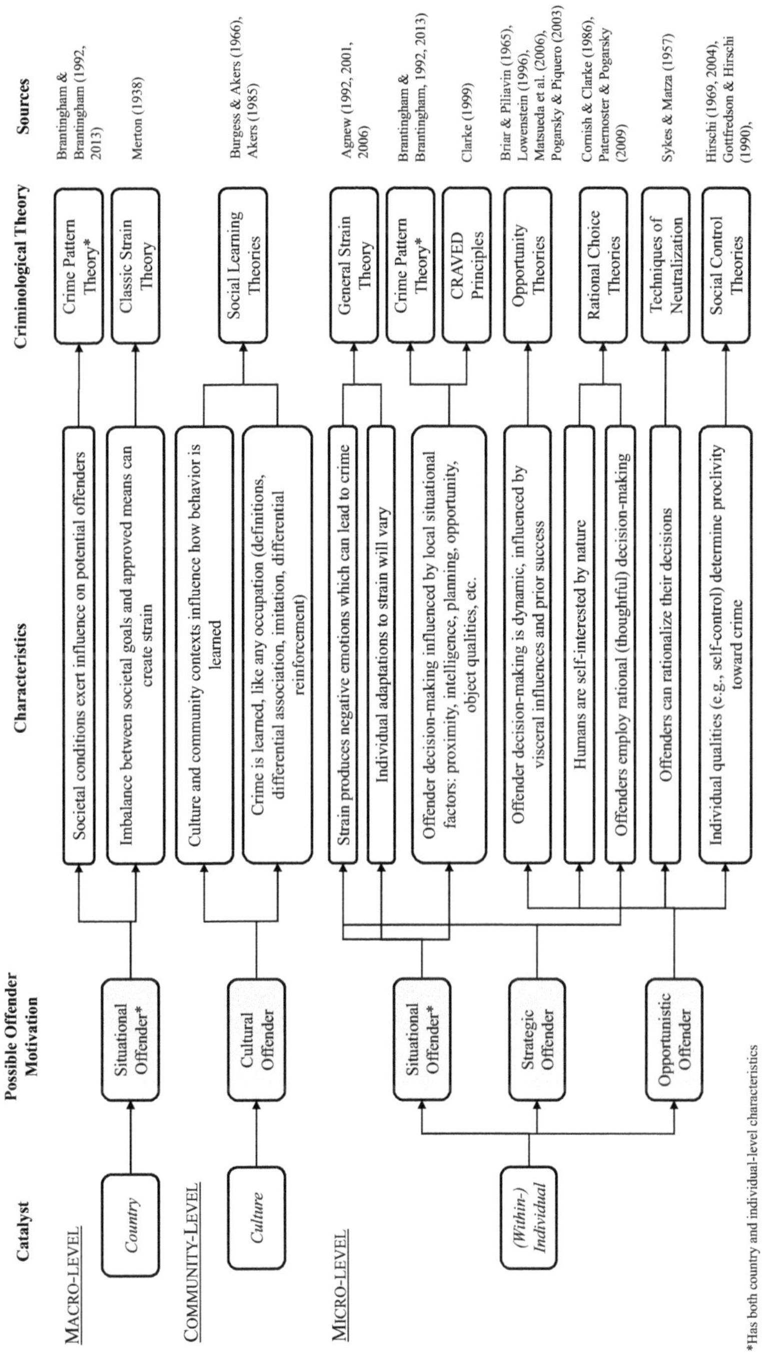

Fig. 2 Catalysts of offender motivation, characteristics, and criminological theories

circumstance. Similarly, cultural (community-level) catalysts may or may not allow for agency in how a potential offender learns norms conducive to criminal activity. The most explicit considerations of agency are at the micro-level. Some theories, like social control dismiss the role of agency while others like rational choice or opportunity theories argue for high levels of agency in decision-making. How these relate to the specific case of antiquities looting is discussed in more depth below.

3.2 Criminological Offender Motivations for Antiquities Looting

Applying these theories to antiquities looting requires understanding both how looters have been viewed in the literature ('looter-victim,' 'cultural' looters, 'professional' looters, 'looter-criminals,' 'resistance' looters) and how offender motivation is accounted for in criminological theory (situational, cultural, strategic, opportunistic). Each of these terms attempt to grapple with the different underlying motivations for action and describe the activities of looters. In doing so, they make assumptions of the offender's agency and the catalyst for their motivation. The term 'victim' implies that the individual has been acted upon, implying a passive role that denies the actor agency. Conversely, 'criminal' and 'resistance' both connote intentional, planned action—whether an act is viewed as a 'crime' is a matter of perspective. 'Professional' refers both to an occupation and organised activity, implying agency and intentionality.

I do not suggest that current groupings of offenders are without merit, merely that they be re-contextualised to be grounded in criminological theories and to allow for layered motivations. In doing so, this study argues that criminological theory can serve as a strategic framework through which offender motivation of antiquities looting can be investigated. The framework presented here is an integration of the characteristics of each looter grouping from the literature with the offender motivations from criminological theory. The resultant new terms describe antiquities looters based on both theory and the extant literature on looting: situational offenders, cultural offenders, opportunistic offenders, and strategic offenders. Figure 3 links these terms to criminological theories, looter terminology, and describes how they would be applied to antiquities looting depending on theoretical approach. Theoretical approach depends on the degree of agency assumed. Duration, frequency, intensity, and whether they act alone or as part of a group will depend on the situational influences.

Situational offenders may be influenced by country (macro-level) or individual, localised factors. In the context of antiquities looting, the catalyst would be macro-level factors that create conditions conducive to looting. Draught, conflict, economic depressions, social or cultural tensions all shape situations that may make looting a favourable outcome. Local or individual situational factors could result from

Motivation	Source of Motivation	Looter Types	Application to Antiquities Looting
Situational Offender	Country (macro-level) catalysts create situational offender motivation that influences decision-making.	Looter-victim Professional looter Resistance looter	**Crime Pattern Theory:** Macro-level factors (e.g., drought, conflict, economic depressions, social or cultural tensions) create conditions conducive to looting. Low agency is assumed. **Classic Strain Theory:** Situationally induced-strain can lead to looting as a reasonable adaptation. Low agency is assumed.
	Individual (micro-level) catalysts create situational offender motivation that influences decision-making.	Looter-victim Professional looter Resistance looter	**Crime Pattern Theory / CRAVED Principles**: Individual situational factors related to an offender's targeting practices. Agency is assumed. **General Strain Theory:** Individual or within-individual situational factors can lead to looting as an adaptation to strain. Low agency is assumed.
Cultural Offender	Culture (community-level) catalysts facilitate the transmission of cultural values that create definitions favorable to crime.	Cultural looter Professional looter	**Social Learning Theory:** offender's motivations are learned through definitions, differential association, imitation, and differential reinforcement. Agency is assumed in the learning and decision-making processes. Offending may occur individually or as part of a group. The specific manifestation of the learning mechanisms may take multiple forms: ❖ Looting as a cultural practice, tied to views of heritage and ownership of the land ❖ Looting as a leisure activity ❖ Looting as an occupation or vocation that often is passed down intergenerationally
Strategic Offender	Individual (micro-level) catalysts facilitate deliberate, intentional actions.	Looter-criminal Professional looter Resistance looter	**Crime Pattern Theory / CRAVED Principles**: Individual offender targeting behaviors based on intelligence or purposive action determine when, how, where, and how often to loot. Specific characteristics of antiquities are included in the determination of looting activities. Agency is assumed. **General Strain Theory:** Individual adaptation to strain may result intentional turn towards looting as an illegal, reasonable adaptation. The reason for rejection of the norms could be tied to political goals and/or emotional responses to strain. Agency is assumed. **Rational Choice Theory / Thoughtfully Reflective Decision-Making:** Looting may achieve a strategic end whose reward outweighs the risks given rational, thoughtful consideration. Agency is assumed.
Opportunistic Offender	Individual (micro-level) catalysts create the opportunity to act based on rational-decision making and individual qualities.	Looter-criminal Professional looter Cultural looter	**Rational Choice Theory:** Looting is a desired outcome based on a rational decision-making process weighing the risks and rewards, bounded by available information and time and influenced by prior success and visceral influences. The opportunity to act is required. Agency is assumed. Offending may occur individually or as part of a group. **Social Control Theory:** Looting will occur if an offender has low self-control. Low agency is assumed.

Fig. 3 A criminological framework for offender motivations in antiquities looting

experienced search practices (leisure looters) or turning to looting to mitigate financial strain. Cultural offenders get their motivation from the cultural and learned norms and definitions in their community. Antiquities looting sees three varieties of this: (1) looting as a cultural practice, tied to views of heritage and ownership of the land (Alderman, 2012; Kersel, 2007; Matsuda, 1998; Paredes Maury, 1999; Patel, 2009); (2) looting as a leisure activity (Kersel, 2007); and (3) looting as an occupation or vocation passed down intergenerationally (Balcells Magrans, 2018; Kersel, 2007; Paredes Maury, 1999).

Strategic offenders may loot antiquities because of a broader connection to organised crime, as someone with expertise exercising their vocation, or as a sign of politically motivated resistance. Finally, whether an opportunistic offender chooses to engage in antiquities looting will depend on what kinds of factors weigh in their rational calculus of risks and rewards, what rationalisations they employ, and the assumed role of individual qualities. Someone who has had successful experiences looting without being caught is more likely to perceive other opportunities as viable given their prior success.

As Fig. 3 demonstrates, offender motivations may overlap, and the same incident may be viewed from multiple perspectives of motivation. For example, in Paredes Maury's (1999, p. 18) interview with Mr. Alpha he notes "A buddy and I were walking in the forest in the Lacandon, locating good trees [*chicozapote*], when we saw a nice mound and decided to try some luck." This account may be viewed as having elements of both cultural and situational motivation. The *chiclero* relationship with their natural environment and cultural norms that do not disparage looting interacts with situational opportunity to produce a looting incident.

4 Considerations for Potential Data and Methods

A significant barrier in the study of antiquities looting—especially to offender motivation—is the lack of data (perceived or actual). Readily available data are difficult to come by and it can be challenging to determine what kind of data would be best suited for a study of offender motivation. This study presents one way to think about what kinds of data could be useful in examining offender motivation within the framework outlined above. The relevant data may or may not already exist in some format depending on the country in question.

In determining what data and methods are appropriate for examining offender motivation, it is important to ensure that the analytical unit of analysis (macro, community, micro) remains consistent across all stages of the research process (see Fig. 4). This study advocates for one approach to research that is grounded in criminological theory. As represented in Fig. 4, the catalyst and offender motivations discussed above inform the choice of theory and the theory and research question inform each other and should be aligned. From theory to analysis, the analytical unit of analysis should remain consistent. A research question interested in cultural motivations for antiquities looting will be best served by data that speaks to

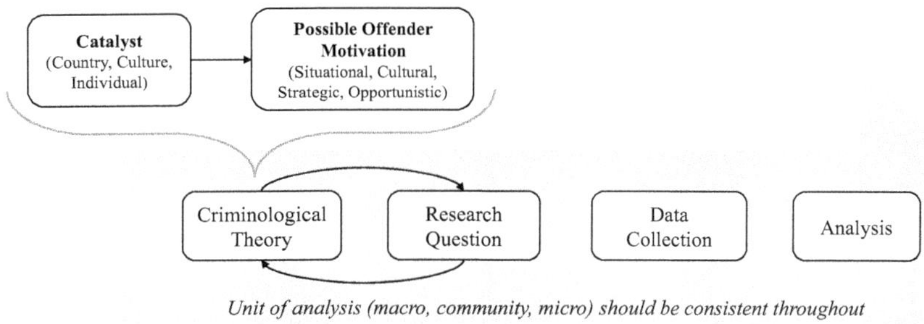

Fig. 4 A criminological theory-grounded approach to research on antiquities looting

community- or individual-level factors. Macro-level data are not appropriate for an analysis of cultural catalysts or motivations since they do not capture individual-level nuance.

The type and quantity of data collected will depend on the available resources and will inform which methods are appropriate for analysis. Figure 5 presents an overview of common data sources and methods that can be used by unit of analysis and offender motivation. Though not an exhaustive list, Fig. 5 presents commonly used data and methods when testing criminological theories and data sources that may be most accessible for studies on antiquities looting. For research interested in cultural offending, data collection could focus on community-level or individual-level sources. A useful data collection tool could be a survey on attitudes and behaviors toward looting. The analysis could then be statistical, thematic, or a combination of approaches. If the question asks about the mechanisms of *how* offenders learn antiquities looting as a trade, then in-person interviews and thematic analysis may be more appropriate.

Thus far, this study has demonstrated how to conceptually link criminological theory and conceptions of offender motivation to data and methods in the context of studying motivations for antiquities looting. The remainder of this chapter demonstrates this approach through a case study examining offender motivation for antiquities looting in Lower Egypt using data from 2015 to 2017 and discussing the implications of the proposed approach for future research.

Unit of Analysis	Possible Offender Motivation	Data	Methods
Macro-level *(Country)*	Situational	Event data	Descriptive: spatial, temporal, spatiotemporal
		Proxies for societal stress	Econometric modeling
		• Economic stress (unemployment, GDP, participation in the labor force, etc.)	Time series analysis
		• Environmental stress (precipitation, crop yield, flooding, fire, water availability)	Simulations
		• Sociopolitical stress (terrorism, protests, riots, armed conflict)	
Community-level *(Culture)*	Cultural	Interviews	Mixed-methods
		Observations	Thematic analysis
		Surveys	Statistical analyses
Micro-level *(Individual or within-individual)*	Situational	Event data (e.g., reports of individual conflict, looting, crime)	Descriptive: spatial, temporal, spatiotemporal
		Surveys	Statistical analyses
		Vignettes	Econometric modeling
		Interviews	Thematic analysis
	Opportunistic	Survey	Network analysis
		Vignettes	
		Proxies for opportunity (e.g., accessibility, proximity, density)	
	Strategic	Event data (e.g., reports of looting)	
		Social network relationships	

Fig. 5 Linking conceptions of offender motivations to expectations for data and methods

5 Motivations for Antiquities Looting in Lower Egypt (2015–2017): A Case Study

Antiquities looting has been documented in Egypt for decades (Boseley, 1997) and looting in Lower Egypt[5] has specifically been of increasing interest to scholars (Fabiani, 2018; Parcak, 2015). However, discussions of motivation for looting have either been omitted or assumed. For this analysis, the primary question is 'what can be said about offender motivations for antiquities looting in Lower Egypt?'

5.1 Conceptualizing Offender Motivation in Lower Egypt

Lower Egypt has a complex environmental backcloth that could motivate an offender or create situations conducive to antiquities looting. Socio-politically, the regime changes from 2011 to 2014 greatly affected Lower Egypt. Religious violence, terrorism, and protests have all continued throughout the country and in Lower Egypt since President Sisi took office in 2014 (Fabiani, 2019). Prolonged economic hardship has also affected Lower Egypt due in part to the 2011 revolution, the role of the military in the economy, and environmental changes (Fabiani, 2019). Finally, Lower Egypt reflects the diversity of Egypt's landscape, containing the fertile Nile delta, desert, and marshland. Lower Egypt also produces most of the country's domestic agriculture, including wheat, rice, cotton, and sugar cane (CAPMAS, 2018). Changes in the landscape due to rapid population expansion has strained the water supply (potable and agricultural) and reduced the amount of available cultivatable land (Fabiani, 2019). Combined with the effects of climate change (reduced rainfall depleting the Nile's capacity and rising sea levels) and the construction of new dams limiting the flow of water, there is considerable strain on Lower Egypt's environment (Fabiani, 2019).

At the individual-level, anecdotal evidence supports the ideas that there are cultural norms favorable to looting. It is considered a "centuries-old business" with high success rates (Boyle, 2014). In 2014, Egypt's Minister for Antiquities Mohamed Ibrahim Ali stated that "the problem is the illicit digging everywhere. In Egypt when you dig, you find something" (Boyle, 2014). Though community- or individual-level sources of data would be ideal to examine these motivations in-depth, currently, so such sources exist that are accessible to the broader research community.[6] Rather than viewing this lack of community-level data as a barrier to

[5]Lower Egypt refers to Egypt's northern Delta region.

[6]One approach would be to seek approval and funding for a community- or individual-level study in the area. Yet there may be any number of reasons such studies have not been undertaken in Egypt–inability to travel to the region of interest (e.g., due to conflict, global pandemics, etc.) or the inability to secure funding and appropriate permissions.

investigating offender motivation, it can be viewed as restricting the unit of analysis on which data can be collected and affecting the types of conclusions the study can draw.

For example, there are macro-level and proxy sources of data that could provide insight. Absent the ability to ask about individual experiences with economic deprivation, research could look for macro-level signs of stress in the economy through internationally recognised measures of economic health (e.g., the gross domestic product (GDP), tourist arrivals in Egypt).[7] Similarly, lacking a community survey looking at the effects of drought or environmental stress and favorability of attitudes towards looting, research could look for a proxy of drought. Drought reflects a lack of healthy vegetation and rainfall, vegetation health indices and precipitation measures from the National Aeronautics and Space Administration (NASA) can proxy the presence of drought. Such proxies cannot speak to any community- or individual-level experiences; they can only speak to a macro-level analysis of offender motivation. That is, on average, which offender motivations might be present overall given certain conditions. Such information is a valuable first step to understanding motivations for antiquities looting and can serve as a foundation from which more granular studies could be conducted. Moreover, since macro-level data exists for most countries, such analyses can facilitate cross-national comparisons. This case study focuses on conceptions of offender motivation that can be examined with macro-level data and proxies—situational and opportunistic offenders.

Theoretically, crime pattern theory has both macro- and micro-level elements and accounts for both situational and opportunistic elements. At the macro-level, examining the degree to which antiquities looting events co-locate (or are near each other in space) could provide insight into situational offending. If one governorate experiences more environmental stress and has more instances of antiquities looting, then that may suggest a situational catalyst for offender motivation rooted in that societal stress. Similarly, the timing of incidents of looting relative to macro-level factors could speak to situational inducements to offending such as financing insurgency or taking advantage of the breakdown in social order following conflict (Fabiani, 2018).[8] It is not possible to directly examine the individual-level offender motivations in crime pattern theory (proximity, opportunity, intelligence-led, and purposive). However, using proxies, it may be possible to speak to the likelihood of some of them as motivations. For example, proximity and opportunity could be examined through the proxies of accessibility of archaeological sites (e.g., proximity to roads).

[7]Tourist arrivals measure the portion of Egypt's economy related to cultural heritage.

[8]It is important to note that none of these theoretical relationships can be examined from a causal perspective in this case study.

5.2 Data and Methods

The data for this case study come from the spatiotemporal database on antiquities looting in Lower Egypt compiled by Fabiani (2019). This database covers almost all Lower Egypt (the Nile Delta)[9] from 2015 to 2017 and contains spatial and temporal data on antiquities looting, demographic data (road networks, capitals, urban designations), and multiple measures each for socio-political, economic, and environmental stress. Data on antiquities looting are coded for evidence of looting per month from satellite images (N = 3119) for 140 archaeological sites in Lower Egypt over the 36-month period.[10] Socio-political measures are coded as geolocated events aggregated to the month and include violent conflict, non-violent conflict, violence against civilians, and an overall measure of socio-political stress.[11] Environmental measures include crop production, vegetation health index, precipitation, and soil moisture content. Economic measures include tourist arrivals, consumer price index, unemployment, and national debt (as a percent of external debt). Both environmental and economic measures include ranges of temporal (monthly, quarterly, yearly) and spatial units (0.05-degree spatial interval to national-level).

This analysis draws on all these variables and aggregates them to the month. Economic and environmental measures are assigned to a 10-km spatial grid to standardise their measurement. Since antiquities looting and the socio-political measures are event data, they were kept as discrete spatial point data.[12] Each measure is operationalised differently for temporal, spatial, spatiotemporal, and statistical analyses. For example, antiquities looting is defined across these dimensions as:

- Temporal: the count of archaeological sites with evidence of looting per month
- Spatial: the average number of months a grid cell has any evidence of looting from 2015 to 2017
- Spatiotemporal: binary measure of whether looting evidence is present at a given site each month
- Statistical: the number of months a site has any evidence of looting[13]

---

[9]Lower Egypt contains 13 governorates (geopolitical border akin to states in the United States) in the Nile Delta: Alexandria, Beheira, Cairo, Damietta, Daqahliyah, Al Gharbiyah, Ismailia, Kafr es Sheikh, Al Minufiyah, Port Said, Qalyubiyah, Al Sharqiyah, and Suez. Suez is excluded from this database due to an inability to identify any geo-coded archaeological site locations.

[10]Coding for evidence of archaeological looting involved a set procedure to ensure consistency of coding: (1) creating a boundary around each site, (2) coding each source of imagery separately according to which has the earliest image per site and comparing sequences of imagery to detect change, (3) reviewing, validating, and aggregating the data. See Fabiani (2019) for a full description of the data collection. Detailed coding procedures are available at www.michellefabiani.com.

[11]Data for socio-political stress were compiled from the Global Terrorism Database (GTD), Armed Conflict Location and Event Database (ACLED), and the Uppsala Conflict Data Program (UCDP).

[12]Overlaying a spatial grid on an area creates uniform more granular spatial units of analysis. See Fabiani (2019) for more information.

[13]Operationalisations for all the variables are discussed in depth in Fabiani (2019).

Data on the macro-level factors and antiquities looting are used to examine situational motivation while the road networks and population density serve as proxies for opportunistic motivation. Figure 6 outlines how these data align with the offender motivations and the analytic methods.

Methodologically, situational and opportunistic motivations are considered separately. To examine situational motivations for looting, this study uses a combination of socio-political, environmental, and economic measures operationalised spatially, temporally, and spatiotemporally. Looking at how these macro-level factors cluster in space and time–and how intensely they cluster ('hot spots')—can help to distinguish between which are likely to have a situational influence on offender motivation. More sophisticated methods could be employed with a larger sample size of archaeological sites. Temporally, econometric models allow an examination of how situational factors (e.g., conflict) and looting change over time in relation to each other and their own history. These models can also distinguish between immediate impacts and delayed reactions. To examine opportunistic motivations for looting, regression analysis is used to test the influence of the proxies for opportunity 'proximity' and 'easily accessible,' measured as the distance to nearest road, city, urban area, and capital.

5.3 *Results*

5.3.1 Situational Offending

Across all dimensions, there is evidence to support a situational view of offender motivation; however, not all macro-level factors appear to be equally important, and this varies by dimension of analysis. Socio-political factors have the most consistent and strongest relationship with antiquities looting from 2015 to 2017. Looking at the spatial distribution of looting and the socio-political indicators in Fig. 7 suggests that there may be some evidence of co-location, though no clear pattern is visible when looking at a snapshot of the entire 36-month period.

Moreover, different socio-political indicators appear to create different situational inducements to offending. Looking at the results in Fig. 8, both violent conflict and non-violent conflict are related to increases in looting in the short-term but not the long-term. Changes in violent conflict in the current or previous month or month are associated with increases in the number of archaeological sites with looting (9.11 and 5.80, respectively). Changes in non-violent protests show an effect 1–2 months prior (1.20 and 1.21, respectively) but not for the current month. By contrast, these results suggest that over the period of 36 months, each additional incident of violence against civilians is associated with an approximately four more sites (4.39) with evidence of antiquities looting.

From the spatiotemporal analyses in Fig. 9, it appears that high value clusters (more locations with looting attempts) increase primarily during 2016 and the first part of 2017. Socio-political indicators show increases in high-value clusters

Unit of Analysis	Possible Offender Motivation	Data	Methods
Macro-level *(Country)*	Situational	Event data: • Antiquities looting (evidence of looting at 140 archaeological sites in sample) • Sociopolitical stress (overall measure of stress, violent conflict, nonviolent conflict, violence against civilians) Proxies for societal stress • Economic stress (consumer price index (general), national debt (% external debt), tourist arrivals, total unemployment) • Environmental stress (precipitation, national vegetation health index - NDVI, soil moisture content, total crop production) • Sociopolitical stress (in form of event data)	Descriptive: • Spatial measures of proximity, clustering • Time series descriptives Econometric modeling (Autoregressive distributed lag models – ARDL) Statistical
Micro-level *(Proxy for Individual)*	Opportunistic	Proxies for opportunity: • Ease of access to archaeological sites (distance from site to nearest road, city, urban area, capital)	Statistical analysis using Ordinary Least Squares (OLS) regression

Fig. 6 Case study data, measures, and methods

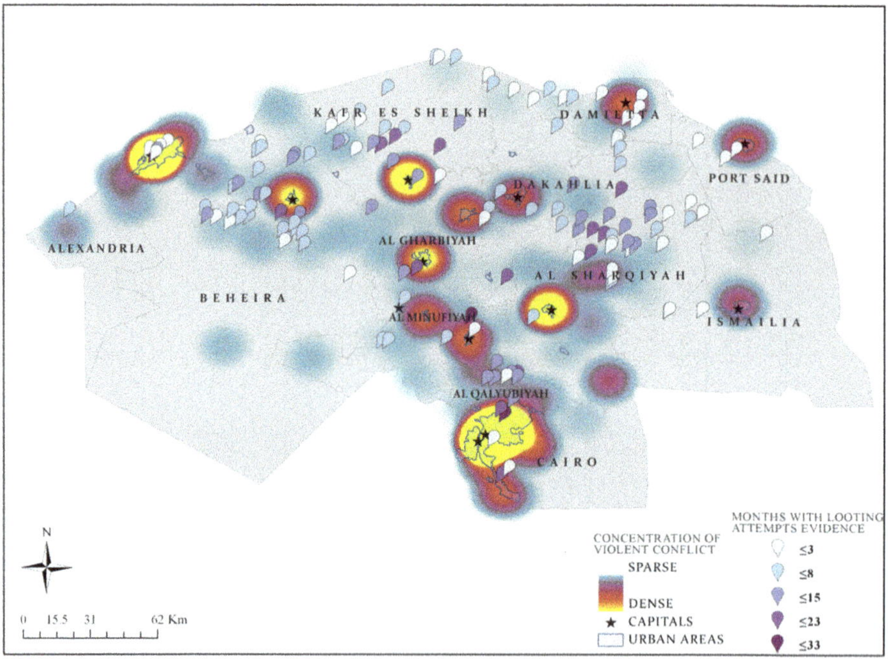

Fig. 7 Antiquities looting vs. socio-political stress (violent conflict) 2015–2017

(locations with more incidents of conflict types) primarily in the end of 2015 and 2016, particularly among violence against civilians. This suggests that there may be some temporal overlap with the clustering of looting attempts and aligns with the long-term findings from the ARDL (autoregressive distributed lag) models. Incidents of violence against civilians in 2015 and 2016 could be a catalyst for looting in 2016 and 2017.

Environmental and economic indicators have a more restricted situational influence on looting, and they are only relevant temporally and spatiotemporally.[14] In the temporal results from Fig. 8, only soil moisture content shows a relationship with antiquities looting—in months where there is less moisture (drier soil), there will be more sites with evidence of looting. Economically, both tourist arrivals and the consumer price index are related to looting. Fewer tourists lead to a slight increase in the number of sites looted (less than one) while consumer prices have a stronger effect. A one percent change in the index from the 2010 baseline leads to an average of three additional sites (3.14) with evidence of looting.[15] Spatiotemporally,

[14]Even with 10-km grid cells, neither environmental nor economic indicators proved granular enough to examine purely from a purely spatial perspective. Economic indicators also could not be examined spatiotemporally.

[15]Total crop production and unemployment were dropped from the final model due to high collinearity with other environmental and economic measures, respectively.

Dependent Variable: Antiquities Looting (N=140)	**Variable**	**Coefficient**	**Std. Error**
Error Correction Term	Antiquities Looting (-1)	**-1.9038***	0.2564
Short-term Relationships	D(Violent Conflict)	**9.1146***	2.4128
	D(Violent Conflict (-1))	**5.8033**	1.9034
	D(Violent Conflict (-2))	3.2715	1.7700
	D(Violent Conflict (-3))	0.1984	0.8488
	D(Violence Against Civilians)	-5.0742	1.9251
	D(Violence Against Civilians (-1))	-2.5826	1.2827
	D(Violence Against Civilians (-2))	-1.2637	0.6187
	D(Violence Against Civilians (-3))	-0.7739	0.4617
	D(Non-Violent Conflict)	1.1976	0.7117
	D(Non-Violent Conflict (-1))	**1.1957***	0.6048
	D(Non-Violent Conflict (-2))	**1.2076***	0.5284
	D(Non-Violent Conflict (-3))	0.5518	0.3253
	Vegetation Health Index	170.7923	67.9757
	Precipitation	0.8246	1.4541
	Soil Moisture Content	**-358.2247**	154.6613
	National Debt (% external)	-11.9904	10.1051
	Tourist Arrivals	**-0.0714***	0.0314
	Consumer Price Index	**3.1409***	5.2367
Long-term Relationships	Violent Conflict	-5.2351	0.9201
	Violence Against Civilians	**4.3949**	1.5777
	Non-Violent Conflict	-0.6513	0.4147

* p ≤ 0.10, ** p ≤ 0.05, *** p ≤ 0.01

Fig. 8 ARDL results for situational analysis

precipitation increases in low-value clusters (corresponding to lower amounts of precipitation) in the end of 2015, 2016, and 2017. As reflected in Fig. 9, when compared with antiquities looting in these time periods, there is some evidence supporting a situational inducement to offending—most sites with looting are in areas of low precipitation (Fig. 10).

5.3.2 Opportunistic Offending

An opportunistic offender as conceptualised here encompasses two of Brantingham's (2012) offender search patterns: 'proximity' and 'opportunity.' Evidence supporting an opportunistic offender motivation would be seen in a positive statistically significant relationship between the measures of proximity (capital, cities, urban area, road) and looting at archaeological sites. Across multiple ways of defining 'distance' (driving on paved vs. dirt roads, straight line distances ignoring roads) the results found no evidence of a statistically significant relationship

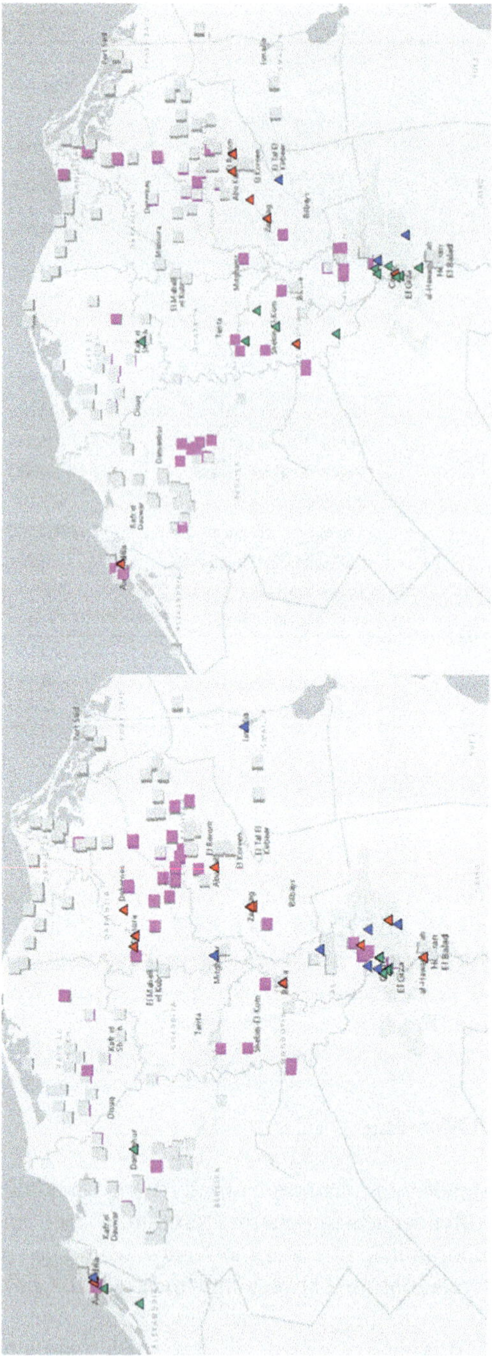

Fig. 9 Socio-political stress by type and looting in October 2015 (left) and December 2016 (right). Blue triangles indicate violence against civilians, green triangles indicate non-violent conflict, and red triangles indicate violent conflict. Purple indicates the presence of looting

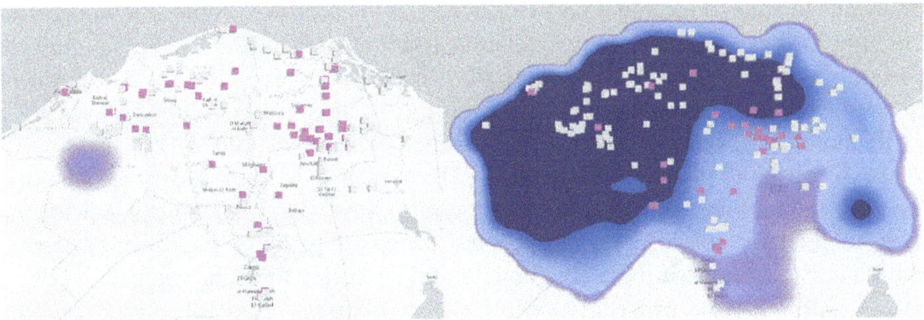

Fig. 10 Precipitation and archaeological looting in August 2015 (left) and October 2015 (right). Darker blue indicates more precipitation. Purple indicates the presence of looting

between proximity and antiquities looting. This suggests that for these data, proximity is not characteristic of an opportunistic offender.

6 Antiquities Looting and Offender Motivation in Lower Egypt

Taken holistically, these results suggest that antiquities looting may be a rationalised behavior resulting from multiple situational motivations. Looking first at socio-political indicators, the suggested immediate impact of violent conflict and nonviolent conflict could indicate looting as a response to *situational opportunity*. Whether it is an armed conflict, terrorism event, or protest turned riot, these socio-political factors can lead to breakdown in social order (either generally or via a mob mentality. In turn this can lead to situational incentives to crime. The same could apply to looting. The long-term relationship between antiquities looting and violence against civilians implies that there is a delayed response between the incident of violence and the looting behavior. With the frequent protests and incidents of violence against civilians in Egypt during this time period (see Fabiani, 2019), discontent with the government is likely. In the aftermath of incidents of violence, it may be easier to rationalise looting an archaeological site. Increases in crime following a community-level breakdown in social control is well documented in criminology (Bell et al., 2014; Carrasco-Jiménez, 2019). It may be that the same mechanisms are at play in these data, though we would need community- or individual-level data to confirm the findings.

The inconsistency of results across dimensions for environmental and economic indicators could suggest overlapping potential motivations. Vegetation health and environmental conditions may dictate which sites experience looting and by whom. Archaeologists often must remove the topsoil (which can be several feet) to get to the archaeological remains using hydraulic equipment or dynamite, depending on the type of soil. If the soil is very difficult to dig through, offenders may be less motivated to attempt looting if they lack access to the necessary tools or it would take too long to dig. Similarly, as precipitation patterns change due to climate change, concerns over the viability of farming may lead to antiquities looting as a form of supplemental income during the dry season.

Economically, only temporal relationships could be examined. Yet the significance of consumer price indices in the ARDL models over tourism arrivals supports the more rationalised view of antiquities looting. Consumer price indices indicate the average prices of basic consumer goods. Increases in these prices signal larger economic stress, supporting a situational motivation tied to economic need.[16]

7 Conclusion

This study provides a framework with which offender motivation can be explicitly examined in the context of antiquities looting, from conceptualisation and criminological theory to data and methods. It then demonstrates this approach with a case study looking at antiquities looting in Lower Egypt from 2015 to 2017. This approach is unique as it seeks to separate offender motivation from assumptions of morality and ethics that have appeared in some prior work on this topic conducted by archaeologists. It also argues that motivation can be layered—multiple overlapping motivations may be present in any given situation. Unpacking the layers of which motivations are most applicable and in what contexts is an important endeavor in the study of antiquities looting (and by extension the broader art market) and could have significant implications for the development of policies aimed at preventing this behavior. Future research should conduct exploratory analysis to identify possible motivations across circumstances and then seek to identify underlying mechanisms, theoretically and empirically. Such studies could advance theories of antiquities looting and help inform the development of policies to reduce and prevent this type of crime.

References

Agnew, R. (1992). Foundation for a general strain theory of crime and delinquency. *Criminology, 30*(1), 47–88. https://doi.org/10.1111/j.1745-9125.1992.tb01093.x

Agnew, R. (2001). Building on the foundation of general strain theory: Specifying the types of strain most likely to lead to crime and delinquency. *Journal of Research in Crime and Delinquency, 38*(4), 319–361. https://doi.org/10.1177/0022427801038004001

Agnew, R. (2006). *Pressured into crime: An overview of general strain theory*. Oxford University Press.

[16]This analysis is exploratory and is unable to speak to causality. It is possible that there is no spatial relationship in evidence.

Akers, R. L. (1985). *Deviant behavior: A social learning approach*. Wadsworth Pub.
Al-Azm, A., & Paul, K. (2019). *Facebook's black market in antiquities: ICOM Red List artifacts offered on Facebook*. The Antiquities Trafficking and Heritage Anthropology Research Project (ATHAR). Retrieved from http://atharproject.org/report2019/
Alder, C., & Polk, K. (2002). Stopping this awful business: The traffic in antiquities examined as a criminal market. *Art, Antiquity, & Law, 7*(1), 35–53.
Alderman, K. L. (2012). Honor amongst thieves: Organized crime and the illicit antiquities trade. *Indiana Law Review, 45*(3), 601–628.
Balcells Magrans, M. (2018). *Contemporary archaeological looting: A criminological analysis of Italian Tomb Robbers*. Unpublished Doctoral Dissertation.
Balestrieri, A. B. B. (2018). Field archaeologists as eyewitnesses to site looting. *Art, 7*(3), 48. https://doi.org/10.3390/arts7030048
Becker, G. (1968). Crime and punishment: An economic approach. *Journal of Political Economy, 76*(2), 1–54.
Bell, B., Jaitman, L., & Machin, S. (2014). Crime deterrence: Evidence from the London 2011 riots. *The Economic Journal, 124*(576), 480–506. https://doi.org/10.1111/ecoj.12137
Bentham, J. (1789). In L. J. Lafleur (Ed.), *An introduction to the principles of morals and legislation*. Hafner.
Bernick, L. (1998). Art and antiquities theft. *Transnational Organized Crime, 4*(2), 91–116.
Borodkin, L. (1995). The economics of antiquities looting. *Columbia Law Review, 95*(2), 377–417.
Boseley, S. (1997, June 19). Raider of Egypt's lost art. *The Guardian*.
Boyle, K. (2014, June 1). Egypt turns to technology in effort to protect ancient treasures from looters. *The Guardian*. Retrieved from http://www.theguardian.com/world/2014/jun/01/egypt-museum-theft-satellite-technology
Brantingham, P. J. (2012). The theory of target search. In F. T. Cullen & P. Wilcox (Eds.), *The Oxford handbook of criminological theory*. Oxford University Press.
Brantingham, P., & Brantingham, P. (1993). Environment, routine and situation: Toward a pattern theory of crime. In R. Clarke & M. Felson (Eds.), *Routine activity and rational choice: Advances in criminological theory* (Vol. 5). Transaction Publishers. Retrieved from https://docdel.umd.edu/illiad/illiad.dll?Action=10&Form=75&Value=1248305
Brantingham, P., & Brantingham, P. (2013). Crime pattern theory. In R. Wortley & L. Green (Eds.), *Environmental criminology and crime analysis* (pp. 87–93). Routledge. https://doi.org/10.4324/9780203118214-13
Briar, S., & Piliavin, I. (1965). Delinquency, situational inducements, and commitment to conformity. *Social Problems, 13*(1), 35–45. https://doi.org/10.2307/799304
Burgess, R., & Akers, R. (1966). A differential association-reinforcement theory of criminal behavior. *Social Problems, 14*(2), 128–147. https://doi.org/10.1525/sp.1966.14.2.03a00020
Carrasco-Jiménez, Edison. (2019). The looting during the social upsurge of October 2019 in Chile. *SocArXiv*. December 10. https://doi.org/10.31235/osf.io/cyegn
Casey, M. (2006). Buried truth: A criminological analysis of the illicit antiquities trade. *Trinity College Law Review, 9*, 119–136.
Central Agency for Public Mobilization and Statistics (CAPMAS). (2018). Statistical yearbook.
Clarke, R. (1999). *Hot products: Understanding, anticipating, and reducing demand for stolen goods* (Paper 112; Police Research Series, pp. 1–48). Home Office Policing and Reducing Crime Unit Research, Development and Statistics Directorate. Retrieved from http://www.popcenter.org/tools/risky_facilities/PDFs/Clarke_1999.pdf
Conklin, J. E. (1994). *Art crime*. Praeger.
Cornish, D. B., & Clarke, R. V. (1986). *The reasoning criminal: Rational choice perspectives on offending*. Transaction Publishers.
Coyne, M. A., & Eck, J. E. (2014). Situational choice and crime events. *Journal of Contemporary Criminal Justice, 31*(1), 12–29. https://doi.org/10.1177/1043986214552605
Cuneo, A., & Danti, M. (2019). Tracking heritage loss in the middle of armed conflict. Archaeology of conflict: Documenting destruction of cultural heritage in the Middle-East and Central Asia. In

J. Bessenay-Prolonge, J.-J. Herr & M. Mura (Eds.), *Archaeology of conflict / Archaeology in conflict–Documenting destruction of cultural heritage in the Middle-East and Central Asia, Routes de l'Orient Actes II* (pp. 265–283). Paris: Association Routes de l'Orient.

Devine, J. A. (2016). Contesting global heritage in the Chicle Workers' Museum. *Latin American Research Review, 51*(3), 101–122. https://www.jstor.org/stable/44000358

Fabiani, M. D. (2018). Disentangling strategic and opportunistic looting: The relationship between antiquities looting and armed conflict in Egypt. *Art, 7*(2), 22. https://doi.org/10.3390/arts7020022

Fabiani, M. D. (2019). Building a baseline: Unifying spatial and temporal methodologies to understand archaeological looting in Egypt [Dissertation, University of Maryland College Park]. https://drum.lib.umd.edu/handle/1903/22107?show=full

Gottfredson, M., & Hirschi, T. (1990). *A general theory of crime*. Stanford University Press.

Hirschi, T. (1969). *Causes of delinquency*. University of California Press.

Hirschi, T. (2004). Self-control and crime. In *Handbook of self-regulation: Research, theory, and applications* (pp. 537–552). The Guilford Press.

Kersel, M. (2007). Transcending borders: Objects on the move. *Archaeologies, 3*(2), 81–98. https://doi.org/10.1007/s11759-007-9013-0

Lowenstein, G. (1996). Out of control: Visceral influences on behavior. Organizational behavior and human decision processes. Retrieved from https://www.alnap.org/help-library/out-of-control-visceral-influences-on-behavior

Lowenthal, D. (2005). Why sanctions seldom work: Reflections on cultural property internationalism. *International Journal of Cultural Property, 12*(3), 393–423.

Mac Ginty, R. (2004). Looting in the context of violent conflict: A conceptualisation and typology. *Third World Quarterly, 25*(5), 857–870.

Mackenzie, S., & Green, P. (Eds.). (2009). *Criminology and archaeology: Studies in looted antiquities*. Hart Publishing.

Mackenzie, S., & Yates, D. (2016). Collectors on illicit collecting: Higher loyalties and other techniques of neutralization in the unlawful collecting of rare and precious orchids and antiquities. *Theoretical Criminology, 20*(3), 340–357.

Matsuda, D. (1998, January). The ethics of archaeology, subsistence digging, and artifact looting in Latin America: Point muted counterpoint. *International Journal of Cultural Property, 7*(1), 87–97. https://doi.org/10.1017/S0940739198770080

Matsueda, R., Kreager, D., & Huizinga, D. (2006). Deterring delinquents: A rational choice model of theft and violence. *American Sociological Review, 71*, 95–122.

McCalister, A. (2005). Organized crime and the theft of Iraqi antiquities. *Trends in Organized Crime, 9*(1), 24–37.

Merton, R. K. (1938). Social structure and anomie. *American Sociological Review, 3*(5), 672–682.

Parcak, S. (2015). Archaeological looting in Egypt: A geospatial view (case studies from Saqqara, Lisht, and el Hibeh). *Near Eastern Archaeology, 78*(3), 196–203.

Paredes Maury, S. (1999). *Surviving in the rainforest: The realities of looting in the rural villages of El Petén, Guatemala*. Foundation for the Advancement of Meso-American Studies (FAMSI).

Patel, S. (2009). Drugs, guns, and dirt. *Archaeology, 62*(2).

Paternoster, R., & Pogarsky, G. (2009). Rational choice, agency, and thoughtfully reflective decision making: The short and long-term consequences of making good decisions. *Journal of Quantitative Criminology, 25*.

Pogarsky, G., & Piquero, A. (2003). Can punishment encourage offending? Investigating the "resetting" effect. *Journal of Research in Crime and Delinquency, 40*(1), 95–120. https://doi.org/10.1177/0022427802239255

Simon, H. (1979). Rational decision making in business organizations. *American Economic Review, 69*(4), 493–513. https://econpapers.repec.org/article/aeaaecrev/v_3a69_3ay_3a1979_3ai_3a4_3ap_3a493-513.htm

Sutherland, E. (Ed.). (1937). *The professional thief by a professional thief.* University of Chicago Press.
Sykes, G. M., & Matza, D. (1957). Techniques of neutralization: A theory of delinquency. *American Sociological Review, 22*(6), 664–670. https://doi.org/10.2307/2089195
United Nations Commission on Crime Prevention and Criminal Justice (UN). (2017). *World crime trends and emerging issues and responses in the field of crime prevention and criminal justice* (E/CN.15/2017/1). United Nations Economic and Social Council.
Weirich, C. (2019). *Situational crime prevention of antiquities trafficking: A crime script analysis.* Unpublished Doctoral Dissertation.

One Flew Over the Cuckoo's Clock

Selling Exclusivity Through Conspicuous Goods on Evolution

Naomi Oosterman and Francesco Angelini

Abstract Despite the increase of specialised law enforcement and commercial art crime databases concerning the registration of luxury products, it remains an often-overlooked category in art crime research. This chapter analyses the market for luxury products, focusing specifically on watches, jewellery, and designer clothing, on defunct anonymous marketplace *Evolution*, which was active between January 2014 and March 2015. We argue that this marketplace works as a way to buy exclusivity through the purchase of both original and counterfeited luxury goods, here called 'conspicuous goods'. The goods we focus on in our analysis endow cultural value, and their possession allows consumers to display a higher level of distinction. However, rather than looking at consumers who desire to differentiate themselves by purchasing these objects, we were more interested in how the market is structured to best sell these products. Therefore, we have implemented a series of statistical analyses on the market supply, focusing on the type of traded object, their brand, and the average prices in Bitcoin, finding that a brand effect on price is at work both in counterfeited and original conspicuous goods. This signals that the market is aware of the dynamics of conspicuous goods and its sellers behave accordingly.

1 Introduction

On 6 November 2014, law enforcement agencies around the world, in a cooperative effort of Europol and the FBI, took part in *Operation Onymous*. During this operation, over 200 online anonymous marketplaces (commonly known as 'dark

---

N. Oosterman (✉)
Department of Arts and Culture Studies, Erasmus University Rotterdam, Rotterdam, Netherlands
e-mail: oosterman@eshcc.eur.nl

F. Angelini
Department of Statistical Sciences "Paolo Fortunati", University of Bologna, Bologna, Italy
e-mail: francesco.angelini7@unibo.it

N. Oosterman, D. Yates (eds.), *Crime and Art*, Studies in Art, Heritage, Law and the Market 1, https://doi.org/10.1007/978-3-030-84856-9_16

markets', 'dark nets', or 'cryptomarkets') were closed down (Afilipoaie & Shortis, 2015). In the operation, over 1 million USD worth of Bitcoin was confiscated, 17 arrests were made, and gold, silver, weapons, computers, and cash were seized. This included high-profile marketplace Silk Road 2.0. Not all marketplaces were closed down. The dark market *Evolution*, which in 2014 was "(. . .) considered to be the market leader, with commentators putting this down to its sleek interface, quick loading times and security features such as multi-signature escrow", saw a 26 percent increase of sales when Silk Road 2.0 went defunct (ibid, pp. 2–3).

There is no systematic or uniform definition for what constitutes a dark market. Overall, the common denominator between different dark marketplaces is that they offer a platform for risk management for participants who wish to make anonymous transactions (Soska & Christin, 2015). They are not, in contradiction to popular belief, in themselves platforms that sell illicit products. Apart from mitigating risk, these online markets can, for example, function as "virtual brokers" that connect multiple vendors, and can even link "online wholesalers with offline retail-level distributors" (Aldridge & Décary-Hétu, 2016, pp. 12–13). What separates the online anonymous marketplace from other online marketplaces such as eBay is the fact that the first ensures complete anonymity, shielding all your personal information (such as IP address), which the latter cannot.

Despite drugs being one of the predominant products sold on online anonymous marketplaces (Aldridge & Décary-Hétu, 2016; Červený & van Ours, 2019; Soska & Christin, 2015), a substantial amount of both original and counterfeit luxury products (such as watches, jewellery, and designer clothes) are offered for sale. These goods can be categorised as so-called 'Veblen goods' or 'conspicuous goods'. These goods, first discussed by Thorstein Veblen in 1899, concern those goods that people with high wealth often consume to great extent to showcase their prosperity to achieve greater social status. In online anonymous marketplaces the supply for these goods indicates a certain demand for objects that can increase the "cultivation of the aesthetic faculty" (Veblen, 1899, p. 75) and indicates a possible driver for distinction that can only be achieved by owning a Veblen good (Bourdieu, 1984; Trigg, 2001). In a certain way, by displaying a form of distinction through material and cultural wealth, "members of higher classes voluntarily incur costs to differentiate themselves from members of lower classes [. . .], knowing that these costs must be large enough to discourage imitation" (Bagwell & Bernheim, 1996, p. 350). These goods however are an often-overlooked category in art crime research, despite the increasing focus of both specialised law enforcement and commercial databases for these objects. The anonymous marketplace positions itself as an ideal location to supply these products as they can be acquired anonymously, and with little risk to the individual seller and buyer.

In this research, we have analysed this category of conspicuous goods by studying the online anonymous market for these objects, specifically focusing on their price and branding mechanisms. We did this by analysing the supply dynamics of both counterfeit and authentic conspicuous goods sold on Evolution. Rather than looking however at the ways in which consumers themselves display patterns of conspicuous consumption, we look at the way the market for these goods is structured. As such, rather than viewing objects as a passive entity, we argue that these objects themselves display an agency of 'desire' and that sellers on this market are aware of the desires these goods provoke. We argue therefore that these goods have criminogenic qualities: in addition to being objects that allow for the idea of upwards social mobility, they also 'invite' acts of criminal behaviour, such as counterfeiting. We argue that this particular illicit market is aware of this, by increasing prices for these goods and framing them as 'desirable' objects by specifying brands and relying on brand effects.

2 The Market for Conspicuous Goods: A New Avenue for Art Crime Research

Studies on crimes in the art world often focus on cultural commodities, and concern, amongst other topics, the theft of cultural artefacts (Kerr, 2015), the policing of art and heritage crime (Oosterman, 2019; Oosterman & Yates, 2020), the illicit trafficking and looting of cultural objects (Mackenzie et al., 2019; Yates, 2015), legislation (Roodt & Carey-Miller, 2013), financial regulation and fraud on the art market (Hufnagel & King, 2020) and the looting of antiquities (Brodie, 2003). An often-overlooked category in art crime research however is that of luxury goods, here called conspicuous goods, such as watches, jewellery, and designer clothes. Despite the lack of academic scrutiny concerning these objects, specialised law enforcement agencies (e.g., Interpol) and commercial databases such as the Art Loss Register (ALR) have recently started including these goods in designated categories within their databases to great extent. At the time of writing, Interpol's *Stolen Works of Art Database* contains over 1000 items in the "Watch/Clock" category, over 2600 items in the "Jewellery" category, and over 180 items in the "Clothing/Textile" category, making up roughly 8 percent of Interpol's entire database. In 2015, the ALR even introduced *The Watch Register*: an online database of stolen wristwatches totalling over 70,000 watches, signalling the significant scale of these goods as distinct categories in both public and commercial databases.[1] Indeed, as mentioned previously, most studies analysing online anonymous marketplaces focus on drugs or arms, but tend to leave out other types of goods that perhaps make up for a small percentage of what the marketplace has on offer, but nevertheless tend to accumulate to tens of thousands of items. Which is quite similar to the distribution of these categories in law enforcement and commercial databases: they make up a small sub-section of a much larger database, but nevertheless encompass as significant number of items. The discussion of the appeal of this market, and the analyses thereof, must therefore consider three things: (1) these overlooked categories need to be included as they make up a significant sub-section of cultural and artistic goods, (2) conspicuous goods, like artistic and cultural objects, can be

[1] At the time of writing, May 2021.

considered as objects of desire that facilitate an aesthetic experience, and (3) that these goods have a symbolic function that operates in an extensive network of social and cultural relations (Albrecht, 1968). These social and cultural relations can turn these desirable goods into so-called criminogenic objects.

Discussing the automobile industry as a criminogenic market structure, Farberman (1975) argues that inequality have "[...] elites play [a powerful role] in controlling society's central master institutions by establishing political and economic policies which set the structural conditions that cause other (lower level) people to commit crime" (p. 438). We understand how these central master institutions create asymmetries in society (Passas, 1999), however little is known about the effect that objects have on people's willingness to commit crime, here art-related crimes. Additionally, different levels of authority correspond to different classes. One can argue that, within the art world, there are dominant and dominated classes, and those who strive for symbolic capital are those in the dominant classes (Bourdieu, 1984). Those without significant knowledge of the field (also dubbed *cultural capital*), economic wealth (*economic capital*), or network (*social capital*) are not able to participate fully in this world and thus become outsiders (ibid). This in turn makes the desire to become a member of this world, even stronger. As we will discuss in our analysis, possibly increasing the desire to own these specific types of goods. Bourdieu (1983, 1984) further emphasises that arts and culture only exist in a social and cultural context and function not only as markers for cultural taste, but also markers of distinction and *place* for individuals. More specifically, they signal one's position within the class society. Discussing luxury products in our analysis, we can connect the theories of Bourdieu to conspicuous goods. As aptly discussed by Trigg (2001), where Veblen (1899) focuses mostly on the 'trickle-down' phenomenon of Veblen goods, where the higher social classes are more inclined to distinguish themselves from the lower classes, Bourdieu also considers the tastes and values of lower classes. A lower (or working) class that actively resists the cultural tastes of those in the higher classes (p. 105). These discussions of the higher classes and the ways in which they position themselves by, amongst other things, the consumption of conspicuous goods to elevate their distinction is not new, but how this relates to the market structures of online anonymous marketplaces, is an under-researched avenue.

The desire of the higher classes to distinguish themselves from the lower classes have also been the subject of conservation within economic discussions of so-called "brand effects" (e.g., Dodds et al., 1991; Erdem & Swait, 2004; Schroeder, 2005). The presence of a brand has an additional influence on the *perceived value* of a good or service. In relation to the *perception* of the brand, this also suggests that the price that people are willing to pay will likely be above market value when a recognisable brand is present on the good. In short, the willingness of people to pay more relies on how *exclusive* the brand is perceived. Studies on brand effects in the art market include the effect of, for example, artist's names on auction and gallery sales prices (e.g., Angelini et al., 2019; Oosterlinck & Radermecker, 2019). What makes these latter examples striking is the turn from cultural value (based on *intangible* indicators) into economic value (*tangible* indicators of currency).[2] Therefore, these goods can provoke what might then be called a criminogenic *desire*. A desire of belonging to a powerful group of elites by displaying markers of distinction, these markers, in this case, can then very well be expensive watches, jewellery, and designer clothes. The increasing presence of these 'markers of distinction' as categories in specialised art crime databases signals the importance and relevance of this category of goods to be studied further.

3 Evolution: Data, Methods, and Analyses

The dataset used for our investigation aimed at analysing which type of objects are available on the platform, comes from the blog post by Compton (2015), who in turn obtained the data from a torrent file that was shared on Reddit in 2015, a few days after the Evolution marketplace was shut down (17 March 2015). The original data was downloaded by an anonymous user with a varying frequency since the creation of the marketplace in early 2014, and consists of two databases. The first consists of all the ads present in the marketplace at the moment of each of the data downloads was made, and the second covers all the sellers that ever operated in the marketplace. We decided to focus on the first of the two, given the aim of our investigation. Therefore, our starting database contains information about objects at sale in the marketplace, for each day the download of data was made. Some objects occur more than once in our dataset: this could be due to the fact that these objects' ads were present in successive downloaded days because they were not sold or because they were sold between two of the downloaded days, but the seller put the same object with the same description at sale in the same range of days. Other information available from the database are: price in Bitcoin, name of the seller, description of the object, date in which the data dump was made,[3] the Bitcoin-EUR and Bitcoin-USD exchange rates on that date, the reputation level of the seller, and the reputation number (that is, the number of feedback votes received by the seller), the percentage of positive feedback,[4] and the categories the goods or services were part of. Our data covers the period from 21 January 2014 to 17 March 2015.

---

[2] Angelini and Castellani (2019) present a critical review on the link between these two values, with a focus on (potential) causal effects.

[3] The dates of the data dumps were not equally distanced, in particular in the first two months, when the download dates were very sparse. In our final data, the distance between one dump and the other goes between two and nine days.

[4] Between the start of Evolution as a marketplace until roughly the end of April 2014, the reputation system did not consist of a numerical value, but only of levels (Freshman, Junior, Senior, Expert, tentatively ordered by us since there is no way to check for this). From May 2014 onwards, the reputation system changed to a numerical value, starting from 0, as in most online marketplace in the legal market, that was associated with a reputation level based on these numbers (Level 1, Level 2, etc.).

As mentioned in the introduction, Evolution was an anonymous online marketplace where the majority of traded objects were drugs, but also other types of objects and services (e.g. weapons, murder for hire, and personal identification information) were on offer, totalling 1,121,087 objects identified by a unique id,[5] and divided into 81 categories, e.g. "Analgesics", "Explosives", and "Bank Logins". Among the available categories, we focused on the existing categories "Counterfeits", "Jewellery", and "Miscellaneous", since these categories are those who most likely contain conspicuous goods. The total number of observations from these three categories was 46,854. In checking the types of goods presented in this subset of the data, we added a series of new variables useful for the empirical analysis, which were the name of the brand of the object (if stated/applicable), a dummy variable equal to 1 if the object is a replica (if stated/applicable), and a variable that describes the sub-category of the object, with 141 different descriptions, among which we found "watches", "clothing", and "jewellery". At this step, we also created the price in EUR and the price in USD for each object, given the price in Bitcoin and the appropriate exchange rates at that time. The selection and the creation of the new variables were made based on the description of the object coming from the original database. In some cases, this description was not completely clear since it used abbreviations and other acronyms which were not directly attributable to any particular type of object linked to conspicuous goods. The dataset after this first manual selection process accounted for 37,478 observations.

In the next step, a series of data cleaning checks were carried out. We picked the statistical observations (hereafter 'observations') whose categories were most related to the focus of our analysis concerning conspicuous goods, dropping 10,085 observations. There were 46 sub-categories left among which we observed diamonds, jewellery, watches, and precious metals. We also removed all the objects with missing or null prices, dropping another 49 observations, so that we ended up with 27,344 objects for our analysis.

Next, we validated the data, checking for potential issues with the variables. We first graphically investigated the prices of our objects and noticed that some of them presented a price which was excessively above the average of other prices for objects of the same sub-category; for example, we dropped a series of replica watches whose prices were above 9000 EUR, when the average price of similar watches was around 145 EUR.[6] This issue may be due to mistakes made by the sellers in reporting the price of the object. In total, we dropped 39 observations, remaining with 27,305. Then, we checked if all the reputation numbers were present, and we found that 22 observations had a N/A reputation number, so we dropped them since we could not identify the reason this information was missing, ending up with 27,283

[5]Notice that each unique id is associated with a certain object that was up on the marketplace in a certain day.

[6]The figures are computed considering the lowest BTC to EUR exchange rate, so they should be taken as the lower boundaries of the ranges of these prices over time, since the exchange rate is highly volatile in the considered period.

Table 1 Descriptive statistics of continuous and dummy variables

Variable name	N	Mean	SD	Min	Max
Price (in BTC)	27,191	0.6637	1.7741	0.0183	39.0998
Price (in EUR)	27,191	168.85	436.16	3.72	9335.27
Price (in USD)	27,191	203.17	523.77	4.31	11,882.38
Reputation number	27,191	151.10	453.59	0	8416
Dummy variable name	N	%			
Replica	20,771	0.957			

The table reports the number of observations (N) for both types of variables, the mean, the standard deviation (SD), the minimum and maximum level for the continuous variables, and the frequency of 1 (in percentage) for the dummy variable. BTC prices are rounded to the fourth digit. EUR and USD prices are rounded to the second digit

observations. Lastly, we graphically investigated how the number of observations and prices were distributed overtime, noticing that some days presented very few observations with respect to all the other days (in particular, 17 October 2014, 07 November 2014, and 24 February 2015); each of these days had less than 40 objects on sale, when the previous and following days had, respectively, 241 and 210, 253 and 197, and 652 and 595. This issue may be due to problems in the downloading of data at the time of the dump and we decided to drop them since the data for each of these days very likely represented only a part of the objects present in the marketplace on those days. By dropping these observations, we reduced our dataset with 92 data points, ending up with a total of 27,191 objects for our analysis.[7] After the cleaning and validation, our data covers the period between the 10 August 2014 and the 17 March 2015. A series of descriptive statistics of the data are presented in Tables 1 and 2.

As we can see in Table 1, the overall price of the products in our database has a high dispersion, ranging from 3.27 EUR to 9335.27 EUR with an average price of 168,85 EUR. The reputation number of the sellers is equally volatile. The highest reputation number is 8416, whereas the lowest is 0, with an average number of 151.10. The standard deviation of the reputation number, explaining the dispersion of the data around the average, is 453.59. Most of the items in our categories, around 96 percent of those that we could identify as such, totalling 20,771 objects, are replicas, namely fake branded products sold as fakes on purpose.

Table 2 displays the ten most frequent brands and sub-categories together with their relative frequencies and average prices. Having selected those conspicuous goods, we can see that certain products are represented more than others. Watches are overrepresented, totalling almost 50 percent of the database (49.6 percent) with an average price of 219.78 EUR. This average price is higher than the average price

[7]Notice that the number of dropped observations in this case would have been higher if we did not drop the N/A reputation number in the previous step, since all the dates before May 2014 presented very few observations with respect to the rest of the period. This might be due to the fact that the marketplace did not start 'at full power' from the beginning, but we have no means to test this hypothesis.

Table 2 Descriptive statistics of categorical variables

Sub-category	Relative frequency (%)	Average price (in EUR)	Brand	Relative frequency (%)	Average price (in EUR)
Watch	49.60	219.78	Rolex	14.73	184.02
Sunglasses	7.13	79.18	Omega	7.09	100.70
Necklace	6.61	108.66	Chanel	6.17	72.92
Bracelet	5.10	44.07	Audemars Piguet	5.75	298.72
Shoes	3.16	114.56	Cartier	5.19	59.60
Pen	3.00	48.81	Louis Vuitton	5.07	87.83
Jacket	2.80	159.61	Emporio Armani	4.43	96.28
Belt	2.68	56.72	Breitling	4.42	143.59
Earrings	2.45	29.20	Montblanc	4.35	51.11
Bag	2.34	147.26	Gucci	3.47	65.89

The table reports the ten most frequent brands and sub-categories, together with their relative frequencies and average price. The values are rounded to the second digit

of the total objects in the database, making watches also amongst the higher price categories of the marketplace. As mentioned previously, watches have become their own distinct sub-category within specialised art crime databases. It therefore does not come as a surprise that Evolutions largest category of conspicuous goods is indeed wristwatches. When combining those conspicuous goods that we can categorise as jewellery,[8] we see a total of 13.2 percent of the marketplace dedicated to these items. The various categories also have strong differences in prices, which overlaps with what we see in Table 1. Concerning brands, there is less of a concentration in one group, although the popular watch brand "Rolex" has the highest number of incidents with 14.73 percent with an average price of 184.04 EUR. There are high differences also in the brand sub-categories, with the brand Audemars Piguet having an average price of 298.72 EUR and Montblanc of 51.11 EUR.

[8]Combining the categories necklace (6.61 percent), bracelet (5.10 percent), and earrings (2.45 percent). Other less represented sub-categories which can be considered as jewels are ring (1.40 percent), cufflinks (0.34 percent), ring and necklace (0.18 percent), keyring (0.07 percent), and money clips (0.01 percent). Some sellers also sold branded boxes of necklaces and bracelets, and these accounted for 0.23 percent of total observations, and branded boxes of watches, accounting for 1.53 percent of all observations.

4 Results

In determining how a market like this one works, we can focus on the demand, on the supply, or on both. In our case, we have no information about the demand, or in that sense about the consumers and we have no means of inferring it in any way,[9] therefore we decided to focus on the supply of the market, from August 2014 up to the closure of the marketplace in March 2015. What we do know however, is the amount of pieces the sellers have sold. This gives us an indication as to what the market demands, regardless. Therefore, we developed two types of analyses: the first studies the time dynamics of this marketplace with a particular focus on the behaviour of the sellers and on the feedback system, while the second aims to understand which of the variables are more important in explaining the price of the objects traded in this market.

4.1 Trends in Price Dynamics

Concerning the time dynamics, we wanted to check if a trend is present in both price dynamics and number of observations. Since the marketplace increased in renown overtime, and it is likely that some sellers (and hence buyers, since this type of market is likely to be supply-driven) moved to Evolution after *Operation Onymous*, we expected to observe both an increase in total price of all objects available in the marketplace and number of objects available, as measures of the importance of the market overtime. In checking if this is the case, one should recall that the data points are irregularly spaced (see footnote 3) and use a particular method to smooth the graph, that is, to remove fluctuations in the figures which are not strictly linked with the trend of the variable we want to analyse. In particular, we used a median filter to smooth the graph, preserving sharp edges in the signal (Ataman et al., 1981; Tukey, 1971). Figures 1 and 2 report the median filtered time series for the price in EUR and for the number of observations, respectively.[10]

From the two figures, it is clear that a strong increasing trend is present in both prices and number of objects at sale in the Evolution marketplace, throughout the considered period. While the number of objects increases almost linearly from Mid-November 2014 onwards, the sum of prices of all the items at sale starts increasing in the same period, then has a small reduction at the beginning of

[9]We cannot know how many of these objects were sold, since we only observed the ads of the sellers and information of consumers is not available. What we can observe is the reputation number as a noisy measure of completed transactions. Inferring remains complex because we cannot assert how many points of the reputation number comes from our examined categories, and how many are from other categories. However, this information is not reproducible from the original dataset.

[10]The median is computed over a moving window of 10 periods, the signal level is estimated at the end of each time window. The computation was implemented using the R package by Fried et al. (2019).

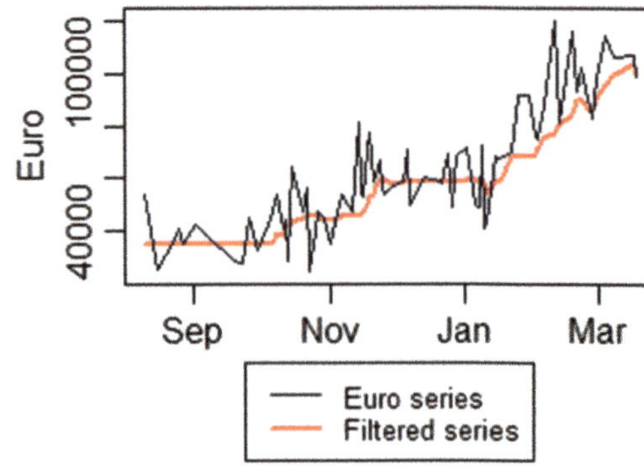

Fig. 1 Median filter for total value of products per day

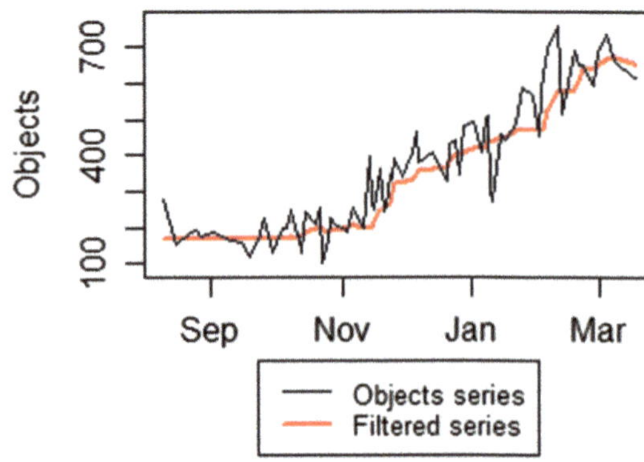

Fig. 2 Median filter for total number of objects per day

January 2015, and then starts increasing again from the second part of January 2015 until the closure of the marketplace. A tentative explanation of this is that, after *Operation Onymous*, several sellers moved to Evolution from other similar marketplaces, increasing the number of ads, but the average price decreased, meaning that the supplied goods presented a lower price. There can be different explanations for this. One explanation could be that sellers with generally lower prices entered the market, and the buyers then moved from the previous sellers to these new sellers. However, in principle, the old sellers might also have left the marketplace, so the price went down and the number of sellers (or the saturation of the market) is the same, or even lower.

4.2 *Seller Behaviour Concerning Number of Objects and Total Price*

Another way to look at the supply side of this marketplace is to consider how the sellers behaved with respect to the number of objects they supplied on the marketplace and to their total price, as a measure of the potential trade flow that each agent could obtain if every object in his/her inventory was sold.

Figure 3 reports the logarithm of the sum of the prices of all the objects each seller put on sale (in blue, on the y axis on the left) and the logarithm of the number of objects at sale (in red, on the y axis on the right).[11]

Figure 3 suggests that not all the sellers behave in the same way, and this is strictly linked to the fact that very different types of objects are part of our dataset. In other words, the average price (which is higher the farther two points in the graph are from each other) can be very different and influenced by the specialization of each seller in a certain type of objects or his/her diversification strategy carried on by focusing on different types of objects. Indeed, the result of the Pearson's Chi-squared test on the contingency of sellers and sub-categories suggests that both specialised sellers as well as sellers that offer more types of objects exist, and this is also confirmed by a network analysis we do not report here, but is available upon request.

4.3 Reputation

Figure 4 reports the logarithm of the reputation number each seller obtained from August 2014 to March 2015 (in blue, on the y axis on the left) and the logarithm of the number of objects at sale (in red, on the y axis on the right). Notice that the number of vendors is smaller than the one in Fig. 3; this is because we focused on those who obtained at least one (1) feedback in the considered period.

Figure 4 indicates that different sellers, under the point of view of the number of completed trades, operate in the marketplace: some sellers have a high number of reviews even though the number of objects at sale are not too high, and the converse combination is also found among other sellers. This suggests that a high number of ads is not strictly linked with a high number of completed trades (and then a high reputation number), even though we must consider that some of these sellers might be selling objects associated with categories we did not consider influencing their reputation score.

4.4 Indicators for Pricing

The second part of the analysis focuses on the variables that play a major role in explaining the price of the objects. One of the simpler ways to check for this kind of relationship in an empirical way is by using an ordinary least squares (OLS)

[11] We reported these values in logarithmic form since the high variability of these values (see Table 1) would impede a graphical comparison otherwise.

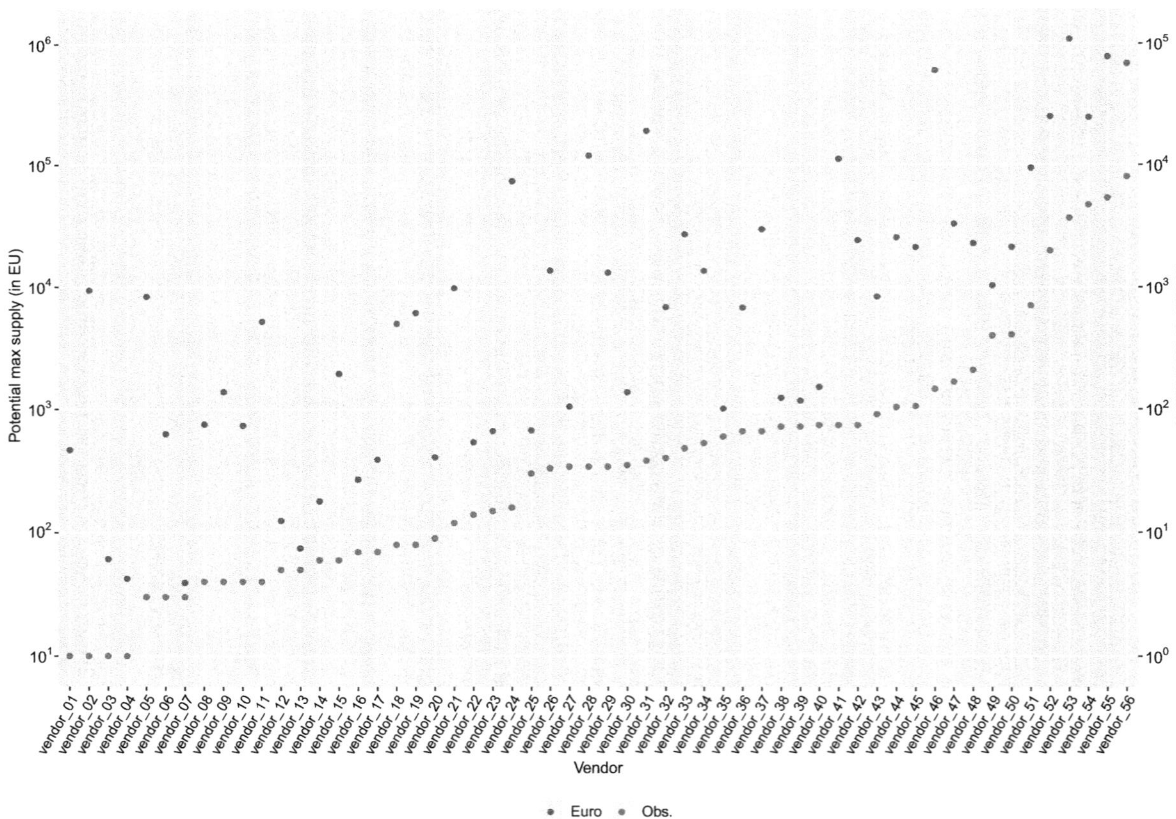

Fig. 3 Logarithm of the sum of prices for all objetcts each seller put on sale (in blue on the x-axis) and the logarithm of the number of objects at sale (in red on the y-axis)

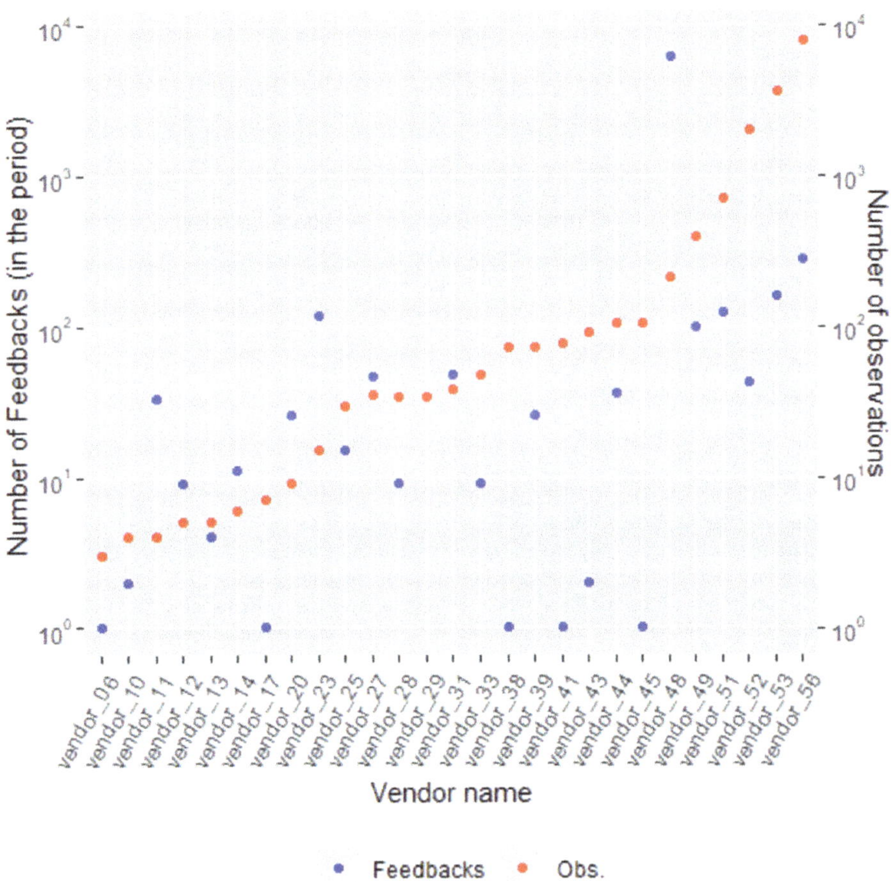

Fig. 4 Logratithm of reputation number each seller obtained from August 2014 to March 2015 (in blue on the y-axis) and the logarithm of the number of objects at sale (in red, on the y axis)

regression (see Wooldridge, 2006). What we want to check is if a series of explanatory variables (such as the brand associated with the product, the object being a replica or authentic piece, etc.) has an impact on the prices of the goods, and if this impact is positive or negative. The direction of the effect (positive versus negative) and its statistical significance (meaning if the effect is indeed significantly different from zero and thus not by chance) will give us hints about what could be the behaviour and beliefs of the sellers in fixing the prices.

In what follows, we will implement the OLS model on different subsamples of our data.[12] The model we are going to use is as follows:

[12] In our analysis, we pool the data at cross-sectional level, meaning that we do not consider time dynamics. This is because our data is irregularly spaced with respect to time and an approach to consider time dynamics with this type of data would be too complex.

Table 3 Regression results

Dependent variable: log(Price in EUR)	(1)	(2)	(3)	(4)	(5)
Intercept	4.068 [0.247] ***	6.109 [0.035] ***	8.479 [0.061] ***	4.984 [0.103] ***	2.570 [0.166] ***
log(Reputation number + 1)	−0.171 [0.003] ***	−0.187 [0.004] ***	−0.045 [0.004] ***	0.044 [0.005] ***	0.049 [0.030]
Replica dummy		−0.298 [0.024] ***		−0.940 [0.046] ***	
Brand dummy variables	Yes	Yes	Yes	Yes	–
Sub-categories dummy variables	Yes	–	Yes	Yes	Yes
Number of observations	26,507	9915	4440	3326	684
Adjusted R^2	0.693	0.484	0.690	0.882	0.847

It is standard practice for the referencing of tests of significance to work with this three-step model. Even despite the fact that we only have levels of significance that are *** (equals <0.001), it is normal for transparency of the results that the other values (equalling both <0.05 and <0.01) to be mentioned, even if non of the statistical results belong to these two values (being */**). Therefore, these values should remain in the legend of table 3 as well. This is standard practice.
*$p < 0.05$
**$p < 0.01$
***$p < 0.001$

$$P_i = \beta_0 + \beta_1 x_{1,i} + \beta_2 x_{2,i} + \ldots + \beta_k x_{k,i} + e_i$$

where the price of the object i, P_i, is explained by k variables ($x_{1,\ i}, x_{2,\ i}, \ldots, x_{k,\ i}$). What we estimate here are the β-s, the coefficients that indicate how each variable is related with the dependent variable P_i. The results of the various OLS regression models we implemented are reported in Table 3.

The values are rounded to three digits and the standard deviation is presented within brackets. Model (1) is computed on all *branded objects*, model (2) on *branded watches* only, model (3) on *jewellery*, model (4) on *branded clothes*, and model (5) on *unbranded objects*.

As we can see, reputation is negatively related to prices in Model 1. Since we primarily consider the supply, it might be the case that those sellers that provide lower-priced items sell more, creating a higher reputation for these respective sellers. Brands impact in Model 1 is statistically significant, some with higher effect than others (consistently with Table 2). When we turn to our biggest conspicuous good in the database, watches, the pattern is similar to what we witnessed in Model 1: the replica dummy variable has a strong negative effect on price.

Jewellery (Model 3) presents the same link between reputation and price that we found in Models 1 and 2. In this model, the dummy variable for the replica is not considered since all the objects in our dataset that are part of jewellery categories are either a replica, or an object whose authenticity is not mentioned in the description.

Clothes (Model 4) behave differently than other branded objects since reputation impact is positive here. Namely high-reputation sellers are those with objects with higher prices, whereas replicas are sold at a lower price. This result might be linked to a different perception of risk of the buyer, which is taken into account by sellers. For example, buyers could perceive the risk differently with respect to the other described models. Namely: buyers perceive a higher risk for these other objects and therefore buy low-priced objects. Meaning that the reputation of the sellers that sell low-priced objects will be higher, and hence the negative direction is visible in the regression, whilst for clothing, this does not occur. Buyers purchase higher-priced objects and therefore the seller of high-priced objects has a higher reputation because they sell more, and this is confirmed by the positive direction in regression analysis. Of course, these are hypotheses of potential power dynamics. However, we have no way to confirm these with certainty. We could say however that clothes in this marketplace are perceived more as Veblen goods than other goods, since people buy high-price clothes, but low-price watches and jewellery.

When we look at objects without a specific brand (Model 5), presented as 'generic' products, the seller's reputation does not seem to be linked with his/her prices in a linear way. In fact, the estimated coefficient related to the seller's reputation is not statistically different from 0. There is a possibility here that these objects are considered as those objects with the highest perceived risk of scam. Additionally, we can argue that these objects are less important in signalling distinction as these specific objects are without brands. They consist mostly of gold, diamonds, and silver, which are objects that are more traditionally kept as 'storage' value, rather than something to display.

5 Analysis

The online anonymous marketplace Evolution showed us that indeed some of the discussed luxury objects are indeed treated as conspicuous goods, selling more frequently for higher prices than for lower ones, *ceteris paribus*. We can argue here that selling distinction through counterfeited luxury objects might be one of the explanations of the appeal of these objects, even if these objects turn out to be counterfeit. We argue that these products are 'objects of desire' that not only create a market for conspicuous consumption, but also a possible driver for criminal behaviour. Already signalling earlier on in this chapter that specialised law enforcement and commercial databases have increased their focus on these type of goods (as aptly visualised by the establishment of The Watch Register in 2015), it is important to note that these objects are indeed circulating in an underground illicit market, and that these are marketed using their brand and their 'exclusive' character. By analysing this marketplace, we can argue that the supply for these products run in the tens of thousands of objects, in just a single marketplace, arguing for these goods to receive increased academic scrutiny, in addition to the increasing focus of law enforcement and commercial databases for these goods.

What distinguishes these goods therefore is that they not only fulfil a material need, but possibly also a strong social need. Within the marketplace, these goods are often labelled as luxury products, and are distinguished as being ‘exclusive’, and thus priced based on their exclusivity. Being able to own or purchase conspicuous goods therefore signals not only the economic wealth of the individual, but also the prestige of the individual. In our analysis of the marketplace, we clearly see that the sellers have an eye for this, actively making use of the products’ brands and offering them through a lens of ‘exclusivity’ and ‘distinction’.

6 Conclusion

Research in art crime, observing some exceptions, has seen little use of statistical inferences, making for a small field of empirically grounded research data to draw upon. Art crime is often reported as the third, or even fourth largest criminal enterprise in the world, however the exact economic and criminal impact of this type of crime, remains unclear. The truth here is that the exact scale is unknown to almost anyone, so we often need to rely on anecdotal evidence or results of small-scale, in-depth studies that are difficult to infer to larger populations. Various factors contribute to this; however, it is mostly due to two specific factors. First, there is the issue of recording. For example, many national police databases rely on the *type* of crime, and not necessarily on the *objects* of theft. So, if a painting is stolen from a private accommodation, thefts are often labelled as property thefts. When a painting is stolen from a museum, it is still often considered as property theft (albeit from a public or commercial institution), however the label ‘cultural property crime’ or ‘art crime’ is more easily given. The second issue concerns determining, or rather understanding, the cultural value of these objects. Next to economic valuations of cultural objects, the exact cultural value of them is difficult to determine since there is no hard determination on how to evaluate this value, especially for non-specialists. Additionally, very little research has been undertaken concerning luxury products.

Of course, this was the very first step in developing art crime related research on this scale in an anonymous online marketplace on this specific category. To further enhance the understanding of these markets, and how their sellers fashion the sales of these goods, further research could explore the narratives of objects for sale (how are objects framed and marketed). Additionally, our formulae and methodology can be applied on notable art crime databases, such as Interpol’s Stolen Works of Art Database or the Art Loss Register. Finally, our results, now specific to Evolution, could work differently in other online marketplaces; a comparison between the sellers’ and consumers’ behaviour of different dark marketplaces could give insights on the generalisability of the results of our analysis.

Acknowledgements We would like to thank Michelangelo Puliga for his assistance with the database.

References

Afilipoaie, S., & Shortis, P. (2015). *Operation Onymous: International law enforcement agencies target the dark net in November 2014*. Swansea University, UK. Retrieved May 30, 2021, from https://www.swansea.ac.uk/media/Operation-Onymous.pdf

Albrecht, M. C. (1968). Art as an institution. *American Sociological Review, 33*(3), 383–397.

Aldridge, J., & Décary-Hétu, D. (2016). Hidden wholesale: The drug diffusing capacity of online drug cryptomarkets. *International Journal of Drug Policy, 35*, 7–15.

Angelini, F., & Castellani, M. (2019). Cultural and economic value: A critical review. *Journal of Cultural Economics, 43*(2), 173–188.

Angelini, F., Castellani, M., & Pattitoni, P. (2019). *Artist names as human brands: Brand strategies in the Italian gallery art market*. Retrieved May 30, 2021, from https://ssrn.com/abstract=3495474

Ataman, E., Aatre, V. K., & Wong, K. M. (1981). Some statistical properties of median filters. *IEEE Transactions on Acoustics, Speech and Signal Processing, 29*(5), 1073–1075.

Bagwell, L. S., & Bernheim, D. (1996). Veblen effects in a theory of conspicuous consumption. *The American Economic Review, 86*(3), 349–373.

Bourdieu, P. (1983). The field of cultural production, or: The economic world reversed. *Poetics, 12* (4–5), 311–356.

Bourdieu, P. (1984). *Distinction: A social critique of the judgment of taste*. Harvard University Press.

Brodie, N. (2003). Stolen history: Looting and illicit trade. *Museum International, 55*(3–4), 10–22.

Červený, J., & Van Ours, J. C. (2019). Cannabis prices on the dark web. *European Economic Review, 120*, 1–11.

Compton, R. (2015). *Darknet market basket analysis*. Retrieved September 15, 2020, from http://ryancompton.net/2015/03/24/darknet-market-basket-analysis.html

Dodds, W. B., Monroe, K. B., & Grewal, D. (1991). Effects of price, brand, and store information on buyers' product evaluations. *Journal of Marketing Research, 28*(3), 307–319.

Erdem, T., & Swait, J. (2004). Brand credibility, brand consideration, and choice. *Journal of Consumer Research, 31*(1), 191–198.

Farberman, H. A. (1975). A criminogenic market structure: The automobile industry. *Sociological Quarterly, 16*(4), 438–457.

Fried, R., Schettlinger, K., & Borowski, M. (2019). robfilter: Robust time series filters. R package version 4.1.2.

Hufnagel, S., & King, C. (2020). Anti-money laundering regulation and the art market. *Legal Studies, 40*(1), 131–150.

Kerr, J. (2015). *The securitization and policing of art theft. The case of London*. Ashgate.

Mackenzie, S., Brodie, N., Yates, D., & Tsirogiannis, C. (2019). *Trafficking culture: New directions in researching the global market in illicit antiquities*. Routledge.

Oosterlinck, K., & Radermecker, A. S. (2019). "The Master of . . .": Creating names for art history and the art market. *Journal of Cultural Economics, 43*, 57–95.

Oosterman, N. (2019). Regional overviews of the policing of art crime in the European Union. In S. Hufnagel & D. Chappell (Eds.), *The Palgrave handbook on art crime* (pp. 213–235). Palgrave Macmillan.

Oosterman, N., & Yates, D. (2020). Policing heritage crime in Latin America. *Revista de Direito Internacional, 17*(3), 275–290.

Passas, N. (1999). Globalization, criminogenic asymmetries and economic crime. *EUR JL Reform, 1*, 399–424.

Roodt, C., & Carey-Miller, D. (2013). Stolen cultural property: Implications of vitium reale in private law and private international law. *Transnational Dispute Management, 10*(5), 1–9.

Schroeder, J. E. (2005). The artist and the brand. *European Journal of Marketing, 39*(11–12), 1291–1305.

Soska, K., & Christin, N. (2015). *Measuring the longitudinal evolution of the online anonymous marketplace ecosystem*. Carnegie Mellon University.
Trigg, A. B. (2001). Veblen, Bourdieu, and conspicuous consumption. *Journal of Economic Issues, 35*(1), 99–115.
Tukey, J. W. (1971). *Exploratory data analysis*. Addison-Wesley Publishing Company.
Veblen, T. (1899). *The theory of the leisure class: An economic study of institutions*. Unwin Book.
Wooldridge, J. (2006). *Introductory econometrics: A modern approach*. Thomson South-Western.
Yates, D. (2015). Illicit cultural property from Latin America: Looting, trafficking, and sale. In F. Desmarais (Ed.), *Countering illicit trafficking in cultural goods. The global challenge of protecting the world's heritage*. ICOM.

www.ingramcontent.com/pod-product-compliance
Ingram Content Group UK Ltd.
Pitfield, Milton Keynes, MK11 3LW, UK
UKHW022213051026
15624UKWH00001B/135
9783030848552